CONTENTS

Cover Picture: Culloden House, Inverness, Scotland (see page 407).

INTRODUCTION BY THE EDITOR

Johansens guides, now in their 15th year, have developed from one single hotel guide into what this year is a set of five – Recommended Hotels, Recommended Inns with Restaurants, Recommended Country Houses and Small Hotels, Recommended Business Meetings Venues and now, for the first time, Johansens Recommended Hotels in Europe. The market place has grown and we have grown with it. Our principles, nevertheless, have remained constant. The annual inspection of candidates for inclusion in our guides reinforced by the thousands of reports from Johansens guide-users sustains our criterion of excellence.

We are publishers and as such we form the link between two groups of clients: hoteliers who, if accepted for membership, pay an annual fee and their guests, who are in many cases purchasers of our guides. We value both these relationships hoping that our contribution to excellence in hospitality, now not only in Britain but in all Europe, will be of great benefit to the diverse clientele which we so proudly serve.

Rodney Exton, Editor.

KEY TO SYMBOLS

13 rms — Total number of rooms	13 rms — Nombre de chambres	13 rms — Anzahl der Zimmer
MasterCard accepted	MasterCard accepté	MasterCard akzeptiert
Visa accepted	Visa accepté	Visa akzeptiert
American Express accepted	American Express accepté	American Express akzeptiert
Diners Club accepted	Diners Club accepté	Diners Club akzeptiert
Quiet location	Un lieu tranquille	Ruhige Lage
Access for wheelchairs to at least one bedroom and public rooms	Accès handicapé	Zugang für Behinderte
Chef-patron	Chef-patron	Chef-patron
M 20 — Meeting/conference facilities with maximum number of delegates	M 20 — Salle de conférences – capacité maximale	M 20 — Konferenzraum-Höchstkapazität
Children welcome, with minimum age where applicable	Enfants bienvenus	Kinder willkommen
Dogs accommodated in rooms or kennels	Chiens autorisés	Hunde erlaubt
At least one room has a four-poster bed	Lit à colonnes	Himmelbett
Cable/satellite TV in all bedrooms	TV câblée/satellite dans les chambres	Satellit-und Kabelfernsehen in allen Zimmern
Direct-dial telephone in all bedrooms	Téléphone dans les chambres	Telefon in allen Zimmern
No-smoking rooms (at least one no-smoking bedroom)	Chambres non-fumeurs	Zimmer für Nichtraucher
Lift available for guests' use	Ascensrur	Fahrstuhl
Indoor swimming pool	Piscine couverte	Hallenbad
Outdoor swimming pool	Piscine de plein air	Freibad
Tennis court at hotel	Tennis à l'hôtel	Hoteleigener Tennisplatz
Croquet lawn at hotel	Croquet à l'hôtel	Krocketrasen
Fishing can be arranged	Pêche	Angeln
Golf course on site or nearby, which has an arrangement with hotel allowing guests to play	Golf	Golfplatz
Shooting can be arranged	Chasse	Jagd
Riding can be arranged	Chevaux de selle	Reitpferd
Hotel has a helicopter landing pad	Hélipad	Hubschrauberlandplatz
Licensed for wedding ceremonies	Cérémonies de noces	Konzession für Eheschliessungen

In association
with MasterCard

Published by
Johansens, 175-179 St John Street, London EC1V 4RP

Tel: 0171-490 3090 Fax: 0171-490 2538

Find Johansens on the Internet at: http://www.johansens.com

Editor:	Rodney Exton
Publishing Director:	Andrew Warren
P.A. to Publishing Director:	Angela Franks
Associate Publisher:	Peter Hancock
Secretary to Associate Publisher:	Carol Sweeney
Regional Inspectors:	Christopher Bond
	Geraldine Bromley
	Julie Dunkley
	Susan Harangozo
	Joan Henderson
	Marie Iversen
	Pauline Mason
	Mary O'Neill
	Brian Sandell
Production Manager:	Daniel Barnett
Production Controller:	Kevin Bradbrook
Designer:	Matthew Davis
Copywriters:	Sally Sutton, Jill Wyatt
Sales and Marketing Manager:	Mike Schwarz
Marketing Executive:	Juliet Brookes
Marketing Assistant:	Rebecca Ford
Managing Director:	Martin Morgan

Copyright © 1995 Johansens

Hobsons Publishing plc,

a subsidiary of the Daily Mail and General Trust plc

ISBN 1 86017 129 X

Printed in England by St Ives plc

Colour origination by Graphic Facilities

Distributed in the UK and Europe by Biblios PDS Ltd, Partridge Green, West Sussex, RH13 8LD. In North America by general sales agent: SunWelcome, INC., Clearwater, Florida (direct sales) and The Cimino Publishing Group, INC. New York (bookstores). In Australia and New Zealand by Bookwise International, Findon, South Australia.

HOW TO USE THIS GUIDE

If you want to identify a Hotel whose name you already know, look for it in the national indexes on pages 480–486.

If you want to find a Hotel in a particular area you can

- Turn to the Maps on page 10 and pages 473–479
- Search the Indexes by County on pages 480–486
- Look for the Town where you wish to stay in the main body of the Guide. This is divided into Countries. Place names in each Country are in alphabetical order.

The Indexes list the Hotels by Counties, they also show those with facilities such as wheelchair access, conference centres, swimming, golf, etc.

The Maps cover all regions including London. Each Hotel symbol (a blue circle) relates to a Hotel in this guide situated in or near the location shown.

Mini Listings page 456–472: The Inns (a red triangle), Country Houses and Small Hotels (a green square) appearing on the Maps are listed in order of place names and divided nationally so that, if you cannot find a Hotel locally, you may be able to find a smaller Johansens Recommendation. Copies of this Guide and of the Guides in which the Inns, Country Houses and Small Hotels appear in full are obtainable from bookshops, by Johansens Freephone 0800 269397 or by using the order coupons on pages 487–496.

Mini listings of Johansens Recommended Hotels in Europe are on pages 469–472.

The Prices, in most cases, refer to the cost of one night's accommodation, with breakfast, for two people. Prices are also shown for single occupancy. These rates are correct at the time of going to press but they should always be checked.

INTRODUCTION

By Martin and Joy Cummings of Amberley Castle, Nr Arundel, West Sussex, Winner of the 1995 Johansens Hotel Award

Hoteliers who appear in Johansens publications reflect in general a pride in our industry that places service to our customers and concern for our staff above all else. To achieve this high level of dedication, given the daily pressures which confront us all, some self-inflicted, others not, we must learn to give relatively more than we take. It is any wonder, therefore, that slowly but surely the reputation of the British hotel scene continues to improve?

Small is, for the most part, beautiful and thanks to Johansens and others, our independence is maintained with an economy of scale in marketing that would be hard to achieve in any other way. The detailed information provided is extremely valuable, and thanks to the ever-increasing demand for quality, I am confident that I'm in good company with those like-minded hoteliers who care more for their customers than for themselves.

We have only traded since 1989 – coincidental with high interest rates, the Gulf War and recession in various parts of the globe. Our international mix relies heavily on the domestic market from Britain (74%) to keep us healthy. It comes as no surprise, indeed I take much satisfaction from the fact, that our home market has a thirst for country hotels, even in difficult economic times, that shows no sign of being quenched. That so many British people should, with the world at their fingertips, choose to visit out establishments is praise indeed. That, especially in the case of Amberley Castle, where our only "real" amenity is simple "peace and quiet", says much for their civilised outlook on life. Add to this the ingredients of history, culture and heritage and you will have the recipe that will appeal to customers the world over.

I wish all those associated with Johansens every success in reaching that market – the independent hotels will surely remain in your debt!

EVERY LANGUAGE SPEAKS MASTERCARD

JOHANSENS AWARDS FOR EXCELLENCE

The names of the winners of the 1996 Awards will be published in the 1997 editions of Johansens guides.

The winners of the 1995 Awards are listed below. They were presented with their certificates at the Johansens Annual Awards dinner, held at The Savoy on 31st October 1994, by Giles Shepard CBE.

WINNERS OF THE
1995 JOHANSENS AWARDS

Johansens Country Hotel Award for Excellence
Amberley Castle, Arundel, West Sussex

Johansens City Hotel Award for Excellence
The Chester Grosvenor, Chester, Cheshire

Johansens Country House Award for Excellence
Coopershill House, Riverstown, Co Sligo

Johansens Inn Award for Excellence
The Lamb, Burford, Oxford

Johansens Most Excellent Value for Money Award
Lower Bache, Leominster, Herefordshire

Johansens Most Excellent Service Award
Hotel Maes-Y-Neuadd, Harlech, Gwynedd

Candidates for awards derive from two main sources: from the thousands of Johansens guide users who send us guest survey reports commending hotels, inn and country houses in which they have stayed and from our team of twelve regional inspectors who regularly visit all properties in our guides. Guest survey report forms can be found on pages 487–496. They are a vital part of our continuous process of assessment and they are the decisive factor in choosing the value for money and the most excellent service awards.

The judges each year are invited from among the winners of previous years awards.

The Judges for the 1995 Awards were:-

David Shentall, Kinloch House, Winner of the 1994 Johansens Country Hotel Award
Malcolm Reed, The Swallow, Birmingham, Winner of the 1994 Johansens City Hotel Award
Hugo Jeune, The Rising Sun, Lynmouth, Winner of the 1991 Johansens Inn Award
Anne McClure, 4 South Parade, York, Winner of the 1994 Johansens Value for Money Award

JOHANSENS demand the highest standards

So we've taken a leaf out of their book.

An entry into Johansens is greatly coveted and hard to achieve.

Not only do levels of service have to be second to none, but the hotels and their surroundings must mirror that commitment to excellence.

Which is where we come in.

Knight Frank & Rutley's Hotel Department reflects those standards. We specialise in acquisitions, disposals, valuations and all other aspects of Hotel Property.

We are dedicated to providing the best hotel property service, tailor-made to your needs.

Knight Frank & Rutley. Is it any wonder we're in Johansen's?

Knight Frank & Rutley
KF+R
INTERNATIONAL
20 Hanover Square, London W1R 0AH
0171-629 8171

INTRODUCTION

By Jonathan Slater, Managing Director of The Chester Grosvenor, Chester, Winner of the 1995 Johansens City Hotel of the Year Award

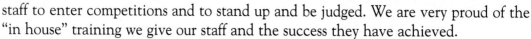

We were absolutely thrilled to learn that we had been awarded the Johansens "City Hotel Award for Excellence" in a month when we also learned that we had retained our RAC Blue Ribbon for the 6th year in succession and been voted "Northern Hotel of the Year" in Life Magazine.

It is always a pleasure to receive awards and accolades, they add the silver baubles to the icing on the cake.

Awards are always unexpected. Having said that, we do actively encourage individual members of staff to enter competitions and to stand up and be judged. We are very proud of the "in house" training we give our staff and the success they have achieved.

At The Chester Grosvenor we are rather like a football team. We have out "colts" whom we develop and train to move into the junior league and eventually into the senior league. Many of our management team have been at The Chester Grosvenor for a number of years.

In an industry that is notorious for a high turnover of staff, I am please to report that ours is well below the industry norm. This provides the hotel with a consistency – something that is manifested throughout the hotel and perhaps one of the reasons we win awards.

Maintaining these standards means hard work. We can all "pull out the stops" for a one-off, but to do it all the time is another ball game.

We will continue to strive and hopefully to keep at the top of the premier division – something that all Johansens hotels strive to do.

HUDSON'S
HISTORIC HOUSES AND GARDENS

including HISTORIC SITES OF INTEREST

The renowned Guide to over 1200 properties in Great Britain

Privately owned, National Trust, English Heritage, National Trust for Scotland and Historic Scotland properties and historic sites open to the public

Over 800 full-colour illustrations.

Descriptions, opening times, admission charges, telephone numbers and directions

Special Events Diary

Listing of Johansens recommended hotels by region

1996 edition on sale from February 1996 in all good bookshops or direct from the publishers.
ISBN: 0 9514157 7 8.   **Price UK: £6.95.**

Hudson's Directory, PO Box 16, Banbury, Oxon OX17 1TF.   Tel: 01295 750750   Fax: 01295 750800

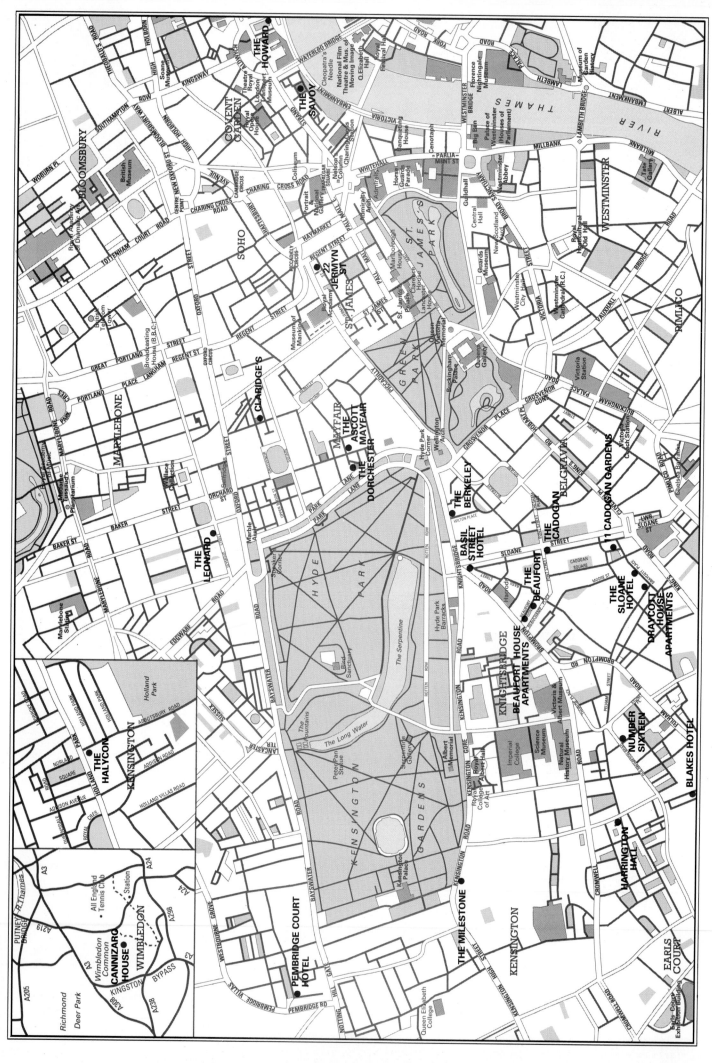

St Paul's Cathedral, London

Johansens Recommended Hotels & Apartments in London

*L*ondon *recommendations represent a fine selection of full service hotels, town house hotels and apartments, from the grand to the petite.*

Our choice is based on location, reputation, value for money and excellence, above all else.

The Johansens guest can be comfortably accommodated within easy reach of the principal shopping areas, museums, galleries, restaurants, theatres and Wimbledon!

*L*ondon is one of the world's most exciting cities – and a city of contrasts. Justly famous for its historic sights, pageantry, heritage and culture, there is also another side to the city, young, glamorous and ever-changing. Even for those who have been to London many times before there is always something new – whether it is the angular reaches of Docklands' ultra-modern architecture or new displays in some of London's favourite museums and galleries...

From May 1996, the Victoria & Albert Museum will celebrate the centenary of William Morris's death with an exhibition of his work including textiles, ceramics, furniture and wallpaper.

At Hyde Park Corner, 'Number 1, London' can be found. This is the popular name for one of the capital's finest private residences, Apsley House. This nineteenth century home of the First Duke of Wellington re-opened in 1995 after extensive refurbishment. It houses the Duke's magnificent collection of paintings, silver, porcelain and furniture; the interiors have been returned to their former glory as the private palace of the 'Iron Duke'.

The London Planetarium in Marylebone Road has reopened after a £4.5 million transformation which included a new star projector, the Digistar 11. This launches visitors on a three dimensional journey through the universe. New space station exhibition areas guide visitors on an interactive voyage of discovery, with scale models of the planets and demonstrations of the effects of a black hole!

The National Gallery in Trafalgar Square houses one of the finest and most extensive collection of paintings in the world and is well worth a visit. So, too, is the British Museum which has acquired two paintings from the ceiling of Henry III's 'Painted Chamber' in medieval Westminster Palace, the earliest surviving English panel paintings.

Heading out of the centre of London, Hampton Court Palace provides an excellent day out in history. The Palace – some 500 years old – sits in splendour on the banks of the River Thames. 1995 saw the completion of one of the most important historic garden restorations ever undertaken, that of the King's Privy Garden which has been returned to the 1702 design when it was at the height of its splendour.

Plant and garden lovers will also be enchanted by the Royal Botanic Gardens Kew, where almost 40,000 different types of plant are growing – at least six of them thought to exist nowhere else.

London's theatre is one of the most vibrant in the world – there is always a new show opening. Even the most sought after shows are sometimes available from reputable ticket agencies or the Half-Price Ticket Booth in Leicester Square, which acts as a clearing house for the theatres' tickets left unsold for the coming matinee/evening. In the summer, there is Shakespeare in the open-air in Regent's Park.

London is famous for music and the performing arts and has two opera houses, The Royal Opera House in Covent Garden and the London Coliseum (where the English National Opera perform in English). Lovers of classical music will appreciate the five world class symphony orchestras which can be found in the capital.

The capital has a very sophisticated transport system including a rail network, buses and an underground train system that is the largest in the world. Visitors can take advantage of travelcards which offer virtually unlimited travel on bus, train and underground within chosen zones. For enquiries about times, fares and journey planning, call London Transport's 24-hour telephone information service on 0171 222 1234. If you do not want to use public transport, the capital's famous taxis are strictly controlled and usually easily accessible in the central area.

Information on London's thousands of attractions, theatre and opera and sporting events is available to personal callers at the Tourist Information Centre on Victoria Station Forecourt. Alternatively, London Tourist Board operates Visitorcall a 24-hour telephone information service on a wide range of topics in London – like 'what's on', 'museums' and 'where to go with children'. Call 0839 123456 for details (calls are charged at 39p a minute cheap rate and 49p at all other times).

Victoria & Albert Museum
Cromwell Road, SW7
Tel: 0171 938 8500

Apsley House
149 Piccadilly, W1
0171 499 5676

London Planetarium
Marylebone Road, NW1
Tel: 0171 486 1121

British Museum
Great Russell Street, WC1
Tel: 0171 636 1555

Hampton Court Palace
East Molesey,
Surrey KT8 9AU
Tel: 0181 781 9500

Royal Botanic Gardens
Kew
Richmond
Surrey TW9 3AB
Tel: 0181 332 5622

Royal Opera House
Covent Garden, WC2
Tel: 0171 304 4000

The London Coliseum
St Martin's Lane, WC2
Tel: 0171 632 8300

Information supplied by

London Tourist Board and Convention Bureau
26 Grosvenor Gardens
Victoria
London SW1W ODU

THE ASCOTT MAYFAIR

49 HILL STREET, LONDON W1
TEL: 0171 499 6868 FAX: 0171 499 0705

This, the latest concept in city centre accommodation, offers all the benefits of a hotel and yet privacy and space in what the brochure describes as "residences", with one, two or three bedrooms, in a spectacular art deco building. The apartments have a 24 hour concierge for security and assistance. Guests have their own maid throughout their stay. There is no restaurant; however, a complimentary Continental breakfast is served on weekdays in The Terrace, overlooking the private gardens. There is an Honour Bar in The Club where guests can mingle or entertain. The Hothouse offers a gym, sauna, steamroom and solarium. The Business Service includes the use of a private boardroom. A marvellous kitchen is provided with everything necessary for entertaining in the versatile dining room. The study area has fax and computer links. The sitting room is extremely comfortable and beautifully decorated. It has satellite television, a music system and video. The luxurious bedrooms have amazing en suite bathrooms, full of soft white towels. The Ascott is in the heart of London – Mayfair being close to all the major shopping centres and best restaurants, theatre-land and sightseeing. **Directions:** Hill Street is off Berkeley Square, near Green Park Underground Station. Price guide: 1 bed from £175 daily–£1,150 weekly; 2 beds from £275 daily–£1,750 weekly.

BASIL STREET HOTEL

BASIL STREET, LONDON SW3 1AH
TEL: 0171-581 3311 FAX: 0171-581 3693 – FROM USA CALL FREE: UTELL 1 800 448 8355

The Basil feels more like an English home than a hotel. Privately owned by the same family for three generations, this Edwardian hotel is situated in a quiet corner of Knightsbridge, on the threshold of London's most exclusive residential and shopping area. Harrods, Harvey Nichols and other famous stores are only minutes away. It is close to museums and theatres. The spacious public rooms are furnished with antiques, paintings, mirrors and *objets d'art*. The lounge, bar and dining room are on the first floor, reached by the striking staircase that dominates the front hall. Bedrooms, all individually furnished, vary in size, style and décor. The hotel has a Carvery/Salad Bar and Wine Bar for lighter meals. Alternatively, the Dining Room is an ideal venue either for unhurried, civilised lunch or dinner by candlelight with piano music. The Parrot Club, a lounge for the exclusive use of ladies, is a haven of rest in delightful surroundings. The Basil combines tradition and caring individual service with the comfort of a modern, cosmopolitan hotel. There is a discount scheme for regular guests, for weekends and stays of five nights or more. **Directions:** Close to Pavilion Road car park. Basil Street runs off Sloane Street. Near Knightsbridge underground and bus routes. Price guide: Single £120–£125; double/twin £175–£180; family room £236–£245.

THE BEAUFORT

33 BEAUFORT GARDENS, KNIGHTSBRIDGE, LONDON SW3 1PP
TEL: 0171 584 5252 FAX: 0171 589 2834

The Beaufort offers the sophisticated traveller all the style and comfort of home – combining warm contempory colourings with the highest possible personal attention. The owner Diana Wallis (pictured below) believes that much of the success of the hotel is due to the charming, attentive staff – a feeling happily endorsed by guests. The Beaufort is situated in a quiet tree-lined square only 100 yards from Harrods and as guests arrive they are all greeted at the front door and given their own door key to come and go as they please. The closed front door gives added security and completes that feeling of home. All the bedrooms are individually decorated, with air conditioning and a great many extras such as shortbread, Swiss chocolates and brandy. The hotel owns a video and cassette library and is home to a magnificent collection of original English floral watercolours. Breakfast is brought to the bedroom – hot rolls and croissants, freshly squeezed orange juice and home-made preserves, tea and coffee. In the drawing room there is a 24-hour honour bar and between 4-5pm every day a free cream tea is served with champagne, scones, clotted cream and jam. The hotel is proud of its no tipping policy and is open all year. **Directions:** From the Harrods exit at Knightsbridge underground station take the third turning on the left. Price guide: Single £110; double/twin from £150; suites £240.

THE BERKELEY

WILTON PLACE, KNIGHTSBRIDGE, LONDON SW1X 7RL
TEL: 0171 235 6000 FAX: 0171 235 4330

Positioned in one of the most elegant residential areas of London, The Berkeley is held to be the last truly deluxe hotel built in Europe. Moved from its original site in Piccadilly in 1972, the new hotel features its own cinema, health club and private garage. Among the many original features retained from the old Berkeley are panelling by Sir Edwin Lutyens and the stunning fireplace and chandeliers. The timeless quality of craftsmanship is reflected not only in the marble entrance hall but throughout the hotel. Originality of design characterises each of the light and spacious bedrooms, some of which have an adjoining terrace and conservatory. French cuisine of the highest standard is presented against a backdrop of English oak panelling and Bartolozzi's 18th century reproductions of the famous Holbein portraits from the Queen's collection. One of the hotel's most innovative features is its roof top swimming pool, designed in the style of an ancient Roman bath with a sliding roof that opens on to the summer sky in fine weather. There is also a gym and sauna or guests may treat themselves to a reviving massage. **Directions:** Close to Knightsbridge tube station. Price guide: Single £190–£220; double/twin £240–£300; suites from £435.

BEAUFORT HOUSE APARTMENTS

45 BEAUFORT GARDENS, KNIGHTSBRIDGE, LONDON SW3 1PN
TEL: 0171 584 2600 FAX: 0171 584 6532 – USA CALL FREE: 1-800- 23-5463

Situated in Beaufort Gardens, a quiet tree-lined Regency cul-de-sac in the heart of Knightsbridge, Beaufort House is an exclusive establishment comprising 22 self-contained and fully serviced luxury apartments. All of the benefits of a first-class hotel are combined with the privacy, discretion and comfort of home. The accommodation ranges in size from an intimate one-bedroomed suite to a spacious, four-bedroomed apartment. Each bedroom has been individually decorated in a stylish fashion and each has its own en suite marble bathroom. Many of the bedrooms have views over Beaufort Gardens while several have west-facing balconys which are particularly attractive for long-stay guests. Fitted kitchens complete with modern appliances are an integral feature of each apartment. A porter is on call 24 hours a day, in addition to a daily maid service. Arrangements can be made for baby-sitting, taxis, tickets for shows, restaurant reservations etc. Conference facilities and executive support services are provided with confidentiality assured at all times. Complimentary membership to Champney's 'The London Club' is offered to all guests for the duration of their stay. **Directions:** Beaufort Gardens leads off Brompton road. Price Guide: From £115 per night. Minimum two night stay.

BLAKES HOTEL

33 ROLAND GARDENS, LONDON SW7 3PF

TEL: 0171 370 6701 FAX: 0171 373 0442 TELEX: 8813500 – FROM USA CALL FREE: 1 800 926 3173

Anouska Hempel, the celebrated London hotelier and fashion designer, created Blakes to offer style and elegance to the travelled connoisseur – and convenience and efficiency to the international business man or woman. *Architectural Digest* described Blakes as 'bedrooms and suites, each a fantasy created with antiques, paintings, rare silks and velvets'. Blakes is just a 5-minute walk through the leafy streets of South Kensington to London's new centre of smart shops in Brompton Cross and a 5-minute taxi ride from Harrods. Its restaurant is one of the finest in London, open until midnight and providing 24-hour room service. If you are travelling on business, you can have a fax in your room, full secretarial facilities, courier service, CNN news and other satellite television stations. *Architectural Digest* called Blakes 'Anouska Hempel's celebrated London refuge'. It is much more than that. It is a delight for all six senses. **Directions:** Roland Gardens is a turning off Old Brompton Road. South Kensington Underground is 5 minutes' walk. Price guide: Single £130; double/twin £155–£240; directors double £305; suite £495–£600.

For hotel location, see map on page 10

THE CADOGAN

SLOANE STREET, LONDON SW1X 9SG
TEL: 0171-235 7141 FAX: 0171-245 0994
FROM THE USA CALL TOLL FREE: Prima Hotels: 800 447 7462; Utell International 1800 44 UTELL

The Cadogan is an imposing late-Victorian building in warm terracotta brick situated in a most desirable location in Sloane Street, Knightsbridge. It is well known for its association with Lillie Langtry, the 'Jersey Lily', actress and friend of King Edward VII, and her house in Pont Street now forms part of the hotel. Playwright and wit Oscar Wilde was a regular guest at The Cadogan. The Cadogan's elegant drawing room is popular for afternoon tea and the meals served in the restaurant combine imaginatively prepared food with value for money. The hotel has 65 comfortable bedrooms and suites all equipped to the highest standards. The Langtry Rooms on the ground floor, once the famous actress's drawing room, make a delightful setting for private parties, wedding receptions and small meetings. The hotel is an excellent base for shopping trips being close to Harrods, Harvey Nichols and Peter Jones. Business visitors will find its central position and easy access make it a most acceptable place to stay when visiting London. **Directions:** The hotel is halfway along Sloane Street at the junction with Pont Street. Price guide: Single £125–£165; double/twin £155–£180; studios/suites £210–£275.

For hotel location, see map on page 10

CANNIZARO HOUSE

WEST SIDE, WIMBLEDON COMMON, LONDON SW19 4UE
TEL: 0181 879 1464 FAX: 0181 879 7338

Cannizaro House, an elegant Georgian Country House, occupies a unique position on the edge of Wimbledon Common and is within an easy walk of Wimbledon Village. Despite the hotel's tranquil location, it is only 20 minutes by train from central London. Cannizaro House, built in 1705, has throughout its long and rich history welcomed royalty and celebrities such as George III, Oscar Wilde and William Pitt, and it is now restored as a hotel which offers the very highest standards of hospitality. The aura of the 18th century age is reflected in the ornate fireplaces and plaster mouldings, gilded mirrors and many antiques in the hotel. All of the hotel's 46 bedrooms are individually designed, with many overlooking beautiful Cannizaro Park. Several intimate rooms are available for meetings and private dining, with larger reception rooms for conferences and weddings. Ray Slade, General Manager of Cannizaro House for many years, ensures the high standards of excellence for which the hotel is renowned, are consistently met. The kitchen is run by award-winning chef Stephen Wilson, who with his brigade produces the finest of modern and classical cuisine, complemented by an impressive list of fine wines. **Directions:** The nearest tube and British Rail station is Wimbledon. Price guide: Single £115–£140; double/twin £135–£190; suite £250–£350. Special weekend rates available.

CLARIDGE'S

BROOK STREET, MAYFAIR, LONDON W1A 2JQ
TEL: 0171-629 8860 FAX: 0171-499 2210

This internationally famous hotel has been the London *pied-à-terre* of some of the world's most prominent families for almost 100 years. The special character of the hotel is immediately apparent in the magnificent entrance hall, with its marble floors and sparkling chandeliers. Claridge's offers a number of newly refurbished rooms and suites, each with a character of its own and furnished in a style more redolent of a private house than an hotel. A waiter, maid or valet can be summoned at the touch of a button. Exceptionally fine food is served in the elegant art deco restaurant, and the Orangery is an ideal setting for small private dinners. In the foyer, for generations one of the most fashionable rendezvous in London, guests are served by liveried footmen and serenaded by Hungarian musicians. A series of private rooms is available for staging meetings, and the ballroom can accommodate a reception for up to 550. 1996 sees the introduction of a magnificent fitness centre. **Directions:** Claridge's is in Brook Street, which runs from Grosvenor Square to Hanover Square, adjacent to Bond Street and many of London's smartest shops. Price guide: Single £185–£220; double/twin £255–£295; suites from £550. A variety of short break arrangements is available from as little as £120 per person.

For hotel location, see map on page 10

THE DORCHESTER

PARK LANE, MAYFAIR W1A 2HJ
TEL: 0171 629 8888 FAX: 0171 409 0114 TELEX: 887704

The Dorchester first opened its doors in 1931, offering a unique experience which almost instantly became legendary. Its reopening in November 1990 after an extensive refurbishment marked the renaissance of one of the world's grand hotels. Its history has been consistently glamorous; from the early days a host of outstanding figures has been welcomed, including monarchs, statesmen and celebrities. The architectural features have been restored to their original splendour and remain at the heart of The Dorchester's heritage. The bedrooms and 52 suites have been luxuriously designed in a variety of materials, furnishings and layouts. All bedrooms are fully air-conditioned and have spectacular Italian marble bathrooms. There are rooms for non-smokers and some equipped for the disabled. In addition to The Grill Room, there is the Oriental Restaurant where the accent is on Cantonese cuisine. Specialised health and beauty treatments are offered in the new Dorchester Spa, with its statues, Lalique-style glass and water fountain. A series of meeting rooms, with full supporting services, is available for business clientèle. As ever, personalised care is a pillar of The Dorchester's fine reputation. **Directions:** Toward the Hyde Park Corner/Piccadilly end of Park Lane. Price guide excluding VAT: Single £210–£235; double/twin £235–£265; suite £350–£1,400.

For hotel location, see map on page 10

DRAYCOTT HOUSE APARTMENTS

10 DRAYCOTT AVENUE, CHELSEA, LONDON SW3 3AA
TEL: 0171-584 4659 FAX: 0171-225 3694

Draycott House stands in a quiet, tree-lined avenue in the heart of Chelsea. Housed in an attractive period building, the apartments have been designed in individual styles to provide the ideal surroundings for a private or business visit, combining comfort, privacy and security with a convenient location. All are spacious apartments, some with three bedrooms and two bathrooms, or a superb penthouse with one or two bedrooms, most having their own balconies or terraces and overlook the private courtyard garden. Each apartment is full of home comforts; a private telephone line and cable television with video and fastext. Answerphones and fax machines can be installed on request.

Complimentary provisions on arrival, milk and newspapers delivered daily. Daily maid service Monday to Friday, 24hr laundry/dry cleaning, laundry room and garage parking included in the rental charge. Additional services arranged, such as cars, catering, travel and theatre arrangements, child minders and an introduction to an exclusive health club. The West End is within easy reach. Knightsbridge within walking distance. **Directions:** Draycott House is situated on the corner of Draycott Avenue and Draycott Place, close to Sloane Square. Price guide: from £940–£2148 + VAT per week: £148-£336 per night. Long term reservations may attract preferential terms.

THE HALCYON

81 HOLLAND PARK, LONDON W11 3RZ
TEL: 0171 727 7288 FAX: 0171 229 8516 – FROM USA CALL FREE: 1 800 457 4000

This small, exclusive hotel in Holland Park offers an exceptional standard of accommodation and service. Essentially a large Town House, its architecture has been meticulously restored to the splendour of the Belle Epoque to take its place amongst the many imposing residences in the area. The generous proprotions of the rooms, along with the striking individuality of their furnishings, creates the atmosphere of a fine country house. Each of the bedrooms and suites has been beautifully furnished and has every modern amenity. All have marble bathrooms and several boast a Jacuzzi. A splendid restaurant, opening onto a ornamental garden and patio, serves distinctive international cuisine complemented by a well chosen wine list. The adjoining bar provides a relaxing environment to enjoy a cocktail and meet with friends. The Halcyon prides itself on offering a superb service and ensuring guests absolute comfort, privacy and security. Secretarial, telex and fax facilities are all available. London's most fashionable shopping areas, restaurants and West End theatres are all easily accessible from The Halcyon. Directions: From Holland Park tube station, turn right. The Halcyon is on the left after the second set of traffic lights. Price guide: Single from £165; double/twin from £235; suite from £275.

HARRINGTON HALL

5-25 HARRINGTON GARDENS, LONDON SW7 4JW
TEL: 0171 396 9696 FAX: 0171 396 9090

The original façade of late Victorian houses cleverly conceals a privately owned hotel of substantial proportions and contempory comfort. Harrington Hall offers 200 air-conditioned luxury bedrooms which have been most pleasantly furnished to the highest international standards and include an extensive array of facilities. A lovely marble fireplace is the focal point in the comfortable and relaxing Lounge Bar, where guests can enjoy a drink in elegant surroundings. The restaurant's mixture of classical decoration and dramatic colour create a delightful setting for the appreciation of fine cuisine. A choice of buffet or à la carte menu is available, both offering a tempting selection of dishes. Ten fully air conditioned conference and banqueting suites, with walls panelled in rich Lacewood and solid cherry, provide a sophisicated venue for conferences, exhibitions or corporate hospitality. Harrington Hall also has a Business Centre for the exclusive use of its guests, along with a private Fitness Centre with multigym, saunas and showers. **Directions:** Harrington Hall is situated in the Royal Borough of Kensington and Chelsea, close to Gloucester Road underground station, two stops from Knightsbridge and Harrods. Price guide: Single/double £120; suites £165.

THE HOWARD

TEMPLE PLACE, THE STRAND, LONDON WC2R 2PR
TEL: 0171 836 3555 FAX: 0171 379 4547 FROM USA TOLL FREE: BTH Hotels 1 800 221 1074

Situated where the City meets the West End, The Howard Hotel is ideal for business and leisure. With décor that echoes the grace of yesteryear, the hotel's interiors are charmingly furnished. Guests can enjoy first-class accommodation, service and cuisine. The air-conditioned bedrooms have French marquetry furniture, marbled bathrooms, satellite television, a fridge-bar and 24-hour room service. Many of them have lovely views across the River Thames. The elegant Temple Bar is the ideal setting in which to relax with a cocktail apéritif before savouring the superb French cuisine in the famous Quai d'Or Restaurant, with its domed ceiling and Renaissance décor. A variety of suites and conference rooms can cater for up to 120 people. The rooms are equally suitable for dinner parties, luncheons, conferences and meetings. Full secretarial support services can be provided. The Howard's sister hotel, The Mirabeau in Monte Carlo, offers luxurious accommodation and is situated overlooking the sea. **Directions:** On the Embankment overlooking the River Thames, 14 miles from Heathrow, 1 mile from Charing Cross station. Temple underground opposite the hotel. Price guide: Single £210; double/twin £236; suite £255–£480.

For hotel location, see map on page 10

22 JERMYN STREET

22 JERMYN STREET, LONDON SW1Y 6HL
TEL: 0171 734 2353 FAX: 0171 734 0750

The winner of many Hotel of the Year awards, 22 Jermyn Street has been in the same family ownership since 1915 and its tradition of providing luxurious accommodation and superb service continues into a third generation with Henry Togna. An ideal choice for guests who appreciate style and comfort, while preferring the personal feel of a smaller hotel to the anonymity of larger establishments. Each room and suite has been designed in complimentary yet different styles, expertly combining antique and contemporary furniture. Among the many services offered are concierge, valet, 24-hour room service, room bars and access to a nearby luxury health club with Nautilus gym, swimming pool and squash courts. There are many excellent restaurants within walking distance, with the hotel's proprietor strongly recommending Le Caprice, Quaglino's, The Square, The Greenhouse and Bistrot Bruno. A host of information covering everything from the arts to shopping, is provided in a room directory. 22 Jermyn Street is located in the heart of London's West End, close to the City, Bond Street's elegant shopping, the main auction houses, fine galleries, the Royal Parks and many of the best theatres and restaurants. **Directions:** Piccadilly Circus tube station is just 50 yards from the hotel. Price guide: Double/twin £199; suites £258.50.

THE LEONARD

15 SEYMOUR STREET, LONDON W1H 5AA
TEL: 0171 935 2010 FAX: 0171 935 6700

Four late 18th century Georgian town houses set the character of this exciting new property due to open in December 1995. There was a hotel at this address in 1926. Now extensive reconstruction has created five rooms and twenty suites decorated individually to a very high standard. Wall coverings present striking colours, complemented by exquisite French furnishing fabrics creating a warm luxurious atmosphere. All rooms are fully air-conditioned and include a private safe, mini-bar, hi-fi system and provision for a PC/fax. Bathrooms are finished in marble and some of the larger suites have a butler's pantry or fully-equipped kitchen. For physical fitness and stress reductions there is an up-to-date exercise room. Experienced staff have been appointed to ensure that guests can enjoy the highest level of attention and service. Breakfast is available in the morning room and light meals are served throughout the day. 24-hour room service is also available. There are, of course, many good restaurants nearby. The Wallace Collection is just a short walk away and one of London's premier department stores, Selfridges, is round the corner in Oxford Street. **Directions:** The Leonard is on the south side of Seymour Street which is just north of Marble Arch and runs west off Portman Square. Car parking in Bryanston Street. Price guide: Double £140–£180; suites £200–£320.

THE MILESTONE

1–2 KENSINGTON COURT, LONDON W8 5DL
TEL: 0171 917 1000 FAX: 0171 917 1010 FROM USA TOLL FREE 1 800 854 7092

The new and luxurious Milestone Hotel is situated opposite Kensington Palace. It enjoys uninterrupted views over Kensington Gardens and a remarkable vista of the royal parklands. A Victorian showpiece, this unique mansion has been meticulously restored to its original splendour while incorporating every modern facility. The 45 rooms and 12 suites are unusual in design, with antiques, elegant furnishings and private balconies. Guests may relax in the comfortable, panelled Park Lounge, which offers a 24-hour lounge service and menu. Cheneston's, the hotel's exceptional restaurant, has an elaborate carved ceiling, original fireplace, ornate windows, panelling and an oratory, which can be used for private dining. The exciting and innovative menu presents the latest in modern international cuisine. Stables Bar, fashioned after a traditional gentlemen's club, makes a convivial meeting place. The health and fitness centre offers guests the use of a solarium, spa bath, sauna and gymnasium. Some of London's finest shops and monuments are within walking distance. **Directions:** At the end of Kensington High Street, at the junction with Princes Gate. Price guide: Single from £200; double/twin £245; suites from £275.

NUMBER ELEVEN CADOGAN GARDENS

11 CADOGAN GARDENS, SLOANE SQUARE, KNIGHTSBRIDGE, LONDON SW3 2RJ
TEL: 0171-730 3426 FAX: 0171-730 5217

Number Eleven Cadogan Gardens was the first of the exclusive private town house hotels in London and now, with the addition of its own in house gymnasium and beauty rooms it continues to take the lead. Number Eleven remains traditional; no reception desk, no endless signing of bills, total privacy and security. It also offers the services you have a right to expect in the 1990s: round the clock room service, a chauffeur-driven Mercedes for airport collection and sightseeing, and a private room which can accommodate 12 for a meeting. Another attraction is the Garden Suite, with a large double bedroom and a spacious drawing room overlooking the gardens. The hotel occupies four stately Victorian houses tucked away between Harrods and Kings Road in a quiet, tree-lined square. Wood-panelled rooms, hung with oil-paintings, are furnished with antiques and oriental rugs in a traditional understated style. The fashionable shops and first-class restaurants of Knightsbridge and Belgravia are within easy walking distance. Theatre tickets can be arranged. **Directions:** Nearest tube is Sloane Square. Price guide: Single £108–£138; double/twin £158–£198; suite £250–£385.

NUMBER SIXTEEN

16 SUMNER PLACE, LONDON SW7 3EG
TEL: 0171 589 5232 FAX: 0171 584 8615

A passer-by may wonder what lies behind the immaculate pillared façade of Number Sixteen. Upon entering the hotel visitors will find themselves in an atmosphere of seclusion and comfort which has remained virtually unaltered in style since its early Victorian origins. The staff are friendly and attentive, regarding each visitor as a guest in a private home. The relaxed atmosphere of the lounge is the perfect place to pour a drink from the bar and meet friends or business associates. A fire blazing in the drawing room in cooler months creates an inviting warmth, whilst the conservatory opens on to a beautiful secluded walled garden which once again has won many accolades and awards for its floral displays. Each spacious bedroom is decorated with a discreet combination of antiques and traditional furnishings. The rooms are fully appointed with every facility that the discerning traveller would expect. A light breakfast is served in the privacy of guests' rooms and a tea and coffee service is available throughout the day. Although there is no dining room at Number Sixteen, some of London's finest restaurants are just round the corner. The hotel is close to the West End, Knightsbridge, Chelsea and Hyde Park. **Directions:** Sumner Place is off Old Brompton Road near Onslow Square. South Kensington Underground Station is 2 minutes' walk away. Price guide: Single £78–£99; double/twin £130–£155.

36 rms   MasterCard   VISA   AMERICAN EXPRESS   ◐   ⚔ 12   ☎   ⬍

PEMBRIDGE COURT HOTEL

34 PEMBRIDGE GARDENS, LONDON W2 4DX
TEL: 0171 229 9977 FAX: 0171 727 4982 – FROM USA TOLL FREE 1 800 709 9882

This gracious Victorian town house has been lovingly restored to its former glory whilst providing all the modern facilities demanded by today's discerning traveller. The 20 rooms are individually decorated with pretty fabrics and the walls adorned with an unusual collection of framed fans and Victoriana. The Pembridge Court is renowned for the devotion and humour with which it is run. Its long serving staff and its two famous cats "Spencer" and "Churchill" assure you of an immensely warm welcome and the very best in friendly, personal service. Over the years the hotel has built up a loyal following amongst its guests, many of whom regard it as their genuine 'home from home' in London. Winner of the 1994 RAC Award for Best Small Hotel in the South East of England, the Hotel is situated in quiet tree-lined gardens just off Notting Hill Gate, an area described by Travel & Leisure magazine as 'one of the liveliest, most prosperous corners of the city. "The Gate" as is affectionately known, is lively, colourful and full of life with lots of great pubs and restaurants and the biggest antiques market in the world at nearby Portobello Road. **Directions:** Pembridge Gardens is a small turning off Notting Hill Gate/Bayswater Road, just 2 minutes from Portobello Road Antiques Market. Price guide: Single £90–£120; double/twin £115–£155.

THE SAVOY

THE STRAND, LONDON WC2R 0EU
TEL: 0171 836 4343 FAX: 0171 240 6040 TELEX: 24234

Built on the site of the medieval Palace of Savoy, the hotel was created in 1889 by Richard D'Oyly Carte, the legendary impresario, as a result of the success of his Gilbert and Sullivan operas. The Savoy has a very English tradition of service and individuality. Bedrooms are decorated and furnished in a variety of styles – traditional, art deco and contemporary – and all share a standard of unrivalled comfort. In the restaurant, with its stunning views of the Thames, classic dishes by the legendary chef Escoffier are recreated, while the Savoy Grill is the meeting place for leading lights in the arts, media and the City. The Savoy Fitness Gallery boasts a roof-top swimming pool and state-of-the-art fitness facilities. Together with its sister hotels in The Savoy Group – The Berkeley in Knightsbridge and Claridge's in Mayfair – The Savoy offers a variety of short-break arrangements, some including dinner, others leaving one free to enjoy London at leisure – call 0171-872 8080 for details. **Directions:** The Savoy is on The Strand, to the west of Lancaster Place and Waterloo Bridge, in the heart of London's theatre district. Price guide: Single £180–£200; double/twin £205–£295, excluding VAT.

THE SLOANE HOTEL

29 DRAYCOTT PLACE, CHELSEA, LONDON SW3 2SH
TEL: 0171 581 5757 FAX: 0171 584 1348 – FROM USA TOLL FREE 1 800 324 9960

A small, intimate hotel set in the heart of London's Chelsea, The Sloane is as luxurious as any of its larger five-star contemporaries. Stunning designs and individual themes are features of the 12 fully air-conditioned bedrooms, which range from the contemporary to the traditional and neo-classical. Beautiful furnishings include vibrant silks, muted tapestries and lace bedspreads. Antique treasures are complemented by modern amenities to ensure maximum comfort. Guests who appreciate fine décor will be pleased to know that all items furnishing the rooms can be purchased. A 24 hour full room service is available with breakfast, light meals or traditional afternoon tea all available in a roof-top reception room, featuring terrace views across Chelsea. The Sloane's business centre provides full technical and secretarial support. The Sloane is situated within walking distance of many of London's most exciting shops, including Harrods and offers easy access to the City and West End. **Directions:** Draycott Place is off Sloane Square. Price guide: Double from £120; deluxe double/twin from £175; suites from £225. Exclusive of VAT.

POTTER & MOORE · Gilchrist & Soames
LONDON

Potter & Moore and Gilchrist & Soames,
both traditional manufacturers of luxury toiletries, offer to the
select and discerning hotelier a wide variety of
high quality bath products.

The perfect touch to the perfect stay.

POTTER & MOORE. GILCHRIST & SOAMES. TELEPHONE: 0733 281000. FAX: 0733 281028

Grasmere, Allan Bank and Helme Crag, Cumbria

Johansens Recommended Hotels in
England

Castles, *cathedrals, museums, great country houses and the opportunity to stay in areas of historical importance, England has much to offer. Whatever your leisure interests, there's a network of more than 550 Tourist Information Centres throughout England offering friendly, free advice on places to visit, entertainment, local facilities and travel information.*

British Travel Centre
12 Regent Street
Piccadilly Circus
London SW1Y 4PQ
(Personal callers only)

English Heritage
Keysign House
429 Oxford Street
London W1R 2HD
Tel: 0171-973 3396
Offers an unrivalled choice of properties to visit.

Historic Houses Association
2 Chester Street
London SW1X 7BB
Tel: 0171-259 5688
Ensures the survival of historic houses and gardens in private ownership in Great Britain.

The National Trust
36 Queen Anne's Gate
London SW1H 9AS
Tel: 0171-222 9251
Cares for more than 590,000 acres of countryside and over 400 historic buildings.

THE HEART OF ENGLAND
Here you have the essence of England, the country's very heart. From the thatched villages of Shakespeare Country, to some of the world's finest potteries in Stoke on Trent.

The Heart of England Tourist Board
PO Box 15
Worcester
Worcestershire WR5 1BR
Tel: 01905 763436

CUMBRIA
England's most beautiful lakes and tallest mountains reach out from the Lake District National Park to a landscape of spectacular coasts, hills and dales.

Cumbria Tourist Board
Ashleigh
Holly Road
Windermere
Cumbria LA23 2AQ
Tel: 015394 44444

NORTHUMBRIA
The north east region of England is steeped in

folklore and history and is celebrated as one of the most important centres of early English Christianity.

Northumbria Tourist Board
Aykley Heads
Durham
Co Durham DH1 5UX
Tel: 0191-384 6905

THE NORTH WEST
This region offers the very best in history and heritage, stunning countryside and vibrant towns and cities including Chester, Lancaster, Liverpool and Manchester.

The North West Tourist Board
Swan House
Swan Meadow Road
Wigan Pier
Wigan WN3 5BB
Tel: 01942 821222

YORKSHIRE & HUMBERSIDE
Scenic coastline with lively resorts, and spectacular seascapes. Unspoilt natural grandeur in dales and moors. Historic cities, picturesque villages, impressive castles and stately homes.

Yorkshire & Humberside Tourist Board
312 Tadcaster Road
York
North Yorkshire YO2 2HF
Tel: 01904 707961

EAST MIDLANDS
This region includes the coastal resorts of Lincolnshire, waterways such as the Grand Union Canal, the Trent & Mersey Canal and the Rivers Trent, Soar and Witham. Most of the Peak District National Park lies in Derbyshire.

East Midlands Tourist Board
Exchequergate
Lincoln
Lincolnshire LN2 1PZ
01522 531521

EAST ANGLIA
A place of farms and pine forests, quiet villages

and thatched cottages, medieval towns and charming cities, lively seaside resorts and quaint villages.

East Anglia Tourist Board
Toppesfield Hall
Hadleigh
Suffolk IP7 5DN
Tel: 01473 822922

WEST COUNTRY
England's favourite holiday destination with a mild climate all year round and over 600 miles of contrasting coastline. Discover another world of legend, mystery and romance.

West Country Tourist Board
60 St Davids Hill
Exeter
Devon EX4 4SY
Tel: 01392 76351

SOUTHERN ENGLAND
This area has connections with great literary figures. In the 19th century, Oxford was a centre for the pre-Raphaelite painters and many of their works can still be viewed in the city.

Southern Tourist Board
40 Chamberlayne Road
Eastleigh
Hampshire SO50 5JH
Tel: 01703 620006

SOUTH EAST
The region has 257 miles of coastline stretching from Gravesend, Kent, to the Witterings, West Sussex. The Channel Tunnel links this corner of England to mainland Europe.

South East England Tourist Board
The Old Brew House
Warwick Park
Royal Tunbridge Wells
Kent TN2 5TU
Tel: 01892 540766

London Tourist Board details appear on page 11.

WENTWORTH HOTEL

WENTWORTH ROAD, ALDEBURGH, SUFFOLK IP15 5BD
TEL: 01728 452312 FAX: 01728 454343

The Wentworth Hotel is ideally situated opposite the beach at Aldeburgh on Suffolk's unspoilt coast. Aldeburgh has maritime traditions dating back to the 15th century which are still maintained today by the longshore fishermen who launch their boats from the beach. It has also become a centre for music lovers: every June the Aldeburgh International Festival of Music, founded by the late Benjamin Britten, is held at Snape Maltings. Privately owned by the Pritt family since 1920, the Wentworth has established a reputation for comfort and service, good food and wine, for which many guests return year after year. Relax in front of an open fire in one of the hotel lounges, or sample a pint of the famous local Adnam's ales in the bar, which also serves meals. Many of the 38 elegantly furnished en suite bedrooms have sea views. The restaurant offers an extensive menu for both lunch and dinner and there is a comprehensive wine list. The garden terrace is the perfect venue for a light lunch *alfresco*. Nearby, the Minsmere Bird Sanctuary will be of interest to nature enthusiasts, while for the keen golfer, two of Britain's most challenging courses are within easy reach of the hotel at Aldeburgh and Thorpeness. Closed December 27 to Jan 9. **Directions:** Aldeburgh is just 7 miles from the A12 between Ipswich and Lowestoft. Price guide: Single £55; double/twin £100.

For hotel location, see maps on pages 473–479

THE ALDERLEY EDGE HOTEL

MACCLESFIELD ROAD, ALDERLEY EDGE, CHESHIRE SK9 7BJ
TEL: 01625 583033 FAX: 01625 586343

This privately owned award-winning hotel, dating from 1850, was refurbished from attic to cellar in 1989. It now has an attractive conservatory, 21 executive rooms and 11 de luxe rooms (each with a whirlpool bath), offering a choice of traditional décor or cottage-style accommodation. Attention is given to the highest standards of cooking; fresh produce, including fish delivered daily, is provided by local suppliers. Specialities include light lunches featuring hot and cold seafood dishes and puddings served piping hot from the oven. The hotel bakery produces a daily selection of unusual and delicious breads. The wonderfully mad wine list features over 1,000 wines and 200 champagnes.

There are special wine tastings held monthly and also gourmet champagne dinners. In addition to the conference room, there is a suite of meeting and private dining rooms. Secretarial services and fax machines are available. The famous Edge walks are nearby, as are Tatton and Lyme Parks, Quarry Bank Mill and Dunham Massey. Manchester's thriving city centre is 15 miles away and the airport is a 20-minute drive. **Directions:** Follow M6 to M56 Stockport. Exit junction 6, take A538 to Wilmslow. Follow signs 1³/₄ miles through Alderley Edge, turn left at Volvo garage and hotel is 200 yards on the right. Price guide: Single £95–£103; double/twin £116–£150.

WHITE LODGE COUNTRY HOUSE HOTEL

SLOE LANE, ALFRISTON, EAST SUSSEX BN26 5UR
TEL: 01323 870265 FAX: 01323 870284

The White Lodge Country House Hotel lies majestically on a rise within 5 acres of glorious Sussex downland in the undisturbed Cuckmere Valley, with picturesque views of the ancient village of Alfriston. Exquisitely furnished with authentic period pieces and elegant drapery, White Lodge is a setting in which to enjoy the style and luxury of a former age, with every comfort and facility of the present day. There are three comfortable lounges, all light and airy, where guests can relax. The cocktail bar is the ideal place to sip an apéritif in congenial surroundings prior to dinner. Whether dining in the attractive Orchid Restaurant or the more intimate dining room, a high standard of service and cuisine is assured. Each bedroom offers every amenity the discriminating guest would expect, with décor to match the quiet elegance which is the hotel's hallmark. White Lodge is only 10 minutes' drive from Glyndebourne, while Brighton, Eastbourne and the port of Newhaven are all within easy reach. The hotel is a romantic setting for wedding celebrations, while for business purposes small conferences and seminars can be catered for. **Directions:** Alfriston is on the B2108 between the A27/A259. Access from the market cross via West Street. Price guide: Single £50; double/twin £80–£110.

For hotel location, see maps on pages 473–479

BREAMISH COUNTRY HOUSE HOTEL

POWBURN, ALNWICK, NORTHUMBERLAND NE66 4LL
TEL: 01665 578544/578266 FAX: 01665 578500

In the heart of Northumberland, close by the rambling Cheviot Hills, Breamish Country House Hotel is a fine Georgian-style building set in five acres of gardens and woodland, offering visitors a uniquely beautiful retreat from the pressures of the working week. The hotel was originally a 17th-century farmhouse converted in the 1800s into a hunting lodge. The owners, Alan and Doreen Johnson, have created an atmosphere of peace and hospitality for their many guests. There are 11 bedrooms, each sumptuously and individually furnished, and are double-glazed with modern conveniences and private facilities. Pre-dinner drinks can be enjoyed in the comfortable drawing room, beside a log fire on winter evenings. In the restaurant, cordon bleu cooks prepare gourmet English cuisine with flair and imagination. To complement the food, the fine cellar offers many wines of distinction at competitive prices. Smoking is not permitted in the dining room. Dogs by prior arrangement. Closed January to mid-February. Activities available locally include riding, golf, course and game fishing. Northumberland is one of Britain's least spoilt regions, with mile upon mile of remote and lovely coastline. The area is also rich in history. **Directions:** Powburn is midway between Morpeth and Coldstream on the A697. Price guide (including dinner): Single: £74; double/twin: £116–£160.

LOVELADY SHIELD COUNTRY HOUSE HOTEL

NENTHEAD ROAD, ALSTON, CUMBRIA CA9 3LF
TEL: 01434 381203 FAX: 01434 381515

Two-and-a-half miles from Alston, England's highest market town, Lovelady Shield nestles in three acres of secluded riverside gardens. Bright log fires in the library and drawing room enhance the hotel's welcoming atmosphere. Owners Kenneth and Margaret Lyons take great care to create a peaceful and tranquil haven where guests can relax. The five-course dinners created by chef Barrie Garton, rounded off by home-made puddings and a selection of English farmhouse cheeses, has won the hotel AA 2 Red Stars and 2 Rosettes for food. Many guests first discover Lovelady Shield en route for Scotland. They then return to explore this beautiful and unspoiled part of England and experience the comforts of the hotel. Golf, fishing, shooting, pony-trekking and riding can be arranged locally. The Pennine Way, Hadrian's Wall and the Lake District are within easy reach. Facilities for small conferences and boardroom meetings are available. Closed 3 January to mid-February. Special Christmas, New Year, winter and spring breaks are offered and special weekly terms. **Directions:** The hotel's driveway is by the junction of the B6294 and the A689, 2¼ miles east of Alston. Price guide (including dinner): Single £72.50–£84.50; double/twin £145–£169.

For hotel location, see maps on pages 473–479

WOODLAND PARK HOTEL

WELLINGTON ROAD, TIMPERLEY, NR ALTRINCHAM, CHESHIRE WA15 7RG
TEL: 0161 928 8631 FAX: 0161 941 2821

The Woodland Park Hotel is a delightful family owned hotel in a secluded residential area. Brian and Shirley Walker offer their guests a warm and friendly welcome, working as a team with their staff to ensure the highest standards of comfort and service. All the bedrooms are individually designed and furnished and some offer the added luxury of an aero spa bath. Guests are invited either to relax in the two comfortable lounges one of which is non-smoking or to enjoy an apéritif in the elegant conservatory adjoining the Terrace Restaurant. The restaurant offers a choice of Brasserie style menu or table d'hôte. The hotel has extensive facilities for business meetings, conferences and weddings. Manchester City Centre is about eight miles away and offers wonderful theatre productions and the famous China Town. The hotel is also a convenient base for visiting Tatton Park, Dunham Park and Capesthorne Hall and the many historical places of interest in Chester. Manchester International Airport is just four miles away. **Directions:** Leave the M56 at Junction 3 and take the A560 towards Altrincham. Turn right onto Wellington Road. The hotel is signposted from the A560. Price guide: Single: £50–£80; double/twin £70–£95.

HOLBECK GHYLL COUNTRY HOUSE HOTEL

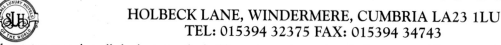

HOLBECK LANE, WINDERMERE, CUMBRIA LA23 1LU
TEL: 015394 32375 FAX: 015394 34743

The saying goes that all the best sites for building a house in England were taken long before the days of the motor car. Holbeck Ghyll has one such prime position. It was built in the early days of the 19th century and is superbly located overlooking Lake Windermere and the Langdale Fells. Today this luxury hotel has an outstanding reputation and is managed personally and expertly by its proprietors, David and Patricia Nicholson. As well as being awarded the RAC Blue Ribbon and AA Red Stars for five consecutive years, they are among an élite who have won an AA Courtesy and Care Award for total consideration of their guests. The majority of bedrooms are large and have spectacular and breathtaking views. All are recently refurbished to a very high standard, are en suite and include decanters of sherry, fresh flowers, trouser presses, fluffy bathrobes and a lot more. The oak-panelled restaurant is a delightful setting for memorable dining and meals are classically prepared, with focus on flavours and presentation, while an extensive wine list reflects quality and variety. The hotel has a billiard room, putting green and new all-weather tennis court. **Directions:** From Windermere, pass Brockhole Visitors Centre, then after $^1/_2$ mile turn right into Holbeck Lane (signed Troutbeck). Hotel is $^1/_2$ mile on left. Price guide (including dinner): Single £90; double/twin £130–£180; suite £180–£220.

KIRKSTONE FOOT COUNTRY HOUSE HOTEL

KIRKSTONE PASS ROAD, AMBLESIDE, CUMBRIA LA22 9EH
TEL: 015394 32232 FAX: 015394 32232

On your next visit to the Lake District, why not visit the Kirkstone Foot Country House Hotel? This charming 17th-century manor house stands in two acres of pretty, flower-filled gardens, overlooking Stock Ghyll which flows through the grounds. Such peace and tranquillity ensure that the tumults of the world will soon be forgotten. Inside, the atmosphere is warm and inviting: Kirkstone Foot's unique ambience has long been enjoyed by its often-returning clientèle. Within the main house are 12 twin, double, family and single rooms, with 15 apartments and cottages in the grounds offering the privacy of self-contained accommodation. The hotel continues to honour the English cultural tradition of good food and hospitality. A five-course dinner menu is changed daily and complemented by an extensive wine list. The staff add to the relaxing character of the hotel by combining attentive service with a friendly, informal manner – a sure recipe for success. With the magnificent scenery of the lakes and fells to golf, riding and water-sports facilities nearby, Kirkstone Foot has plenty to offer. The whole area inspired Wordsworth. Closed 3 January to early February. **Directions:** On Kirkstone Pass Road, off A591 at north end of Ambleside. Price guide (including dinner): Single £54–£70; double/twin £108–£120; suites £120.

ROTHAY MANOR

ROTHAY BRIDGE, AMBLESIDE, CUMBRIA LA22 0EH
TEL: 015394 33605 FAX: 015394 33607

Situated half a mile from Lake Windermere, this Georgian listed building stands in 1½ acres of grounds. The bedrooms include three beautifully furnished suites, two of which are in the lodge beside the manor and afford an unusual measure of space and privacy. One suite is equipped for five people and designed with particular attention to the comfort of guests with disabilities: it has a ramp leading to the garden and a spacious shower. Care and consideration are evident throughout. The menu is varied and meals are prepared with flair and imagination to high standards, complemented by an interesting wine list. For the actively inclined, residents have free use of the nearby Low Wood Leisure Club, with swimming pool, sauna, steam room, Jacuzzi, squash, sunbeds and a health and beauty salon. Permits are available for fishing, while locally guests can play golf, arrange to go riding, take a trip on a steam railway or visit Wordsworth's cottage. Small functions can be catered for with ease. Closed 2 January to 11 February. Represented in the USA by Josephine Barr: 800-323 5463. Each winter a full programme of special breaks with reduced rates is offered, as well as music, silver and antiques, walking and painting courses. **Directions:** ¾ mile from Ambleside on A593, the road to Coniston. Price guide: Single £76–£80; double/twin £110–£130; suite £156–£160.

ESSEBORNE MANOR

HURSTBOURNE TARRANT, ANDOVER, HAMPSHIRE SP11 0ER
TEL: 01264 736444 FAX: 01264 736725

Esseborne Manor is small and unpretentious, yet stylish. The present house was built at the end of the 19th century and carries the name used to record details of the local village in the *Domesday Book*. It is set in a pleasing garden amid the rich farmland of the North Wessex Downs in a designated area of outstanding natural beauty. Ian and Lucilla Hamilton, who manage the house, have established the restful atmosphere of a private country home where guests can unwind and relax. There are just 10 comfortable bedrooms, some reached via a courtyard, each decorated and furnished to a high standard, with views of the gardens and surrounding countryside. During the winter, a log fire glows in the sitting room, where guests can enjoy an apéritif before dinner. The pretty dining room reflects the importance the owners place upon service and good food. Chef Nick Watson creates imaginative menus from carefully selected, fresh seasonal produce. In the grounds there is a herb garden, an all-weather tennis court, a croquet lawn and plenty of good walking beyond. Nearby Newbury racecourse has a busy programme of steeplechasing and flat racing. Places to visit include Highclere Castle, Stonehenge, Salisbury, Winchester and Oxford. **Directions:** Midway between Newbury and Andover on the A343, 1½ miles north of Hurstbourne Tarrant. Price guide: Single £84; double/twin £95–£125.

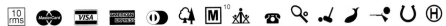

APPLEBY MANOR COUNTRY HOUSE HOTEL

ROMAN ROAD, APPLEBY-IN-WESTMORLAND, CUMBRIA CA16 6JB
TEL: 017683 51571 FAX: 017683 52888

Set in one of the most picturesque towns in the North, Appleby Manor is an ideal base for those wishing to explore the lovely surrounding countryside or for guests simply seeking peace and relaxation. Owned and run to the best traditional standards by the Swisloe family, it provides a friendly atmosphere and service. The high quality, well equipped accommodation includes seven coach house bedrooms where dogs are permitted. The award winning dining room offers a choice of four menus and a selection of over 70 malt whiskies are available from the bar. The hotel has a splendid leisure club with a small swimming pool, Jacuzzi, sauna, steam-room, solarium and fitness room. There is also a games room with table tennis, snooker and pool. Recreational facilities within easy reach include tennis courts, squash courts, cricket pitch, pony trekking and a bowling green. The town also has an impressive 18-hole golf course, set against the magnificent backdrop of the northern Pennines. Appleby provides an ideal base for exploring the Lake District, Yorkshire Dales and Bowes Museum at Barnard Castle. Directions: From the South take junction 38 of the M6 and then the B6260 to Appleby (13 miles). Drive through the town to a T-junction, turn left, first right and follow road for two-thirds of a mile. Price guide: Single £59–£64; double/twin £88–£108.

TUFTON ARMS HOTEL

MARKET SQUARE, APPLEBY-IN-WESTMORLAND, CUMBRIA CA16 6XA
TEL: 017683 51593 FAX: 017683 52761

This distinguished Victorian coaching inn, owned and run by the Milsom family, has been refurbished to provide a high standard of comfort. The bedrooms evoke the style of the 19th century, when the Tufton Arms became one of the premier hotels in Victorian England. The kitchen is run under the auspices of David Milsom, who spoils guests for choice with a gourmet dinner menu as well as a grill menu. The AA rosette and RAC Merit awarded restaurant is renowned for its fish dishes. Complementing the cuisine is an extensive wine list. There are conference and meeting rooms including the recently refurbished Hothfield Suite which can accommodate up to 120 people. 1995 RAC/Consort Hotel of the Year. RAC award for hospitality. Appleby, the historic county town of Westmorland, stands in splendid countryside and is ideal for touring the Lakes, Yorkshire Dales and Pennines. It is also a convenient stop-over en route to Scotland. Superb fishing for wild brown trout on a 24-mile stretch of the main River Eden, salmon fishing can be arranged on the lower reaches of the river. Shooting parties for grouse, duck and pheasant are a speciality. Appleby has an 18-hole moorland golf course. **Directions:** In centre of Appleby (bypassed by the A66), 38 miles west of Scotch Corner, 13 miles east of Penrith (M6 junction 40), 12 miles from M6 junction 38. Price guide: Single £55–£70; double/twin £85–£125; suite £140.

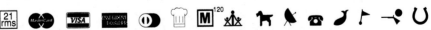

AMBERLEY CASTLE

AMBERLEY, NR ARUNDEL, WEST SUSSEX BN18 9ND
TEL: 01798 831992 FAX: 01798 831998

Winner of the Johansens 1995 Country Hotel Award, Amberley Castle is over 900 years old and is set between the rolling South Downs and the peaceful expanse of the Amberley Wildbrooks. Its towering battlements give breathtaking views while its massive, 14th-century curtain walls and mighty portcullis bear silent testimony to its fascinating history. Resident proprietors, Joy and Martin Cummings, have transformed this medieval fortress into a unique country castle hotel. They offer a warm, personal welcome and their hotel provides the ultimate in contemporary luxury, while retaining an atmosphere of timelessness. Guests can choose from four-poster, twin four-poster or brass double-bedded rooms. Each room is individually designed and has its own Jacuzzi bath. The exquisite 12th-century Queen's Room Restaurant is the perfect setting for the creative cuisine of new head chef Simon Thyer and his team. Amberley Castle is a natural first choice for romantic or cultural weekends, sporting breaks or confidential executive meetings. It is ideally situated for opera at Glyndebourne, theatre at Chichester and racing at Goodwood and Fontwell. It is easily accessible from London and the major air and channel ports. **Directions:** Amberley Castle is on the B2139, off the A29 between Fontwell and Bury. Price guide: Single £100; double/twin £130–£225.

BAILIFFSCOURT

CLIMPING, WEST SUSSEX BN17 5RW
TEL: 01903 723511 FAX: 01903 723107

Bailiffscourt is a perfectly preserved "medieval" house, built in the 1930s using material from historic old buildings. Gnarled 15th century beams and gothic mullioned windows combine to recreate a home from the Middle Ages. Set in 22 acres of beautiful pastures and walled gardens, it provides guests with a wonderful sanctuary in which to relax or work. The bedrooms are all individually decorated and luxuriously furnished, with many offering four poster beds, open log fires and beautiful views over the surrounding countryside. The restaurant offers a varied menu and summer lunches can be taken alfresco in a rose-clad courtyard or the walled garden. A good list of well-priced wines accompanies meals. Private dining rooms are available for weddings, conferences and meetings, and companies can hire the hotel as their 'country house' for 2 or 3 days. Bailiffscourt, which is AA three rosettes accredited, is surrounded by tranquil parkland with a golf practice area, outdoor pool and tennis courts. Climping Beach, 100 yards away, is ideal for windsurfing. Nearby are Arundel with its castle, Chichester and Goodwood. **Directions:** Three miles south of Arundel, off the A259. Price guide: Single £80; double from £95.

PENNYHILL PARK HOTEL AND COUNTRY CLUB

LONDON ROAD, BAGSHOT, SURREY GU19 5ET
TEL: 01276 471774 FAX: 01276 473217

Bagshot has been a centre of hospitality since the early Stuart sovereigns James I and Charles I had a hunting lodge there. Pennyhill Park Hotel continues to uphold that tradition. Built in 1849, this elegant mansion reflects its journey through Victorian and Edwardian times while providing every modern amenity. The bedrooms are outstanding: no two are identical, and infinite care has been invested in creating practical rooms with distinctive features. Impeccable service is to be expected, as staff are trained to classical, Edwardian standards. Cuisine is served in the welcoming setting of the Latymer Restaurant, accompanied by a wine list that includes many rare vintages. During the day a light meal may be taken in the Orangery, which is part of the Pennyhill Country Club. Recreational facilities are available within the grounds, which span 120 acres and include landscaped gardens, a 9-hole golf course, a swimming pool and a three acre lake. Pennyhill Park is conveniently located only 27 miles from central London and not far from Heathrow, Windsor Castle, Ascot, Wentworth and Sunningdale. **Directions:** From the M3, exit 3, take A322 towards Bracknell. Turn left on to A30 signposted to Camberley. 3/4 mile after Bagshot; turn right 50 yards past the Texaco garage. Price guide: Single from £125; double/twin from £140; suite from £205.

For hotel location, see maps on pages 473–479

THE ROYAL BERKSHIRE

LONDON ROAD, SUNNINGHILL, ASCOT, BERKSHIRE SL5 0PP
TEL: 01344 23322 FAX: 01344 27100/01344 874240

For over 100 years The Royal Berkshire was the home of the Churchill family. Now it is an elegant hotel, ideally located between Ascot racecourse and the Guards Polo Club. This Queen Anne mansion, built in 1705 by the Duke of Marlborough for his son, is set in 15 acres of gardens and woodlands. Guests have access to a wide range of leisure facilities including a putting green, indoor heated pool, squash court, whirlpool spa and sauna. The spacious interiors are smartly decorated in contemporary pastel shades, with the full-length windows bathing the rooms in light. Tea or drinks can be enjoyed in the drawing rooms or on the terrace with views across the lawns. The menu offers an eclectic choice of dishes to please connoisseurs of fine food. All meals are carefully prepared with meticulous attention to presentation. Some interesting vintages are included on the wine list. A series of well-equipped function rooms, combined with easy accessibility from Heathrow and central London, makes the Royal Berkshire a popular venue for business events. For golfers, Swinley, Sunningdale and Wentworth are all nearby. Royal Windsor and Eton are a short drive away. **Directions:** One mile from Ascot on the corner of A329 and B383. Nearest M25 exit is junction 13. Price guide: Single from £120; double/twin from £165; weekend rate £49.50 per person per night.

CALLOW HALL

MAPPLETON ROAD, ASHBOURNE, DERBYSHIRE DE6 2AA
TEL: 01335 343403 FAX: 01335 343624

The approach to Callow Hall is up a tree-lined drive through the 44-acre grounds. On arrival visitors can take in the splendid views from the hotel's elevated position, overlooking the valleys of Bentley Brook and the River Dove. The majestic building and Victorian gardens have been restored by resident proprietors, David, Dorothy and their son, Anthony Spencer, who represent the fifth and sixth generations of hoteliers in the Spencer family. Mineral water and home-made biscuits can be found in the spacious period bedrooms. Fresh local produce is selected daily for use in the kitchen, where the term 'home-made' comes into its own. Home-cured bacon, sausages, fresh bread, traditional English puddings and melt-in-the-mouth pastries are among the items prepared on the premises. Visiting anglers can enjoy a rare opportunity to fish for trout and grayling along a mile-long private stretch of the Bentley Brook, which is mentioned in Izaak Walton's *The Compleat Angler*. Callow Hall is ideally situated for touring the Peak District and Dovedale. Closed Christmas. **Directions:** Take the A515 through Ashbourne towards Buxton. At the Bowling Green Inn on the brow of a steep hill, turn left, then take the first right, signposted Mappleton, and the hotel is over the bridge on the right. Price guide: Single £65–£80; double/twin £90–£120.

HOLNE CHASE HOTEL

NR ASHBURTON, DEVON TQ13 7NS
TEL: 01364 631471 FAX: 01364 631453

A hunting estate in the 11th century, this ETB 4 Crowns Highly Commended hotel has been run in a professional yet friendly and informal fashion by the Bromage family since 1972. Most of the rooms at Holne Chase, including many of the individually furnished bedrooms, offer spectacular views over the Dart Valley. Deep sofas, easy chairs, log fires and books create a relaxing atmosphere, confirming the proprietors' aim to provide a sanctuary from the hustle and bustle of everyday life. A productive kitchen garden supplies the restaurant, where good quality, regional cooking can be enjoyed. Fly-fishermen can enjoy the hotel's mile-long stretch of the River Dart, in quest of salmon and sea trout. Guided walks can be arranged from Holne Chase, which is a good base for exploring Dartmoor's open moorland and deep wooded valleys. It is also an area of archaeological interest, having the largest concentration of Iron Age and prehistoric sites in Northern Europe. Canoeing, golfing and riding can all be organised. Special breaks are available. **Directions:** Holne Chase is three miles north of Ashburton. To find the hotel, take the Ashburton turning off the A38, and follow the signs for Two Bridges. The hotel turning is on the right just after the road crosses the River Dart. Price guide: Single from £65; double/twin £90–£100; suite £115.

EASTWELL MANOR

BOUGHTON LEES, ASHFORD, KENT TN25 4HR
TEL: 01233 219955 FAX: 01233 635530

In the midst of a 3,000-acre estate, set in 62 acres of lovely grounds, lies Eastwell Manor. It was once the home of Queen Victoria's second son, Prince Alfred, and his wife. The Queen and her elder son, later to become Edward VII, were frequent visitors here. The elegant bedrooms are named after past owners, lords, ladies and gentlemen, bearing witness to the hotel's rich history. Each room is individually and gracefully furnished and offers every modern comfort. Huge open fireplaces with stone mantles, carved panelling, leather Chesterfield sofas and fine antique furniture are features of the lounges, billiard room and bar. A choice of traditional English and French cuisine is served in the handsome wood panelled dining room, matched by an excellent cellar of carefully chosen wines. Guests are invited to take advantage of the hotel's tennis court and croquet lawn, while a variety of other leisure pursuits are available locally. The Manor is conveniently located for visiting the historic cathedral city of Canterbury, Leeds Castle and a number of charming market towns. **Directions:** M20 junction 9. A28 towards Canterbury, then A251 signed Faversham. Hotel is three miles north of Ashford in the village of Boughton Lees. Price guide: £107.50–£137.50; double/twin £140–£190; suites £235–£255.

RIVERSIDE COUNTRY HOUSE HOTEL

ASHFORD-IN-THE-WATER, NR BAKEWELL, DERBYSHIRE DE4 1QF
TEL: 01629 814275 FAX: 01629 812873

Ashford-in-the-Water lies in a limestone ravine of the River Wye in the Peak District National Park. Mentioned in the *Domesday Book*, it is a picture-postcard village of quaint, stone-built cottages. Near the village centre stands the Riverside Country House, a small ivy-clad Georgian mansion, bounded by an acre of mature garden and river frontage. Oak panelling and inglenook fireplaces in the lounge create a sense of warmth – an ideal place to chat or curl up with a book. Using seasonally available game from the nearby Chatsworth estate and freshly caught fish, Master Chef Simon Wild creates a series of exciting dishes. Dinner, complemented by fine wines, is served at antique tables set with

gleaming silver, sparkling crystal and illuminated by candle-light. Lunch is always available and the Terrace Room is open all day. All the prettily decorated bedrooms, with hand-made soft furnishings, all have private facilities. Ideally situated for Chatsworth, Haddon Hall and Hardwick Hall, the hotel is also convenient for the Derbyshire Dales, Lathkill and Dovedale. Bargain breaks offered for two to five-night stays. **Directions:** 1½ miles north of Bakewell on the A6 heading towards Buxton. Ashford-in-the-Water lies on the right side of the river. The hotel is at the end of the village main street next to the Sheepwash Bridge. Price guide: Single from £75; double/twin from £99.

TYTHERLEIGH COT HOTEL

CHARDSTOCK, AXMINSTER, DEVON EX13 7BN
TEL: 01460 221170 FAX: 01460 221291

Originally the village cider house, this 14th-century Grade II listed building has been skilfully converted into a spacious modern hotel, idyllically situated in the secluded village of Chardstock on the Devon/Dorset/Somerset borders. The hotel is owned and run by Frank and Pat Grudgings, who extend a warm welcome. The bedrooms, converted from former barns and outbuildings, are all individually designed, some with four-poster or half-tester beds and double Jacuzzis. The beautifully designed restaurant is housed in a Victorian-style conservatory, overlooking an ornamental lily pond with cascading fountain and wrought-iron bridge. Imaginative menus based on local ingredients are complemented by a carefully selected wine list. Awarded AA Red Rosette for food. Special house parties are held at Christmas and New Year and bargain break weekends can be arranged. The hotel has an outdoor heated swimming pool, sauna, solarium and mini-gym. Riding, tennis, golf and clay pigeon shooting can be arranged locally. The hotel is ideally located for guests to explore the varied landscape of the South West and there are many historic houses and National Trust properties nearby. **Directions:** From Chard take A358 Axminster road; Chardstock signposted on right about 3 miles along. Price guide: Single £55; double/twin £98–£123.50.

HARTWELL HOUSE

OXFORD ROAD, NR AYLESBURY, BUCKINGHAMSHIRE HP17 8NL
TEL: 01296 747444 FAX: 01296 747450 – FROM USA FAX FREE: 1 800 260 8338

Standing in 90 acres of gardens and parkland landscaped by a pupil of 'Capability' Brown, Hartwell House has both Jacobean and Georgian façades. This beautiful house, brilliantly restored by Historic House Hotels, was the residence in exile of King Louis XVIII of France from 1809 to 1814. The large ground floor reception rooms, with oak panelling and decorated ceilings, have antique furniture and fine paintings which evoke the elegance of the 18th century. There are 47 individually designed bedrooms and suites, some in the house and some in Hartwell Court, the restored 18th-century stables. The dining room at Hartwell is the setting for memorable meals produced by head chef Alan Maw. The Hartwell Spa adjacent to the hotel includes an indoor swimming pool, whirlpool spa bath, steam room, gymnasium, hairdressing and beauty salon. Situated in the Vale of Aylesbury, the hotel, which is a member of Relais & Chateaux, is only an hour from London and 20 miles from Oxford. Blenheim Palace, Waddesdon Manor and Woburn Abbey are nearby. Dogs are permitted only in the Hartwell Court bedrooms. **Directions:** On the A418 Oxford Road, 2 miles from Aylesbury. Price guide: Single £98; double/twin £150–£235; suites £195–£350.

THE PRIORY HOTEL

HIGH STREET, WHITCHURCH, AYLESBURY, BUCKINGHAMSHIRE HP22 4JS
TEL: 01296 641239 FAX: 01296 641793

The Priory Hotel is a beautifully preserved, timber-framed house dating back to 1360. It is set in the picturesque conservation village of Whitchurch, 5 miles north of Aylesbury. With its exposed timbers, leaded windows and open fires, it retains all its traditional character and charm – a refreshing alternative to the all-too-familiar chain hotels of today. All 11 bedrooms are individually furnished and many of them have four-poster beds. At the heart of the hotel is La Boiserie Restaurant, where classical French cuisine is served in intimate surroundings. An imaginative à la carte fixed-price menu is offered, including a range of seasonal dishes. Start, for example, with a rich terrine of partridge, wild mushrooms and pistachios, then perhaps choose marinated saddle of venison in Cognac butter sauce and garnished with truffles. Specialities include fresh lobster and flambé dishes. The self-contained conference suite can be used for private lunches, dinners and receptions. Among the places to visit locally are Waddesdon Manor, Claydon House, Silverstone motor circuit and Oxford. Closed between Christmas and New Year's Eve; the restaurant also closes on Sunday evenings. **Directions:** Situated on the A413 4 miles north of Aylesbury. Price guide: Single £60–£80; double/twin £90–£110; suite from £102.

For hotel location, see maps on pages 473–479

HASSOP HALL

HASSOP, NR BAKEWELL, DERBYSHIRE DE45 1NS
TEL: 01629 640488 FAX: 01629 640577

The recorded history of Hassop Hall reaches back 900 years to the *Domesday Book*, to a time when the political scene in England was still dominated by the power struggle between the barons and when the only sure access to that power was through possession of land. By 1643, when the Civil War was raging, the Hall was under the ownership of Rowland Eyre, who turned it into a Royalist garrison. It was the scene of several skirmishes before it was recaptured after the Parliamentary victory. Since purchasing Hassop Hall in 1975, Thomas Chapman has determinedly pursued the preservation of its outstanding heritage. Guests can enjoy the beautifully maintained gardens as well as the splendid countryside of the surrounding area. The bedrooms, some of which are particularly spacious, are well furnished and comfortable. A four-poster bedroom is available for romantic occasions. A comprehensive dinner menu offers a wide and varied selection of dishes, with catering for most tastes. As well as the glories of the Peak District, places to visit include Chatsworth House, Haddon Hall and Buxton Opera House. Christmas opening – details on application. **Directions:** From M1 exit 29 (Chesterfield), take A619 to Baslow, then A623 to Calver; left at lights to B6001. Hassop Hall is 2 miles on right. Price guide: Single £65–£85; double/twin £75–£95. Inclusive rates available on request.

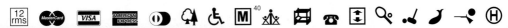

THE PLOUGH

BOURTON ROAD, CLANFIELD, OXFORDSHIRE OX18 2RB
TEL: 01367 810222 FAX: 01367 810596

The Plough at Clanfield is an idyllic hideaway for the romantic at heart. Set in a sleepy Oxfordshire village on the edge of the Cotswolds, The Plough dates from 1560 and is a fine example of well-preserved Elizabethan architecture. When Hatton Hotels refurbished the hotel several years ago, great care was taken to preserve the charm and character of the interiors. Because there are only six bedrooms, guests can enjoy an intimate atmosphere and attentive, personal service. All the bedrooms are beautifully appointed to the highest standard and all have en suite bathrooms, four with whirlpool baths. At the heart of the hotel is the award-winning Tapestry Room Restaurant, regarded as one of the finest in the area. The cuisine is superbly prepared and impeccably served, with an interesting selection of wines. Two additional dining rooms are available for private entertaining. The hotel is an ideal base from which to explore the Cotswolds or the Thames Valley. There are many historic houses and gardens in the area, as well as racing at Newbury and Cheltenham. A member of Hatton Hotels. **Directions:** From Oxford, take the A420 for about 15 miles, then turn right to Faringdon. Go straight through the village on the main road. Clanfield is about four miles further on. Price guide: Single £65; double/twin £85–£100.

WROXTON HOUSE HOTEL

WROXTON ST MARY, NR BANBURY, OXFORDSHIRE OX15 6QB
TEL: 01295 730777 FAX: 01295 730800

Built of honeyed local stone, Wroxton House has undergone a sensitive restoration linking three village houses, dating from the 17th century, with a delightful clocktower wing and conservatory lounge. The relaxing character of the hotel is created by the carefully selected staff, who combine attentive service with friendliness and informality. The spacious and bright lounges contain thoughtfully chosen furnishings, comfortable armchairs and a profusion of flowers and plants. The 32 en suite bedrooms have been individually decorated and the original timbers preserved in many of the older rooms. The classic English styles complement the deeply polished woods of the furniture. Guests may dine by candlelight in the intimate restaurant, where a traditional Cotswold atmosphere is evoked by original beams, inglenooks, carved oak recesses, horse brasses and pewter. The expertly prepared menus display a personal interpretation of classic British dishes which make imaginative use of the freshest local produce. Wroxton House Hotel is a popular choice with businessmen, as it offers good meeting facilities in a quiet setting. Golf and riding can be arranged locally. **Directions:** Easily reached via M40, Wroxton is two miles outside Banbury on the A422 Stratford-upon-Avon road. Price guide: Single £75–£85; double/twin £95–£125.

HALMPSTONE MANOR

BISHOP'S TAWTON, NR BARNSTAPLE, DEVON EX32 0EA
TEL: 01271 830321 FAX: 01271 830826

Set in 200 acres of rolling, north Devonshire countryside, Halmpstone Manor continues a 400-year tradition of hospitality. The name Halmpstone means 'holy boundary stone', from its original links with the ecclesiastical lands of Bishop's Tawton. Proprietors Jane and Charles Stanbury have achieved a delightful combination of the formal and informal, to create a relaxing atmosphere of genuine warmth and quiet charm. Dinner is served in the distinctive early 16th-century wood-panelled dining room, where in winter an inviting log fire glows. Gourmet cuisine is prepared to the highest standards, with imaginative use of fresh local and exotic ingredients. Gleaming silver, sparkling glassware and beautiful china make for superbly presented meals. The tastefully co-ordinated bedrooms, luxuriously furnished with either four-poster or brass and coronet beds, all have sumptuous en suite facilities. Attentive and friendly service ensures that all guests' requirements are met. 2 AA Red Rosettes. Dogs are permitted in one of the bedrooms. **Directions:** A361 to Barnstaple; A377 to Bishop's Tawton. At end of village, turn left opposite BP filling station. Travel 2 miles further, turn right at Halmpstone Manor sign. Price guide: Single £65; double/twin £100–£130.

TYLNEY HALL

ROTHERWICK, NR HOOK, HAMPSHIRE RG27 9AZ
TEL: 01256 764881 FAX: 01256 768141

Arriving at this hotel in the evening, with its floodlit exterior and forecourt fountain, you can imagine that you are arriving for a party in a private stately home. Grade II listed and set in 66 acres of stunning gardens and parkland, Tylney Hall typifies the great houses of the past. Apéritifs are taken in the wood-panelled library bar; haute cuisine is served in the glass-domed Oak Room restaurant, complemented by conscientious service. The hotel was the 1990 winner of the AA Care and Courtesy Award and holds 2 AA Rosettes for food and also AA 4 Red Stars. Extensive leisure facilities include indoor and outdoor heated swimming pools, multi-gym, sauna, tennis, croquet and snooker, while hot-air ballooning, archery, clay pigeon shooting, golf and riding can be arranged. Surrounding the hotel are wooded trails ideal for rambling or jogging. Functions for up to a hundred are catered for in the Tylney Suite or Chestnut Suite, while more intimate gatherings are held in one of the other seven meeting rooms. The cathedral city of Winchester and Stratfield Saye House are all nearby. **Directions:** M4, junction 11, towards Hook and Rotherwick – follow signs to hotel. M3, junction 5, 3rd exit, A287 towards Newnham – over A30 into Old School Road. Left for Newnham and right onto Ridge Lane. Hotel is on the left after one mile. Price guide: Single from £104; double/twin from £124; suite from £214.

CAVENDISH HOTEL

BASLOW, DERBYSHIRE DE45 1SP
TEL: 01246 582311 FAX: 01246 582312

Dating from the late-18th century, the original Peacock Hotel has been considerably upgraded and was re-opened as the Cavendish in 1975. Set on the Duke and Duchess of Devonshire's estate at Chatsworth, the hotel occupies a unique position and makes a marvellous base for visitors who wish to explore this part of Derbyshire. A warm welcome is assured from proprietor Eric Marsh who greets guests personally. All the well-equipped bedrooms overlook the estate and have en suite facilities. The hotel has a relaxed, homely feel which is enhanced by crackling log fires in cooler weather. The tasteful furnishings include antiques and fine art from the Devonshire Collection.

Meals are served throughout the day in the Garden Room Restaurant, where the informal atmosphere is in contrast to the other, more formal, dining room. Chef Nicholas Buckingham and his team have won many commendations for their creative cuisine. A footpath connects the hotel to the Chatsworth Estate where guests are welcome to stroll. Hardwick Hall, Haddon Hall, the Treak Cliff Cavern (the Blue John mine) and the Tramway Museum at Crich are all nearby. **Directions:** The hotel is on the A619 in Baslow, 9 miles west of Chesterfield; 15 miles from M1, junction 29. Price guide (excluding breakfast): Single £79; double/twin £99.

For hotel location, see maps on pages 473–479

FISCHER'S

BASLOW HALL, CALVER ROAD, BASLOW, DERBYSHIRE DE45 1RR
TEL: 01246 583259 FAX: 01246 583818

Situated on the edge of the magnificent Chatsworth Estate, Baslow Hall enjoys an enviable location surrounded by some of the country's finest stately homes and within easy reach of the Peak District's many cultural and historical attractions. Standing at the end of a winding Chestnut tree-lined driveway, this fine Derbyshire manor house was tastefully converted by Max and Susan Fischer into an award winning country house hotel in 1989. Since opening Fischer's has consistently maintained its position as one of the finest establishments in the Derbyshire/South Yorkshire regions earning the prestigious Egon Ronay 'Restaurant of the Year' award in 1995. Whether you are staying in the area for private or business reasons, it is a welcome change to find a place that feels less like a hotel and more like a home combining comfort and character with an eating experience which is a delight to the palate. Max presides in the kitchen. His Michelin starred cuisine can be savoured either in the more formal main dining room or in 'Café Max' – where the emphasis is on more informal eating and modern tastes. Baslow Hall offers facilities for small conferences or private functions. Baslow is within 12 miles of the M1 motorway, Chesterfield and Sheffield. Fischer's is on the A623 in Baslow. Price guide: Single £70–£85; double/twin £95–£120; suite £120.

COMBE GROVE MANOR HOTEL & COUNTRY CLUB

BRASSKNOCKER HILL, MONKTON COMBE, BATH, AVON BA2 7HS
TEL: 01225 834644 FAX: 01225 834961

This is an exclusive 18th-century country house hotel situated two miles from the beautiful city of Bath. Built on the hillside site of a Roman settlement, Combe Grove Manor is set in 82 acres of formal gardens and woodland, with magnificent views over the Limpley Stoke Valley. In addition to the Georgian Restaurant, where superb food is served prepared by chef Paul Mingo-West, there is a private dining room, plus a wine bar and restaurant with a terrace garden. After dinner guests may relax with drinks in the elegant drawing room or library. The bedrooms are lavishly furnished, all individually designed with en suite facilities, two of which have Jacuzzi baths. Within the grounds are some of the finest leisure facilities in the South West, including indoor and outdoor heated pools, a spa bath and steam room, four all-weather tennis courts, a 5-hole par 3 golf course and a two-tiered driving range. Guests may use the Nautilus gym, aerobics studio, saunas and solaria or relax in the Clarins beauty rooms where a full range of treatments is offered. Separate from the Manor House is the Garden Lodge which is ideal for conferences. ETB 5 Crowns Highly Commended. AA 4 Stars. 2 Rosettes. **Directions:** Set south-east of Bath on Brassknocker Hill, between Combe Down and Monkton Combe. Map can be supplied on request. Price guide: Single £98; double/twin from £98; suite from £195.

For hotel location, see maps on pages 473–479

HOMEWOOD PARK

HINTON CHARTERHOUSE, BATH, AVON BA3 6BB
TEL: 01225 723731 FAX: 01225 723820

Standing amid 10 acres of beautiful grounds and woodland on the edge of Limpley Stoke Valley, a designated area of natural beauty is Homewood Park, one of Britain's finest privately-owned smaller country house hotels. This lovely 19th century building has an elegant interior, adorned with beautiful fabrics, antiques, oriental rugs and original oil paintings. Lavishly furnished bedrooms offer the best in comfort, style and privacy. Each of them has a charm and character of its own and all have good views over the Victorian garden. The outstanding cuisine has won the hotel an excellent reputation. The à la carte menu uses wherever possible produce both from local suppliers and from Homewood itself. A range of carefully selected wines, stored in the hotel's original mediaeval cellars, is available augment lunch and dinner. Before or after a meal guests can enjoy a drink in the comfortable bar or drawing room, both of which have a log fire during the cooler months. The hotel is well placed for guests to enjoy the varied attractions of the wonderful city of Bath with its unique hot springs, Roman remains, superb Georgian architecture and American Museum. **Directions:** On the A36 six miles from Bath towards Warminster. Price guide: Single £90; double/twin £95–£130.

LUCKNAM PARK

COLERNE, NR BATH, WILTSHIRE SN14 8AZ
TEL: 01225 742777 FAX: 01225 743536

For over 250 years Lucknam Park has been a focus of fine society and aristocratic living, something guests will sense immediately upon their approach along the mile-long avenue lined with beech trees. Built in 1720, this magnificent Palladian mansion is situated just six miles from Bath on the southern edge of the Cotswolds. The delicate aura of historical context is reflected in fine art and antiques dating from the late Georgian and early Victorian periods. The Michelin-starred cuisine can be savoured in the elegant restaurant, at tables laid with exquisite porcelain, silver and glassware, accompanied with wines from an extensive cellar. Set within the walled gardens of the hotel is the Leisure Spa, comprising an indoor pool, sauna, solarium, steam room, whirlpool spa, gymnasium, beauty salon and snooker room. Numerous activities can be arranged on request, including hot-air ballooning, riding, golf and archery. Bath, described by the Romans as "the most magnificent city west of the Alps" remains one of the most beautiful cities in Europe. Bowood House, Corsham Court and Castle Combe are among the many other local places of interest. **Directions:** Fifteen minutes from M4, junctions 17 and 18, located between A420 and A4 near the village of Colerne. Price guide: Single £110; double/twin £160; suite from £300.

THE PRIORY HOTEL

WESTON ROAD, BATH, AVON BA1 2XT
TEL: 01225 331922 FAX: 01225 448276

Lying in the seclusion of landscaped grounds, The Priory Hotel is in easy reach of some of Britain's finest architecture. Within walking distance of Bath city centre, this Gothic-style mellow stone building dates from 1835, when it formed part of a row of fashionable residences on the west side of the city. Visitors will sense the luxury as they enter the hotel: antique furniture, plush rugs and *objets d'art* add interest to the two spacious reception rooms and the elegant drawing room. Well-defined colour schemes lend an uplifting brightness throughout, particularly in the tastefully appointed bedrooms. Chef Michael Collom's French classical style is the primary inspiration for the cuisine, served in three interconnecting dining rooms which overlook the garden. An especially good selection of wines can be recommended to accompany meals. Private functions can be accommodated both in the Drawing Room and the Orangery, with garden access an added bonus. The Roman Baths, Theatre Royal, Museum of Costume and a host of bijou shops offer plenty for visitors to see. **Directions:** Leave M4 at junction 18 to Bath on A46. Enter city on A4 London road and follow signs for Bristol. Turn right into Park Lane which runs through Royal Victoria Park. Then turn left into Weston Road. The hotel is on the left. Price guide: Single £85; double/twin £155–£195.

THE QUEENSBERRY

RUSSEL STREET, BATH, AVON BA1 2QF
TEL: 01225 447928 FAX: 01225 446065 – FROM USA TOLL FREE 1 800 323 5463

When the Marquis of Queensberry commissioned John Wood to build this house in Russel Street in 1772, little did he know that 200 years hence guests would still be being entertained in these elegant surroundings. An intimate town house hotel, The Queensberry is in a quiet residential street just a few minutes' walk from Wood's other splendours – the Royal Crescent, Circus and Assembly Rooms. Bath is one of England's most beautiful cities. Regency stucco ceilings, ornate cornices and panelling combined with enchanting interior décor complement the strong architectural style. However, the standards of hotel-keeping have far outpaced the traditional surroundings, with high-quality en suite bedrooms, room service and up-to-date office support for executives. The Olive Tree Restaurant is one of the leading restaurants in the Bath area. Proprietors Stephen and Penny Ross, who in the 1980's gained their admirable reputation at Homewood Park, are thoroughly versed in offering hospitality. Represented in America by Josephine Barr. The hotel is closed for one week at Christmas. **Directions:** From junction 18 of M4, enter Bath along A4 London Road. Turn sharp right up Lansdown Road, left into Bennett Street, then right into Russel Street opposite the Assembly Rooms. Price guide: Single £89; double/twin £98–£164.

For hotel location, see maps on pages 473–479

In association with MasterCard

THE ROYAL CRESCENT

ROYAL CRESCENT, BATH, AVON BA1 2LS
TEL: 01225 739955 FAX: 01225 339401

The Royal Crescent Hotel is part of the Royal Crescent itself a 500ft curve of 30 houses with identical façades. The Crescent was conceived in the latter part of the 18th century and is one of the greatest European architectural masterpieces. The hotel comprises the two central houses and within its beautiful gardens are The Pavilion, The Garden Villa and The Dower House. In the front hall of the hotel is a unique collection of original Bath landscapes and portraits of the famous people who have lived in the city. The bedrooms are individually decorated to suit every taste and each has its own character, while the suites are the last word in comfort. The Beau Nash suite, for example, has its own large spa pool room. Luxurious furnishings and tasteful décor are also a striking feature of the various reception rooms. Nestling in the gardens, the Dower House Restaurant offers a delicious table d'hôte menu which combines flair with imagination and originality. The restaurant has received three AA rosettes and an Egon Ronay Star. The hotel has peaceful conference facilities in The Royal Crescent Mews. Apart from the delights of Bath, there are innumerable local activities. These include motor racing at the Castle Combe Circuit and hot air ballooning. **Directions:** Detailed directions are available from the hotel on booking. Price guide Single: £98–£120; double/twin £145–£205; suites £275.

STON EASTON PARK

STON EASTON, BATH, SOMERSET BA3 4DF

TEL: 01761 241631 FAX: 01761 241377 e-MAIL stoneaston@cityscape.co.uk

The internationally renowned hotel at Ston Easton Park is a Grade I Palladian mansion of notable distinction. A showpiece for some exceptional architectural and decorative features of its period, it dates from 1739 and has recently undergone extensive restoration, offering a unique opportunity to enjoy the opulent splendour of the 18th century. A high priority is given to the provision of friendly and unobtrusive service. The hotel has won innumerable awards for its décor, service and food. Jean Monro, an acknowledged expert on 18th century decoration, supervised the design and furnishing of the interiors, complementing the original features with choice antiques, paintings and *objets d'art*.

Fresh, quality produce, delivered from all parts of Britain, is combined with herbs and vegetables from the Victorian kitchen garden to create English and French dishes. To accompany the meal, a wide selection of rare wines and old vintages is stocked in the house cellars. The grounds, landscaped by Humphry Repton in 1793, consist of romantic gardens and parkland. The 17th-century Gardener's Cottage, close to the main hotel on the wooded banks of the River Norr, provides private suite accommodation. A Relais et Châteaux member. **Directions:** Eleven miles south of Bath on the A37 between Bath and Wells. Price guide: Single from £95; double/twin £145–£300.

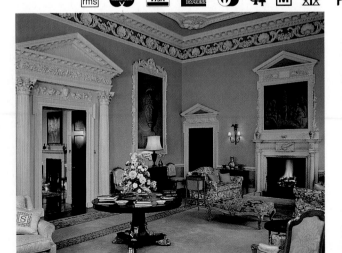

POWDERMILLS HOTEL

POWDERMILL LANE, BATTLE, EAST SUSSEX TN33 0SP
TEL: 01424 775511 FAX: 01424 774540

Situated outside the historic Sussex town famous for the 1066 battle, Powdermills is an 18th century listed country house which has been skilfully converted into an elegant hotel. Nestling in 150 acres of parks and woodland, the beautiful and tranquil grounds feature a 7-acre specimen fishing lake, as well as three smaller lakes stocked with trout which guests may fish. Wild geese, swans, ducks, kingfishers and herons abound and a rare breed of Scottish sheep grazes nearby. Privately owned and run by Douglas and Julie Cowpland, the hotel has been carefully furnished with locally acquired antiques. On cooler days, log fires burn in the entrance hall and drawing room. The bedrooms – two with four-posters –

are all individually furnished and decorated. The Orangery Restaurant has received many accolades and offers fine classical cooking by chef Paul Webbe. Guests may dine on the terrace in summer, looking out over the swimming pool and grounds. Light meals and snacks are available in the library. The location is ideal from which to explore the beautiful Sussex and Kent countryside and there are many villages and small towns in the area.
Directions: From centre of Battle take the Hastings road south. After $\frac{1}{4}$ mile turn right into Powdermill Lane. After sharp bend, entrance is on right; cross bridge and lakes to reach hotel. Price guide: Single £35–£55; double/twin £75–£120.

THE MONTAGU ARMS HOTEL

BEAULIEU, NEW FOREST, HAMPSHIRE SO42 7ZL
TEL: 01590 612324 FAX: 01590 612188

Situated at the head of the River Beaulieu in the heart of the New Forest, The Montagu Arms Hotel carries on a tradition of hospitality started 700 years ago. As well as being a good place for a holiday, the hotel is an ideal venue for small conferences. Each of the 24 bedrooms has been individually styled and many are furnished with four-poster beds. Choose from sumptuous suites, luxurious junior suites, superior and standard accommodation. All rooms are equipped with colour television, direct-dial telephones, radio and a trouser press. Dine in the oak-panelled restaurant overlooking the garden, where you can enjoy cuisine prepared by award-winning chef Simon Fennell. The menu is supported by an outstanding wine list. The hotel offers complimentary membership of an exclusive health club 6 miles away. Facilities there include a supervised gymnasium, large indoor ozone pool, Jacuzzi, steam room, sauna and beauty therapist. With much to see and do around Beaulieu why not hire a mountain bike? Visit the National Motor Museum, Exbury Gardens or Bucklers Hard, or walk for miles through the beautiful New Forest. Special tariffs are available throughout the year. **Directions:** The village of Beaulieu is well signposted and the hotel commands an impressive position at the foot of the main street. Price guide: Single £69.90–£75.90; double/twin £98.90–£149.90; suite £175.90.

WOODLANDS MANOR

GREEN LANE, CLAPHAM, BEDFORD, BEDFORDSHIRE MK41 6EP
TEL: 01234 363281 FAX: 01234 272390

Woodlands Manor is a secluded period manor house, set in acres of wooded grounds and gardens, only two miles from the centre of Bedford. The hotel is privately owned and a personal welcome is assured. In the public rooms, stylish yet unpretentious furnishings preserve the feel of a country house, with open fires in winter. The en suite bedrooms are beautifully decorated and have extensive personal facilities. All have views of the gardens and surrounding countryside. The elegantly proportioned restaurant, once the house's main reception room, provides an agreeable venue for dining. The menus balance English tradition with the French flair for fresh, light flavours, complemented by wines from well-stocked cellars. The private library is well suited to business meetings and intimate dinner parties. Woodlands Manor is conveniently located for touring: the historic centres of Ely, Cambridge and Oxford are within easy reach, and stately homes such as Woburn Abbey and Warwick Castle are not far away. The hotel is two miles from the county town of Bedford, with its riverside park and the Bunyan Museum. Other places of interest nearby include the RSPB at Sandy and the Shuttleworth Collection of aircraft at Biggleswade. **Directions:** Clapham village is two miles north of the centre of Bedford. Price guide: Single £59.50–£75; double/twin ££85.

THE MANOR HOUSE

NORTHLANDS, WALKINGTON, EAST YORKSHIRE HU17 8RT
TEL: 01482 881645 FAX: 01482 866501

Set in 3 acres of tree-lined grounds, overlooking horse paddocks and parkland, The Manor House occupies a secluded position on the gentle, wooded flanks of the rolling Yorkshire Wolds. This late 19th century retreat is perfect for those seeking relaxation. The bedrooms, with their open, attractive views, are individually furnished and decorated to the highest standard; guests will find themselves pampered with unexpected and useful personal comforts. Chef-patron Derek Baugh, formerly of The Dorchester has evolved a distinctive, creative style of cuisine, and the connoisseur will find Lee Baugh's confections irresistible. Believing that the gourmet requires a sympathetic alliance between what he or she is eating and drinking, Derek has ensured that the wine list reflects his informed interest in world wide wines. On summer evenings, dinner may be taken in the conservatory, overlooking the south terrace and lawns. Horse-riding, clay pigeon shooting and golf can all be enjoyed locally, while there is racing at nearby Beverley, York and Doncaster. The Manor House won the 1994 RAC Restaurant Award. **Directions:** From Walkington on B1230 towards Beverley, turn left at traffic lights (following the brown hotel signs), then left and left again for the hotel. Price guide: Single £74–£80; double/twin £93–£120.

THE SWAN HOTEL AT BIBURY

BIBURY, GLOUCESTERSHIRE GL7 5NW
TEL: 01285 740695 FAX: 01285 740473

The Swan Hotel at Bibury in the South Cotswolds, a 17th century coaching inn, is a perfect base for both leisurely and active holidays which will appeal especially to motorists, fishermen and walkers. The hotel has its own fishing rights and a moated ornamental garden encircled by its own crystalline stream. Bibury itself is a delightful village, with its honey-coloured stonework, picturesque ponds, the trout filled River Coln and its utter lack of modern eyesores. The beautiful Arlington Row and its cottages are a vision of old England. When Liz and Alex Furtek acquired The Swan, they had the clear intention of creating a distinctive hotel in the English countryside which would acknowledge the needs of the sophisticated traveller of the 1990s. A programme of refurbishment and upgrading of the hotel and its services began with the accent on unpretentious comfort. Oak-panelling, plush carpets and sumptuous fabrics create the background for the fine paintings and antiques that grace the interiors. The 18 bedrooms are superbly appointed with luxury bathrooms and comfortable furnishings. Guests may dine in either the restaurant or the brasserie which serves meals all day. Dogs by arrangement. **Directions:** Bibury is signposted off A40 Oxford–Cheltenham road, on the left-hand side. Price guide: Single £85–£175; double/twin £115–£280.

NEW HALL

WALMLEY ROAD, ROYAL SUTTON COLDFIELD, WEST MIDLANDS B76 1QX
TEL: 0121 378 2442 FAX: 0121 378 4637

Set in 26 acres of private gardens and surrounded by a lily-filled moat, New Hall dates from the 12th century and is reputedly the oldest fully moated manor house in England. This prestigious hotel offers a warm welcome to both the discriminating business visitor and leisure guest. Much acclaimed, New Hall proudly holds the coveted RAC Blue Ribbon Award and is the AA Inspectors' Hotel of the Year for England 1993/4. It was also the highest rated hotel in the Birmingham area Egon Ronay 1994. The cocktail bar and adjoining drawing room overlook the terrace from which a bridge leads to the yew topiary, orchards and sunlit glades. Individually furnished bedrooms and suites offer every modern comfort and amenity with lovely views. A new 9-hole golf course is available for guests' use. Surrounded by a rich cultural heritage, New Hall is convenient for Lichfield Cathedral, Warwick Castle, Stratford-upon-Avon, the NEC and the ICC in Birmingham (only seven miles away). The Belfry Golf Centre is also nearby. Details of champagne weekend breaks, opera, ballet and other weekends are available on request. **Directions:** From exit 9 of M42, follow A4097 (ignoring signs to A38 Sutton Coldfield). At B4148 turn right. New Hall is one mile on the left. Price guide: Single £95–£114; double/twin £110–£160; suite £175–£300.

THE SWALLOW HOTEL

12 HAGLEY ROAD, FIVEWAYS, BIRMINGHAM B16 8SJ
TEL: 0121 452 1144 FAX: 0121 456 3442

Upon opening this very special hotel became the first in the Midlands to achieve five stars and since then has won innumerable awards. These include the Caterer and Hotelkeeper's 'Hotel of the Year 1992', AA Courtesy and Care award and four AA Red Stars. Two of the most highly regarded accolades have been given recently – English Tourist Board 'England for Excellence Award' 1993 (the Lanesborough in 1992 and the Chewton Glen in 1991) and Johansens 'City Hotel of the Year' 1994. Awards, however, do not give the whole picture. The Swallow Hotel offers business and leisure travellers an oasis of calm and warm hospitality in a fascinating and culturally diverse city. Service and surroundings are quite outstanding. Ninety eight luxuriously comfortable bedrooms and suites offer all one would expect from an hotel of this calibre. Dining is memorable whether in the Sir Edward Elgar Restaurant or in Langtry's which warrant an Egon Ronay 'Star' and three AA Rosettes: traditional afternoon tea in the Drawing Room is a favourite indulgence with all guests. Nowhere is luxury more apparent than in the Swallow Leisure Club with its theme of Ancient Egypt – including hieroglyphics. **Directions:** Fiveways roundabout – junction 1 (M5) 5 miles, junction 6 (M6) 5½ miles. Price guide from: Single £125; double/twin £145; suite £299.

For hotel location, see maps on pages 473–479

79

DOWN HALL COUNTRY HOUSE HOTEL

HATFIELD HEATH, NR BISHOP'S STORTFORD, HERTFORDSHIRE CM22 7AS
TEL: 01279 731441 FAX: 01279 730416

Down Hall is an Italian-style mansion set in over 100 acres of woodland, park and landscaped gardens. The hotel is a splendid example of quality Victorian craftmanship, with many of the architectural details reproduced in the recently added West Wing. There is superb attention to detail throughout. The well-proportioned bedrooms have antique-style inlaid mahogany furniture and brass chandeliers. Italian granite is a feature of the luxurious en suite bathrooms. The hotel's public rooms offer comfort in the grand manner, with high ceilings, crystal chandeliers and paintings on the walls. There are two restaurants, offering English and international cuisine, with a wide selection of unusual dishes. For conferences, there are 26 meeting rooms, including 16 purpose-built syndicate rooms. Indoor and outdoor leisure facilities include a heated pool, whirlpool, sauna, croquet and putting lawns, giant chess, tennis courts and fitness trail. Down Hall is within access of London and Stansted Airport. For excursions, Cambridge, Constable country and the old timbered village of Thaxted are all within a few miles. **Directions:** Exit at junction 7 of M11. Follow the A414 towards Harlow. At the 4th roundabout follow the B183 to Hatfield Heath. Bear right towards Matching Green and the hotel is 1.3 miles on the right. Price guide: Single £86; double/twin £115.

For hotel location, see maps on pages 473–479

THE DEVONSHIRE ARMS COUNTRY HOUSE HOTEL

BOLTON ABBEY, SKIPTON, NORTH YORKSHIRE BD23 6AJ
TEL: 01756 710441 FAX: 01756 710564

The Devonshire reflects its charming setting in the Yorkshire Dales: a welcome escape from a busy and crowded world, peace and quiet, beauty, and the perfect place to relax. The hotel is owned by the Duke and Duchess of Devonshire and is set in 12 acres of parkland on their Bolton Abbey estate, in the Yorkshire Dales National Park. Many antiques and paintings from Chatsworth in the public rooms and bedrooms (several of which are themed) add to the country house atmosphere, which is complemented by excellent service and an award-winning restaurant. As well as a wide choice of outdoor activities and themed or activity breaks, The Devonshire Club is adjacent to the hotel and offers a full range of leisure, health and beauty therapy facilities including: heated indoor swimming pool, steam room, sauna, spa bath, cold water plunge pool, high-powered sunbed, fully equipped gymnasium, beauty therapy rooms – staffed by "Matis" trained therapists, health and relaxation treatments. In addition to the highest ETB rating (5 Crowns De Luxe), three AA Red Stars and two Rosettes the Devonshire is a member of 'Small Luxury Hotels of the World', was YHTB 'Hotel of the Year' for 1992, 1993 and 1994 and an ETB Silver Award Winner for 1993. **Directions:** Off the A59 Skipton–Harrogate road at junction with the B6160. Price guide: Single £95–£105; double/twin £130–£155; suite £200.

THE CARLTON HOTEL

EAST OVERCLIFF, BOURNEMOUTH, DORSET BH1 3DN
TEL: 01202 552011 FAX: 01202 299573

Bournemouth's premier hotel, The Carlton, has provided hospitality to royalty, heads of state and ministers of the Crown for generations. Perfectly positioned on the town's much favoured East Cliff, with miles of golden sands below, it creates a world of discreet luxury for its guests, offering impeccable service and unrivalled comfort. The interiors are a rich combination of classical furniture and contemporary decoration, creating an impression of space and opulence. The bedrooms are spacious, beautifully furnished and equipped with every modern facility, while the suites are unashamedly luxurious. Dining at the hotel is a memorable experience. In the beautifully decorated two-tier restaurant, guests are assured of international cuisine and fine wines. The versatile Meyrick Suite is suitable for banquets, wedding receptions, conferences or promotional events. For smaller functions, The Carlton offers its business suites, impressively furnished and featuring state-of-the-art equipment. Relaxation is provided by the facilities of the Health Club, with its sauna, solarium, Jacuzzi, gymnasium and heated outdoor pool. Luxury breaks, 2 nights or more from £59.50 per person including 4-course dinner. **Directions:** The Carlton is on the corner of East Overcliff Drive and Meyrick Road, on the sea front. Price guide: Single from £95; double/twin from £120; suites from £185.

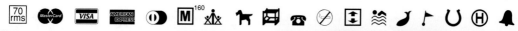

For hotel location, see maps on pages 473–479

THE EDGEMOOR

HAYTOR ROAD, BOVEY TRACEY, SOUTH DEVON TQ13 9LE
TEL: 01626 832466 FAX: 01626 834760

Built in 1870, The Edgemoor Country House Hotel, owned and managed by Rod and Pat Day, stands in a peaceful location in two acres of grounds literally on the eastern boundary of the Dartmoor National Park. There are 12 charming bedrooms, two of which are on the ground floor. All have en suite bathrooms and some have four-poster beds. The public rooms look over the hotel grounds and provide comfortable and sophisticated surroundings in which to enjoy your stay. In the restaurant, chef Edward Elliott prepares modern English and French cuisine using local produce whenever possible. The wine list offers an interesting and varied selection. Bar meals are available at lunch time and in the evenings. Children are welcome and a special high-tea is provided for them. With the hotel's close proximity to Dartmoor, walkers and naturalists are well catered for. Shooting, fishing and riding can be arranged locally. The Edgemoor is also a good touring base for the West Country. Worth a visit are Castle Drogo, Becky Falls and Haytor. **Directions:** On leaving the M5, join the A38 in the direction of Plymouth. At Drumbridges roundabout, take A382 towards Bovey Tracey. At the second roundabout turn left and, after approximately 1/2 mile, fork left at the sign for Haytor. Price guide: Single £44.75–£57.95; double/twin £82.50–£93.90.

THE VICTORIA HOTEL

BRIDGE STREET, BRADFORD, WEST YORKSHIRE BD1 1JX
TEL: 01274 728706 FAX: 01274 736358

Built as the showpiece of the Lancashire and Yorkshire railway in 1875, The Victoria has been totally restored and refreshed since its purchase in January 1995 by the owners of the award-winning 42 The Calls in Leeds. Emphasis has been placed on producing an outstandingly comfortable hotel, but with service scaled down to keep room rates substantially below other hotels with comparable comforts. The bedrooms all have stereos, video players, trouser presses, hairdryers and superb bathrooms with power showers. Vic and Bert's Grill au Feu de Bois is a modern interpretation of a Parisian Brasserie with a selection of dishes prepared under the supervision of Bradford's only Michelin starred chef. The excellent facilities include a small gym and sauna, The Pie Eyed Parrot Pub and a beautiful banquetting room for special events. Bradford is a base from which to visit Herriot country and the Brontë parsonage, whilst the world-famous National Museum of Film, Photography and Television, the new Transperience Museum and the Alhambra Theatre are within walking distance. **Directions:** From M62 take junction 26 onto the M606, then the A6177 and A611. At end of dual carriageway take right exit at roundabout to Hallings. Turn right at traffic lights and the hotel is on the left. Price guide: Single £79–£99; double/twin £89–£109; suites £109–£119.

WOOLLEY GRANGE

WOOLLEY GREEN, BRADFORD-ON-AVON, WILTSHIRE BA15 1TX
TEL: 01225 864705 FAX: 01225 864059

Woolley Grange is a 17th century Jacobean stone manor house set in 14 acres of formal gardens and paddocks. Standing on high ground, it affords southerly views of the White Horse at Westbury and beyond. Furnished with flair and an air of eccentricity, the interior décor and paintings echo the taste of owners, Nigel and Heather Chapman. Woolley Grange is gaining a reputation for outstanding cuisine and is highly rated in *The Good Food Guide*. Using local farm produce and organically grown fruit and vegetables from the Victorian kitchen gardens, the chef has created a sophisticated style of country house food which aims to revive the focus on flavours. Children are particularly welcome; the owners have four of their own and they do not expect their young visitors to be 'seen but not heard'. In the Victorian coach house there is a huge games room and a well-equipped nursery with a full-time nanny available to look after guests' children 10am–6pm every day. A children's lunch and tea are provided daily. Nearby attractions include medieval Bradford-on-Avon, Georgian Bath, Longleat and prehistoric Stonehenge. Riding can be arranged. **Directions:** From Bath on A363, fork left at Frankleigh House after town sign. From Chippenham, A4 to Bath, fork left on B3109; turn left after town sign. Price guide: Single £80; double/twin £95–£165.

FARLAM HALL HOTEL

BRAMPTON, CUMBRIA CA8 2NG
TEL: 016977 46234 FAX: 016977 46683

Farlam Hall was opened in 1975 by the Quinion and Stevenson families who over the years have managed to achieve and maintain consistently high standards of food, service and comfort. These standards have been recognised and rewarded by all the major guides and membership of Relais et Châteaux. This old border house, dating in parts from the 17th century, is set in mature gardens which can be seen from the elegant lounges and dining room, creating a relaxing and pleasing environment. The fine silver and crystal in the dining room complement the quality of the English country house cooking produced by Barry Quinion and his team of chefs. There are 12 individually decorated bedrooms varying in size and shape, some having Jacuzzi baths, one an antique four-poster bed, and there are two ground floor bedrooms. This area offers many different attractions: miles of unspoiled countryside for walking, eight golf courses within 30 minutes of the hotel, Hadrian's Wall, Lanercost Priory and Carlisle with its castle, cathedral and museum. The Lake District, Scottish Borders and Yorkshire Dales each make an ideal day's touring. Winter and spring breaks are offered. Closed Christmas. **Directions:** Farlam Hall is 2½ miles east of Brampton on the A689, not in Farlam village. Price guide (including dinner): Single £95–£110; double/twin £170–£220.

MONKEY ISLAND HOTEL

BRAY-ON-THAMES, MAIDENHEAD, BERKSHIRE SL6 2EE
TEL: 01628 23400 FAX: 01628 784732

The name Monkey Island derives from the medieval Monk's Eyot. Circa 1723 the island was purchased by Charles Spencer, the third Duke of Marlborough, who built the fishing lodge now known as the Pavilion, and the fishing temple, both of which are Grade I listed buildings. The Pavilion's Terrace Bar, overlooking acres of riverside lawn, is an ideal spot for a relaxing cocktail, and the Pavilion Restaurant, perched on the island's narrowest tip with fine views upstream, boasts fine English cuisine, an award-winning cellar and friendly service. The River Room is suitable for weddings or other large functions, while the Regency-style boardroom is perfect for smaller parties. It is even possible to arrange exclusive use of the whole island for a truly memorable occasion. The Temple houses not only the comfortable bedrooms and suites but also the Wedgwood Room, with its splendid ceiling in high-relief plaster, and the octagonal Temple Room below. Monkey Island is one mile downstream from Maidenhead, within easy reach of Royal Windsor, Eton, Henley and London. Closed from 26 December to mid-January. Weekend breaks from £65 p.p. **Directions:** Take A308 from Maidenhead towards Windsor; turn left following signposts to Bray. Entering Bray, go right along Old Mill Lane, which goes over M4; the hotel is on the left. Price guide: Single £70–£90; double/twin £80–£120; suites from £145.

TOPPS HOTEL

17 REGENCY SQUARE, BRIGHTON, EAST SUSSEX BN1 2FG
TEL: 01273 729334 FAX: 01273 203679

Quietly situated in Regency Square at the heart of Brighton, the Topps Hotel and Restaurant is only 2 minutes' walk from the sea and the Metropole Conference Centre, with the Lanes and Royal Pavilion nearby. This charming hotel offers an attractive alternative to the more anonymous large establishments in the vicinity and is under the personal supervision of resident proprietors, Paul and Pauline Collins. With its friendly welcome and efficient service, the Topps Hotel is certainly deserving of its name. The bedrooms are all elegantly appointed and every need of the discerning visitor has been anticipated. In the basement is the comfortable restaurant, where the emphasis is on freshness and simplicity. English and French influences are combined to create good but unpretentious cuisine. Brighton is often described as 'London-by-the-sea' – its urbane atmosphere and wide range of shops, clubs and theatres make it a popular town for visitors. Glyndebourne, Arundel, Chichester and Lewes are within easy reach and London is only 52 minutes away by train. **Directions:** Regency Square is off King's Road (A259), opposite the West Pier. Price guide: Single £45–£89; double/twin £79–£99.

SWALLOW ROYAL HOTEL

COLLEGE GREEN, BRISTOL, AVON BS1 5TA
TEL: 0117 9255100 FAX: 0117 9251515

The Swallow Royal Hotel enjoys a superb central position next to Bristol Cathedral and overlooking College Green. It was much admired by Queen Victoria and Sir Winston Churchill and it survived the ravages of Second World War bombs and fires. In 1991 the hotel was reopened following a painstaking restoration programme. Today it is returned to its former glory and is Bristol's leading luxury hotel. The warmest of welcomes await guests, who are invited to savour the combined experience of Victorian elegance and modern day comfort. There are 242 rooms including 16 luxurious suites, all individually designed and furnished to the highest standards and many offer superb views over the city and harbour. There is a choice of two restaurants; the imposing Victorian Palm Court with its spectacular glass roof or the less formal Terrace Restaurant which overlooks Cathedral Square. Awarded 2 AA Rosettes. The Swallow Leisure Club, designed with Ancient Rome in mind, boasts handpainted murals, mosaics and Roman columns and offers an ideal environment for those seeking either energetic pursuits or relaxation. Facilities include a large heated indoor swimming pool, sauna, spa bath, steam room, sunbeds and fitness room. The hotel has its own car park. **Directions:** At the end of the M32 keep right and follow the signs for the City Centre. Price guide: Single from £95; double/twin from £120; suites £150–£300.

HUNSTRETE HOUSE

HUNSTRETE, CHELWOOD, NR BRISTOL, AVON BS18 4NS
TEL: 01761 490490 FAX: 01761 490732

In a classical English landscape on the edge of the Mendip Hills stands Hunstrete House. This hotel, surrounded by lovely gardens, is largely 18th century, although the history of the estate goes back to 963AD. Each of the bedrooms is individually decorated and furnished to a high standard, combining the benefits of a hotel room with the atmosphere of a charming private country house. Many offer uninterrupted views over undulating fields and woodlands. The reception areas exhibit warmth and elegance and are liberally furnished with beautiful antiques. Log fires burn in the hall, library and drawing room through the winter and on cooler summer evenings. The Terrace dining room looks out on to an Italianate, flower filled courtyard. A highly skilled head chef offers light, elegant dishes using produce from the extensive garden, along with the best of English meat and fish. The menu changes regularly and the hotel has an excellent reputation for the quality and interest of its wine list. In a sheltered corner of the walled garden there is a heated swimming pool for guests to enjoy. For the energetic, the all weather tennis court provides another diversion and there are riding stables in Hunstrete village, a five minute walk away. **Directions:** From Bath take the A4 towards Bristol and then the A368 to Wells. Price guide: Single £115; double/twin £145.

DANESWOOD HOUSE HOTEL

CUCK HILL, SHIPHAM, NR WINSCOMBE, SOMERSET BS25 1RD
TEL: 01934 843145 FAX: 01934 843824

A small country house hotel, Daneswood House stands in a leafy valley in the heart of the Mendip Hills – on a clear day, the views stretch as far as Wales. It was built by the Edwardians as a homeopathic health hydro and under the enthusiastic ownership of David and Elise Hodges it has been transformed into a charming hotel. Each bedroom is well furnished and individually decorated with striking fabrics. The honeymoon suite, with its king-sized bed, frescoed ceiling and antiques, is particularly comfortable. First-class cooking places equal emphasis on presentation and taste. Each dish is carefully prepared in a style that combines traditional English and French cooking with a nouvelle influence. During the summer, guests can dine alfresco and enjoy barbecued dishes such as Indonesian duck and baked sea bass with fennel and armagnac. There is a carefully selected wine list and a wide choice of liqueurs. The private conference lounge makes a quiet setting for meetings, while private functions can be catered for with ease. Awarded 2 AA Rosettes. Cheddar Gorge is 2 miles away, and Wells, Glastonbury, Bristol and Bath are nearby. Guide dogs only accommodated. **Directions:** Shipham is signposted from A38 Bristol–Bridgwater road. Go through village towards Cheddar; hotel drive is on left leaving village. Price guide: Single £57.50–£69.50; double/twin £69.50–£79.50; suite £112.

BUCKLAND MANOR

BUCKLAND, NR BROADWAY, GLOUCESTERSHIRE WR12 7LY
TEL: 01386 852626 FAX: 01386 853557

Set in an idyllic Cotswold valley, this fine gabled mansion house – parts of which date back to the 13th century – was tastefully converted in 1982 into an award-winning country house hotel. Guests can find respite far from the everyday hurly-burly and enjoy being cossetted in this friendly house. The bedrooms are of the highest standard, exquisitely furnished, with luxury bathrooms fed from the Manor's own spring water. Downstairs, the lounge and reception rooms feature impressive fireplaces, burnished oak panelling, antiques and plentiful displays of fresh flowers. Buckland Manor's resident manager is Nigel Power, previously of The Savoy and Hôtel du Rhône, Geneva. The head chef, Martyn Pearn, trained at the Connaught and Claridge's in London and was previously head chef of La Reserve in Bordeaux. Given sufficient notice he will be happy to cook to order, and whatever the dish, only the best provisions are selected to meet the hotel's exacting standards. There are good recreational facilities at Buckland Manor in addition to the putting green and extensive gardens. Nearby attractions include Cheltenham and Stratford-upon-Avon. The 'Cotswold Way' which is behind the manor has magnificent views and is excellent for walking. **Directions:** Off the B4632, 2 miles south of Broadway. Price guide: Single £150–£315; double/twin £160–£325.

Dormy House

WILLERSEY HILL, BROADWAY, WORCESTERSHIRE WR12 7LF
TEL: 01386 852711 FAX: 01386 858636

This former 17th-century farmhouse has been beautifully converted into a delightful hotel which retains much of its original character. With its oak beams, stone-flagged floors and honey-coloured local stone walls it imparts warmth and tranquillity. Dormy House provides a wealth of comforts for the most discerning guest. Each bedroom is individually decorated – some are furnished with four-poster beds – and suites are available. Head Chef, Alan Cutler, prepares a superb choice of menus and the restaurant, expertly managed by Saverio Buchicchio, offers an extensive wine list includes many half bottles. The versatile Dormy Suite is an ideal venue for conferences, meetings or private functions – professionally arranged to individual requirements. The hotel has its own leisure facilities which include a games room, gym, sauna/steam, room, croquet lawn and putting green. Mountain bikes are available for hire. Broadway Golf Club is adjacent. The locality is idyllic for walkers. Stratford-upon-Avon, Cheltenham Spa, Hidcote Manor Garden and Sudeley Castle are all within easy reach. USA representative: Josephine Barr, 1-800-323-5463. Closed 4 days at Christmas. **Directions:** Hotel is ½ mile off A44 between Moreton-in-Marsh and Broadway. Taking the turning signposted Saintbury, the hotel is first on left past picnic area. Price guide: Single £60–£80; double/twin £120–£145.

THE LYGON ARMS

BROADWAY, WORCESTERSHIRE WR12 7DU
TEL: 01386 852255 FAX: 01386 858611

The Lygon Arms, a magnificent Tudor building with numerous historical associations, stands in Broadway, acclaimed by many as 'the prettiest village in England', in the heart of the Cotswolds. Over the years much restoration has been carried out, emphasising the outstanding period features, such as original 17th century oak panelling and an ancient hidden stairway. The bedrooms are individually and tastefully furnished and offer guests every modern luxury combined with the elegance of an earlier age. The Great Hall, complete with a 17th century minstrels' gallery, and the smaller private dining rooms provide a fine setting for a well-chosen and imaginative menu. Conference facilities including the new look state-of-the-art Torrington Room are available for up to 70 participants. Guests can enjoy a superb range of leisure amenities including all-weather tennis, indoor pool, gymnasium, billiard room, beauty salon, steam room, solarium, saunas and table tennis. Golf can be arranged locally. The many Cotswold villages; Stratford-upon-Avon, Oxford and Cheltenham are nearby, while Broadway itself is a paradise for the antique collector. **Directions:** Set on the right-hand side of Broadway High Street on the A44 in the direction of London to Worcester. Price guide: Single from £90; double/twin from £140 including Continental breakfast, excluding VAT.

CAREYS MANOR HOTEL

BROCKENHURST, NEW FOREST, HAMPSHIRE SO42 7RH
TEL: 01590 623551 FAX: 01590 622799

Careys Manor, an elegant country house, dates from 1888 and is built on the site of a royal hunting lodge used by Charles II. Situated in 5 acres of landscaped grounds and surrounded by glorious New Forest countryside, the hotel is proud of the personal welcome and care it extends to its visitors. The comfortably furnished bedrooms are appointed to the highest standards. In the Garden Wing, there is a choice of luxury bedrooms, some opening directly onto the lawns and others with a balcony overlooking the pretty gardens. The restaurant offers fine English and French cuisine, prepared and presented to gourmet standards. A prestigious sports complex comprises a large indoor swimming pool with Jacuzzi, sauna, solarium and a Turkish steam room. In addition, guests can work out in the professionally supervised gymnasium, where there is also a room for massage, sports injury and beauty treatments. Wind-surfing, riding and sailing can all be enjoyed locally, while Stonehenge, Beaulieu, Broadlands, Salisbury and Winchester are a short distance away. Business interests can be catered for – there are comprehensive self-contained conference facilities. **Directions:** From M27 junction 1, follow A337 to Lymington. Careys Manor is on the left after 30 mph sign at Brockenhurst. Price guide from: Single £69–£79; double/twin £109–£129; suite £159.

NEW PARK MANOR

LYNDHURST ROAD, BROCKENHURST, NEW FOREST, HAMPSHIRE SO42 7QH
TEL: 01590 623467 FAX: 01590 622268

Escape from the crowds to one of the New Forest's finest country house hotels. A former hunting lodge of Charles II, the building is grade II listed and dates back to the 16th century. The en suite bedrooms are all individually decorated, keeping in mind the style and grandeur of the old manor; most offer superb views over the surrounding parkland with its wandering ponies and deer. Enjoy a romantic evening with fine wines and French influenced cuisine in the Stag Head Restaurant or relax with a good book from the library in front of the open log fire in the historic Rufus Bar. The New Forest suite creates a wonderful setting for all types of functions – tailor made to suit your personal requirements. For the more energetic New Park Manor offers riding from its own equestrian centre with BHS trained stable crew, a tennis court and an outdoor heated swimming pool. There is something for everyone so why not get away from it all and escape to the peace and tranquility, topped with service par excellence, of the New Park Manor? **Directions:** New Park Manor is $1/2$ mile off the A337 between Lyndhurst and Brockenhurst easily reached from M27 via Cadnam. Price guide: Single £82.50; double/twin £110–£140.

RHINEFIELD HOUSE HOTEL

RHINEFIELD ROAD, BROCKENHURST, HAMPSHIRE SO42 7QB
TEL: 01590 22922 FAX: 01590 22800

Known locally as the 'jewel in the forest', at first sight the sheer grandeur of Rhinefield House surpasses all expectaitions. A hint of Italian Renaissance sweeps across ornamental gardens, with canals reflecting the mellow stonework. Lovingly restored to their original 1890s design, over 5,000 yew trees form the maze and formal parterres where a grass ampitheatre has been carved out of the western slopes for summer evening concerts. The interiors are equally impressive, the journey through the rooms is a voyage of discovery. Authentically created in the style of a Moorish Palace, the Alhambra Room has Islamic inscriptions, onyx pillars and mosaic flooring. Fine cuisine is served in the elegant Armada Restaurant – so called after its splendid carving depicting the Spanish Armada. An airy sun-lit conservatory and attractive bedrooms appointed in accordance with the style of the house all add up to Rhinefield's appeal. The Grand Hall is an exact replica of Westminster Hall – an ideal setting for balls, society weddings and stylish banquets. A wide range of conference rooms and equipment is available for business events. Guests may unwind in the Atlantis Leisure Club with its plunge pool, solarium, sauna and gymnasium. Directions: A35 from Lyndhurst, or along Rhinefield Road from Brockenhurst. Price guide: Single £85; double/twin £110; suite £155–£170.

GRAFTON MANOR COUNTRY HOUSE HOTEL

GRAFTON LANE, BROMSGROVE, WORCESTERSHIRE B61 7HA
TEL: 01527 579007 FAX: 01527 575221

Closely associated with many of the leading events in English history, Grafton Manor's illustrious past can be traced back to Norman times. Commissioned in 1567, the present manor is set in several acres of gardens leading to a lake. Modern comfort and style are combined with the atmosphere of an earlier age. Pot-pourri from the hotel's 19th-century rose gardens scents the rooms and over 100 herbs are grown in a unique, chessboard-pattern garden. All the herbs are in regular use in the restaurant kitchen, where Simon Morris aims to 'produce only the best' for guests. Preserves made from estate produce are on sale. Meals are served in the 18th-century dining room, the focal point of Grafton Manor. Damask-rose petal and mulberry sorbets are indicative of the inspired culinary style. Indian cuisine is Simon's award winning hobby and Asian dishes often complement the traditional English cooking. The fully equipped bedrooms have been meticulously restored and furnished, some with open fires on cooler evenings. Grafton Manor is ideally placed for Birmingham, the NEC and the International Conference Centre. It is an equally good base from which to explore the Worcestershire countryside. **Directions:** From M5 junction 5 proceed via A38 towards Bromsgrove. Bear left at first roundabout; Grafton Lane is first left after 1/2 mile. Price guide: Single £85; double/twin £95; suite £150.

THE BAY TREE HOTEL AND RESTAURANT

SHEEP STREET, BURFORD, OXON OX18 4LW
TEL: 01993 822791 FAX: 01993 823008

The Bay Tree has been expertly refurbished so that it retains all its Tudor splendour while offering every modern facility. The oak-panelled rooms have huge stone fireplaces, and a galleried staircase leads upstairs from the raftered hall. All the bedrooms are en suite, three of them furnished with four-poster beds and two of the five suites have half-tester beds. In the summer, you can relax in the delightful walled gardens, featuring landscaped terraces of lawn and flower beds. A relaxing atmosphere is enhanced by the staff's attentive service in the flagstoned dining room where the head chef's creative cuisine is complemented by a comprehensive selection of fine wines. Light meals are served in a country-style bar, while the conservatory lounge is the place to unwind and enjoy the view over the grounds. Burford, often described as the gateway to the Cotswolds, is renowned for its assortment of antique shops and the Tolsey Museum of local history. The Bay Tree Hotel makes a convenient base for day trips to Stratford-upon-Avon, Stow-on-the-Wold and Blenheim Palace. Golf, clay pigeon shooting and riding can be arranged locally. **Directions:** Burford is on the A40 between Oxford and Cheltenham. Proceed halfway down the hill into Burford, turn left into Sheep Street and The Bay Tree Hotel is 30 yards on your right. Price guide: Single £60–£80; double/twin £110–£115.

THE BROOKHOUSE

ROLLESTON-ON-DOVE, NR BURTON UPON TRENT, STAFFORDSHIRE DE13 9AA
TEL: 01283 814188 FAX: 01283 813644

Originally built as a farmhouse in 1694, this attractive, ivy-clad William and Mary house stands in a tranquil position beside a gently flowing brook and lush gardens. Grade II listed, the building was converted into a hotel in 1976, and since then it has earned a reputation for its friendly service and hospitality. Of particular interest are the pretty bedrooms, with four-poster, half-tester or Victorian brass beds. The bedding is trimmed with Nottingham lace. Downstairs, the décor and antique furniture are in keeping with the cosy cottage style. In the restaurant, soft wall-lighting and candles create an intimate atmosphere, while polished wooden tables are set with silver and crystal. The food is of a consistently high quality. An extensive menu presents a wide choice to suit all tastes. Small private functions can be catered for: fax, photo-copying and secretarial services can be arranged for business meetings. Serious hikers and ramblers alike will find plenty of good walking in the nearby Derbyshire Dales and Peak District. Notable local attractions include the Shugborough Estate, Calke Abbey, Haddon and Kedleston Halls. **Directions:** Rolleston is just outside Burton upon Trent between the A50 to Stoke-on-Trent and the A38 to Derby. Price guide: Single £65–£75; double/twin £85–£95.

THE ANGEL HOTEL

BURY ST EDMUNDS, SUFFOLK IP33 1LT
TEL: 01284 753926 FAX: 01284 750092

Immortalised by Charles Dickens as the hostelry where Mr Pickwick enjoyed an excellent roast dinner, The Angel Hotel is renowned for its first-class service to travellers, continuing the tradition since first becoming an inn in 1452. Visitors have the immediate impression of a hotel that is loved and nurtured by its owners. In the public rooms, guests will appreciate the carefully chosen ornaments and pictures, fresh flowers and log fires. Bedrooms are individually furnished and decorated and all have en suite bathrooms. The elegant dining room has been awarded 2 rosettes by the AA for excellent food and service. Overlooking the ancient abbey, the restaurant serves classic English cuisine, including local speciality dishes and succulent roasts. The Angel can offer a wide range of quality conference and banqueting facilities catering for private dinners, meetings and weddings from 10–120 persons. The hotel is within an hour of east coast ferry ports and 45 minutes from Stansted Airport. Nearby there is racing at Newmarket and several golf courses within easy reach. Bury St Edmunds is an interesting and historic market town and an excellent centre for touring East Anglia. **Directions:** The hotel is situated in the centre of the town. Price guide: Single £65; double/twin £85–£95; suite £115. Weekend rates £34 per person bed and breakfast.

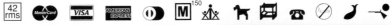

RAVENWOOD HALL

ROUGHAM, BURY ST EDMUNDS, SUFFOLK IP30 9JA
TEL: 01359 270345 FAX: 01359 270788

Nestling within 7 acres of lovely lawns and woodlands deep in the heart of Suffolk lies Ravenwood Hall. Now an excellent country house hotel, this fine Tudor building dates back to 1530 and retains many of its original features. The restaurant, still boasting the carved timbers and huge inglenook from Tudor times, creates a delightfully intimate atmosphere in which to enjoy imaginative cuisine. The menu is a combination of adventurous and classical dishes, featuring long forgotten English recipes. The Hall's extensive cellars are stocked with some of the finest vintages, along with a selection of rare ports and brandies. A cosy bar offers a less formal setting in which to enjoy some unusual snacks.

Comfortable bedrooms are furnished with antiques, reflecting the historic tradition of the Hall, although each is equipped with every modern facility. A wide range of leisure facilities is available to guests, including a hard tennis court, a croquet lawn and heated swimming pool. There are golf courses and woodland walks to enjoy locally and both hunting and shooting can be arranged. The many places of interest nearby include the famous medieval wool towns of Lavenham and Long Melford, and the historic cities of Norwich and Cambridge are also within easy reach. **Directions:** Situated 2 miles east of Bury St Edmunds off the A14. Price guide: £59–£77; double/twin: £77–£97.

BUXTED PARK COUNTRY HOUSE HOTEL

BUXTED, UCKFIELD, EAST SUSSEX TN22 4AY
TEL: 01825 732711 FAX: 01825 732770

Buxted Park is set in over 312 acres of parkland, boasting a herd of deer and lakes stocked with rare species of ducks, swans and geese. The estate dates back to 1725. In 1940 the house was redesigned by Basil Ionides, interior designer of The Savoy and Clarige's. The hotel has recently been extensively renovated and refurbished, including the magnificent Victorian conservatory-now The Orangery restaurant. Spacious and attractively decorated bedrooms offer every modern amenity, some have balconies and others direct access to the gardens. The two restaurants provide elegant surroundings in which to enjoy excellent English cuisine, with a strong Thai influence. A full range of fine wines is available to complement the meal. The stunning Coat of Arms drawing room and the Ballroom each provide an ideal venue for all types of social and corporate entertaining and there are a number of other drawing rooms for conferences. The Cellar Bar is ideal for informal meetings, the Library for smaller gatherings. Full Health Club facilities are available, including a well equipped gym, sauna, outdoor heated swimming pool (indoor pool to open spring 1996) and snooker room. **Directions:** The hotel is on the A272, east of its junction with the A22. Price guide Single from £75; double/twin from £95; master room/suites from £135. Special two night breaks available.

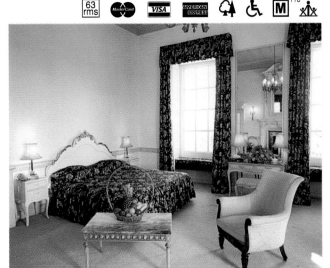

HOWFIELD MANOR

CHARTHAM HATCH, NR CANTERBURY, KENT CT4 7HQ
TEL: 01227 738294 FAX: 01227 731535

At Howfield Manor great care has been taken to preserve a long tradition of hospitality dating back to 1181, while discreetly providing modern comforts. Originally part of the Priory of St Gregory, this historic country house is set in 5 acres of secluded grounds with a formal English rose garden. The hotel has an authentic priest hole and, in the Priory Bar, striking *trompe l'oeil* murals. Illuminated under the floor of the Old Well Restaurant is the ferned ancient well, which was the main source of water for the monks who lived here 800 years ago. Guests can choose from an extensive range of menus to cater for every occasion – from an intimate à la carte meal for two to a gourmet dinner party in the self-contained conference and banqueting suite. The well-furnished bedrooms have been thoughtfully equipped. Located only 2 miles from the cathedral city of Canterbury, Howfield Manor makes an ideal base for touring this area and as a stopping-off point to and from the continent. Special weekend breaks are also available. **Directions:** From A2 London–Dover road, follow signs for Chartham Hatch after the Gate Service Station, then follow straight on for 2 1/4 miles. Hotel is on left at junction with A28. Price guide: Single £62.50; double/twin £82.50–£95.

For hotel location, see maps on pages 473–479

THE MANOR HOUSE

CASTLE COMBE, CHIPPENHAM, WILTSHIRE SN14 7HR
TEL: 01249 782206 FAX: 01249 782159

The Manor House at Castle Combe enjoys a setting of idyllic tranquillity: 26 acres of gardens and parkland, a gently flowing trout stream, and the romance of a terraced Italian garden. All the rooms have been lovingly restored in sympathy with their historical significance. The House bedrooms are individually furnished to a luxurious standard, in keeping with the history of the house. A friendly relaxed atmosphere, excellent service, food and guest care are combined in this charming country house. The Manor House has recently acquired the exclusive Castle Combe Golf Club which adjoins the Manor House grounds. Designed by Peter Allis and Clive Clark, this championship 18-hole 6340 yard par 73 course is one of the most spectacular and challenging courses in the South of England. It is set in 200 acres of wooded valley and downland, in an area of outstanding natural beauty. A stroll through the village of Castle Combe, unchanged for almost 200 years and believed by many to be 'England's prettiest village', is itself a magical experience. **Directions:** Fifteen minutes' drive from junctions 17 and 18 of the M4, or 20 minutes from the M5/M4 intersection. Twelve miles from Bath (two hours from central London). Approached directly from A420 and B4039. Price guide: Single £95; double/twin from £115; suite from £225.

THE PRIEST HOUSE

KINGS MILLS, CASTLE DONINGTON, DERBYSHIRE DE74 2RR
TEL: 01332 810649 FAX: 01332 811141

Magnificently situated on the banks of the River Trent, The Priest House is surrounded by 54 acres of mature unspoilt woodlands. Each of the bedrooms has been individually styled and the splendid Heron and Stocker suites are designed within the original Gothic Tower. Opening onto the private courtyard garden, the elegant library provides a perfect environment in which to read and relax. The traditional Mill Bar offers a selection of real ales and is a popular venue for guests and nonresidents alike, along with the 'Malt Room' which boasts over 80 different malt whiskies. The Riverside Restaurant enjoys a growing reputation for the imaginative cuisine that it provides at both lunch and dinner, complemented by an excellent wine list. A number of spacious suites are available for banquets, receptions, weddings and private parties. A variety of leisure activities are available within the hotel complex, including clay pigeon shooting, coarse fishing and go-karting. Places of interest nearby include Calke Abbey and Donington Park race circuit. **Directions:** From M1, junction 24, follow the signs A6 towards Derby. At first roundabout take left turn signposted Castle Donington. At first traffic lights turn right into park Lane and follow road for 1½ miles to The Priest House. Price guide: Single £78; double/twin £88; four-poster £108; suites £130.

BROCKENCOTE HALL

CHADDESLEY CORBETT, NR KIDDERMINSTER, WORCESTERSHIRE DY10 4PY
TEL: 01562 777876 FAX: 01562 777872

The Brockencote estate consists of 70 acres of landscaped grounds surrounding a magnificent hall. There are a gatehouse, half-timbered dovecote, lake, some fine European and North American trees and an elegant conservatory. The estate dates back 300 years and the style of the building reflects the changes which have taken place in fashion and taste over the years. At present, the interior combines classical architectural features with contemporary creature comforts. As in most country houses, each of the bedrooms is different: all have their own character, complemented by tasteful furnishings and décor. The friendly staff provide a splendid service under the supervision of owners Alison and Joseph Petitjean. Head chef, Didier Philipot specialises in traditional French cuisine with occasional regional and seasonal specialities. Brockencote Hall is an ideal setting for those seeking peace and quiet in an unspoiled corner of the English countryside. Located a few miles south of Birmingham, it is convenient for business people and sightseers alike – it makes a fine base for touring historic Worcestershire. **Directions:** Exit 4 from M5 or exit 1 from M42. Brockencote Hall is set back from the A448 at Chaddesley Corbett between Bromsgrove and Kidderminster. Price guide: Single £80; double/twin £110–£135.

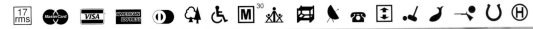

GIDLEIGH PARK

CHAGFORD, DEVON TQ13 8HH
TEL: 01647 432367 FAX: 01647 432574

Gidleigh Park enjoys an outstanding reputation among connoisseurs for its comfort and gastronomy. It has collected a clutch of top culinary awards for its imaginative cuisine (The Times Hotel Restaurant of the Year 1989, Egon Ronay Hotel of the Year 1990), and the Gidleigh Park wine list is one of the best in Britain. Service throughout the hotel is faultless. The en suite bedrooms – two of them in a converted chapel – are luxuriously furnished with antiques. The public rooms are elegantly appointed, and during the cooler months a fire burns merrily in the lounge's impressive fireplace. Set amid 40 secluded acres in the Teign Valley, Gidleigh Park is 1½ miles from the nearest public road. Two croquet lawns, an all-weather tennis court, a bowling lawn and a splendid water garden can be found in the grounds. A 730 foot, par 27 putting course designed by Peter Alliss was opened in 1995. Guests can swim in the river or explore Dartmoor on foot or horse-back. There are 14 miles of trout, sea trout and salmon fishing, as well as golf facilities nearby. Gidleigh Park is a Relais et Châteaux member. **Directions:** Approach from Chagford: go along Mill Street from Chagford Square. Fork right after 150 yards, cross into Holy Street at factory crossroads and follow lane for two miles. Price guide (including dinner): Single £205–£335; double/twin £290–£375.

For hotel location, see maps on pages 473–479

THE WEBBINGTON HOTEL

LOXTON, SOMERSET BS26 2XA
TEL: 01934 750100 FAX: 01934 750100

At the foot of the southern slopes of the Mendip Hills, overlooking the picturesque hamlet of Loxton, is The Webbington Hotel. The original Edwardian manor house was built at the turn of the century, but over the years it has been extended. Today it nevertheless retains the elegance and style of a country house and includes many interesting architectural features, such as the oak panelled library. All the bedrooms are individually styled and well equipped and the public rooms are very well furnished and comfortable. The Tiark Restaurant offers a choice of table d'hote and à la carte menus, accompanied by an extensive selection of fine wines. The hotel has its own leisure club, where guests can enjoy a wide range of activities. The heated swimming pool is situated in a large Edwardian conservatory offering panoramic views over the valley towards the sea and there is a fully equipped gym where qualified staff offer supervised training sessions. The Webbington is ideally located for guests who enjoy walking and horse riding. Within easy reach are Glastonbury, the Cheddar Caves and Gorge, Bath, and the tiny city of Wells with its magnificent Cathedral and moated Bishop's Palace. **Directions:** Exit M5 junction 22, follow A38 towards Bristol. After five miles at Lower Weare turn left just after the Lamb Inn. The hotel is signposted. Price guide: Single £60; doubler/twin £70–£85.

CHEDINGTON COURT

CHEDINGTON, NR BEAMINSTER, DORSET DT8 3HY
TEL: 01935 891265 FAX: 01935 891442

Situated in the Dorset Hills near the borders of Somerset and Devon, Chedington Court stands 600 feet above sea level and commands magnificent views over the surrounding countryside. This striking Jacobean-style mansion which is a member of 'Romantik Hotels' is set in 10 acres of grounds which contain ancient trees, a variety of shrubs, sweeping lawns, terraces and an ornamental water garden. Proprietors Philip and Hilary Chapman aim to provide a high standard of comfort, delicious food and a good selection of fine wines in beautiful surroundings. All ten bedrooms, some of which are huge, have antique furnishings and en suite bathrooms. The equally fine public rooms include a conservatory full of unusual plants. One mile from the hotel, and taking pride of place among the leisure facilities, is the 6,754-yard, par 74, 9-hole golf course with a further 9 holes being built, which attracts players of all handicaps. There is also a billiard room, a croquet lawn and a putting green. In this part of the world there are numerous small, unspoiled villages and charming towns to explore. Lulworth Cove, Lyme Regis, Dorchester, Weymouth and the splendid coastlines of Dorset and South Devon can be easily reached by car. **Directions:** Just off the A356, $4\frac{1}{2}$ miles south-east of Crewkerne at Winyard's Gap. Price guide: (including dinner) Single £89–£102; double/twin £158–£184.

For hotel location, see maps on pages 473–479

PONTLANDS PARK COUNTRY HOTEL & RESTAURANT

WEST HANNINGFIELD ROAD, GREAT BADDOW, NR CHELMSFORD, ESSEX CM2 8HR
TEL: 01245 476444 FAX: 01245 478393

Pontlands Park is a fine Victorian mansion, originally built for the Thomasin-Foster family in 1879. It became a hotel in 1981. The Victorian theme is still much in evidence, tempered with the best of contemporary interior styling. Immaculate public rooms – the conservatory-style Garden Room, the residents' lounge with its deep sofas and the relaxed ambience of the Victorian bar – are designed with guests' comfort in mind. Beautifully furnished bedrooms have co-ordinated fabrics and well-defined colour schemes. Diners are offered a selection of imaginative menus, with fine wines and attentive service. Within the grounds, Trimmers Leisure Centre has indoor and outdoor swimming pools, Jacuzzis, saunas and a solarium. The beauty salon offers many figure-toning, hairstyling and beauty treatments. Meetings and private dinners for from 2 to 36 guests can be accommodated, and functions for up to 200 guests can be held in the marquee. Closed 26 December to 4 January (but open for New Year's Eve). **Directions:** Pontlands Park is only about 30 miles from London. From A12 Chelmsford bypass take Great Baddow intersection (A130). Take first slip-road off A130 to Sandon/Great Baddow; bear left for Great Baddow, then first left for West Hanningfield Road. Price guide: Single £85; double/twin £120.

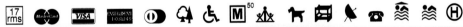

THE GREENWAY

SHURDINGTON, CHELTENHAM, GLOUCESTERSHIRE GL51 5UG
TEL: 01242 862352 FAX: 01242 862780

Set amid gentle parkland with the rolling Cotswold hills beyond, The Greenway is an Elizabethan country house with a style that is uniquely its own – very individual and very special. Renowned for the warmth of its welcome, its friendly atmosphere and its immaculate personal service, The Greenway is the ideal place for total relaxation. The public rooms with their antique furniture and fresh flowers are elegant and spacious yet comfortable, with roaring log fires in winter and access to the formal gardens in summer. The 19 bedrooms all have private bathrooms and are individually decorated with co-ordinated colour schemes. Eleven of the rooms are located in the main house with a further eight rooms in the converted Georgian coach house immediately adjacent to the main building. The award winning conservatory dining room overlooks the sunken garden and lily pond, providing the perfect backdrop to superb cuisine of international appeal complemented by an outstanding selection of wines. Situated in one of Britain's most charming areas, The Greenway is well placed for visiting the spa town of Cheltenham, the Cotswold villages and Shakespeare country. **Directions:** On the outskirts of Cheltenham off the A46 Cheltenham–Stroud road, 2½ miles from the city centre. Price guide: Single £87.50; double/twin £130–£195.

For hotel location, see maps on pages 473–479

HOTEL ON THE PARK

EVESHAM ROAD, CHELTENHAM, GLOUCESTERSHIRE GL52 2AH
TEL: 01242 518898 FAX: 01242 511526

Hotel On The Park is an exclusive Town House Hotel situated in the elegant spa town of Cheltenham. It enjoys an envied position overlooking the beautiful Pittville Park. A classic example of a Regency villa, the atmosphere inside is one of warmth and sophistication, akin to that of a traditional country house. The 12 intimate and restful bedrooms are individually styled and furnished with antiques, offering everything that one would expect to find in a small, luxury hotel. Each room has a private bathroom en suite, colour satellite television, direct-dial telephone, hairdryer and refreshments. A board meeting room for 18 people is available. Guests can enjoy some of the best modern European cooking on offer today in The Restaurant, where fresh produce is meticulously prepared with imagination and flair to produce well-balanced menus. The wine list has been carefully selected to offer something for all tastes. Cheltenham, with its Regency architecture, attractive promenade and exclusive shops, has plenty to offer visitors and is set in the heart of the Cotswolds. Cheltenham racecourse has a busy National Hunt programme. For details of terms during Gold Cup week, apply well in advance. Dogs accommodated by prior arrangement. **Directions:** Opposite Pittville Park, 5 minutes' walk from town centre. Price guide: Single from £77.75; double/twin from £100.50; suites from £115.50.

BROXTON HALL COUNTRY HOUSE HOTEL

WHITCHURCH ROAD, BROXTON, CHESTER, CHESHIRE CH3 9JS
TEL: 01829 782321 FAX: 01829 782330

Built in 1671 by a local landowner, Broxton Hall is a black-and-white half-timbered building set in five acres of grounds and extensive gardens amid the rolling Cheshire countryside. The medieval city of Chester is eight miles away. The hotel provides every modern comfort while retaining the ambience of a bygone age. The reception area reflects the character of the entire hotel, with its magnificent Jacobean fireplace, plush furnishings, oak panelled walls and carved mahogany staircase. On cool evenings log fires are lit. The small but well-appointed bedrooms are furnished with antiques and have en suite bathrooms as well as every modern comfort. Overlooking the gardens, the restaurant receives constant praise from regular diners. French and English cuisine is served, using local game in season and freshly caught fish. There is an extensive wine list. Breakfast may be taken in the sunny conservatory overlooking the lawned gardens. The hotel is an ideal venue for business meetings and conferences. Broxton Hall is the perfect base from which to visit the North Wales coast and Snowdonia. There are a number of excellent golf courses nearby, and racecourses at Chester and Bangor-on-Dee. **Directions:** Broxton Hall is on the A41 Whitchurch–Chester road, eight miles between Whitchurch and Chester. Price guide: Single £60–£65; double/twin £70–£105.

THE CHESTER GROSVENOR

EASTGATE, CHESTER CH1 1LT
TEL: 01244 324024 FAX: 01244 313246

The Chester Grosvenor, in the heart of the historic City of Chester, is owned by the Duke of Westminster's Grosvenor Estate. The hotel is renowned for its fabulous cuisine and has two restaurants – the award winning Arkle Restaurant, named after the famous racehorse, and an informal Parisian style Brasserie. The extensive wine cellars hold over 900 bins. All 86 bedrooms and suites are beautifully appointed, fully air conditioned with 24-hour room service provided and all the amenities you would expect from a de luxe hotel. The hotel has its own leisure suite with a multi-gymnasium, sauna and solarium and has membership of a local country club with indoor and outdoor swimming pools, tennis and squash. The hotel is situated within the Roman walls of the city and is a stroll away from Chester Cathedral, Chester race course and the River Dee. It is adjacent to the Chester Rows with their boutiques and exclusive shops. **Directions:** In the centre of Chester on Eastgate. 24-hour NCP car parking – follow signs to Grosvenor Precinct Car Park. Price guide: Weekend break rate £140 per double room per night – bed, breakfast and VAT included. Single from £130; double/twin from £190; suites £270.

CRABWALL MANOR

PARKGATE ROAD, MOLLINGTON, CHESTER, CHESHIRE CH1 6NE
TEL: 01244 851666 FAX: 01244 851400

Crabwall Manor can be traced back to Saxon England, prior to the Norman Conquest. The present Grade II listed manor at the heart of the hotel is believed to have originated from a Tudor farmhouse, with successive occupants enlarging the building over the ages. Set in 11 acres of wooded parkland on the outer reaches of Chester, the hotel has achieved a fine reputation under the ownership of Carl Lewis. A relaxed ambience is enhanced by staff who combine attentive service with friendliness and care. Bathrobes and sherry are among the many extras to be found in the bedrooms and luxury suites. Brightly printed drapes and pastel shades lend a freshness to the décor of the spacious lounge and reception areas, while a log fire crackling away in the inglenook fireplace adds warmth. Chef Michael Truelove, formerly of The Box Tree Restaurant in Ilkley, introduces a classic French influence to traditional English dishes. Manchester and Liverpool Airports are 30 minutes away by road. Chester, the Wirral and North Wales are all easily accessible. **Directions:** Go to end of M56, ignoring signs to Chester. Follow signs to Queensferry and North Wales, taking the A5117 to the next roundabout. Left onto the A540, towards Chester for 2 miles. Crabwall Manor is on the right. Price guide: Single £99; double/twin £125; suite £135–£155. Weekend rates available.

ROWTON HALL HOTEL

WHITCHURCH ROAD, ROWTON, CHESTER CH3 6AD
TEL: 01244 335262 FAX: 01244 335464

Standing in eight acres of gardens and pastureland on the outskirts of the city of Chester, Rowton Hall enjoys far-reaching views across the Cheshire Plains to the Welsh hills. Built as a private residence in 1779, the hall is renowned for the informal country-house atmosphere which welcomes all its guests. It retains many original features, including a Robert Adam fireplace and superb carved staircase. The conservatory-style Hamilton Lounge, overlooking the garden, is the perfect place to enjoy morning coffee, afternoon tea or cocktails, while the Cavalier Bar is ideal for a lunchtime snack. The bedrooms are furnished with chintzy fabrics and all have en suite bathrooms. In the Langdale Restaurant, which has earned a first-class reputation, chef Roger Price's à la carte and table d'hôte menus can be sampled in elegant and restful surroundings. Fresh vegetables and herbs are supplied by the hall's kitchen garden. Hotel guests have complimentary use of Hamiltons Leisure Club – facilities include a swimming pool, multi-gym, sauna and solarium. There are five conference/meeting rooms accommodating up to 200. The hotel offers special weekend rates. **Directions:** From the centre of Chester, take the A41 towards Whitchurch. After three miles, turn right to Rowton village. The hotel is in the centre of the village. Price guide: Single £67–£82; double/twin £88–£95; suite £125.

THE MILLSTREAM HOTEL

BOSHAM, NR CHICHESTER, WEST SUSSEX PO18 8HL
TEL: 01243 573234 FAX: 01243 573459

A village rich in heritage, Bosham is depicted in the Bayeux Tapestry and is associated with King Canute, whose daughter is buried in the local Saxon church. Moreover, sailors from the world over navigate their way to Bosham, which is a yachtsman's idyll on the banks of Chichester Harbour. The Millstream consists of a restored 18th-century malthouse and adjoining cottages linked to The Grange, a small English manor house. Cane and pine bedroom furnishings are complemented by chintz fabrics and pastel décor. Period furniture, a grand piano and bowls of freshly cut flowers feature in the drawing room. A stream meanders past the front of the delightful gardens, where traditional herbs are grown for use by the *chef de cuisine*. Whatever the season, care is taken to ensure that the composition and presentation of the dishes reflect high standards. An extensive buffet selection is offered in the summer months and includes specialities like lobster, crab and salmon. During the winter, good-value 'Hibernation Breaks' are available. **Directions:** From A259, 4 miles west of Chichester, take Walton Lane to Bosham; the hotel is situated on the right. Price guide: Single £59–£79; double/twin £89–£109.

STANTON MANOR

STANTON SAINT QUINTIN, NR CHIPPENHAM, WILTSHIRE SN14 6DQ
TEL: 01666 837552 FAX: 01666 837022

Near to the M4 just off the beaten track in five acres of leafy gardens, there has been a habitation at Stanton Manor for over 900 years. The original house was listed in the *Domesday Book* and was later owned by Lord Burghley, Elizabeth I's chief minister. The Elizabethan dovecote in the garden bears witness to that period, although the present building dates largely from the 19th century. The bedrooms are furnished in a homely, country style and several offer views over Wiltshire farmland. Choices from the à la carte menu might include a starter of king prawns and mussels provençale or chicken liver parfait followed, for a main course, by saddle of spring lamb in a brandy, tomato

and tarragon sauce. A variety of light meals is available in either the lounge or the bar. Proprietors Elizabeth and Philip Bullock are usually on hand to ensure that a friendly, personal service is extended to all their visitors. The Roman city of Cirencester, Chippenham, and a wealth of pretty villages all invite exploration. **Directions:** Leave the M4 at junction 17 and join the A429 towards Cirencester. After 200 yards, turn left to Stanton Saint Quintin; Stanton Manor is on the left in the village. Price guide: Single £68; double/twin £82.

CHARINGWORTH MANOR

NR CHIPPING CAMPDEN, GLOUCESTERSHIRE GL55 6NS
TEL: 01386 593555 FAX: 01386 593353

The ancient manor of Charingworth lies amid the gently rolling Cotswold countryside, just a few miles from the historic towns of Chipping Campden and Broadway. The 14th-century manor house overlooks its own 50-acre grounds and offers peace, tranquillity and enthralling views. Inside, Charingworth is an historic patchwork of intimate public rooms with log fires burning during the colder months. There are 24 individually designed bedrooms, all furnished with antiques and fine fabrics. Outstanding cuisine is regarded as being of great importance and guests at Charingworth are assured of imaginative dishes. Great emphasis is placed on using only the finest produce and the AA has awarded the cuisine two Rosettes. There is an all-weather tennis court within the grounds, while inside, a beautiful swimming pool, sauna, steam room, solarium and billiard room are available, allowing guests to relax and unwind. Hidcote Manor Gardens, Batsford Arboretum, Stratford-upon-Avon, Oxford and Cheltenham are all within easy reach. Short-break rates are available on request. **Directions:** Charingworth Manor is on the B4035 between Chipping Campden and Shipston-on-Stour. Price guide: (including full breakfast) Single from £90; double/twin from £150.

THE COTSWOLD HOUSE

HIGH STREET, CHIPPING CAMPDEN, GLOUCESTERSHIRE GL55 6AN
TEL: 01386 840330 FAX: 01386 840310

The Cotswold House takes pride of place on Chipping Campden's historic High Street, described by Trevelyn as 'the most beautiful street left in this island'. The beauty and harmony of this unique setting are reflected within the hotel, where antiques, choice fabrics, works of art and vast bowls of freshly cut flowers complement the elegant Regency architecture, creating a warm and welcoming atmosphere where friendly, efficient service is the hallmark. There are 15 very comfortable bedrooms, ranging from the whimsical Aunt Lizzie's Room to a wonderfully 'over the top' Four-Poster Room. In the Restaurant, menus combine fresh local produce with seasonal variety imparting a new meaning to the words 'English cooking'. The award of AA Rosettes and Red Stars, together with the RAC's coveted Blue Ribbon, acknowledge exceptional all-round standards. A private room is available for small parties, weddings and conferences. The Cotswold House is perfectly located for visiting the many famous houses and gardens nearby and is just a short drive from Stratford-upon-Avon, Warwick, Oxford and Cheltenham Spa. Special short-stay breaks are available all year, except at Christmas when the hotel is closed.
Directions: Chipping Campden lies 2 miles north-east of the A44 on the B4081. Price guide: Single from £72; double/twin from £105; four poster from £155.

THE ARDENCOTE MANOR

LYE GREEN ROAD, CLAVERDON, WARWICK CV35 8LS
TEL: 01926 843111 FAX: 01926 842646

Set in the heart of Shakespeare country the Ardencote Manor Hotel and Country Club combines Victorian elegance with the finest leisure and beauty facilities. Recently nominated for the AA Courtesy and Care Award and the Best Hotel Newcomer 1996 Award, the hotel is a former gentlemans residence adorned by beautifully designed landscaped gardens boasting its own four-acre trout lake and fishermans lodge. The bedrooms are elegantly furnished, all with en suite facilities and many offering splendid country views. Guests have the choice of dining in the Palms conservatory, whose doors open onto wonderful gardens, or in the intimate Oak panelled fine dining restaurant. The country club facilities include an indoor heated swimming pool, Jacuzzi, sauna and steam room, a fully equipped gymnasium, four squash courts and a jogging track. This is all complemented with fully equipped beauty treatment and therapy rooms and designer hair salon. The hotel is within easy reach of Stratford-upon-Avon, Warwick, the National Exhibition Centre, Indoor Arena and National Agricultural Showground. **Directions:** From junction 16 of M40 take A3400 to Henley-in-Arden and then B4095 to Claverdon. Lye Green Road is on the left. Price guide: Single £72.95–£82.95; double/twin £100–£115; suites £115–£135.

WOODLANDS PARK HOTEL

WOODLANDS LANE, STOKE D'ABERNON, COBHAM, SURREY KT11 3QB
TEL: 01372 843933 FAX: 01372 842704

Set in 10 acres of parkland, Woodlands Park Hotel is an ideal location for touring the surrounding Surrey and Berkshire countryside. At the turn of the century, the then Prince of Wales and famous actress Lillie Langtry were frequent visitors to this splendid Victorian mansion. Well equipped en suite bedrooms retain an appealing Victorian theme and ambience, despite having been refurbished to the highest standards. Each offers its guests luxury, comfort and every modern amenity. The Oak Room Restaurant serves imaginative English and French cuisine in elegant surroundings, while Langtry's Bar and Brasserie, offering a daily blackboard menu and a wide selection of dishes from the speciality menu, is designed for those who prefer less formal dining. Small meeting rooms can be reached from the Grand Hall and can accommodate between 10 and 60 for private dinners or meetings, while the modern Prince of Wales Suite seats up to 300. Nearby are Wisley Gardens, Hampton Court and Brooklands Museum. Kempton Park and Sandown are within a short distance for those who enjoy racing. **Directions:** On the M25 take junction 9 or 10. The hotel is east of Cobham at Stoke d'Abernon on the A245. Price guide: Single £105; twin/double £135–£180; suites £215.

FIVE LAKES HOTEL, GOLF & COUNTRY CLUB

COLCHESTER ROAD, TOLLESHUNT KNIGHTS, MALDON, ESSEX CM9 8HX
TEL: 01621 868888 FAX: 01621 869696

Set in 320 acres of Essex countryside, Five Lakes is a superb 21st century hotel which combines the latest in leisure, health, beauty and sporting activities with state-of-the-art conference, meeting and banqueting facilities. The 114 bedrooms are furnished to a high standard and offer every comfort and convenience. With its two 18-hole courses, the Lakes course being a championship course used annually by the PGA European Tour as a qualifying venue. The hotel is already recognised as one of East Anglia's leading golf venues. Guests are also invited to take advantage of the championship tennis centre with four indoor and four outdoor tennis courts, three squash courts, and a comprehensive leisure, spa and fitness centre. There is a choice of restaurants, where good food is complemented by excellent service. Lounges and cocktail bars provide a comfortable environment in which to relax and enjoy a drink. Extensive facilities are available for meetings and conferences, designed to cater for from four to four hundred delegates. There are 13 rooms, all offering natural daylight and providing a full range of appropriate equipment.
Directions: Approximately 35 minutes from junction 28 of the M25 follow A12 towards Colchester and take B1024 at Kelvedon. Price guide: Single £85; double/twin £105–£115; suites £145.

For hotel location, see maps on pages 473–479

THE WHITE HART HOTEL & RESTAURANT

MARKET END, COGGESHALL, ESSEX CO6 1NH
TEL: 01376 561654 FAX: 01376 561789

A historic, family-run hotel, The White Hart is situated in the Essex town of Coggeshall, where it has played an integral part for many years. In 1489 The White Hart became the town's meeting place when most of the adjoining Guildhall was destroyed by fire. Part of that original Guildhall now forms the residents' lounge, and features magnificent roof timbers hewn from sweet chestnut. Sympathetically restored throughout, the hotel has been comfortably appointed with much attention to detail. All the en suite bedrooms have been decorated with bright fabrics to reflect the hotel's colourful character. Heavily timbered and spacious, the restaurant enjoys a good reputation locally. The table d'hôte and à la carte menus feature a choice of Italian dishes with a particular emphasis on seafood and shellfish. Pasta is freshly made, and aromatic sauces and tender cuts of meat figure prominently on the menu. The hotel has recently received merit awards from the RAC for comfort and its restaurant, which already holds 2 AA rosettes and an Egon Ronay recommendedation. Coggeshall is noted for its antiques shops. It is also convenient for Colchester and Chelmsford and the ferry ports of Felixstowe and Harwich. **Directions:** Coggeshall is just off the A120 between Colchester and Braintree. From the A12 follow signs through Kelvedon, then take B1024. Price guide: Single £61.50; double/twin £82–£130.

TREGLOS HOTEL

CONSTANTINE BAY, NR PADSTOW, CORNWALL PL28 8JH
TEL: 01841 520727 FAX: 01841 521163

The atmosphere of a large country house pervades Treglos Hotel, which enjoys a superb position overlooking the spectacular North Cornish coastline. Most of the hotel's bedrooms and suites enjoy magnificent views over Constantine Bay and Trevose Head. All are equipped to a very high standard and a daily laundry service, room service and night porter are all available. Spacious lounges, warmed on chilly days by roaring log fires, are the perfect place to relax, and in warmer weather guests may enjoy the tranquillity of the beautifully landscaped gardens. The restaurant enjoys a good reputation and offers an extensive menu catering for every need. Specialities include fresh local seafood, traditional roasts and vegetables from the kitchen garden. A lovely heated swimming pool and Jacuzzi open onto the lawns and gardens and the patio, overlooking the bay, is a favoured place to enjoy delicious cream teas and early evening drinks. Nearby, the picturesque harbour at Padstow provides fishing from mackerel to shark, along with boat trips around the off shore islands. Several National Trust properties are within easy reach. Trevose golf links and sandy beaches are just a short stroll from the hotel. **Directions:** Constantine Bay and Treglos are signposted from St Merryn (B3276 from Padstow. Newquay Airport is eight miles away. Price guide: Single £49–£72; double/twin £96–£136; suites £132–£180.

In association with MasterCard

TILLMOUTH PARK HOTEL

CORNHILL-ON-TWEED, NORTHUMBERLAND TD12 4UU
TEL: 01890 882255 FAX: 01890 882540

Designed by Sir Charles Barry, the famous Victorian architect of the Houses of Parliament in Westminster, Tillmouth Park offers the same warm welcome today as it did when it was an exclusive private country house. It is situated in a rich countryside farmland of deciduous woodland and moor. The generously sized bedrooms have been recently refurbished in a distinctive old fashioned style with period furniture, although all offer modern day amenities. The kitchen prides itself on traditional country fare, with the chef using fresh local produce to create imaginative and well presented dishes. The restaurant serves a fine table d'hôte menu, while the Bistro is less formal. Fresh salmon and game are always available with 24 hours' notice. A well chosen wine list and a vast selection of malt whiskies complement the cuisine. Tillmouth Park is an ideal centre for country pursuits including field sports, fishing, hill walking, shooting, riding, birdwatching and golf. For the spectator there is rugby, curling and horse racing during the season. Places of interest nearby include stately homes such as Floors, Manderston and Paxton. Flodden Field, Lindisfarne and Holy Island are all within easy reach and the coast is just 15 minutes away. **Directions:** Tillmouth Park is on the A698 Cornhill-on-Tweed to Berwick-on-Tweed road. Price guide: Single £70–£90; twin/double £105–£125.

COOMBE ABBEY

BRINKLOW ROAD, BINLEY, WARWICKSHIRE CV3 2AB
TEL: 01203 450450 FAX: 01203 635101

Coombe Abbey is approached by travelling along a lovely avenue of lime trees and chestnuts, crossing a moat and passing through a cloistered entrance. Originally a Cistercian Abbey dating back to the 11th century, this hotel lies in the heart of 500 acres of parkland and formal gardens. Deep colours, carefully selected fabrics and antique furnishing and lighting are all features of its restful bedrooms. Room designs, often eccentric or mischievous, include hidden bathrooms, four poster beds and the occasional hand painted Victorian bath in the centre of the room. Many bedrooms overlook the grounds with their splendid 80 acre lake.

The restaurants and private dining rooms each have their individual charm and offer a variety of settings suitable for all occasions. Sophisticated and creative menus provide a good choice of delightful dishes and the service is attentive but never intrusive. The hotel is an ideal venue for conferences and weddings. Among the local attractions are Kenilworth Castle and Stratford and the surrounding area is excellent for walking and birdwatching. **Directions:** Leave the M40 at junction 15 and take the A46 towards Binley. Coombe Abbey is on the B4027. Price guide: Single £95–£105; twin/double £120–£295; suite £225.

NAILCOTE HALL

NAILCOTE LANE, BERKSWELL, NR COVENTRY, WARWICKSHIRE CV7 7DE
TEL: 01203 466174 FAX: 01203 470720

Nailcote Hall is a charming Elizabethan country house hotel set in 15 acres of gardens and surrounded by Warwickshire countryside. Built in 1640, the house was used by Cromwell during the Civil War and damaged by his troops prior to the assault on Kenilworth Castle. Ideally located in the heart of England, Nailcote Hall is within 15 minutes' drive of the castle towns of Kenilworth and Warwick, Coventry Cathedral, Birmingham International Airport/Station and the NEC. Situated at the centre of the Midlands motorway network, Birmingham city centre, the ICC and Stratford-upon-Avon are less than 30 minutes away. Leisure facilities include indoor swimming pool, gymnasium, solarium and sauna. Outside are all-weather tennis courts, petanque, croquet, a 9-hole par-3 golf course and putting green. The hotel is associated with Stoneleigh Deer Park Golf Club. In the intimate Tudor surroundings of the Oak Room restaurant, the chef will delight you with superb cuisine, while the cellar boasts an extensive choice of international wines. Forty en suite bedrooms offer luxury accommodation, and elegant facilities are available for conferences, private dining and corporate hospitality. **Directions:** Situated 6 miles south of Birmingham International Airport/ NEC on the B4101 Balsall Common–Coventry road. Price guide: Single £110–£125; double/twin £120–£165.

CRATHORNE HALL HOTEL

CRATHORNE, NR YARM, NORTH YORKSHIRE TS15 0AR
TEL: 01642 700398 FAX: 01642 700814

Part of the Virgin group, Richard Branson's Crathorne Hall was the last great stately home built in the Edwardian era. Now a splendid country house hotel, it is set in 15 acres of woodland overlooking the River Leven and the Cleveland Hills. True to their original fashion, the interiors have elegant antique furnishings complementing the grand architectural style. There is no traffic to wake up to here: just the dawn chorus, all the comforts of a luxury hotel and, if desired, a champagne breakfast in bed. From a simple main course to a gastronomic dinner, the food is of the highest quality, complemented by a comprehensive wine list. Whether catering for conferences, product launches, wedding receptions or a quiet weekend for two, professional, courteous service is guaranteed. In the grounds guests can play croquet, follow the jogging track or try clay pigeon shooting with a tutor on a layout designed to entertain the beginner and test the expert. Hot-air ballooning, fishing, archery and tennis can be arranged. The Yorkshire Dales, Durham and York are nearby. **Directions:** From A19 Thirsk–Teesside road, turn to Yarm and Crathorne. Follow signs to Crathorne village; hotel is on left. Teesside Airport and Darlington rail station are both seven miles; a courtesy collection service is available. Price guide: Single £99; double/twin £135–£180.

OCKENDEN MANOR

OCKENDEN LANE, CUCKFIELD, WEST SUSSEX RH17 5LD
TEL: 01444 416111 FAX: 01444 415549

Set in 9 acres of gardens in the centre of the Tudor village of Cuckfield, this hotel is an ideal base from which to discover Sussex and Kent, the Garden of England. First recorded in 1520, Ockenden Manor has become a hotel of great charm and character. The bedrooms all have their own individual identity: climb your private staircase to Thomas or Elizabeth, look out across the lovely Sussex countryside from Victoria's bay window or choose Charles, with its handsome four-poster bed. The restaurant, with its beautifully painted ceiling, is a dignified setting in which to enjoy acclaimed cuisine. 'Modern English' is how the chef describes his culinary style, offering an à la carte menu with a daily table d'hôte choice to include fresh seasonal produce and herbs from the hotel garden. An outstanding, extensive wine list offers, for example, a splendid choice of first-growth clarets. Spacious and elegantly furnished, the Ockenden Suite welcomes private lunch and dinner parties. A beautiful conservatory is attached to the Ockenden Suite, this opens on to the lawns, where marquees can be set up for summer celebrations. The gardens of Nymans, Wakehurst Place and Leonardslee are nearby, as is the opera at Glyndebourne. **Directions:** In the centre of Cuckfield on the A272. Less than 3 miles east of the A23. Price guide: Single from £85; double/twin from £115–£195.

HEADLAM HALL

HEADLAM, NR GAINFORD, DARLINGTON, COUNTY DURHAM DL2 3HA
TEL: 01325 730238 FAX: 01325 730790

This magnificent Jacobean mansion is set in three acres of formal gardens in the quiet countryside of rural Teesdale. Originally built in the 17th century, the hall was home for 150 years to the Brocket family and more recently to Lord Gainford. Since 1979 Headlam Hall has been owned and personally run by the Robinson family. The grounds include a small private trout water enclosed by ancient yew and beech hedges. The hotel has a tennis court, croquet lawn, a fine swimming pool, sauna and snooker room. All the bedrooms are individually furnished, and the restaurant provides the best of traditional English cuisine. The main hall features a magnificent carved oak fireplace and open staircase, while the Georgian drawing room opens onto a stepped terrace overlooking the lawns. There are four separate conference and meeting rooms including the Edwardian Suite holding up to 200 people. A free night's accommodation and champagne breakfast are provided for newly-weds holding their reception here. Fishing and golf can be enjoyed nearby and Barnard Castle and Durham are only a short drive away. Stephenson's first railway engine is on view in Darlington. Dogs by prior arrangement. **Directions:** Headlam is two miles north of Gainford off the A67 Darlington–Barnard Castle road. Price guide: Single £55–£75; double/twin £70–£85; suite £90.

BRANDSHATCH PLACE HOTEL

FAWKHAM VALLEY ROAD, FAWKHAM, KENT DA3 8NQ
TEL: 01474 872239 FAX: 01474 879652

Set amidst 12 acres of private parkland and gardens, Brandshatch Place is a distinguished Georgian residence built in 1806. Approached along an impressive tree-lined drive, it offers a peaceful getaway from London, only 20 miles to the north. The hotel has been carefully renovated and now has every modern amenity, from banqueting and conference rooms to a fully equipped leisure club. All the bedrooms are pleasantly decorated, 12 of which are located in the recently converted mews. Dine in the award-winning Hatchwood Restaurant where chefs create dishes of originality using only the best produce available.

After your meal enjoy a relaxing drink in the library bar. You are always welcome to use Fredericks, the sports and leisure complex with its indoor pool, three squash courts, supervised gymnasium, dance studio, hair and beauty salon, sauna, steam room, two solariums, snooker room and tennis courts. Business and private functions are easily accommodated in the eight meeting rooms. **Directions:** From M25 junction 3 follow A20 south, then signs to Fawkham Green, hotel is on the right about $^1/_2$ mile before Fawkham village. Price guide: Single: £79–£89; double/twin £98–£120.

ROWHILL GRANGE

WILMINGTON, DARTFORD, KENT DA2 7QH
TEL: 01322 615136 FAX: 01322 615137

An unexpected find in this area, Rowhill Grange nestles in nine acres of woodlands and mature gardens descending to a picturesque lake. A combination of top service and friendliness makes Rowhill Grange the perfect venue for everything from weekend breaks to special occasions such as weddings and anniversaries. All the luxurious bedrooms are named after flowers and boast individual character and decoration, with a full range of facilities available to ensure maximum comfort and convenience for guests. The Garden Restaurant has been recently refurbished and the team of top chefs has taken a fresh look at the menus. The result is superb cuisine, ranging from the traditional to the exotic. From late spring and through the summer months guests may take dinner on the terrace, sharing a scenic view with the swans and ducks. For special occasions, the private oak panelled dining room is available. The Clockhouse Suite is a self contained functions annexe with a dining/dancing area, comfortable lounge and a bar. Extensive health and beauty spa opens spring 1996. **Directions:** M20 junction 1/M25 junction 3. Take the B2173 into Swanley and B258 north at Superstore roundabout. After Hextable Green the entrance is almost immediately on the left. Price guide: Double/twin £80–£125.

DEDHAM

MAISON TALBOOTH

STRATFORD ROAD, DEDHAM, COLCHESTER, ESSEX CO7 6HN
TEL: 01206 322367 FAX: 01206 322752

In the north-east corner of Essex, where the River Stour borders with Suffolk, is the Vale of Dedham, an idyllic riverside setting immortalised in the early 19th century by the paintings of John Constable. One summer's day many years later, in 1952, the young Gerald Milsom enjoyed a 'cuppa' in the Talbooth tea room and soon afterwards took the helm at what would develop into Le Talbooth Restaurant. Business was soon booming and the restaurant built itself a reputation as one of the best in the country. By 1969 Gerald had branched out, and Maison Talbooth was created in a nearby Victorian rectory, to become, as it still is, a standard bearer for Britain's premier country house hotels. Indeed, in 1982 Gerald

Milsom became the founder member of the Pride of Britain group. With its atmosphere of opulence, Maison Talbooth has ten spacious guest suites which all have an air of quiet luxury. Every comfort has been provided, and for an extra touch of romance, some of the bathrooms have large round baths with gold taps. Full breakfast is served in the suites. Le Talbooth Restaurant is a pleasant half mile stroll away or a courtesy car can drive you where first-class cuisine is served. The hotel arranges special Constable tours. **Directions:** Dedham is about a mile from the A12 between Colchester and Ipswich. Price guide: Single £85–£110; double/twin £105–£140. Telephone for details of special short breaks.

MAKENEY HALL COUNTRY HOUSE HOTEL

MAKENEY, MILFORD, DERBYSHIRE DE56 0RU
TEL: 01332 842999 FAX: 01332 842777

Set in a restful location on the River Derwent, Makeney Hall is surrounded by over 6 acres of beautifully landscaped gardens just 10 minutes' drive from Derby. Founded by the Strutt family with cotton-spinning wealth, this quiet, capacious hotel, with its mid-Victorian features, offers guests a warm, distinctive welcome. The carefully chosen décor imparts an air of bygone comfort. Bedrooms in the main house are spacious and individually appointed and many overlook the gardens. A splendid covered courtyard gives access to a further eighteen new rooms. Guests may dine in Lavinia's AA rosetted restaurant, where expert cooking and fresh local produce create cuisine of the highest standard. The fare is British in flavour and a selection of fine wines is available. Makeney Hall's Conference and Banqueting suites can accommodate wedding receptions and business meetings of up to 130 visitors. Places of interest locally include the Derwent Valley – an area of outstanding natural beauty – the Peak District, the stately homes of Chatsworth and Haddon Hall, and Alton Towers. **Directions:** From M1 (exits 25 or 28) head for Derby and A38 northbound. Follow A6 (signposted Matlock). Makeney is signposted at Milford, 6 miles NW of Derby. Price guide: Double-twin: from £65; suite: from £135.

MICKLEOVER COURT

ETWALL ROAD, MICKLEOVER, DERBYSHIRE DE3 5XX
TEL: 01332 521234 FAX: 01332 521238

This modern up-to-date hotel, set on the edge of Mickleover, offers comfortable accommodation and excellent service. The air conditioned bedrooms are pleasantly furnished and well equipped with all the latest accessories. The main restaurant, the Avesbury, which has received wide acclaim including an AA Rosette, offers a fixed table d'hôte and à la carte menu. Both these menus provide a good variety by imaginative dishes. The second restaurant, the Stelline, specialises in Italian food, particularly pastas and pizzas. Guests are invited to take advantage of the Castaway leisure club with state-of-the-art gymnasium, 15 metre swimming pool, and hair and beauty salon.

The hotel's conference and banqueting suites can accommodate up to 200 people. An extensive range of activities and country pursuits available in the vicinity includes golf, windsurfing, riding, gliding, clay pigeon shooting, water-skiing, dry-skiing, flying, sailing, car racing tuition and ballooning. Places of interest nearby include Alton Towers, Uttoxeter Racecourse and the Peak District. **Directions:** From M1 junction 28 follow signs to Derby. Ignore signs for city centre and take first exit signposted to Uttoxeter A516 and then first exit for Mickleover. The hotel is on the right before the roundabout. Price guide: Single from £85; double/twin from £99.50.

WENTBRIDGE HOUSE HOTEL

WENTBRIDGE, NR PONTEFRACT, WEST YORKSHIRE WF8 3JJ
TEL: 01977 620444 FAX: 01977 620148

Wentbridge House dates from 1700 and is set in 20 acres of grounds in the beautiful Went Valley. This fine building was once owned by the Bowes Lyon family and is renowned for its antiques and Thompson of Kilburn furniture. It is surrounded by superb lawns and trees and provides guests with a wonderful setting in which to enjoy a break. All the bedrooms, one of which boasts a resident ghost called Mary, are individually furnished and decorated to a high standard, including the spacious Oak Room with its four-poster bed, antiques and Persian rugs. The award-winning Fleur de Lys restaurant enjoys an excellent reputation for its cuisine and interesting selection of unusual and great wines.

The hotel is ideal for executive meetings and conferences. The Leatham Suite can accommodate 40 delegates theatre style, while the elegant oak beamed and panelled Tudor Room offers an exceptional setting for a maximum of 20 people. The Crystal Suite, which overlooks the courtyard, is eminently suitable for presentations, conferences and wedding receptions. Wentbridge House is recommended by Egon Ronay, Michelin and The Good Food Guide and has the English Tourist Board's 4 Crowns Highly Commended rating. Directions: Wentbridge is half a mile off the A1, four miles south of the M62/A1 interchange. Price guide: Single £65–£90; double/twin £75–£99.

LUMLEY CASTLE HOTEL

CHESTER-LE-STREET, COUNTY DURHAM DH3 4NX
TEL: 0191 389 1111 FAX: 0191 389 1881/0191 387 1437

This magnificent 14th century castle offers an exciting blend of ancient history and modern convenience. The hotel has 60 bedrooms each individually styled and appointed to a high standard. The King James Suite is Lumley's hallmark of taste and distinction. The public areas of the hotel, amply supported by medieval pillars, captivate the attention and imagination of all visitors. The subdued lighting and hidden corridors enhance the exciting atmosphere that pervades this amazing building. The Black Knight Restaurant will tease the most experienced palate. Lumley Castle's Medieval Memories weekend breaks offer a magnificent 'get-away' opportunity. These include an evening at the award-winning Elizabethan Banquet, full of fun, feasting (5-course meal) and merriment. The sharp wit and musical talent of the Castle's entertainers in their striking costumery offer a night to remember. The golf course adjoining the hotel is a must for the golfing enthusiast and Durham's new County Cricket Ground is a short walk away. For the more serious minded, Lumley has a number of conference and meeting rooms which provide an unusual setting for business matters. **Directions:** From A1(M) northbound take A693/A167 to Chester-le-Street and Durham. At the second roundabout take first left to Lumley Castle. Price guide: Single £82–£110; double/twin £110–£140; suite £180.

SUMMER LODGE

SUMMER LANE, EVERSHOT, DORSET DT2 0JR
TEL: 01935 83424 FAX: 01935 83005

A charming Georgian building, idyllically located in Hardy country, the Summer Lodge was formerly the dower house of the Earls of Ilchester. Now it is a luxurious hotel where owners Nigel and Margaret Corbett offer their visitors a genuinely friendly welcome, encouraging them to relax as if in their own home. The bedrooms have views over the 4-acre sheltered gardens or overlook the village rooftops across the meadowland. In the dining room, with its French windows that open on to the garden, the cuisine is highly regarded. Fresh local produce is combined with the culinary expertise of chef Donna Horlock to create a distinctive brand of English cooking. The unspoiled Dorset countryside, and coastline 12 miles south, make for limitless exploration, and bring to life the setting of *Tess of the d'Urbevilles, The Mayor of Casterbridge, Far from the Madding Crowd* and the other Hardy novels. Many National Trust properties and gardens in the locality are open to the public. There are stables, golf courses and trout lakes nearby. Summer Lodge has earned the distinction of becoming a member of Relais et Châteaux. **Directions:** The turning to Evershot leaves the A37 halfway between Dorchester and Yeovil. Once in the village turn left into Summer Lane and the hotel entrance is 150 yards on the right. Price guide: Single £100; double/twin £125–£225.

THE EVESHAM HOTEL

COOPERS LANE, OFF WATERSIDE, EVESHAM, WORCESTERSHIRE WR11 6DA
TEL: 01386 765566 RESERVATIONS: 0800 716969 FAX: 01386 765443

National awards for 'friendly eccentricity' suggest that a stay at The Evesham Hotel will be memorable. Indeed, the emphasis here is on unconventional hotel-keeping, informality and fun! Originally a Tudor farmhouse, the hotel was extended and converted into a Georgian mansion house in 1810. Privately owned and managed by the Jenkinson family since the mid-1970s, guests can be assured of prompt, friendly service and a relaxed atmosphere. Each of the 40 en suite bedrooms is furnished complete with a teddy bear and a toy duck for the bath. The restaurant offers delicious cuisine from a very imaginative and versatile menu, accompanied by a list of unusual wines. John Jenkinson claims that the eclectic wine list 'enjoys great notoriety' and that the hotel can offer a wide selection of drinks. The indoor swimming pool has a seaside theme, and guests have access to squash and tennis at a nearby sports club. The peace of the 2¹/₂-acre garden belies the hotel's proximity to the town – a 5-minute walk away. In the gardens are six 300 year-old mulberry trees and a magnificent Cedar of Lebanon, planted in 1809. The hotel is a good base from which to explore the Cotswolds, Stratford-upon-Avon and the Severn Valley. Closed Christmas. **Directions:** Coopers Lane lies just off Waterside (the River Avon). Price guide: Single £60–£68; double/twin £88–£98.

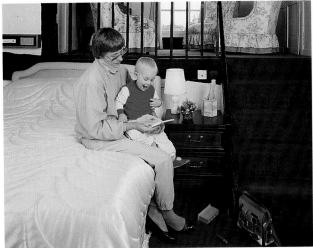

St Olaves Court Hotel

MARY ARCHES STREET, EXETER, DEVON EX4 3AZ
TEL: 01392 217736 FAX: 01392 413054

St Olaves Court, famous for its restaurant and home from home atmosphere, stands just 400 yards from Exeter Cathedral. It is a lovely Georgian building which is secluded in its own walled garden an oasis in the city centre. The rooms are very well cared for and range from single and twins to luxurious double bedrooms with Jacuzzi. The hotel has been discretely furnished, partly with antiques, and the public rooms are spacious and comfortable. A particularly attractive cocktail bar overlooks the garden. The level of service provided is first rate and reassuringly old fashioned. Central to the enjoyment of St Olaves is the excellence of the cooking. The candle-lit restaurant one of the best in south west England is renowned for its outstanding cuisine. The Head Chef, winner of the young Irish Chef of the Year competition, achieves taste, texture and colour as well as excellence in presentation. The restaurant has won two AA Rosettes for good food, an RAC Food Merit Award and many other prestigious accolades. St Olaves Court Hotel is ideally placed for visiting famous National Trust gardens like Killerton and for exploring the City of Exeter as well as the South Devon coastline and the beauties of Dartmoor National Park. **Directions:** From Exeter city centre follow signs to 'Mary Arches P'. The hotel entrance is directly opposite. Price guide: Single £70–£85; double/twin £85–£110.

For hotel location, see maps on pages 473–479

NORTHCOTE MANOR

BURRINGTON AT PORTSMOUTH ARMS, TAW RIVER VALLEY, NORTH DEVON EX37 9LZ
TEL: 01769 560501 FAX: 01769 560770

Northcote Manor is beautifully situated in superb Devon countryside, midway between Exmoor and Dartmoor and the north and south Devon coasts. For nearly 300 years the home of a local squire, this 17th century building is set in the seclusion of 20 acres of sweeping lawns, landscaped gardens and lush woodland. It offers a peaceful and relaxed environment, combining today's comfort with an atmosphere of a past era. The luxurious bedrooms are equipped with every modern amenity and the public rooms are both spacious and elegant. The manor's new owners place great emphasis on providing an excellent service which caters for the most individual requirements. Creative first class cuisine relies mainly on home-grown and local produce for which the county is famous. In the grounds there are horses to take out for a ride and a number of leisure facilities, including a tennis court and an area to practise golf. The 18-hole Libbaton golf course is just round the corner, and arrangements for salmon and sea trout fishing in the nearby River Taw can be made in season. The Manor is ideally placed for touring the whole of Devon, the Cornish coasts, Somerset and beyond. **Directions:** About 25 miles from Exeter on the A377 at Portsmouth Arms turn into private drive. Do not enter Burrington Village. Price guide: Single £79–£129; double/twin £109–£129; suites £169.

BUDOCK VEAN GOLF & COUNTRY HOUSE HOTEL

MAWNAN SMITH, FALMOUTH, CORNWALL TR11 5LG
TEL: 01326 250288 FAX: 01326 250892

The elegant Budock Vean Golf and Country House Hotel is set in 65 acres of beautiful gardens and parklands, with a private foreshore to the tranquil Helford River. Most of the comfortably furnished bedrooms enjoy stunning views over the hotel's sub-tropical gardens, some have adjoining sitting rooms and all are well equipped with modern amenities. Keen appetites will be well satisfied by the variety of dishes offered on the hotel's excellent and original menus. Seafood, including local lobsters and oysters, is an obvious speciality. In addition to traditional food, there is a choice of dishes with an international flavour. The hotel has its own tennis courts, golf course and swimming pool and activities including watersports, horse riding, yachting, boating and fishing are all within easy reach of the hotel. Numerous places of interest nearby include the Seal Sanctuary at Gweek, several heritage sites, and many magnificent gardens and properties of the National Trust. **Directions:** Follow A39 to Falmouth and head for Mawnan Smith. In Mawnan Smith take the right at the Red Lion. Pass Trebah Gardens and the turning for Helford Passage – Budock Vean is on the left. Price guide (including dinner): Single £52–£83; double/twin £105–£166; suites £119–£181.

For hotel location, see maps on pages 473–479

MEUDON HOTEL

MAWNAN SMITH, NR FALMOUTH, CORNWALL TR11 5HT
TEL: 01326 250541 FAX: 01326 250543

Set against a delightfully romantic backdrop of densely wooded countryside between the Fal and Helford Rivers, Meudon Hotel is a unique, superior retreat: a luxury, family-run establishment which has its origins in two humble 17th century coastguards' cottages. The French name comes from a nearby farmhouse built by Napoleonic prisoners of war and called after their eponymous home village. Set in nearly nine acres of fertile gardens – laid out by landscape gardener 'Capability' Brown, and now coaxed annually into early bloom by the mild Cornish climate – Meudon is safely surrounded by 200 acres of beautiful National Trust land and the sea. All bedrooms are en suite and enjoy spectacular views over sub-tropical gardens. Many a guest is enticed by the cuisine to return: in the restaurant (or the gardens during warm weather), fresh seafood and kitchen garden produce is served with wines from a judiciously compiled list. There are opportunities locally for fishing, sailing and walking. Golf is free. **Directions:** From Truro A39 to Hillhead roundabout turn right and the hotel is four miles on the left. Price guide (including dinner): Single £83–£100; double/twin £146–£170; suite £204–£240.

NANSIDWELL COUNTRY HOUSE

MAWNAN, NR FALMOUTH, CORNWALL TR11 5HU
TEL: 01326 250340 FAX: 01326 250440

Lying at the head of a wooded farmland valley running down to the sea, Nansidwell Country House is bounded by several acres of grounds between National Trust coastland and the Helford River. The house has five acres of sub-tropical gardens with Camellias coming out in December and also extraordinary banana trees, sometimes bearing tiny fruit. The philosophy of proprietors Jamie and Felicity Robertson is that their guests should experience the atmosphere of an amiable, well-run country house. That so many guests return each year is a credit to the hotel. The bedrooms are prettily furnished and offer every comfort. Chef Anthony Allcott places an emphasis on fresh, local produce, particularly seafood such as lobster, mussels and oysters. For the sports enthusiast, there are five 18-hole golf courses within a short drive, as well as sea fishing and reservoir trout fishing and the hotel has a tennis court. Wind-surfing, sailing, riding and bowls can all be enjoyed in the vicinity and there is the natural beauty of Falmouth's great harbour, the Helford River and Frenchman's Creek. Closed 2 January to 1 February. **Directions:** From A39, take A394 Helston road. After one mile follow sign for Mabe/Mawnan Smith. Price guide Single from £110; double/twin from £145 to include dinner and continental breakfast. Bed and breakfast rates available.

TRELAWNE HOTEL

MAWNAN SMITH, NR FALMOUTH, CORNWALL TR11 5HS
TEL: 01326 250226 FAX: 01326 250909

A very friendly welcome awaits guests, who will be enchanted by the beautiful location of Trelawne Hotel, on the coast between the Rivers Fal and Helford. Large picture windows in the public rooms, including the attractively decorated, spacious lounge, ensure that guests take full advantage of the panoramic views of the ever-changing coastline. The bedrooms are charming, many with views of the sea. The soft colours of the décor, the discreet lighting and attention to detail provide a restful atmosphere, in harmony with the Wedgwood, fresh flowers and sparkling crystal in the restaurant. The menu changes daily and offers a variety of inspired dishes, including local seafood, game and fresh vegetables. Recreational facilities include a putting green and a games room, with snooker, table-tennis and darts. The Royal Duchy of Cornwall is an area of outstanding beauty, with many National Trust and English Heritage properties to visit and a range of leisure pursuits to enjoy. Trelawne Hotel offers its own golf package at no less than ten fine courses. 'Slip Away Anyday' spring, autumn and winter breaks. Closed January. A Hospitality Hotel of Cornwall. AA Rosette. **Directions:** From A39 take A394 Helston road. After one mile follow sign for Mabe/Mawnan Smith. Price guide (including dinner): Single £45–£73; double/twin £90–£132.

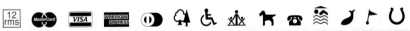

FLITWICK MANOR

CHURCH ROAD, FLITWICK, BEDFORDSHIRE MK45 1AE
TEL: 01525 712242 FAX: 01525 718753

Flitwick Manor is a Georgian gem, classical in style, elegant in décor, comfortable in appointment, a country house hotel that remains true to the traditions of country house hospitality. Nestling in acres of glorious rolling parkland complete with lake, grotto and church, the manor has the intimacy and warmth that makes it the ideal retreat for both pleasure and business. The fifteen bedrooms, with their distinctive characters and idiosyncrasies, add to the charm of the reception rooms: a soothing withdrawing room, a cosy library and pine panelled morning room, the latter two doubling up as both meeting and private dining rooms. Fine antiques and period pieces, easy chairs and inviting sofas, winter fires and summer flowers, they all blend effortlessly together to make a perfect whole. The restaurant is highly acclaimed by all the major food guides and indeed the AA, with its bestowal of three Rosettes, rates Flitwick Manor as the county's best and amongst the top one hundred establishments in the country. Outside pleasures are afforded by the all-weather tennis court, croquet lawns and putting green as well as a range of local attractions such as Woburn Abbey and Safari Park. **Directions:** Flitwick is on the A5120 just north of the M1 junction 12. Price guide: Single £90–£190; double/twin/suite £125–£225. Special weekend rates available.

ALEXANDER HOUSE

TURNER'S HILL, WEST SUSSEX RH10 4QD
TEL: 01342 714914 FAX: 01342 717328

Alexander House is a magnificent mansion with its own secluded 135 acres of park, including a gently sloping valley which forms the head of the River Medway. Records trace the estate from 1332 when a certain John Atte Fen made it his home. Alexander House is now a modern paragon of good taste and excellence. Spacious rooms throughout this luxurious hotel are splendidly decorated to emphasise their many original features and the bedrooms are lavishly furnished to the highest standards of comfort. The House is renowned for its delicious classic English and French cuisine, rare wines and vintage liqueurs. Music recitals and garden parties are among the events held here and

there are good conference facilities available. Guests are invited to take part in activities including clay pigeon shooting, croquet, snooker and tennis. There is also a new fitness room and solarium, along with a resident beautician. A chauffeured Daimler can take guests to Gatwick Airport in under 15 minutes. Antique shops, National Trust properties, museums and the Royal Pavilion in Brighton are nearby. **Directions:** Alexander House lies on the B2110 road between Turner's Hill and East Grinstead, six miles from junction 10 of the M23 motorway. Price guide: Single £95–£150; double/twin £125; suites £150–£195.

For hotel location, see maps on pages 473–479

ASHDOWN PARK HOTEL

WYCH CROSS, FOREST ROW, ASHDOWN FOREST, EAST SUSSEX RH18 5JR
TEL: 01342 824988 FAX: 01342 826206

Ashdown Park is a grand, rambling 19th century mansion overlooking almost 200 acres of landscaped gardens to the forest beyond. Built in 1867, the hotel is situated within easy reach of Gatwick Airport, London and the South Coast, and provides the perfect backdrop for every occasion, from a weekend getaway to a honeymoon or business convention. The hotel is subtly furnished throughout to satisfy the needs of escapees from urban stress. The 95 en suite bedrooms are beautifully decorated – several with elegant four-poster beds, all with up-to-date amenities. The Anderida restaurant offers a painstakingly compiled menu and wine list, complemented by discreetly attentive service in soigné surroundings. Guests seeking relaxation can retire to the indoor pool and sauna, pamper themselves with a massage, before using the solarium, or visiting the beauty salon. Alternatively, guests may prefer to amble through the gardens and nearby woodland paths; the more energetic can indulge in tennis, squash pitch and putt, croquet or use the newly opened Fitness Studio. There is also an indoor driving range, a lounge/bar and a 9-hole par 3 golf course is on line for play at the end of August 1995 with an outdoor driving range. **Directions:** East of A22 at Wych Cross on road signposted to Hartfield. Price guide: Single from £94; double/twin from £115; suite from £150–£230.

LANGSHOTT MANOR

LANGSHOTT, HORLEY, SURREY RH6 9LN
TEL: 01293 786680 FAX: 01293 783905

A warm welcome and old fashioned hospitality await visitors to Langshott Manor. This beautiful and lovingly restored Elizabethan manor house is set in 3 acres of tranquil gardens, with woodland and countryside walks all around. The seven bedrooms in the house are most comfortably furnished and have king-size, top quality beds made up with fine linen. Big log fires roar in the oak-panelled reception rooms when the weather is cold. Traditional English cuisine is served either in the dining room or the privacy of The Gallery, which is ideal for small conferences, business meetings and social events. Free parking (2 weeks) and luxury courtesy car to Gatwick Airport are available. Although Langshott Manor is only 8 minutes' drive away from the airport, the house is tucked away down a quiet country lane and offers its guests peace and seclusion from the flight path. Hever Castle, Chartwell, Knole Park, Brighton Pavilion and many other properties are all within 30 minutes' drive. **Directions:** From A23 in Horley take Ladbroke Road (Chequers Hotel roundabout) to Langshott. The manor is three quarters of a mile (one kilometer) on the right. Price guide: Single £86–£91; double/twin £106–£144.

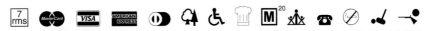

SOUTH LODGE HOTEL

LOWER BEEDING, NR HORSHAM, WEST SUSSEX RH13 6PS
TEL: 01403 891711 FAX: 01403 891766

From its elevated position in the heart of West Sussex, South Lodge has commanding views over the rolling South Downs. The house was originally built as a family home by Frederick Ducane Godman, an eminent 19th-century botanist and explorer, and the hotel's 90-acre grounds are evidence of his abiding passion – many of the shrubs and trees were planted by him. The hotel prides itself on the warm welcome extended to guests, ensuring a memorable stay. Wood panelling and open fires in the reception rooms create an atmosphere of comfortable elegance and the luxuriously appointed bedrooms offer every modern amenity. From the south-facing dining room there are views over the rolling Sussex countryside, from where comes much of what features on the menu, perfectly complemented by a comprehensive yet carefully chosen wine list. Private and business functions can be catered for in one of the private rooms. South Lodge offers a wide variety of sporting and leisure facilities, including croquet, tennis and clay pigeon shooting, golf at Mannings Heath just minutes from the hotel, fishing and riding. Nearby attractions include Glyndebourne and Chartwell, Leonardslee gardens and racing at Goodwood, Plumpton and Brighton. **Directions:** South Lodge is situated on the A 281 at Lower Beeding, south of Horsham. Price guide: Single from £110; double/twin from £135; suite from £205.

THE WIND IN THE WILLOWS

DERBYSHIRE LEVEL, GLOSSOP, DERBYSHIRE SK13 9PT
TEL: 01457 868001 FAX: 01457 853354

"Not so much an hotel, more a delightful experience" said a guest recently of this charming country house where guests will discover a convivial combination of friendliness and professionalism. The hotel has benefited from the continuity provided by proprietors Anne Marsh and Peter Marsh, a mother-and-son team who have been running The Wind in the Willows for over 14 years. In 1994, a conference room was added which can be incorporated into the present dining room, and also four extra bedrooms not shown in picture. Set in the marvellous scenery of the Peak District National Park and the Pennine Hills, the totally relaxed atmosphere of this early Victorian house is further protected by five acres of land and gardens on three sides and the Park and golf course on the other. In recognition of its high standards, the hotel was voted the 1991 RAC Best Small Hotel in the North of England. Home-cooked food at its best is served in a private dining room. The pretty bedrooms have interesting individual features and all have private shower/bathrooms; the Erika Louise room has an attractive Victorian bathroom. Riding, golf, pot-holing and gliding can be arranged locally. **Directions:** One mile east of Glossop on the A57, 400 yards down the road opposite the Royal Oak. Price guide: Single £57–£75; double/twin £67–£95.

HATTON COURT HOTEL

UPTON HILL, UPTON ST LEONARDS, GLOUCESTERSHIRE GL4 8DE
TEL: 01452 617412 FAX: 01452 612945

This old ivy-clad Cotswold manor is set in seven acres of beautifully maintained gardens and 30 acres of green pastures. Nestling in the hills of Upton St Leonards, it enjoys stunning views over the Severn Valley towards the Malvern Hills. Extensive refurbishment of the manor has sought to combine modern comfort and sophistication with 17th century charm and character. Lavishly furnished bedrooms, many featuring Jacuzzis, offer a host of amenities and a number of personal extras including fresh fruit, mineral water, home-made cookies and bathrobes. Carrington's, Hatton Court's restaurant, boasts delightful decor, panoramic views and gastronomic delights.

Classical traditional dishes and food cooked in the modern French style are complemented by wines from some 300 bins. Riding, golf and dry skiing are available just minutes from the hotel. Places to visit nearby include the elegant spa towns of Bath and Cheltenham, the Wildfowl and Wetlands Trust at Slimbridge, Prinknash Abbey, Berkeley Castle and Stratford-upon-Avon. Special breaks are available and details of these can be supplied on request. A member of Hatton Hotels. **Directions:** Hatton Court is located three miles south of Gloucester on the B4073 Gloucester–Painswick road, off the A46. Price guide: Single £85–£95; double/twin £95–£110; suite £125.

In association with MasterCard

GRAYTHWAITE MANOR

FERNHILL ROAD, GRANGE-OVER-SANDS, CUMBRIA LA11 7JE
TEL: 01539 532001 FAX: 01539 535549

This beautifully furnished, traditionally run country house has been owned and run by the Blakemore family since 1937 and extends a warm welcome to its guests. It enjoys a superb setting in eight acres of private landscaped gardens and woodland on the hillside overlooking Morecambe Bay. Each bedroom is decorated and furnished in the best of taste and many offer superb views across the gardens and bay to the Pennines beyond. Elegant, spacious lounges with fresh flowers and antiques provide an exclusive setting and log fires are lit to add extra cheer on chillier nights. The Manor enjoys an excellent reputation for its cuisine and guests can look forward to a six course dinner comprising carefully prepared dishes complemented by the right wine from the extensive cellar. A few miles inland from Grange-over-Sands are Lake Windermere and Coniston Water and some of the most majestic scenery in the country. Nearby are the village of Cartmel, Holker Hall, Levens Hall and Sizergh Castle. The area abounds with historic buildings, gardens and museums.
Directions: Take M6 to junction 36 and then the A65 towards Kendal, followed by the A590 towards Barrow. At roundabout take B5277 to Grange-over-Sands and go through town turning right opposite the fire station into Fernhill Road. The hotel is on the left. Price guide: Single £40–£50; double/twin £80–£95.

MICHAELS NOOK

GRASMERE, CUMBRIA LA22 9RP
TEL: 015394 35496 FAX: 015394 35645

Built in 1859 and named after the eponymous shepherd of Wordsworth's poem, Michaels Nook has long been established as one of Britain's leading country house hotels. Opened as a hotel in 1969 by Reg and Elizabeth Gifford, it overlooks Grasmere Valley and is surrounded by gardens and trees. Reg is a respected antiques dealer, and the hotel's interior reflects his appreciation of English furniture, rugs, prints and porcelain. There are two suites, and twelve individually designed bedrooms, all with en suite bathrooms. In the acclaimed restaurant, polished tables are set with fine crystal and china. The best ingredients are used to create dishes memorable for their delicate flavours and artistic presentation. The panelled Oak Room, with its stone fireplace and gilt furnishings, can be booked for private parties and executive meetings. Leisure facilities at the nearby Wordsworth Hotel are available to guests, as is free golf at Keswick Golf Club, Monday–Friday. Michaels Nook is, first and foremost, a home where comfort is the watchword. **Directions:** Approaching Grasmere on the A591 from the south, ignore signs for Grasmere Village and continue to The Swan Hotel on the right. There turn sharp right and follow the lane uphill for 400 yds to Michaels Nook. Price guide (including dinner): Single from £120; double/twin £160–£290; suite £300–£350.

For hotel location, see maps on pages 473–479

THE WORDSWORTH HOTEL

GRASMERE, NR AMBLESIDE, CUMBRIA LA22 9SW
TEL: 015394 35592 FAX: 015394 35765

In the very heart of the English Lakeland, The Wordsworth Hotel combines AA 4 Star standards with the magnificence of the surrounding fells. Set in its own grounds in the village of Grasmere, the hotel provides first-class, year-round facilities for both business and leisure travellers. It has a reputaion for the high quality of its food, accommodation and hospitality. The comfortable bedrooms have well-equipped bathrooms, and there are two suites with whirlpool baths. 24-hour room service is available for drinks and light refreshments. Peaceful lounges overlook landscaped gardens, and the heated indoor pool opens on to a sun-trap terrace. There is a Jacuzzi, mini-gym, sauna and solarium. As well as a Cocktail Bar, the hotel has its own pub, "The Dove and Olive Branch", which has received accolades from The Good Pub Guide. In "The Prelude Restaurant" menus offer a good choice of dishes, prepared with skill and imagination from the freshest produce. The Wordsworth Hotel is a perfect venue for conferences, incentive weekends and corporate entertaining. Three function rooms are available with highly professional back-up. Lakeland's principal places of interest are all within easy reach. **Directions:** The hotel is located next to Grasmere village church. Price guide: Single £59–£75; double/twin £104–£152; suite £195.

THE ANGEL POSTING HOUSE AND LIVERY

91 THE HIGH STREET, GUILDFORD, SURREY GU1 3DP
TEL: 01483 64555 FAX: 01483 33770

The Angel, a delightful historic coaching inn on the old Portsmouth road, now a luxurious small hotel, has stood in Guildford High Street since the 16th century. This timber-framed building has welcomed many famous visitors, including Lord Nelson, Jane Austen and Charles Dickens. Today, with easy access to Gatwick, Heathrow, the M4, M3 and M25, The Angel is ideally placed for both business and pleasure. The galleried lounge with its oak-beamed Jacobean fireplace and 17th-century parliament clock is a welcome retreat from the bustle of the nearby shops. The Crypt Restaurant, with its vaulted ceiling and intimate atmosphere, serves a wide choice of superb English and Continental cuisine together with fine wines and impeccable service. The charming bedrooms and suites, decorated with soft furnishings and fabrics, are all unique. Excellent communications, presentation facilities and 24-hour service make this a good choice for business meetings. Private dinners, buffets, dances and wedding receptions can also be catered for. **Directions:** From M3 junction 3 take the A322; or from M25 junction 10 take the A3. The Angel is in the centre of Guildford, within the pedestrian priority area – guests should enquire about vehicle access when booking. Price guide (room only): Double/twin £105–£140; suite £160.

WEST LODGE PARK

COCKFOSTERS ROAD, HADLEY WOOD, BARNET, HERTFORDSHIRE EN4 0PY
TEL: 0181 440 8311 FAX: 0181 449 3698

West Lodge Park is a country house hotel which stands in 34 acres of Green Belt parklands and gardens. These include a lake and an arboretum with hundreds of mature trees. Despite this idyllic setting, the hotel is only 1 mile from the M25 and within easy reach of London. Run by the Beale family for 50 years, West Lodge Park was originally a gentleman's country seat, rebuilt in 1838 on the site of an earlier keeper's lodge. In the public rooms, antiques, original paintings and period furnishings create a restful atmosphere, while a Regency style conservatory adds space and offers excellent views over the surrounding countryside. All the bright and individually furnished bedrooms, many of which enjoy country views, have a full range of modern amenities. Well presented cuisine is available in the elegant restaurant. Residents enjoy free membership and a free taxi to the nearby David Lloyd leisure centre, which has excellent facilities. Hatfield House and St Albans Abbey are 15 minutes' drive away. The hotel is credited with AA 4 stars and rosette, RAC 4 stars plus 2 merit awards and is the 1995 County Hotel of the Year in the Which? Hotel Guide. **Directions:** The hotel is situated on A111 one mile north of Cockfosters underground station and one mile south of junction 24 on the M25. Price guide: Single £64.50–£96; double/twin from £99.

HOLDSWORTH HOUSE

HOLDSWORTH ROAD, HOLMFIELD, HALIFAX, WEST YORKSHIRE HX2 9TG
TEL: 01422 240024 FAX: 01422 245174

Holdsworth House is a retreat of quality and charm standing three miles north of Halifax in the heart of Yorkshire's West Riding. Built in 1633, it was acquired by the Pearson family over 30 years ago. With care, skill and professionalism they have created a hotel and restaurant of considerable repute. The interior of the house, with its polished panelling and open fireplaces, has been carefully preserved and embellished with fine antique furniture and ornaments. The comfortable lounge opens onto a pretty courtyard and overlooks the herb garden and gazebo. The restaurant comprises three beautifully furnished rooms, ideally arranged for private dinner parties. Exciting modern English and continental cuisine is meticulously prepared and presented by Eric Claveau, complemented by a thoughtfully compiled wine list. The restaurant now has two AA Rosettes. Each bedroom has its own style – from the four split-level suites to the two single rooms designed for wheelchair access. This is the perfect base from which to explore the Pennines, the Yorkshire Dales and Haworth – the home of the Brontë family. Closed at Christmas. **Directions:** From M1 junction 42 take M62 westbound to junction 26. Follow A58 to Halifax (ignore signs to town centre). At Burdock Way roundabout take A629 to Keighley; after 1½ miles go right into Shay Lane; hotel is one mile, on right. Price guide: Single £72.50–£82; double/twin £90–£95; suite £110.

THE BALMORAL HOTEL

FRANKLIN MOUNT, HARROGATE, NORTH YORKSHIRE HG1 5EJ
TEL: 01423 508208 FAX: 01423 530652

Set in award-winning gardens, The Balmoral is four minutes walk from the delightful Victorian spa town of Harrogate. The hotel's nine four-poster bedrooms are elegantly decorated and furnished, offering the highest standards of comfort. Each bed is of carved mahogany, walnut or oak and draped in a different style. The remaining bedrooms are equally tasteful and luxurious and all provide an extensive range of modern amenities. For those seeking the ultimate in luxury, the Windsor Suite boasts a whirlpool bath. Guests can relax in the exquisite Oriental Bar or opt for a quiet drink in the cosy snug before taking dinner. The restaurant, with its unique "magical theme", enjoys a good reputation with locals and serves modern English cuisine, complemented by an extensive wine list of predominantly New World wines. Tea rooms, antique shops, art galleries, theatre and a host of recreational facilities are all close by. Guests also have the use of the Academy Leaisure Health and Fitness Centre. The town is an excellent base for visiting Brontë and Herriot country and the many historic homes and castles in the area. **Directions:** From the centre of Harrogate go North on the A61 to Parliament Street and at the Conference Centre traffic lights turn right on to Kings Road. The hotel is $^1/_2$ a mile on the right. Price guide: Single £77–£88; double/twin £96–£100; suites £105–£163.

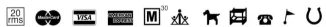

THE BOAR'S HEAD HOTEL

THE RIPLEY CASTLE ESTATE, HARROGATE, NORTH YORKSHIRE HG3 3AY
TEL: 01423 771888 FAX: 01423 771509

Imagine relaxing in a four star hotel at the centre of a historic 1700 acre private country estate in England's incredibly beautiful North Country. The Ingilby family who have lived in Ripley Castle for 28 generations invite you to enjoy their hospitality at The Boar's Head Hotel. There are 25 luxury bedrooms, individually decorated and furnished, most with king-size beds. The restaurant menu is outstanding, presented by a creative and imaginative kitchen brigade, and complemented by a wide selection of reasonably priced, good quality wines. There is a welcoming bar serving traditional ales straight from the wood, and popular bar meal selections. When staying at The Boar's Head, guests can enjoy complimentary access to the delightful walled gardens and grounds of Ripley Castle, which include the lakes and a deer park. A conference at Ripley is a different experience – using the idyllic meeting facilities available in the castle, organisers and delegates alike will appreciate the peace and tranquility of the location which offers opportunities for all forms of leisure activity outside meeting hours. **Directions:** Ripley is very accessible, just 10 minutes from the conference town of Harrogate, 20 minutes from the motorway network, and Leeds/Bradford Airport, and 40 minutes from the City of York. Price guide: Single £75–£90; double/twin £85–£120.

For hotel location, see maps on pages 473–479

GRANTS HOTEL

SWAN ROAD, HARROGATE, NORTH YORKSHIRE HG1 2SS
TEL: 01423 560666 FAX: 01423 502550

Towards the end of the last century, Harrogate became fashionable among the affluent Victorian gentry, who came to 'take the waters' of the famous spa. Today's visitors have one advantage over their Victorian counterparts – they can enjoy the hospitality of Grants Hotel, the creation of Pam and Peter Grant. The friendly welcome, coupled with high standards of service, ensures a pleasurable stay. All the bedrooms are attractively decorated and have en suite bathrooms. Downstairs, guests can relax in the comfortable lounge or take refreshments out to the terrace gardens. Drinks and light meals are available at all times from the cocktail bar, whereas dinner is a more formal occasion in the air-conditioned Chimney Pots restaurant. Cooking is in the modern English style, with old favourites adapted to accommodate more contemporary tastes – a blend which meets with the approval of local gourmets. Located less than five minutes' walk from Harrogate's Conference and Exhibition Centre, Grants offers its own luxury suite of meeting and syndicate rooms, the Herriot Suite. The Royal Pump Room Museum and the Royal Baths Assembly Rooms are nearby. Guests have free use of "The Academy Leisure and Fitness Club". **Directions:** Swan Road is in the centre of Harrogate, off the A61 to Ripon. Price guide: Single £90–£99; double/twin £99–£139.

HOB GREEN HOTEL AND RESTAURANT

MARKINGTON, HARROGATE, NORTH YORKSHIRE HG3 3PJ
TEL: 01423 770031 FAX: 01423 771589

Hob Green is a small country house hotel set in 870 acres of farm and woodland. The gardens, which include a croquet lawn, have won awards regularly in the Harrogate District Best Kept Garden Competition. The hall and drawing room are furnished with a combination of antique and contemporary furniture, while crackling fires in the winter months create a warm and welcoming atmosphere. Overlooking manicured lawns, with views towards the ha-ha, fields and woodland, is the restaurant, where guests can enjoy interesting and varied cooking, incorporating fresh vegetables from the garden. The comfortably appointed bedrooms also have fine views. Markington is the perfect setting for equestrian enthusiasts, as the Yorkshire Riding Centre, run by two former Olympic dressage team members, is located in the village and offers some of the best riding facilities in Europe. Golf, fishing, cricket and horse-racing are all within easy reach of the hotel. Fountains Abbey, Markenfield Hall, Ripley Castle and the cathedral cities of York and Ripon are also nearby. **Directions:** Follow the A61 Harrogate–Ripon road for about four miles, then turn left to Markington at Wormald Green. Go through the village of Markington and the hotel is one mile on the left. Price guide: Single £70; double/twin £85–£95; suite £110.

BEL ALP HOUSE

HAYTOR, NR BOVEY TRACEY, SOUTH DEVON TQ13 9XX
TEL: 01364 661217 FAX: 01364 661292

Peace and seclusion are guaranteed at the Bel Alp House with its spectacular outlook from the edge of Dartmoor across a rolling patchwork of fields and woodland to the sea, 20 miles away. Built as an Edwardian country mansion and owned in the 1920s by millionairess Dame Violet Wills, Bel Alp has been lovingly restored by proprietors Roger and Sarah Curnock, whose personal attention ensures their guests' enjoyment and comfort in the atmosphere of a private home. Sarah takes charge of the cooking and the set dinner is changed nightly. She uses only the best local produce and her meals are accompanied by Roger's well-chosen and comprehensive wine list. Of the nine en suite bedrooms, two still have their original Edwardian basins and baths mounted on marble plinths, and all have views over the gardens. An abundance of house plants, open log fires and restful colours complements the family antiques and pictures to create the perfect environment in which to relax. AA Rosette. Bel Alp is ideally situated for exploring Devon and parts of Cornwall: Plymouth, famed for Drake and the Pilgrim Fathers, Exeter with its Norman cathedral, and National Trust properties Castle Drogo and Cotehele Manor House are all within an hour's drive. **Directions:** Bel Alp is off the B3387 Haytor road, 2½ miles from Bovey Tracey. Price guide: Single £78–£87; double/twin £120–£156.

THE CARLTON HOTEL

ALBERT STREET, HEBDEN BRIDGE, WEST YORKSHIRE HX7 8ES
TEL: 01422 844400 FAX: 01422 843117

The Carlton is an unusual town house hotel, centrally situated on the first and second floors of the old Co-operative Society building, dating from 1867. Following a full refurbishment of this Victorian emporium, The Carlton Hotel was able to continue serving the local community, while also attracting a much wider, international clientèle. A lift takes visitors from the entrance hall up to the elegant reception area where a friendly welcome waits. The 18 en suite bedrooms are individually appointed with attractive furnishings, satellite T.V. and hospitality bars. In the Hawkstones Restaurant imaginative menus combining European and traditionally English food are prepared daily by the kitchen team under the direction of head chef Earl McIniess. As an alternative to the restaurant a fine selection of hearty bar snacks is available daily in the Wragley Bar. Conference parties and banquets can be accommodated in the Hardcastle Suite. Situated at the head of the Calder Valley, Hebden Bridge is a thriving mill town, with a motor car museum and many quaint antique and craft shops. The Carlton Hotel is well placed for walkers to explore the Yorkshire Dales and nearby Howarth. **Directions:** Entering Hebden Bridge on the A646, turn down Hope Street, which runs into Albert Street. The Carlton Hotel is on the left. Price guide: Single £49–£69; double/twin £69–£79.

THE PHEASANT

HAROME, HELMSLEY, NORTH YORKSHIRE YO6 5JG
TEL: 01439 771241/770416

The Pheasant, rich in oak beams and open log fires, offers two types of accommodation, some in the hotel and some in a charming, 16th century thatched cottage. The Binks family, who built the hotel and now own and manage it, have created a friendly atmosphere which is part of the warm Yorkshire welcome all guests receive. The bedrooms and suites are brightly decorated in an attractive, cottage style and all are complete with en suite facilities. Traditional English cooking is the speciality of the restaurant, many of the dishes prepared using fresh fruit and vegetables grown in the hotel gardens. During the summer, guests may chat or relax on the terrace overlooking the pond. The opening of a new indoor heated swimming pool is an added attraction. Other sporting activities available locally include swimming, riding, golf and fishing. York is a short drive away, as are a host of historic landmarks including Byland and Rievaulx Abbeys and Castle Howard of *Brideshead Revisited* fame. Also nearby is the magnificent North York Moors National Park. Dogs by arrangement. Closed Christmas, January and February. **Directions:** From Helmsley, take the A170 towards Scarborough; after 1/4 mile turn right for Harome. Hotel is near the church in the village. Price guide: Single £55–£65; double/twin £110–£130. (Including five-course dinner).

THE POLURRIAN HOTEL

MULLION, LIZARD PENINSULA, SOUTH CORNWALL TR12 7EN
TEL: 01326 240421 FAX: 01326 240083

The Polurrian Hotel, a building of splendid Edwardian elegance perched on 300 foot cliffs, is set in beautiful landscaped gardens and surrounded by National Trust coastline. Comfort is the key and there are a host of modern amenities including a baby-listening device. Daily changing, four course menus offer excellent food, with fresh fish among the specialities. Guests are invited to take advantage of the luxurious Leisure Club where there is a heated pool, solarium, sauna and gym. Other activities within the hotel and its grounds include tennis, badminton, snooker, croquet and squash. The pleasures of the 18-hole Mullion golf course are just two miles away. Polurrian Hotel also offers a number of self-catering bungalows and apartments. Places of interest nearby include RNAS Culdrose, home of the Sea King helicopters, Goonhilly Earth Station, The Lizard, Gweek Seal Sanctuary, and Land's End. There are plenty of leisure activities available in the vicinity, such as fishing, sailing and spectacular coastal walks. **Directions:** From Helston follow A3083 towards the The Lizard. After six miles turn right onto the B3296 to Mullion. Price guide (including dinner): Single £42–£86; double/twin £84–£172; suites £116–£184.

For hotel location, see maps on pages 473–479

In association
with MasterCard

NUTHURST GRANGE

HOCKLEY HEATH, WARWICKSHIRE B94 5NL
TEL: 01564 783972 FAX: 01564 783919

The most memorable feature of this friendly country house hotel is its outstanding restaurant. Chef-patron David Randolph and his team have won many accolades for their imaginative menus, described as 'English, cooked in the light French style'. Diners can enjoy their superb cuisine in the three adjoining rooms which comprise the restaurant and form the heart of Nuthurst Grange. The rest of the house is no less charming – the spacious bedrooms have a country house atmosphere and are appointed with extra luxuries such as an exhilarating air-spa bath, a trouser press, hairdryer and a safe for valuables. For special occasions there is a room furnished with a four-poster bed and a marble bathroom. There are fine views across the 7$\frac{1}{2}$ acres of landscaped gardens. Executive meetings can be accommodated at Nuthurst Grange – within a 12-mile radius of the hotel lie Central Birmingham, the NEC, Stratford-upon-Avon, Coventry and Birmingham International Airport. Sporting activities available nearby include golf, canal boating and tennis. **Directions:** From M42 exit 4 take A3400 signposted Hockley Heath (2 miles, south). Entrance to Nuthurst Grange Lane is $\frac{1}{4}$ mile south of village. Also, M40 (exit 16 – southbound only), take first left, entrance 300 yards. Price guide: Single £89; double/twin £105–£125; suite £135.

THE WORSLEY ARMS HOTEL

HOVINGHAM, YORK, NORTH YORKSHIRE YO6 4LA
TEL: 01653 628234 FAX: 01653 628130

The Worsley Arms is an attractive stone-built Victorian coaching inn in the heart of Hovingham, a pleasant and unspoiled Yorkshire village with a history stretching back to Roman times. The hotel, which overlooks the village green and is set amid delightful gardens, was built in 1841 by the baronet Sir William Worsley. It is still owned by the Worsley family whose home, Hovingham Hall, is nearby. Elegant, traditional furnishings and open fires create a welcoming and restful atmosphere. The spacious sitting rooms are an ideal place to relax over morning coffee or afternoon tea, or to meet friends and chat in the comfortable bar. The award-winning Wyvern Restaurant (2 AA Rosettes) offers creatively prepared dishes, including game from the estate, cooked and presented with flair. The en suite bedrooms range in size and are all prettily decorated and well appointed, with room service available. There is plenty to do nearby, including tennis, squash, jogging, golf and scenic walks along nature trails. Also, guests can explore the majestic beauty of the Dales and spectacular Yorkshire coastline or discover the many historic abbeys, battlefields, stately homes and castles nearby including Castle Howard just five miles away. **Directions:** Hovingham is on the B1257, eight miles from Malton and Helmsley. Price guide: (including dinner) Single £82.50; double/twin £125.

For hotel location, see maps on pages 473–479

BAGDEN HALL HOTEL & GOLF COURSE

WAKEFIELD ROAD, SCISSETT, NR HUDDERSFIELD, WEST YORKSHIRE HD8 9LE
TEL: 01484 865330 FAX: 01484 861001

Bagden Hall is set in 40 acres of parkland, yet less than 10 minutes from the M1. It was built in the mid-19th century by local mill owner George Norton as a home for his family, whose portraits still hang in the foyer. Lovingly restored by current owners the Braithwaite family, Bagden has been transformed into an elegant hotel. The grounds comprise magnificent lawns, superb landscaped gardens, a lake and an 18th century boathouse. Inside, the hotel has recently undergone a major programme of renovation and now has all the facilities one would expect of a modern hotel while retaining its original character. Each of the 17 bedrooms – one with four-poster – has en suite facilities. The oak-panelled lounge bar and conservatory have views over the lawns to the lake, an ideal setting for a drink before moving on to the Glendale Restaurant. Here, traditional and modern English food with classical French influences is served amid tasteful surroundings. There is a fine wine list to complement the food. For golfers, there is a 9-hole par 3/4 golf course on site. Conference facilities are available. **Directions:** From south, leave M1 at junction 38, taking A637 towards Huddersfield. Take A636 to Denby Dale. From north, leave M1 at junction 39, taking A636 to Denby Dale. Hotel is $1/_2$ mile through Clayton West on left. Price guide: Single £60; double/twin £80–£100.

THE OLD BRIDGE HOTEL

1 HIGH STREET, HUNTINGDON, CAMBRIDGESHIRE PE18 6TQ
TEL: 01480 452681 FAX: 01480 411017

The Old Bridge is a handsome, 18th-century edifice standing on the banks of the River Ouse close to the centre of Huntingdon, a thriving market town and the birthplace of Oliver Cromwell. The hotel has been decorated in keeping with its original character. In the panelled dining room and main lounge, sumptuous fabrics, quality prints and beautiful furnishings impart a sense of elegance. Each of the 26 guest rooms is unique in its style and décor – all have been luxuriously appointed with every attention to detail, and with a full complement of facilities. The menu exemplifies British cooking at its best – traditional dishes are interpreted with imagination and flair, and is balanced by an exceptional and award winning wine list. The restaurant menu is also offered in the more informal setting of The Terrace which has a delightful series of murals painted by Julia Rushbury. Private parties or business lunches can be accommodated in the Cromwell Room and a fully integrated business centre is available for executive meetings. Guests can enjoy boating trips from the private jetty or visit nearby Cambridge, Ely and Newmarket. **Directions:** Situated off the A1 where it joins both the A1–M1 link and the M11/A14. The hotel is just off the inner ring road. Price guide: Single £69.50; double/twin £85–£120.

For hotel location, see maps on pages 473–479

YE OLDE BELL

HIGH STREET, HURLEY, BERKSHIRE SL6 5LX
TEL: 01628 825881 FAX: 01628 825939

Built in 1135 as the guest house for a 12th century Benedictine Monastery, Ye Olde Bell is reputed to be the oldest inn in England. It prides itself on living up to the old monastic rule that visitors must be received with warmth and respect – the service is excellent. The bedrooms, which include three with four poster beds, have wooden beams, leaded windows and comfortable chairs. Despite a delightful ambience of days gone by, they nevertheless offer a full range of modern amenities such as remote control satellite TV, hairdryer, trouser press, mini bar and tea and coffee making facilities. 'No smoking' rooms are available and baby sitting can be arranged. In the bar guests can relax in front of an open fire and enjoy a quiet drink before moving into the restaurant. Here they can enjoy a full range of traditional and continental dishes which have won the award of an AA Rosette. Modern hi-tech telecommunications systems and their associated paraphernalia are discreetly hidden in oak timbers, knarled floors and rafters so that business meetings can take place in this charming old inn. A host of attractions nearby include Windsor, Henley-on-Thames, Marlow, Royal Ascot Racecourse and Cliveden House. **Directions:** From M40 exit 4 follow signs to Henley-on-Thames. The hotel is in the village of Hurley. Price guide: Single £95; double/twin £105; suites £150.

THE FERNIE LODGE HOTEL

BERRIDGES LANE, HUSBANDS BOSWORTH, LUTTERWORTH, LEICESTERSHIRE LE17 6LE
TEL: 01858 880551 FAX: 01858 880014

The Fernie Lodge is a long established Georgian country house hotel, set in the heart of the rolling Leicestershire landscape, where the charm of a bygone age combines with the very best of modern comfort and facilities. Each bedroom is individually decorated and possesses its own unique character. Dining at the hotel is always a memorable experience. Creative cuisine, skilfully prepared by chefs using only the finest fresh produce and highest quality ingredients, has won it an excellent culinary reputation. Enticing dishes are complemented by an extensive range of wines. A traditional conservatory, where the resident pianist regularly entertains in time honoured style, is a perfect place to relax after a meal. For business meetings, Fernie Lodge offers a wide choice of rooms sizes and lay outs and a full range of audio visual equipment is provided. The hotel prides itself on a friendly, cheerful and quietly professional service and nothing is ever too much trouble. Fernie Lodge is within easy driving distance of Northampton, Leicester and many smaller historic towns. Originally famous for hunting, the area now offers a wide range of equine pursuits, along with clay pigeon shooting, trout fishing, golfing, gliding and sailing. **Directions:** Take Junction 20 from M1. At Lutterworth take A427 to Husbands Bosworth. Price guide: Single £55; double/twin £67.

ILSINGTON HOTEL

ILSINGTON, NEWTON ABBOT, DEVON TQ13 9RR
TEL: 01364 661452 FAX: 01364 661307

The Ilsington Hotel stands in six acres of beuatiful private grounds within the Dartmoor National Park. Run by charming owners, Howard and Karen Astbury, the delightful furnishings and friendly ambience offer a most comfortable environment in which to relax. Stylosh bedrooms and suites all boast outstanding views across the rolling pastoral countryside and every comfort and convenience to make guests feel at home, including English toiletries. The distinctive candle-lit dining room is perfect for savouring the superb cuisine created by talented chefs from fresh local produce. The library is ideal for an intimate dining party or celebration whilst the Victorian conservatory is the place for morning coffee or a Devon cream tea. There is a fully equipped purpose built gymnasium, heated indoor pool, sauna and spa – also experienced masseurs. Some of England's most idyllic and unspoilt scenery surrounds Ilsington, with the picturesque villages of Lustleigh, Widecombe-in-the-Moor and Manaton all closeby. Footpaths lead from the hotel on to Dartmoor. Riding, fishing and many other country pursuits can be arranged nearby. **Directions:** From M5 join A38 at Exeter following Plymouth signs. After approximately 12 miles exit for Moretonhamstead and Newton Abbot. At roundabout follow signs for Ilsington. Price guide: (including dinner) Single £65; double/twin £100.

THE COMMODORE

MARINE PARADE, INSTOW, DEVON EX39 4JN
TEL: 01271 860347 FAX: 01271 861233

The Commodore Hotel is set in the charming waterside village of Instow and overlooks the sandy beach at the mouth of the Taw and Torridge Estuaries. Originally a Georgian Gentleman's residence, it has been sympathetically extended and converted and offers its guests every modern comfort. The individually designed bedrooms are spacious, airy and tastefully decorated to a high standard. Sea facing rooms have the benefit of balconies and all rooms are provided with reclining sun loungers. Among a full range of modern amenities are thoughtful extras such as hairdryers and trouser presses. A spacious and inviting restaurant offers table d'hôte and à la carte seasonally adjusted menus with seafood specialities. A varied choice of bar meals is served in the lounge areas of the hotel, or during the summer months on the patio terrace. Instow is ideally situated for discovering Henry Williamson's Tarka Country, set between the historic market towns of Bideford and Barnstaple and within easy reach of the Exmoor and Dartmoor National Parks. Places of interest nearby include a number of excellent museums and art galleries, while other recreational activities include sailing, windsurfing and water skiing. **Directions:** Exit M5 junction 27. Join A361 link road to Barnstaple, then A39. Sign for Instow is just before Torridge bridge. Price guide: Single £55–£70; double/twin: £90–£110.

BELSTEAD BROOK MANOR HOTEL

BELSTEAD BROOK PARK, BELSTEAD ROAD, IPSWICH, SUFFOLK IP2 9HB
TEL: 01473 684241 FAX: 01473 681249

An oasis on the edge of Ipswich, the Belstead Brook Manor Hotel is surrounded by eight acres of landscaped gardens and woodlands. It combines the charms and tranquility of the original 16th century country house with every modern day comfort and convenience. Traditional hospitality and service of the highest quality are guaranteed to guests. The bedrooms are pleasantly furnished and many overlook the traditional English garden where resident peacocks stroll. The hotel offers a choice of table d'hôte and à la carte menus, complemented by a comprehensive cellar. The intimate oak panelled bar is the perfect place in which to relax before or after a meal. For weddings, conferences or banquets, the hotel offers private dining rooms and a choice of purpose built meeting and syndicate rooms to accommodate up to 60 guests or delegates. Places of interest nearby include Ipswich (birthplace of Cardinal Wolsey), Woodbridge, medieval Kersey, Flatford Mill and the castles at Orford and Framlingham. **Directions:** From the A12/A14 interchange take Ipswich West Exit. First roundabout take third exit (Pinewood). Second roundabout take third exit (Shepherd Drive). Third roundabout take second exit (Belmont Road). Right at T-junction (Ellenbrook Road). Left at T-junction. Hotel down lane, left at Belstead Road. Price guide: Double/twin £68–£78; suites £98.

For hotel location, see maps on pages 473–479

HINTLESHAM HALL

HINTLESHAM, IPSWICH, SUFFOLK IP8 3NS
TEL: 01473 652268 FAX: 01473 652463

The epitome of grandeur, Hintlesham Hall is a house of evolving styles: its splendid Georgian façade belies its 16th-century origins, to which the red-brick Tudor rear of the hall is a testament. The Stuart period also left its mark, in the form of a magnificent carved-oak staircase leading to the north wing of the hall. The combination of styles works extremely well, with the lofty proportions of the Georgian reception rooms contrasting with the timbered Tudor rooms. The décor throughout is superb – all rooms are individually appointed in a discriminating fashion. Iced mineral water, toiletries and towelling robes are to be found in each of the comfortable bedrooms. The herb garden supplies many of the flavours for the well-balanced menu which will appeal to the gourmet and the health-conscious alike, complemented by a 300-bin wine list. Bounded by 175 acres of rolling countryside, leisure facilities include the Hall's own 18-hole championship golf course, gymnasium, saunas, steam room, spa bath, tennis, croquet and snooker. Guests can also explore Suffolk's 16th-century wool merchants' villages, its pretty coast, 'Constable country' and Newmarket. **Directions:** Hintlesham Hall is 4 miles west of Ipswich on the A1071 Sudbury road. Price guide: Single £85; double/twin £110; suite £210.

THE BORROWDALE GATES COUNTRY HOUSE HOTEL

GRANGE-IN-BORROWDALE, KESWICK, CUMBRIA CA12 5UQ
TEL: 01768 777204 FAX: 01768 777254

Built in 1860, Borrowdale Gates is surrounded on all sides by the rugged charm of the Lake District National Park. It affords panoramic views of the Borrowdale Valley and surrounding fells and nestles in two acres of wooded gardens on the edge of the ancient hamlet of Grange, close to the shores of Derwentwater. Tastefully decorated bedrooms offer every modern comfort and command picturesque views of the surrounding scenery. The comfortable lounges and bar, decorated with fine antiques and warmed by glowing log fires in cooler months, create the perfect setting in which to enjoy a drink and forget the bustle of everyday life. Fine food is served in the restaurant, with menus offering a wide and imaginative selection of dishes. The cuisine is complemented by a thoughtfully chosen wine list and excellent service. This Lakeland home is a haven of peace and tranquillity and is ideally located for walking, climbing and touring. There are also many places of literary and historical interest within easy reach, for example Wordsworth's birthplace in Cockermouth. The hotel is closed throughout January. **Directions:** M6 junction 40 A66 into Keswick. B5289 to Borrowdale. After four miles right into Grange over double hump back bridge. Price guide: Single £55–£75; double/twin £100–£130. (Including dinner).

UNDERSCAR MANOR

APPLETHWAITE, NEAR KESWICK, CUMBRIA CA12 4PH
TEL: 017687 75000 FAX: 017687 74904

This beautiful Italianate house, recently extensively refurbished, was built in Victorian times and enjoys an elevated position with panoramic views over Derwentwater and the mountains beyond. It is set in 40 acres of serene gardens and woodlands, home of roe deer and red squirrels. Individually created bedrooms offer ever-changing views over the lakes and mountains and the public rooms provide an ideal atmosphere in which to relax. The house is operated by Pauline and Derek Harrison with Pauline's brother Robert Thorton the Head Chef – for dinner, choose from a tantalising selection of dishes, including local Herdwick lamb cutlets, pan fried with home-made herb cake and served on a chive and tarragon sauce, and roast guinea fowl, served with chicken livers on an orange flavoured sauce. Excellent fishing is available on the local lakes and tarns, while golfers may chose from Keswick (four miles), Penrith, Silloth, Workington and Carlisle golf courses. There are regular horse races at Carlisle, Cartmel and Hexham. For walking, pony trekking, sailing, bird watching or paragliding opportunities, the Lakes can match and excell anywhere in Britain. **Directions:** From M6, junction 40, take A66 bypassing Keswick. At roundabout take A591 exit, then turn immediately right and Underscar Manor is a short distance. Price guide: Single £95; double/twin £150–£250 (including dinner).

MEADOW HOUSE

SEA LANE, KILVE, SOMERSET TA5 1EG
TEL: 01278 741546 FAX: 01278 741663

With its origins dating from around 1600, Meadow House was enlarged in Georgian times to become a rectory. Standing in eight acres of grounds, the hotel is entirely surrounded by countryside with rolling meadows and woodland and has views encompassing the nearby Quantocks, Bristol Channel and Welsh coast. A stream feeds the hotel pond as it wends its way to the sea only a few minutes' walk away. Unspoiled Kilve Beach is renowned for its rock formations, fossils and spectacular cliff views. The spacious bedrooms are comfortably furnished and guests will find mineral water, fresh flowers and biscuits when they arrive. French windows open on to a large, south-facing

terrace overlooking the garden, which is a profusion of colour during the summer. Antiques, curios and books abound in the drawing room and study, while log fires create a cosy atmosphere in winter. Guests may dine in the main restaurant or in the adjoining conservatory. The frequently changing menu pays particular attention to English recipes, usir ¦ fruit and vegetables from the kitchen garden whenever possible. The wine list is exceptional. Dogs can be accommodated in some rooms. **Directions:** Leave M5 at junction 23. Join A39 at Bridgwater. Turn right at Kilve into Sea Lane; hotel is ½ mile on left. Price guide: Single from £55–£75; double/twin from £75–£110.

CONGHAM HALL

GRIMSTON, KING'S LYNN, NORFOLK PE32 1AH
TEL: 01485 600250 FAX: 01485 601191

Dating from the mid-18th century, this stately manor house is set in 40 acres of paddocks, orchards and gardens, including its own cricket pitch. The conversion from country house to luxury hotel in 1982 was executed with care to enhance the elegance of the classic interiors. Proprietors Christine and Trevor Forecast have, however, retained the atmosphere of a family home. Christine's particular forte is the herb garden and flower arranging, and her displays enliven the décor throughout, while the delicate fragrance of home-made pot-pourri perfumes the air. Winners of the Johansens Hotel Award for Excellence 1993. In the Orangery restaurant, guests can relish modern English cooking. The origin of many of the flavours is explained by the herb garden, with over 100 varieties for the chef's use. Even the most discerning palate will be delighted by the choice of wines. Congham Hall is an ideal base for touring the countryside of West Norfolk, as well as Sandringham, Fakenham races and the coastal nature reserves. A video of the hotel and vicinity is available. **Directions:** Go to the A149/A148 interchange northeast of King's Lynn. Follow the A148 towards Sandringham/Fakenham/Cromer for 100 yards. Turn right to Grimston. The hotel is then $2^1/_2$ miles on the left. Price guide: Single £75–£85; double/twin £99–£130; suites from £165.

MILL HOUSE HOTEL

KINGHAM, OXFORDSHIRE OX7 6UH
TEL: 01608 658188 FAX: 01608 658492

Superbly converted Cotswold stone Mill House listed in the *Domesday Book* and set in nine tranquil acres with its own trout stream in the heart of the Cotswolds between Burford, Chipping Norton and Stow-on-the-Wold. The 23 luxury en suite bedrooms are all elegantly appointed and overlook the surrounding Cotswold countryside. There is a comfortable lounge with deep armchairs and sofas, and the bar features the ancient beamed ceiling and orginal bread ovens of the landfall flour mill. Open log fires are a feature throughout the winter; in summer, all rooms are enhanced by beautiful flour arrangements and fragrant pot-pourri. The heart of the hotel is the Marionette Room restaurant which provides cuisine of the highest standards. The menus are changed daily to take advantage of the very best of fresh, seasonal produce. With the whole of the Cotswolds within easy reach, the Mill House is the ideal base from which to explore: Broadway, Chipping Campden, Moreton-in-Marsh, the Slaughters and Bourton-on-the-Water are all within 30 minutes drive. The Mill House has AA 3 Stars and 2 Rosettes for food; RAC 3 Stars withHospitality, Comfort and Restaurant Awards. **Directions:** South of Kingham village midway between Chipping Norton and Stow-on-the-Wold just off the B4450. Price guide: Single £55–£65; double/twin £90–£110.

BUCKLAND-TOUT-SAINTS

GOVETON, KINGSBRIDGE, DEVON TQ7 2DS
TEL: 01548 853055 FAX: 01548 856261

Situated in rural South Devon, Buckland-Tout-Saints was built in 1690, when William, Prince of Orange, and Mary were on the throne of England. The hotel is in a beautiful and peaceful situation. It has 7 acres of lovely gardens. John and Tove Taylor, with their son George, are here to care for you. They are continuing the tradition of country house entertaining, promoting the feeling of being a privileged guest in a private house. On the first floor, four de luxe rooms and three suites are decorated in harmony with the period setting. Six smaller rooms on the second floor have Provence-style shuttered windows and lovely views. In the pine-panelled Queen Anne Restaurant, simple, crisp linen, china and glassware provide elegant surroundings for dinner. 2 AA Rosettes, Pride of Britain. Chef David Newland prepares imaginative English and French dishes which are presented in the modern English style. An extensive range of wines provides something to enhance each meal. Kingsbridge, 2 miles away, is a bustling market town, while Dartmouth is further round the coast. The wilds of Dartmoor, Dartington Glassworks, numerous quaint fishing ports and several National Trust properties are nearby. Children and dogs by prior arrangement. **Directions:** Signposted from the A381 between Totnes and Kingsbridge. Price guide: (including dinner) Single £75; double/twin £150–£170; suite £190.

PENRHOS COURT

KINGTON, HEREFORDSHIRE HR5 3LH
TEL: 01544 230720 FAX: 01544 230754

Penrhos was built in 1280, the year when Edward I, King of England, took Kington away from the Welsh. This unique farm building is set in six acres of grounds and stands on the border of Herefordshire and Wales. Many years of devoted work by the owners have transformed Penrhos into a delightful small hotel, offering seclusion and high standards of comfort and service. Chef-patronne Daphne Lambert prepares the dishes served in the hotel's restaurant and over the years has evolved her own style of cooking. She uses only fresh ingredients of the highest quality, preparing them in a way that does not mask the natural flavours nor strip the food of its nutritional value. The four-course evening menu, which changes every day, offers a choice for all tastes. All meat served is organic or additive free. The food is complemented by a list of rare and unusual wines from small, dedicated growers. Special events held at the hotel throughout the year include wine and whisky tasting evenings and exhibitions of art and sculpture. Penrhos is within easy reach of five golf courses and other activities available in the area include riding, hang-gliding, rally driving and go-carting. Also nearby are Hay-on-Wye, the Wye Valley and Hereford. **Directions:** Half mile south of Kington on the A44. Price guide: Single £50–£90; double/twin £80–£100; suites £120.

RAMPSBECK COUNTRY HOUSE HOTEL

WATERMILLOCK, LAKE ULLSWATER, NR PENRITH, CUMBRIA CA11 0LP
TEL: 017684 86442 FAX: 017684 86688

A beautifully situated hotel, Rampsbeck Country House stands in 18 acres of landscaped gardens and meadows leading to the shores of Lake Ullswater. Built in 1714, it first became a hotel in 1947, before the present owners acquired it in 1983. Thomas and Marion Gibb, with the help of Marion's mother, Marguerite MacDowall, completely refurbished Rampsbeck with the aim of maintaining its character and adding only to its comfort. Most of the well-appointed bedrooms have lake and garden views. Three have a private balcony and the suite overlooks the lake. In the elegant drawing room, a log fire burns and French windows lead to the garden. Guests and non-residents are welcome to dine in the intimate candle-lit restaurant. Imaginative menus offer a choice of delicious dishes, carefully prepared by head chef Andrew McGeorge and his team. A good bar lunch menu offers light snacks as well as hot food. Guests can stroll through the gardens, play croquet or fish from the lake shore, around which there are designated walks. Lake steamer trips, riding, golf, sailing, windsurfing and fell-walking are available nearby. Closed from the first week in January to mid-February. Dogs by arrangement only. **Directions:** Leave M6 at junction 40, take A592 to Ullswater. At T-junction at lake turn right; hotel is 1½ miles on left. Price guide: Single £48–£90; double/twin £90–£170; suite £170.

THE ARUNDELL ARMS

LIFTON, DEVON PL16 0AA
TEL: 01566 784666 FAX: 01566 784494

A 250-year-old former coaching inn near Dartmoor, The Arundell Arms is one of England's best-known sporting hotels. Americans travel 3,000 miles to fish the hotel's 20 miles of private waters on the River Tamar for salmon, trout and sea trout. The Arundell has two professional fishing instructors and runs a wide range of fly-fishing courses throughout the year. Also renowned as a shooting lodge, the driven snipe shoots have an international following. The hotel takes great pride in its 2 AA Rosette restaurant presided over by Master Chef Philip Burgess, formerly of L'Écu de France in London. With its slate floors, crackling fires, paintings and antiques, The Arundell Arms epitomises old-world charm and is a splendid base for visits to the historic houses and gardens, the moors and quaint fishing villages of Devon and Cornwall. Only 45 minutes' drive from Exeter and Plymouth, it is also ideal for the business executive, as it can be reached by fast roads from all directions: an elegant and spacious conference suite is available. **Directions:** Lifton is approximately 1/4 mile off the A30 and 2 miles east of Launceston and the Cornish border. Price guide: Single £58–£62; double/twin £93–£95.

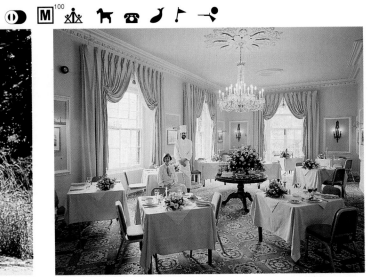

HOPE END HOTEL

HOPE END, LEDBURY, HEREFORDSHIRE HR8 1JQ
TEL: 01531 633613 FAX: 01531 636366

Hope End is a most romantic small hotel, set in 40 acres of restored 18th-century listed parkland. This very individual Georgian hotel provides total peace and an opportunity to enjoy an idle holiday amid rural surroundings. Formerly the childhood home of poet Elizabeth Barrett Browning, the building has been refurbished to offer discreet comfort. Nine en suite bedrooms are furnished with antiques and paintings, while the absence of TV ensures complete tranquillity. An extraordinary range of organic fruit, vegetables and herbs is grown in the walled kitchen garden. Free-range eggs, milk, yoghurt, local beef, lamb, fish and game in season are used in the kitchen. Fresh home-made bread is always available, along with a wide selection of farmhouse cheeses and the hotel's own spring water. Chef-patronne Patricia Hegarty prepares delicious dishes in the English country style to a high standard that has earned both national acclaim and 3 AA Rosettes. The wine list includes over 150 labels, with some rare vintages. Hope End is an ideal touring base as the Welsh Marches, Cotswolds and Malvern Hills are nearby. Ledbury itself is an interesting old market town with black and white houses. Closed from mid-December to early February. **Directions:** Two miles north of Ledbury, just beyond Wellington Heath. Price guide: Single £87; double/twin £99.

For hotel location, see maps on pages 00

Hope End Georgian Domestic Park and Garden

A listed Georgian Park and Gardens of forty acres laid out by J.C. Loudon in 1809 for Edward Moulton Barrett, father of Elizabeth Barrett Browning, in the Picturesque Manner, restored over the last five years and containing various wooded walks and prospects, a temple, grotto, carp pools and shady seats which are part of a nature reserve.

In contrast, the mid-18th century, brick-walled, domestic kitchen garden extending to over an acre is arranged to produce an extensive display of fruit, vegetable and herbs using many modern and interesting organic techniques to maintain 18th century traditions.

This is a new concept in garden visiting as access is available by booking only and the number of visitors is limited at any one time at the discretion of the proprietors to maintain the quiet and romantic atmosphere of the gardens.

Teas and light refreshments available.

Ledbury, Herefordshire HR8 1JQ Tel: 01531 633613 Fax: 01531 636366

42 THE CALLS

42 THE CALLS, LEEDS, WEST YORKSHIRE LS2 7EW
TEL: 0113 244 0099 FAX: 0113 234 4100

This remarkable hotel is absolutely unique. Converted from an old riverside corn mill, it is run as a very personal and luxurious hotel by Jonathan Wix and his general manager John Knaggs, in a peaceful location in the centre of Leeds. Shops, offices and theatres are within a few minutes' walk. The bedrooms have been individually decorated and furnished, taking full advantage of the many original features from small grain shutes to massive beams, girders and old machinery. Each room has 10 channel TV, a fresh filter coffee machine, complimentry toffees and cordials, luxury toiletries, trouser press and hair dryer. Stereo CD players are fitted in all the bedrooms and a library of disks is available to guests. Every comfort has been provided with full-size desks, handmade beds and armchairs, a liberal scattering of eastern rugs and beautiful bathrooms. Valet car parking and 24-hour room service are offered. Next door to the hotel is the simple but stylish Brasserie 44 and the superb Pool Court at 42 where guests' bills can be charged to their hotel account. **Directions:** M1 junction 46, follow signs to Harrogate, turn right by Tetley's Brewery. Go over Crown Point Bridge, then second left keeping the parish church on your left. Turn left again by Calls Landing and 42 will be directly in front of you. Price guide: Single £95–£135; double/twin £125–£140; suite £150–£220.

HALEY'S HOTEL & RESTAURANT

SHIRE OAK ROAD, HEADINGLEY, LEEDS, WEST YORKSHIRE LS6 2DE
TEL: 0113 278 4446 FAX: 0113 275 3342

Just two miles from Leeds City Centre, yet set in a quiet leafy lane in the Headingley conservation area close to the cricket ground and the university, Haley's is truly the country house hotel in the city. Each of the 22 guest rooms offers the highest levels of comfort, and are as individual as the fine antiques and rich furnishings which grace the hotel. The Bramley Room and Library are popular venues for private meetings, lunch or dinner parties. Haley's Restaurant has an enviable reputation, holding two AA rosettes, and was voted County Restaurant of the Year in the 1994 Good Food Guide. An imaginative menu of modern English cuisine is complemented by a fine wine list. Guests at Haley's frequently comment on the high standards of food and service they receive from courteous and dedicated staff. Not suprisingly, Haley's has won a host of accolades: the highest AA quality rating in the city and the two AA rosettes, also very complimentary write-ups in most leading guidebooks. (Haley's loos are also a four-times winner of Loo of the Year Award!) **Directions:** Two miles north of Leeds City Centre off the main A660 Otley Road – the main route to Leeds/Bradford Airport, Ilkley and Wharfedale. Price guide: Single £95; double/twin £112; suite £185. Weekend tariff also available.

MONK FRYSTON HALL

MONK FRYSTON, LEEDS, NORTH YORKSHIRE LS25 5DU
TEL: 01977 682369 FAX: 01977 683544

This mellow old manor house, with origins dating back to the time of William the Conqueror, is of great architectural interest. The mullioned and transom windows, and the family coat of arms above the doorway, are reminiscent of Monk Fryston's fascinating past. In 1954 the hall was acquired by the Duke of Rutland, who has since created an elegant hotel for the 20th century, while successfully preserving the strong sense of heritage and tradition. The bedrooms, ranging from cosy, to airy and spacious, all have private en suite bathrooms and are appointed to a high standard. A comprehensive menu offers a wide choice of traditional English dishes with something to suit all tastes. From the hall, the terrace leads to landscaped Italian gardens which overlook an ornamental lake and are a delight to see at any time of year. Wedding receptions and dinner-dances are catered for in the oak-panelled Haddon Room with its splendid carved fireplace. The Rutland Room makes a good conference venue. Monk Fryston Hall is an ideal choice for business people, tourists or those seeking a relaxing break. York is 16 miles, Leeds 14 miles and Harrogate 18 miles away. **Directions:** Three miles off A1, on the A63 towards Selby in the centre of Monk Fryston. Price guide: Single £66–£72; double/twin £94–£110.

QUORN COUNTRY HOTEL

66 LEICESTER ROAD, QUORN, LEICESTERSHIRE LE12 8BB
TEL: 01509 415050 FAX: 01509 415557

Originally Leicestershires most exclusive private club, based around the original 17th century listed building. This award winning hotel, set in four acres of landscaped gardens is the only non-city centre hotel in Leicestershire to be awarded 4 stars by the AA. For the ninth consecutive year the hotel has recieved RAC merit awards for excellence in cuisine, hospitality and comfort. The bedrooms are equipped to the very highest standards with attention given to every detail. From the businessman who needs an 'office in the bedroom' to weekend guests seeking those extra 'touches' which help create the ideal peaceful retreat. Ladies travelling alone can feel reassured that their special needs are met and indeed exceeded. Particular emphasis is given to the enjoyment of food with a declared policy of using, whenever possible, the freshest local produce. Your stay will be enhanced by the choice of two different dining experiences. You can choose between the Shires Restaurant with its alcoves and low beamed ceiling and full à la carte service, or the Light Bright, airy atmosphere of the Orangery Brasserie. **Directions:** Situated just off the A6 Leicester to Nottingham main road, in the bypassed village of Quorn (Quorndon), five miles from junction 23 of the M1 from north, junction 21A from South, East and West. Price Guide: Single £80 ; double/twin £92 ; suite £120.

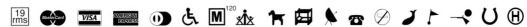

HOAR CROSS HALL HEALTH SPA RESORT

HOAR CROSS, NR YOXALL, STAFFORDSHIRE DE13 8QS
TEL: 01283 575671 FAX: 01283 575652

Hoar Cross Hall is a health spa resort in a stately home. Rated one of the top three health spas in Britain, this Grade II listed building, situated in acres of formal gardens and woodland, has all the charm of a luxury country residence, combined with the most innovative and comprehensive health spa facilities on offer. Eighty six luxury en suite bedrooms are furnished with either half-tester, crown-tester or four-poster beds. The opulent public areas retain most original features including panelling, mouldings and fireplaces. Dining is an experience combining healthy eating with à la carte choices. Fully equipped meeting facilities for up to 150 delegates offers the ideal venue for 'Healthy Executive'

conferences. Specialising in hydrotherapy, over 40 beauty & fitness therapists are on hand to relieve life's stresses. Outdoor activities range from hard-court tennis and 9-hole pitch and putt to croquet and bicycles. Price includes accommodation, breakfast, lunch, dinner, unlimited use of all indoor and outdoor facilities in addition to a number of inclusive treatments. (For your complete relaxation minimum guest age is 16 years). Corporate half-board rates available – details on request. AA four star rating.
Directions: From Lichfield turn off A51 onto A515 towards Ashbourne. Go through Yoxall and turn left to Hoar Cross. Price guide (fully inclusive, see above): Single £98; double/twin £196.

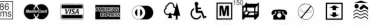

SWINFEN HALL

SWINFEN, NR LICHFIELD, STAFFORDSHIRE WS14 9RS
TEL: 01543 481494 FAX: 01543 480341

Swinfen Hall is a luxurious country house hotel built in the mid-18th century under the supervision of local architect Benjamin Wyatt. The money lavished on this dream residence is evident today in Swinfen Hall's balustraded Minstrels' Gallery and superb stucco ceilings crafted by Italian artisans. Elsewhere, fine architectural touches include the splendid carved-wood lobby ceiling, plus magnificent panelling and tiled fireplaces perfect in every detail. Owned by Helen and Victor Wiser, Swinfen is expertly managed by Paul Gilmore, who ensures a quality of service and hospitality befitting such a setting. In the restaurant and private dining room, guests can select from fresh fish, beef and local game (the breakfast menu is famed for its choice and value). A sun-filled banqueting hall with oak-panelled walls and magnificent Grinling Gibbons carvings is available for receptions and dinner dances. Bedrooms, decorated in pastel shades, are light, airy and comfortable, with period furnishings and modern conveniences including hospitality trays and hairdryers. Birmingham, and the International Airport are only 20 minutes away, and places to visit include Tamworth Castle and Lichfield Cathedral. **Directions:** Exit M42 at junctions A5. Lichfield is signposted off A5. Price guide: Single £65–£85; double/twin £85–£95; suite £105–£125.

THE WOOLTON REDBOURNE HOTEL

**ACREFIELD ROAD, WOOLTON, LIVERPOOL, MERSEYSIDE L25 5JN
TEL: 0151 428 2152/421 1500 FAX: 0151 421 1501**

The Woolton Redbourne Hotel is a fine Grade II listed building which was built in the grand country house style by the great Victorian industrialist, Sir Henry Tate. Set amidst beautiful landscaped gardens and lawns, the hotel is a refuge of peace and tranquillity. Completely refurbished in original Victorian splendour by the Collins family, the Woolton Redbourne has quickly established itself as one of the region's foremost hotels. Whether for business or pleasure the hotel succeeds in creating a very homely atmosphere with highly personal and friendly service. The hotel is filled with intriguing Victorian antiques and each bedroom is delightfully decorated and furnished in period style. For those seeking the ultimate in comfort, the hotels five suites are highly recommended. In the dining room an imaginative select table d'hote menu is served and a meal at the Woolton Redbourne Hotel has become an integral part of the experience. A full wine list is offered. The hotel caters for small business meetings and is just five miles from the city centre.**Directions:** At the end of the M62, junction 4, turn left onto the A5058. At second traffic lights turn left onto Woolton Road. The hotel is two miles on the left. Price guide: Single £62–£90; double/twin £86–£140; suite £150.

LOWER SLAUGHTER MANOR

LOWER SLAUGHTER, NR BOURTON-ON-THE-WATER, GLOUCESTERSHIRE GL54 2HP
TEL: 01451 820456 FAX: 01451 822150

One of the best kept secrets in the Cotswolds. In three years, Audrey and Peter Marks have transformed this magnificent 17th century manor house into one of the highest rated country house hotels in England. The Manor has been awarded the prestigious three Red Star rating and the Courtesy and Care Award from the AA. It is also the recipient of a Blue Ribbon Award from the RAC. Flowers abound in all the elegant public rooms where fine antiques, works of art and blazing log fires in the winter add to the very special atmosphere. Exceptionally spacious bedrooms look out onto the picturesque gardens. Michael Benjamin's cuisine has gained much praise from the guides including the award of 3 AA Rosettes.

There is a fine range of wines from the old and new worlds and the Manor was awarded Egon Ronay's guides 'Californian Wine Cellar of the Year 1994'. The emphasis is on style, comfort and service. There is an indoor heated swimming pool, sauna, all-weather tennis court, croquet lawn and putting green. The Manor is ideally located as a base from which to tour the Cotswolds and as an excellent venue for discreet meetings in the private conference suite. **Directions:** From the A419, follow the signs to The Slaughters; the Manor is on the right entering the village. Price guide: All prices include English breakfast and dinner from the à la carte menu. Single £140–£195; double/twin £205–£275; suites £290.

WASHBOURNE COURT HOTEL

LOWER SLAUGHTER, GLOUCESTERSHIRE GL54 2HS
TEL: 01451 822143 FAX: 01451 821045

Situated in the centre of the village of Lower Slaughter, in the heart of the Cotswolds, Washbourne Court Hotel is a magnificent 17th century building. Owned and managed by the Pender family and assisted by a professional team, the hotel prides itself on offering high quality accommodation and friendly, personal service. Much of the original character and charm of the place has been retained, with traditional beamed ceilings, flagstone floors and mullioned windows. During the summer months, guests can enjoy a drink on the riverside terrace or, in winter, indoors in front of an old-fashioned log fire. Modern English cuisine is served to a high standard in the Riverside

Restaurant, where guests dine by candlelight. The menus make full use of local produce and there is a fine wine list. The restaurant has recently been awarded two AA Rosettes. There are several bedrooms in the main building; alternatively, choose one of the Barn rooms, incorporating the original beams, or one of the cottage-style suites with private lounge. The surrounding area is renowned for its beauty and there are many gentle walks. The Fosse Way, one of the famous Roman roads, is $\frac{1}{2}$ a mile away. **Directions:** Washbourne Court is $\frac{1}{2}$ a mile from the A429 Fosse Way between Stow-on-the-Wold and Cirencester. Price guide: Single £78; double/twin £88; suite £130.

DINHAM HALL

LUDLOW, SHROPSHIRE SY8 1EJ
TEL: 01584 876464 FAX: 01584 876019

Built in 1792 Dinham Hall is situated in the historic town of Ludlow. It lies only 40 metres from the Castle which, having played an important part in England's history, today hosts the Shakespearian productions which form the major part of the annual Ludlow Festival. Dinham's enviable location provides its guests with the combination of ready access to the town and picturesque views over the open Shropshire countryside. There is a magnificent fireplace in the sitting room, with log fires in the winter. In the restaurant flowers help to provide a subtle atmosphere in which to enjoy prize-winning cuisine while the Merchant Suite, with its 14th century timbers, is an ideal setting for private dinners and meetings. During the summer afternoon teas are served on the terrace overlooking the walled garden. The décor of the bedrooms is a harmony of modern facilities and period design, a number of rooms having four-poster beds. The restaurant and many bedrooms command views over the gardens and Teme Valley to wooded hills. Guests may also enjoy a visit to Ludlow races or spend a few hours browsing in the town's antique shops. South Shropshire is one of the most beautiful parts of the country with Ludlow amongst the finest market towns. **Directions:** In the centre of Ludlow overlooking the castle. Price guide: Single £65–£75; double/twin £89–£110.

PASSFORD HOUSE HOTEL

MOUNT PLEASANT LANE, LYMINGTON, HAMPSHIRE SO41 8LS
TEL: 01590 682398 FAX: 01590 683494

Set in nine acres of picturesque gardens and rolling parkland, the Passford House Hotel lies midway between the charming New Forest village of Sway and the Georgian splendour of Lymington. Once the home of Lord Arthur Cecil, it is steeped in history and the traditions of leisurely country life. Pleasantly decorated bedrooms include a number of de luxe rooms, while comfort is the keynote in the four public lounges. The hotel prides itself on the standard and variety of cuisine served in its delightful restaurant and the extensive menu aims to give pleasure to the most discerning of palates. Meals are complemented by a speciality wine list. The hotel boasts a superb leisure centre, catering for all ages and activities. In addition to two heated swimming pools, there is a multi-gym, sauna, solarium, pool table, croquet lawn, and magnificent tennis court. Just a short drive away are Beaulieu, the cathedral cities of Winchester and Salisbury and ferry ports to the Isle of Wight and France. The New Forest area has five golf courses and, for those interested in riding, there are many stables and trekking centres. Milford-on-Sea, four miles away, is the nearest beach. **Directions:** At Lymington leave the A337 at the Tollhouse Inn, then take the first turning right and the hotel is on the right. Price guide: £75: double/twin £110–£135.

PARKHILL HOTEL

BEAULIEU ROAD, LYNDHURST, NEW FOREST, HAMPSHIRE SO43 7FZ
TEL: 01703 282944 FAX: 01703 283268

Reached by way of a winding drive through glorious parkland from the scenic route between Lyndhurst and Beaulieu, Parkhill, situated in an elevated position with superb views across open forest and heathland, is perfect for a restful break or holiday and makes the ideal venue for special business meetings and small conferences, offering a charming New Forest remoteness coupled with an excellence of standards and service. Dining at Parkhill is very much an integral part of your overall pleasure. The award winning restaurant offers a most tranquil setting with fine views across the lawns, where deer can frequently be seen grazing. Cuisine is a delicious blend of modern and classical English cooking, where local fresh produce is used to create appetising menus, balanced by a carefully chosen and well-stocked cellar. Parkhill is also an ideal base for touring not only the delightful surrounding areas, but also the many places of interest which are all within easy driving distance, including Exbury Gardens, home to one of the world's finest collections of rhododendrons and azaleas, Broadlands, the home of Lord Mountbatten, the *Mary Rose* in Portsmouth Dockyard, and the graceful cathedral cities of Salisbury and Winchester. **Directions:** From Lyndhurst take the B3056 toward Beaulieu; Parkhill is about 1 mile from Lyndhurst on your right. Price guide: Single from £54–£76; double from £94–£132.

THE LYNTON COTTAGE HOTEL

NORTH WALK, LYNTON, NORTH DEVON EX35 6ED
TEL: 01598 752342 FAX: 01598 752597

Once the residence of a knight of the realm, The Lynton Cottage Hotel has a panoramic view of the Lyn Valley and Lynmouth Bay – a spectacular sight to greet visitors approaching along the winding drive. Dating back to the 17th century, the hotel combines period charm with modern comforts. The 16 en suite bedrooms and suites are individually decorated with taste and style and equipped to reflect the perfectionist approach of enthusiastic proprietors John and Maisie Jones. Under the auspices of chef Leon Balanche, innovative cuisine is prepared with flair, finesse and an influence of French culinary style. AA Rosette awarded. Gastronomic house parties have proved popular on regular weekends throughout the year, offering guests an opportunity to enjoy the finest gourmet cooking accompanied by wines carefully selected for the occasion. Other special breaks available include mystery whodunnit and champagne weekends. Riding, clay pigeon shooting, golf and salmon fishing are all available locally and the hotel is an ideal base from which to discover the rugged beauty of Exmoor and the Valley of Rocks. Closed January. **Directions:** From M5 take A39 to Porlock then on to Lynton, where the hotel is on the North Walk. Price guide (including dinner): Single £57–£75; double/twin £110–£140.

CLIVEDEN

TAPLOW, BERKSHIRE SL6 0JF
TEL: 01628 668561 FAX: 01628 661837

Cliveden, Britain's only 5 Red AA star hotel that is also a stately home, is set in 376 acres of National Trust private gardens and parkland, overlooking the Thames. As the former home of Frederick, Prince of Wales, three Dukes and the Astor family, Cliveden has been at the centre of Britain's social and political life for over 300 years. It is exquisitely furnished in a classically English style, with a multitude of oil paintings, antiques and *objets d'art* set against elaborate carved panelling, chiselled colonnades and ornate plasterwork. The spacious guest rooms and suites are appointed to the most luxurious standards, with every comfort assured. One of the greatest pleasures of eating at Cliveden is in the choice of dining rooms and the scope of the menus. The French Dining Room, with its original Madame de Pompadour rococo decoration, is the finest 18th-century *boiserie* outside France. Alternatively, relish the Michelin-starred cuisine of chef Ron Maxfield in Waldo's Restaurant. The Pavilion offers a full range of health and fitness facilities and beauty therapies. Guests can ride Cliveden's horses over the estate or enjoy a leisurely cruise on an Edwardian launch. Comprehensively equipped, the two boardrooms provide self-contained business meeting facilities. **Directions:** Situated on B476, 2 miles north of Taplow. Price guide: Single £210; double/twin £240; suites from £395.

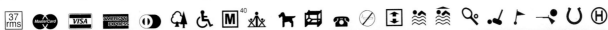

FREDRICK'S HOTEL & RESTAURANT

SHOPPENHANGERS ROAD, MAIDENHEAD, BERKSHIRE SL6 2PZ
TEL: 01628 35934 FAX: 01628 771054

'Putting people first' is the guiding philosophy behind the running of this sumptuously equipped hotel and, indeed, is indicative of the uncompromising service guests can expect to receive. Set in two acres of grounds, Fredrick's overlooks the fairways and greens of Maidenhead Golf Club beyond. The immaculate reception rooms are distinctively styled to create something out of the ordinary. Minute attention to detail is evident in the 37 bedrooms, all immaculate with gleaming, marble-tiled bathrooms, while the suites have their own patio garden or balcony. A quiet drink can be enjoyed in the light, airy Wintergarden lounge before entering the air-conditioned restaurant. Amid the elegant décor of crystal chandeliers and crisp white linen, fine gourmet cuisine is served which has received recognition from leading guides for many years. Particularly suited to conferences, four private function rooms with full secretarial facilities are available. Helicopter landing can be arranged. Easily accessible from Windsor, Henley, Ascot, Heathrow and London. Closed 24-30 December. **Directions:** Leave M4 at exit 8/9, take A404(M) and leave at first turning signed Cox Green/White Waltham. Turn into Shoppenhangers Road; Fredrick's is on the right. Price guide: Single £138–£148; double/twin £168–£178; suite £250.

CHILSTON PARK COUNTRY HOUSE

SANDWAY, LENHAM, NR MAIDSTONE, KENT ME17 2BE
TEL: 01622 859803 FAX: 01622 858588 TELEX: 966154 CHILPK G

This magnificent Grade I listed mansion, one of England's most richly decorated hotels, was built in the 13th century and remodelled in the 18th century. Now sensitively refurbished, the hotel's ambience is enhanced by the lighting at dusk each day of over 200 candles. The marble hall and drawing room offer guests an opportunity to relax and to admire the outstanding collection of antiques. Owners Martin and Judith Miller, who are renowned antiques experts (their annual *Miller's Guide to Antiques* is a bestseller), have made the entire hotel a treasure trove for their many interesting *objets d'art*. The opulently furnished bedrooms are fitted to a high standard and many have four-poster beds. Good, fresh English cooking is offered in each of Chilston's five dining rooms, where outstanding menus are supported by an excellent wine list. In keeping with the traditions of a country house, a wide variety of sporting activities is available, golf and riding nearby, fishing in the natural spring lake and punting. **Directions:** Take junction 8 off the M20, then A20 to Lenham Station. Turn left into Boughton Road. Go over the crossroads and M20; Chilston Park is on the left. Price guide: Single £70–£145; double/twin £90–£190.

CRUDWELL COURT HOTEL

CRUDWELL, NR MALMESBURY, WILTSHIRE SN16 9EP
TEL: 01666 577194 FAX: 01666 577853

Crudwell Court is a 17th-century rectory, set in three acres of Cotswold walled gardens. The pretty, well-established grounds have lily ponds and a garden gate leading through to the neighbouring Saxon church of All Saints. Completely refurbished in recent years, the old rectory has been decorated with bright, cheery colours. Sunshine yellow in the sitting room, warm apricot in the drawing room and shades of buttercream and blue in the bedrooms lend a fresh feel to this hotel. Visitors enter through a flagstoned hall to discover rooms with comfortable seating and plenty of books to read. In the panelled dining room guests will find a weekly changing menu, which is best described as modern Anglo-French. Cooked to order, the meals are a feast for the eye as well as the palate. The restaurant has recently been extended into a new conservatory, which may also be used for private functions. Malmesbury has a magnificent Norman abbey church and a curious market cross. Nearby are the towns of Tetbury and Cirencester, the picturesque villages of Castle Combe and Lacock and numerous stately homes. **Directions:** Crudwell Court is on the A429. Travelling towards Cirencester, when you reach the village of Crudwell turn right (signposted Oaksey) opposite the Plough Inn, and the hotel is on the left. Price guide: Single £50; double/twin £90.

THE OLD BELL

ABBEY ROW, MALMESBURY, WILTSHIRE SN16 0AG
TEL: 01666 822344 FAX: 01666 825145

The Old Bell was established by the Abbot of Malmesbury during the reign of King John as a place to refresh guests who came to consult the Abbey's library. Situated at the edge of the Cotswolds, this Grade I listed building may well be England's most ancient hotel. Inside, the Great Hall boasts a medieval stone fireplace, while each bedroom is decorated and furnished with an individual style and character. A classic and imaginative menu exemplifies the best in English cooking, with meals ranging from four-course dinners complemented by fine wines in the Edwardian dining room, to informal snacks on the terrace. The oak-beamed lounges, which were built in the 16th century for the steward of Malmesbury Abbey, open on to a quiet terrace and traditional English garden complete with gazebo. Families are particularly welcomed at The Old Bell; there is no charge for children sharing parents' rooms and children's menus are available. The 'Den' is equipped with a multitude of toys and open every day. Malmesbury is only 30 minutes from Bath and is close to a number of other beautiful villages such as Castle Combe, Bourton-on-the-Water and Lacock. Outdoor places of interest include the mysterious stone circle at Avebury and the Westonbirt Arboretum. **Directions:** Near the market cross in the centre of Malmesbury. Price guide: Single £60–£70; double/twin £75–£115; suites £125.

WHATLEY MANOR

NR EASTON GREY, MALMESBURY, WILTSHIRE SN16 0RB
TEL: 01666 822888 FAX: 01666 826120

This Grade II listed manor, set around a central courtyard, stands in 12 acres of grounds running down to a peaceful stretch of the River Avon. Originally built in the 17th century, Whatley Manor was refurbished by a wealthy sportsman in the 1920s and many of the present buildings date from that period. While the hotel's interior is furnished to a high standard, an emphasis has always been placed on maintaining a relaxed, informal atmosphere, enhanced by pine and oak panelling, log fires and the effect of warm colours in the lounge and drawing room. The dining room similarly combines elegance with intimacy and it overlooks the gardens. Ten of the bedrooms are in the 'Courthouse'. Snooker and table-tennis facilities are provided in the original saddle rooms and there is also a sauna, solarium and Jacuzzi. Close for gardening enthusiasts is Hodges Barn at Shipton Moyne. With the Cotswolds, the cities of Bath and Bristol plus Tetbury, Cirencester, Westonbirt Arboretum, Longleat, Stourhead Gardens and many places of historic interest nearby, Whatley Manor is the perfect place for long weekend breaks, for which the special terms ensure good value. Two night weekend breaks from £121. **Directions:** The hotel is on the B4040 three miles west of Malmesbury. Price guide: Single £85–£96; double/twin £112–£136.

THE COTTAGE IN THE WOOD

HOLYWELL ROAD, MALVERN WELLS, WORCESTERSHIRE WR14 4LG
TEL: 01684 575859 FAX: 01684 560662

The Malvern Hills – the home and inspiration for England's most celebrated composer, Sir Edward Elgar – are the setting for The Cottage in the Wood. The hotel occupies 7 acres of thickly wooded grounds, perched high on the hillside. With its spectacular outlook across the Severn Valley plain, it won acclaim from the *Daily Mail* for 'the best view in England'. Formerly attached to the Blackmore Park seat of Sir Thomas Hornyold, it now comprises three buildings: the Georgian Dower House, Beech Cottage and Coach House. The cottage-style furnishings of all the bedrooms give it an intimate and cosy feel, and the Coach House bedrooms have sun-trap balconies and patios. An essentially English menu is complemented by an extensive wine cellar comprising over 260 bins. To counter any gastronomic indulgence, guests can take an exhilarating trek straight from the hotel grounds to the breezy summits of the Malverns. The Victorian spa town of Great Malvern is nearby, as are the Three Counties Showground and the cathedral cities of Worcester, Gloucester and Hereford. The hotel is personally run by John and Sue Pattin and their family. **Directions:** Three miles south of Great Malvern on A449, turn into Holywell Road opposite Jet petrol station. Hotel is 250 yards on right. Price guide: Single £68; double/twin £89–£135. Bargain breaks available.

ETROP GRANGE

THORLEY LANE, MANCHESTER AIRPORT, GREATER MANCHESTER M90 4EG
TEL: 0161 499 0500 FAX: 0161 0790

Tucked away near Manchester Airport lies Etrop Grange, a beautiful country house hotel and restaurant. The original house was built in 1780 and more than 200 years on has been lovingly restored. Today, the hotel enjoys a fine reputation for its accommodation, where the luxury, character and sheer elegance of the Georgian era are evident in every feature. The magnificent restaurant offers a well balanced mix of traditional and modern English cuisine, complemented by an extensive selection of fine wines. Attention to detail ensures personal and individual service. In addition to the obvious advantage of having an airport within walking distance, the location of Etrop Grange is ideal in many other ways. With a comprehensive motorway network and InterCity stations minutes away, it is accessible from all parts of the UK. Entertainment for visitors ranges from the shopping, sport and excellent nightlife offered by the city of Manchester to golf, riding, clay pigeon shooting, water sports and outdoor pursuits in the immediate countryside. Cheshire also boasts an abundance of stately homes, museums and historical attractions. **Directions:** Leave M56 at junction 5 towards Manchester Airport. At roundabout take first exit and follow signs for Etrop Grange. Price guide: Single £74–£120; double/twin £84–£130; suites £110–£155.

For hotel location, see maps on pages 473–479

THE IVY HOUSE HOTEL

HIGH STREET, MARLBOROUGH, WILTSHIRE SN8 1HJ
TEL: 01672 515333 FAX: 01672 515338

The Ivy House Hotel is an 18th-century Grade II listed building, overlooking Marlborough High Street. Built in 1707 for the Earl of Aylesbury, it has been refurbished to display the many architectural features of the changing eras. Beyond the reception area, guests may relax in the Churchill Lounge, with its antique furniture. Facing the sun terrace, at the rear of the building, is the elegant Palladian-style Garden Restaurant. The cooking is of a high standard, reflecting both traditional and progressive styles. The purpose-built Beeches Conference and Banqueting Suite provides a venue for business meetings, while the Marlborough Suite is suitable for private dinner parties. The Ivy House is professionally run by owners David Ball and Josephine Scott, who offer guests a comfortable stay which is extremely good value for money. The ancient archaeological sites of Silbury Hill, Stonehenge and Avebury are easily accessible by car, as are the Marlborough Downs and the Savernake Forest. Close by are the stately homes of Bowood House, Corsham Court and Blenheim Palace. **Directions:** The hotel is in Marlborough High Street, just off the A4 from Bath. Price guide: Single £55–£65; double/twin £68–£75.

For hotel location, see maps on pages 473–479

213

DANESFIELD HOUSE

MEDMENHAM, MARLOW, BUCKINGHAMSHIRE SL7 2EY
TEL: 01628 891010 FAX: 01628 890408

Danesfield House is set in 65 acres of gardens and parkland overlooking the River Thames and offering panoramic views across the Chiltern Hills. It is the third house since 1664 to occupy this lovely setting and it was designed and built in sumptuous style at the end of the 19th century. After years of neglect the house has been fully restored, combining its Victorian splendour with the very best modern hotel facilities. Among the many attractions of its luxury bedrooms, all beautifully decorated and furnished, are the extensive facilities they offer. These include two telephone lines (one may be used for personal fax), satellite TV, mini bar, trouser press, hair dryers, bath robes and toiletries. Guests can relax in the magnificent drawing room with its galleried library or in the sunlit atrium. There is a choice of two restaurants the Oak Room and Loggia Brasserie both of which offer a choice of international cuisine. The hotel also has six private banqueting and conference rooms. Leisure facilities include a squash court, swimming pool, croquet, tennis court and jogging and walking trails. Also within easy reach are Windsor Castle, Disraeli's home at Hughenden Manor, Milton's cottage and the caves of West Wycombe. **Directions:** Between the M4 and M40 on the A4155 between Marlow and Henley-on-Thames. Price guide: Single £125; double/twin £145; suites £195.

In association with MasterCard

MATLOCK (Riber)

RIBER HALL

MATLOCK, DERBYSHIRE DE4 5JU
TEL: 01629 582795 FAX: 01629 580475

A listed historical building, starred in its class, Riber Hall dates from the 1400s, although much of the manor house is Elizabethan. Having survived through the ages, Riber Hall underwent extensive restoration in 1970 to attain its present status as a prestigious hotel. The original features are very much in evidence, with exposed beams and large fireplaces creating a fitting backdrop to the antique furniture and period décor. Quietly located around an attractive courtyard, the bedrooms are all appointed to a high standard with many thoughtful extras. Acknowledged as a restaurant of distinction, Riber Hall offers a comprehensive wine list, game when in season and a wide choice of delicious dishes in an intimate atmosphere, enhanced by fine Wedgwood bone china and cut glass. Conferences, wedding receptions and small dinner parties can be privately catered for. The tranquillity of the setting can be appreciated in the walled garden and orchard. AA nominated as one of 'The Most Romantic Hotels in Britain'. The Peak National Park beyond beckons explorers, while Chatsworth, Haddon Hall, Hardwick Hall and Calke Abbey are nearby. **Directions:** Twenty minutes from junction 28 of M1, off A615 at Tansley; 1 mile further to Riber. Price guide: Single £79.50; double/twin £98.

For hotel location, see maps on pages 473–479

215

PERITON PARK HOTEL

MIDDLECOMBE, NR MINEHEAD, SOMERSET TA24 8SW
TEL: 01643 706885 FAX: 01643 706885

Bordering on the northern fringe of the Exmoor National Park, the elevated position of this handsome country house gives the visitor magnificent views of the West Somerset hills, with flashes of the Bristol Channel beyond. Through the dawn mists the early riser may be rewarded by the spectacle of a herd of red deer grazing on the moorland below the hotel. Set in 4 acres of woodland, this residence, built in 1875, is now owned by Richard and Angela Hunt whose aim is to run a select hotel in the style of a country gentleman's home. In this they have succeeded – the décor and furnishings in the well-proportioned rooms have been enlivened with warm autumn colours to create a restful impression. The wood-panelled restaurant, with its double aspect views over the grounds, has been completely renovated. Imaginative use of Somerset and West Country produce has earned Periton Park a reputation for gastronomic excellence. The combination of heathered moorland, sheltered combes and rugged coastline makes the hotel an ideal base for walking and field sports, while riding is available from the stables adjacent to the hotel. **Directions:** Periton Park is situated off the A39 on the left just after Minehead, in the direction of Lynmouth and Porlock. Price guide: Single £65; double/twin £90.

THE ANGEL HOTEL

NORTH STREET, MIDHURST, WEST SUSSEX GU29 9DN
TEL: 01730 812421 FAX: 01730 815928

The Angel Hotel, is a stylishly restored 16th century coaching inn which has earned widespread praise from national press and guidebooks. Sympathetically renovated to combine contemporary comfort with original character, the Angel bridges the gap between town house bustle and country house calm. To the front, a handsome Georgian façade overlooks the high street,while at the rear, quiet rose gardens gardens lead to the parkland and ruins of historic Cowdray Castle. There are 25 bedrooms, all offering private bathrooms and modern amenities. Individually furnished with antiques, many rooms feature original Tudor beams. The hotel has been widely acclaimed for the quality of its food, which draws on influences as diverse as British, French, Italian and Caribbean cookery, and can be in the informal atmosphere of the brasserie or in the elegant setting of the Cowdray Room restaurant. For business guests the hotel offers two attractive meeting rooms, presentation aids and secretarial services. The historic market town of Midhurst is well placed for visits to Petworth House, Arundel Castle and the South Downs. **Directions:** From the A272, the hotel is on the left as the town centre is approached from the east. Price guide: Single £65–£95; double/twin £75–£150.

THE SPREAD EAGLE HOTEL

SOUTH STREET, MIDHURST, WEST SUSSEX GU29 9NH
TEL: 01730 816911 FAX: 01730 815668

Dating from 1430, when guests were welcomed to the tavern here, The Spread Eagle is one of England's oldest hotels. Throughout the centuries, including its time as a famous coaching inn, the influences of successive eras have been preserved both in the architecture and decorative features of the hotel. Heavy polished timbers, Tudor bread ovens and a series of Flemish stained-glass windows are among the many noteworthy features. Innovative cooking forms the basis of the meals, served in the dining room, with its huge, coppered inglenook fireplace and dark oak beams hung with traditional Sussex Christmas puddings. Colourful, co-ordinated fabrics and antique furnishings make for attractive bedrooms, all fully appointed. The 17th-century Jacobean Hall is an ideal venue for meetings – or perhaps a medieval banquet complete with minstrels! A secluded courtyard garden is flanked, in the summer, by climbing roses and clematis. The stately homes at Petworth, Uppark and Goodwood are all within a short drive, with Chichester Cathedral, the Downland Museum and Fishbourne Roman Palace among the many local attractions. Cowdray Park Polo Club is only 1 mile away. **Directions:** Midhurst is on the A286 between Chichester and Milford. Price guide: Single from £69; double/twin from £79.

MOORE PLACE HOTEL

THE SQUARE, ASPLEY GUISE, MILTON KEYNES, BEDFORDSHIRE MK17 8DW
TEL: 01908 282000 FAX: 01908 281888

This elegant Georgian mansion was built by Francis Moore in the peaceful Bedfordshire village of Aspley Guise in 1786. The original house, which is set on the village square, has been sympathetically extended to create extra rooms. The additional wing has been built around an attractive courtyard with a rock garden, lily pool and waterfall. The pretty Victorian-style conservatory restaurant, with its floral tented ceiling and festooned drapes, serves food that rates among the best in the area. Vegetarian options can always be found on the menus, which offer dishes prepared in the modern English style and balanced with a selection of fine wines. The 54 bedrooms are well appointed with many amenities, including a trouser press, hairdryer, welcome drinks and large towelling bath robes. Banquets, conferences and dinner parties can be accommodated in five private function rooms: all are decorated in traditional style yet are equipped with the latest audio-visual facilities. The hotel is close to Woburn Abbey, Silverstone, Whipsnade Zoo, Stowe and Milton Keynes. The convenient location and accessibility to the motorway network makes Moore Place Hotel an attractive choice, whether travelling on business or for pleasure. **Directions:** Only two minutes' drive from the M1 junction 13. Price guide: Single £65; double/twin £90–£165; suite £165.

THE BEACON COUNTRY HOUSE

BEACON ROAD, MINEHEAD, SOMERSET TA24 5SD
TEL: 01643 703476 FAX: 01643 702668

This elegant Edwardian building is surrounded by 20 acres of grounds visited by red deer and home to badgers and peacocks. From the hotel's woods there is direct access to Exmoor and to a winding coastal path. Although extensively refurbished, the building has maintained the character of a fine country house. All the public rooms are tastefully furnished to create a comfortable and relaxing atmosphere, and a superb, domed, glass conservatory affords views of the gardens and sea beyond. Co-owner and master chef, Pennie Fulcher-Smith, compiles an imaginative menu which places emphasis on fresh local produce, and, although a wide variety of dishes is offered, Pennie is happy to cater for all tastes. There is also an extensive wine list. The individually styled bedrooms are as elegantly furnished as the rest of the hotel and provide every modern facility. There is a livery adjacent to the hotel and riding or shooting breaks are available by arrangement. The Beacon Country house is an ideal base for those touring the West Country and Exmoor. **Directions:** Leave the M5 at junction 25 to Minehead on the A358. Continue along Townsend Road; right at T-junction, second left at Blenheim Road, first left into Marlett Road. Straight over into Burgundy Road; round hairpin bend, hotel is at end of Beacon Road on the right. Price guide: Single £55; double/twin £75–£85.

For hotel location, see maps on pages 473–479

THE MANOR HOUSE HOTEL

MORETON-IN-MARSH, GLOUCESTERSHIRE GL56 0LJ
TEL: 01608 650501 FAX: 01608 651481

This former 16th-century manor house and coaching inn is set in beautiful gardens in the Cotswold village of Moreton-in-Marsh. The Manor House Hotel has been tastefully extended and restored, yet retains many of its historic features, among them a priest's hole and secret passages. The 39 well-appointed bedrooms have been individually decorated and furnished. The restaurant offers imaginative French cooking and traditional English dishes using only the freshest ingredients, accompanied by an expertly selected wine list. For the guest seeking relaxation, leisure facilities include an indoor heated swimming pool, spa bath and sauna. Sports enthusiasts will also find that tennis, golf, riding and squash can be arranged locally. The spacious conference facilities are set apart from the rest of the hotel. Modern business facilities, combined with the peaceful location, make this an excellent venue for executive meetings. It is also an ideal base for touring, with many attractions nearby, including Stratford-upon-Avon, Warwick and the fashionable centres of Cheltenham, Oxford and Bath. **Directions:** The Manor House Hotel is on the A429 Fosse Way near the junction of the A44 and A429 north of Stow, on the Broadway side of the intersection. Price guide: Single £55; double/twin £85–£125.

THE MANOR HOUSE HOTEL AND GOLF COURSE

MORETONHAMPSTEAD, DEVON TQ13 8RE
TEL: 01647 440355 FAX: 01647 440961

This fine mansion is set in 270 acres of private estate, on the edge of Dartmoor National Park and within easy reach of 'the English Riviera'. The Manor House, a favoured location for both business and pleasure, is complete with its own 18-hole championship golf course which provides a combination of natural beauty and ideal golfing terrain. Luxury en suite bedrooms are equipped with every modern amenity to ensure maximum comfort and convenience. The elegant restaurant offers interesting and well-balanced menus. Irresistible cream teas are served on the South Terrace during the summer, while in winter they can be enjoyed in front of the open fires of the oak-panelled lounge. Leisure activities offered by the hotel include game and fly fishing, tennis, billiards, croquet, a challenging par three practice course and a new leisure centre is anticipated to open in spring 1996. The Manor House is a perfect location for conferences, seminars and training events. The Bowden Room can accommodate up to 120 delegates and smaller rooms are also available. Places of interest nearby include Dartmoor, Torbay and Exeter Cathedral. **Directions:** Exit M5 at junction 31. Follow Okehampton A30 road for approximately ten miles, then take A382 to Moretonhampstead, then B3212 towards Princetown. The hotel drive is on the left. Price guide: Single £72.50; double/twin £82.50–£130.

ROOKERY HALL

WORLESTON, NANTWICH, NR CHESTER, CHESHIRE CW5 6DQ
TEL: 01270 610016 FAX: 01270 626027

Built in 1816 by a wealthy English landowner, Rookery Hall is set in 200 acres of gardens and pastures fringing the banks of the River Weaver. Later that century Baron William Von Schroder of the banking world purchased the hall and changed the traditional Georgian mansion into a fine Victorian house with a hint of his ancestry coming to the fore in the form of a magnificent Schloss-like tower. Internally, the beautifully proportioned reception rooms are noted for the elegance of the Salon, the spendid main staircase in English oak and the highly polished mahogany and walnut panelling in the dining room. Guest rooms are all individually designed and many overlook the gardens. The restaurant offers fine dining and has recently been awarded 3 AA Rosettes for cuisine. Excellent conference facilities are provided within the converted stables. A wide range of outdoor activities are available within the grounds including motorised sports, team challenges, clay shooting and falconry. Conveniently located for visiting the nearby potteries and historic Chester. ETB 5 Crown Deluxe, North West Tourist Board Hotel of the Year 1995 and RAC Blue Ribbon award. **Directions:** From M6 junction 16 take the A500 to Nantwich, then the B5074 to Worleston. Price guide: Single £98.50–£150; double/twin £150–£190; suite £198–£250.

CHEWTON GLEN

CHEWTON GLEN, NEW MILTON, HAMPSHIRE BH25 6QS
TEL: 01425 275341 FAX: 01425 272310

Chewton Glen, a shrine that merits many a pilgrimage, has a setting of lovely gardens, woodland and lawns. The original mansion was built in the short-lived Palladian style of the early 18th century and despite renovations it essentially retains the unique character of an English country house. There are antiques, paintings, memorabilia of the famous author, Captain Marryat, who lived there and wrote *Children of the New Forest* and *Mr Midshipman Easy*, and arrays of fresh flowers. Many bedrooms have balconies that give guests the chance to enjoy beautiful views of the surrounding parkland scenery. The menu in the Marryat Restaurant is a delicious harmony of the classical and the modern, gastronomically accompanied by a list of over 400 wines. The hotel has a health club with a magnificent swimming pool, spa, steam room, saunas and gym. There are excellent conference facilities. Among the other pursuits on hand are golf, tennis, snooker, shooting and riding. Places of interest nearby include Beaulieu, Broadlands, Exbury Gardens, The Solent, Kingston Lacy and Stonehenge. **Directions:** A35 from Lyndhurst to Bournemouth.Turn left at Walkford (approx 10 miles afterLyndhurst). Turn left before round about, hotel is on the right. Price guide: Single from £185; double/twin from £195; suites from £295.

THE PENTIRE ROCKS HOTEL

NEW POLZEATH, NR ROCK, NORTH CORNWALL PL27 6US
TEL: 01208 862213 FAX: 01208 862259

Set amid the spectacular scenery of the North Cornwall coast, the Pentire Rocks Hotel is a small, friendly hotel owned and managed by Clive and Christine Mason. It retains the personal touch that only family ownership can bring and provides the perfect base from which to explore this picturesque area of the West Country. The conservatory lounge is the ideal place to relax and there is an open fire on chilly evenings. There is also a smaller TV lounge. The bar area is a comfortable meeting place for an apéritif. All 15 bedrooms have en suite facilities and offer a level of comfort that more than justifies the hotel's AA 2-star status. Two AA Rosettes for cuisine. Guests may choose from the à la carte or table d'hôte menus. The wine list would satisfy the most discerning palate. Service is attentive and friendly. There is a superb outdoor heated swimming pool. The North Cornwall coastal footpath runs just outside the hotel, while for the less energetic there are many magnificent houses and gardens to visit nearby. Surfers are well catered for at Polzeath, one of the safest and cleanest beaches in the West Country. **Directions:** From Launceston bypass, follow North Cornwall sign to Camelford and Wadebridge. Then head towards Port Isaac and follow signs to New Polzeath. Price guide: Single £38–£48; double/twin £76–£96. Special golf/breaks are available on request. Open Christmas and New Year.

DONNINGTON VALLEY HOTEL & GOLF COURSE

OLD OXFORD ROAD, DONNINGTON, NEWBURY, BERKSHIRE RG14 3AG
TEL: 01635 551199 FAX: 01635 551123

Uncompromising quality is the hallmark of this hotel and its 18-hole golf course that opened in 1991. The grandeur of the Edwardian era has been captured by the striking décor of the hotel's reception area with its splendid wood-panelled ceilings and impressive overhanging gallery. Each individually designed bedroom has been thoughtfully equipped to guarantee comfort and peace of mind. In addition to the standard guest rooms Donnington Valley offers a number of non-smoking rooms, family rooms, superior executive rooms and luxury suites. With its open log fire and elegant surroundings, the Piano Bar is an ideal place to meet friends or, alternatively, to enjoy the relaxed ambience of the Golf Bar. Guests may dine in the Gallery Restaurant which offers fine international cuisine complemented by an extensive choice of wines and liqueurs. The golf course is the perfect place to spend a relaxing weekend working on your handicap or to mix business with pleasure. Special corporate golfing packages are offered and tournaments can be arranged. Purpose-built conference suites provide the flexibility to meet the demands of today's executive meeting. **Directions:** Leave the M4 at junction 13, go south towards Newbury on A34, then follow signs for Donnington Castle. Price guide: Single £65–£108; double/twin £90–£128.

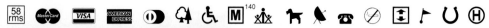

FOLEY LODGE HOTEL

STOCKCROSS, NEWBURY, BERKSHIRE RG20 8JU
TEL: 01635 528770 FAX: 01635 528398

Set in the heart of beautiful Berkshire, this former Victorian hunting lodge has been developed into a luxury Country House Hotel. The individually designed and furnished bedrooms overlook trees, garden and open countryside. The attractive Victorian décor in the award-winning à la carte restaurant reflects the superb quality of the hotel's fine French and traditional English cuisine. Head Chef, Ian Webb, uses the best ingredients to prepare his inventive dishes. Le Café Jardin Bistro offers a more informal alternative to the à la carte restaurant. The grand octagonal pagoda pool is surrounded by lush greenery and some exercise equipment, with an adjoining room housing a pool table and bar billiards. Comprehensive facilities are available to ensure that conference and business meetings run smoothly. Themed activity breaks can be arranged for racing weekends with visits to Newbury races and Lambourn stables, hot-air ballooning, or fishing and shooting. Within an hour's drive are the nearby attractions of Oxford, Salisbury, Winchester, Hungerford, Highclere and Windsor Castle. **Directions:** Foley Lodge is in the village of Stockcross on the B4000, 1¹/₂ miles west of Newbury and close to the M4, A4 and A34. Price guide: Single £50–£95; double/twin £70–£115; suite from £110.

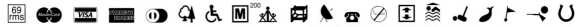

HOLLINGTON HOUSE HOTEL

WOOLTON HILL, NR NEWBURY, BERKSHIRE RG20 9XA
TEL: 01635 255100 FAX: 01635 255075

Hollington House Hotel, one of England's foremost luxury country house hotels, opened in July 1992. The Elizabethan-style house, built in 1904, is set in 25 acres of mature woodland gardens, adjacent to 250 acres of private parkland. Prior to returning to the UK after an absence of 32 years, John and Penny Guy created and owned Burnham Beeches Hotel, near Melbourne, which became Australia's first Relais et Châteaux hotel. No expense has been spared in their endeavours to achieve similar standards of excellence here. The 20 individually designed bedrooms are furnished with antiques and paintings and have sumptuous bathrooms. Elegant reception rooms, an oak-panelled, galleried hall and private boardroom are among the many splendid features of the house. Chef David Lake serves a modern style of cooking with flair and innovation, based on traditional English and French cuisine. Indoors there is a swimming pool and a full-size snooker table, outdoors a solar-heated swimming pool, a tennis court and a croquet lawn. The surrounding countryside offers opportunities for walking, shooting, hunting and horse-racing. Conference, wedding and weekend packages available.
Directions: From A343 Newbury– Andover road, follow signs for Hollington Herb Garden. Price guide: Single from £95; deluxe double/twin from £135; junior suite from £195.

LINDEN HALL HOTEL AND HEALTH SPA

LONGHORSLEY, MORPETH, NORTHUMBERLAND NE65 8XF
TEL: 01670 516611 FAX: 01670 788544

Ivy-clad, hidden away among 450 acres of fine park and woodland in mid-Northumberland, Linden Hall is a superb Georgian country house within easy reach of Newcastle-upon-Tyne. An impressive mile-long drive sweeps up to its main door where, upon entering, the visitor will discover a relaxed, dignified atmosphere enhanced by gracious marble hearths, antiques and period pieces. Those wishing to escape the urban stress will be delighted to find every fitness and relaxation requirement catered for at the health and beauty spa: beauty therapy treatments, fitness and steam room, swimming pool, sun terrace and solarium are all available on the premises. The 50 bedrooms are individually and elegantly furnished. Some rooms have four-poster beds; each has its own private bathroom, supplied with thoughtful extras. The Linden Pub serves informal drinks and the Dobson Restaurant, with panoramic views of the Northumberland coastline, serves delicious food, imaginatively prepared. Wedding receptions, banquets, dinner parties and business conferences can be held in comfort in any one of Linden Hall's conference and banqueting suites. **Directions:** From Newcastle take A1 north for 15 miles, then A697 toward Coldstream and Wooler. The hotel is one mile north of Longhorsley. Price guide: Single £97–£105; double/twin £125–£185; suite: £195.

SLALEY HALL

SLALEY, HEXHAM, NR NEWCASTLE-UPON-TYNE, NORTHUMBERLAND NE47 0BY
TEL: 01434 673350 FAX: 01434 673962

Slaley Hall was built as a private residence by the Hunting family in the true splendour of the Edwardian age. Now a hotel with a championship golf course, it is set in 1,000 acres of grounds which include woods, parks, moorland and the rarest Japanese gardens in Britain. Guests have a choice of restaurants, all of which serve superb food. The 142 bedrooms and suites are exquisitely designed with comfort in mind, while the furnished public rooms offer an ideal environment in which to relax and enjoy the wonderful surroundings. Elegant conference and banqueting suites have been designed to accommodate the most prestigious corporate and private events for up to 400 guests. In addition to one of the finest international championship golf courses in the North, the Tyne Valley offers some of the best salmon fishing in England. Sporting challenges such as clay pigeon shooting, off-road driving, riding and archery are available at Slaley Hall. There is also a fully-equipped gymnasium, sauna, steam, beauty treatment rooms and a 23 meter indoor swimming pool in landscaped surroundings. The area is rich in history and boasts some fine examples of medieval castles. It is close to Newcastle's international airport and the famous Metro Centre. **Directions:** From Newcastle take A69 towards Carlisle and then the A68 south. Slaley Hall is signposted from the road. Price guide: Single £107–£118; double/twin £125–£145; suites £270

PASSAGE HOUSE HOTEL

KINGSTEIGNTON, NEWTON ABBOT, DEVON TQ12 3QH
TEL: 01626 55515 FAX: 01626 63336

Overlooking the Teign Estuary, the Passage House Hotel has been designed to take advantage of the clear and panoramic views. Drawing inspiration from the natural beauty of the surrounding landscapes, the interior colour schemes are soft, muted shades of grey, blue and pink. The bedrooms provide every comfort, while the Penthouse rooms have a private terrace. The relaxing theme is continued in the reception rooms, with natural pale wood and mirrors enhancing the sense of space and light. Five-course table d'hôte and à la carte menus offer imaginatively prepared Devon recipes, using the freshest local fare, including Teign salmon, oysters and game. Throughout the hotel the service is extremely friendly and efficient. For active guests, there is a fully equipped leisure club, comprising indoor pool, hydro-spa, steam room, sauna, solarium and gymnasium. Sailing, water-skiing and golf are available locally. Racing fans should note that the hotel is located adjacent to Newton Abbot racecourse. The Devon heartland is rich in historical monuments, and the rugged scenery of Dartmoor is only minutes from the hotel. Special rate breaks available. **Directions:** Turn off A380 onto A381, follow signs to racecourse. Turn left at mini-roundabout; hotel is first left. Price guide: Single £59; double/twin £75–£85; suite £125.

REDWORTH HALL HOTEL & COUNTRY CLUB

REDWORTH, NR NEWTON AYCLIFFE, COUNTY DURHAM DL5 6NL
TEL: 01388 772442 FAX: 01388 775112 FAX (C&B): 01388 775660

Redworth Hall, a Grand Heritage Hotel, is a 17th-century, tastefully converted manor house situated in 25 acres of woodland. There are 100 en suite bedrooms, several of which are suitable for guests with disabilities. The furnishings throughout range from antique to fine reproduction. The hotel's health club includes a heated indoor swimming pool, with a hoist for guests with disabilities, a spa bath, sunbeds, steam bath, squash courts, sauna, snooker tables, all-weather tennis courts and a fully equipped gymnasium. There is an indoor play area and an outdoor adventure playground for children. There are 16 function rooms which can accommodate from 3 to 300 guests,

making the hotel ideal for conferences, training courses and weddings. In addition, Medieval Banquets are held in the Great Hall at various times throughout the year. Guests may choose between two restaurants: the elegant Crozier Blue Room offering innovative cuisine or the airy Conservatory which features a traditional carvery and contemporary à la carte menu. The hotel has 4 stars AA, RAC, 5 Crowns Highly Commended ETB and 2 AA Rosettes for food and service. **Directions:** A1(M) exit 58, A68 to Corbridge, then A6072 to Bishop Auckland; hotel two miles on left. Price guide: Single £98–£108; double/twin £115–£155; four-poster £150.

BROOKDALE HOUSE RESTAURANT AND HOTEL

NORTH HUISH, SOUTH BRENT, DEVON TQ10 9NR
TEL: 01548 821661 FAX: 01548 821606

This Grade II listed Tudor Gothic mansion is hidden away in a sequestered valley with four acres of picturesque gardens, lawns and woodland. It was originally built in the mid 19th century as a rectory and recently has been sensitively restored and renovated to its former glory. Fine examples of moulded ceilings, Gothic windows and beautiful marble fireplaces have been retained. The hotel's bedrooms, tastefully decorated and furnished with antiques, offer every modern comfort and convenience. The restaurant is at the heart of Brookdale House and the à la carte menu enjoys an excellent reputation locally. The proprietors have concentrated on providing high quality food using local produce: additive free meat, fresh organically grown vegetables and a range of unpasteurised Devon cheeses. The hotel, which prides itself on providing excellent and personal service, offers good facilities for small conferences of up to 40 people. Places of interest nearby include Dartmoor, Plymouth and Exeter, while leisure activities include riding, lawn tennis, hunting, fishing and walking. Dartington Hall is a short drive away, also Totnes and the Elizabethan Museum. **Directions:** Exit A38 at South Brent and follow signs to Avonwick. At Avon Inn turn right, then next left to North Huish. Price guide: Single £45–£55; double/twin £60–£90.

PARK FARM COUNTRY HOTEL & LEISURE

HETHERSETT, NORWICH, NORFOLK NR9 3DL
TEL: 01603 810264 FAX: 01603 812104

Park Farm Hotel occupies a tranquil and secluded location in beautifully landscaped grounds south of Norwich. There are executive rooms for additional comforts, with four poster beds and Jacuzzi baths. Additional bedrooms have been sympathetically converted from traditional buildings and new buildings to reflect the style of the six rooms available in the main house. A superb leisure complex to suit all ages has been carefully incorporated alongside the original Georgian house to include, heated swimming pool, sauna, steam room, solarium, spa bath, gymnasium and aerobics studio. The croquet lawn, putting green and hard tennis court are situated in the grounds. Associated with the hotel is a superb golf course. The delightful Georgian restaurant is renowned for high standards of cuisine and service, with a wide selection of dishes and fine choice of wines. Conference facilities cater for up to 120 candidates, (24 hour and daily delegate rates available). The Norfolk broads, the coast, Norwich open market, Castle museum and Cathedral are nearby.
Directions: By road, just off A11 on B1172, Norwich Airport eight miles, Norwich rail station six miles and Norwich bus station five miles. A light aircraft landing strip and helipad are in the grounds. Price guide: Single £60–£100; double/twin £70–£115; suite £120.

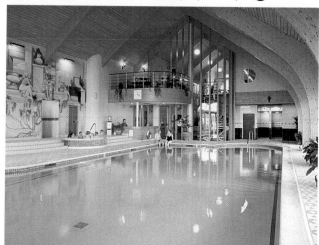

PETERSFIELD HOUSE HOTEL

LOWER STREET, HORNING, NR NORWICH, NORFOLK NR12 8PF
TEL: 01692 630741 FAX: 01692 630745

Petersfield House Hotel is set slightly back from the banks of one of the most attractive reaches of the River Bure. Surrounded by 2 acres of landscaped gardens, it occupies a choice position at the heart of Broadland. The charming location and private moorings are discreetly secluded, away from the crowds. However, in Broadland there are plenty of things to do: sailing can be enjoyed throughout the area and there are open regattas in the summer. Horning is midway between the medieval city of Norwich and the sweeping Norfolk coast. At the hotel, a regular Saturday night dinner-dance attracts many guests and non-residents. Varied fixed price and extensive à la carte menus are offered in the restaurant, where a comprehensive list of over 60 wines provides the ideal accompaniment to dinner. The bedrooms, many recently refurbished, are bright, comfortable and with en suite bathrooms. Most rooms overlook the well-tended gardens which feature a delightful lily pond, fountain and flintstone moon gate that links the gardens to a small woodland glade. The Petersfield is family-owned and managed, and guests can be assured of personal attention at all times. **Directions:** From Norwich ring road, take A1151 to Wroxham. At Hoveton take the A1062 to Horning; hotel is in centre of the village. Price guide: Single £60; double £75.

SPROWSTON MANOR HOTEL

SPROWSTON PARK, WROXHAM ROAD, NORWICH, NORFOLK NR7 8RP
TEL: 01603 410871 FAX: 01603 423911

This imposing country house, built originally in 1559 and then largely rebuilt in the 19th century, stands at the end of an oak-lined driveway in 10 acres of grounds, just 3 miles from Norwich. The bedrooms, all en suite and some with four-posters, have views over the hotel's parkland setting and are spacious and comfortable. The hotel has two restaurants. In The Orangery, lavishly draped Gothic arched windows provide the perfect atmosphere in which to enjoy the finest table d'hôte cuisine. The more traditional Manor Restaurant has been restored to classic splendour with mahogany columns, oil paintings and crystal chandeliers. The à la carte menu offers a good choice of dishes.

The large health spa with indoor swimming pool and leisure club, with spa bath, pool bar, fitness studio, steam rooms and sauna, are open to hotel residents free of charge. Solarium and beauty salon charged as taken. With its well-equipped conference rooms, the hotel is an excellent venue for social and business functions. Adjoining the hotel is the 18-hole Sprowston Park Golf Club, with floodlit driving range. The city of Norwich, Sandringham, the Norfolk Broads and the Norfolk coast are all within easy reach. **Directions:** From Norwich, take the Wroxham Road (A1151) and follow signs to Sprowston Park. Price guide: Single £79–£105; double/twin £85–£105.

LANGAR HALL

LANGAR, NOTTINGHAMSHIRE NG13 9HG
TEL: 01949 860559 FAX: 01949 861045

Set in the Vale of Belvoir, Langar Hall is the family home of Imogen Skirving. Built in 1830, it combines the standards of good hotel-keeping with the hospitality and style of country house living. Having received a warm welcome, guests can enjoy the atmosphere of a private home that is much loved and cared for. The 10 en suite bedrooms are individually designed and comfortably appointed. The public rooms feature fine furnishings and most rooms afford beautiful views of the garden, park and moat. As well as a collection of paintings from the 19th and 20th centuries on display in the pillared dining room, exhibitions by contemporary artists are regularly held here. Imogen and her kitchen team collaborate to produce an excellent, varied menu of modern British food. For the perfect start to the weekend it is worth booking early for a special Friday night break which combines a leisurely dinner with an entertaining in-house opera or theatre performance. It is an ideal venue for small boardroom meetings. Dogs can be accommodated by arrangement. **Directions:** Langar is accessible via Bingham on the A52, or via Cropwell Bishop from the A46 (both signposted). The house adjoins the church and is hidden behind it. Price guide: Single £60–£80; double/twin £85–£125.

HAMBLETON HALL

HAMBLETON, OAKHAM, RUTLAND, LEICESTERSHIRE LE15 8TH
TEL: 01572 756991 FAX: 01572 724721

Hambleton Hall, originally a comfortable Victorian house, was converted into a superb country house hotel in 1979. It enjoys a spectacular lakeside setting in a charming and unspoilt area of Rutland. The hotel's tasteful interiors have been designed to create elegance and comfort, retaining individuality by avoiding a catalogue approach to furnishing. Delightful displays of flowers, an artful blend of ingredients from local hedgerows and Nine Elms market, complement many rooms. In the restaurant, the chef and his enthusiastic team offer a menu which is strongly seasonal. Grouse, Scottish ceps and chanterelles, partridge and woodcock are all available at just the right time of year, accompanied by the best vegetables, herbs and salads from the Hall's garden. The dishes are beautifully presented and supported by a list of interesting wines at reasonable prices. For the energetic there are lovely walks around the lake and opportunities for tennis and swimming, golf, riding, bicycling, trout fishing, and sailing. Burghley House and Belton are nearby, as are the antique shops of Oakham, Uppingham and Stamford. Hambleton Hall is a Relais et Chateaux member. **Directions:** In the village of Hambleton, signposted from the A606, 1 mile east of Oakham. Price guide: Single £105; double/twin £105–£270.

CHEVIN LODGE COUNTRY PARK HOTEL

YORKGATE, OTLEY, WEST YORKSHIRE LS21 3NU
TEL: 01943 467818 FAX: 01943 850335 FREEPHONE RESERVATIONS 0500 340560

A quite unique hotel – you would probably need to travel to Scandinavia to discover a similar complex to Chevin Lodge. Built entirely of Finnish logs and surrounded by birch trees, it is set in 50 acres of lake and woodland in the beauty spot of Chevin Forest Park. The spacious, carefully designed bedrooms are furnished with pine and wicker and some have patio doors leading to the lakeside gardens. In addition, there are several luxury lodges tucked away in the woods, some with their own kitchen, which provide alternative accommodation to the hotel bedrooms. Imaginative and appetising meals are served in the beautiful balconied restaurant, which overlooks the lake.

Chevin Lodge offers conference facilities in the Woodlands Suite which is fully equipped for all business requirements. For the sporty there is a games room, all-weather tennis court and jogging and cycling trails that wind through the woods. Hotel guests also enjoy free membership of an exclusive nearby leisure club. Hotel swimming pool opens February 1996. Leeds, Bradford and Harrogate are within 20 minutes' drive. Special weekend breaks are available. **Directions:** From A658 between Bradford and Harrogate, take the Chevin Forest Park road, then left into Yorkgate for Chevin Lodge. Price guide: Single £85–£95; double/twin £95–£115.

LE MANOIR AUX QUAT' SAISONS

GREAT MILTON, OXFORDSHIRE OX44 7PD
TEL: 01844 278881 FAX: 01844 278847

Situated in secluded grounds a few miles south of the historic city of Oxford in rural Cotswold countryside, the restaurant and the country house hotel of Le Manoir aux Quat' Saisons are among the finest in Europe. Le Manoir is the inspired creation of Raymond Blanc whose extraordinary cooking has received the highest tributes from all international guides to culinary excellence. Uniquely, the London Times gives Blanc's cooking 10 out of 10 and rates it 'the best in Britain'. The atmosphere throughout is one of understated elegance while all nineteen bedrooms and suites offer guests the highest standards of comfort and luxury. Every need is anticipated, for service is a way of life here, never intrusive but always present. For dedicated 'foodies', Le Petit Blanc, Raymond Blanc's highly successful cookery school, is a must. Five-day courses are run from October to April and participation is restricted to eight guests to ensure the highest level of personal tuition. Participants stay at Le Manoir and their partners are welcome to stay free of charge although their meals and drinks are charged separately. **Directions:** From London, M40 and turn off at junction 7 (A329 to Wallingford). From the North, leave M40 at junction 8 and follow signs to Wallingford (A329). After $1^1/_2$ miles, take second turning on right, Great Milton Manor. Price guide: Double/twin £175–£275; suites £325–£375.

STUDLEY PRIORY

HORTON-CUM-STUDLEY, OXFORD, OXFORDSHIRE OX33 1AZ
TEL: 01865 351203 FAX: 01865 351613

Studley Priory, its exterior little altered since Elizabethan days, is conveniently located only 7 miles from both the main London–Oxford road and the dreaming spires of Oxford. There is a sense of timeless seclusion in the setting of 13 acres of wooded grounds with their fine views of the Cotswolds, the Chilterns and the Vale of Aylesbury. The bedrooms range from single rooms to the Elizabethan Suite, which has a half-tester bed dating from around 1700. Cots are available for young children. The restaurant, offering the best of English and French cuisine, provides a seasonally changing menu created from fresh local produce and complemented by an extensive and well-balanced wine list. Good conference facilities are available, and wedding parties and banquets can be accommodated. Studley Priory is ideally placed for visits to Blenheim Palace, the Manors of Waddesdon and Milton, Broughton Castle, the Great Western Museum of Railways and also horse-racing at Ascot, Newbury and Cheltenham. Clay pigeon shooting and many other activities can be arranged at the hotel and there are riding facilities nearby. A member of the Hatton Hotels Group. **Directions:** Leave M40 at junction 8. The hotel is situated at the top of the hill in the village of Horton-cum-Studley. Price guide: Single £90; double/twin £100–£150; suite £210.

THE SEAFOOD RESTAURANT & ST PETROC'S

RIVERSIDE, PADSTOW, CORNWALL PL28 8BY
RESERVATIONS: 01841 532485 FAX: 01841 533344

The Seafood Restaurant stands on the estuary bank in the enchanting North Cornish fishing port of Padstow, along a stretch of coastline noted for its outstanding natural beauty. Annexed to the restaurant is St Petroc's House, a charming 18th century Merchant's House which is now a little hotel with its own bistro. The chefs from the Seafood Restaurant, who have built up an international reputation for the most innovative fish and shellfish cuisine, also prepare the food for St Petroc's hotel. Opposite the restaurant is the quay where the lobster boats and trawlers unload their haul, so the fish comes straight from the sea into the kitchen and onto the table. The menus are simple, relying on the delights that only freshly caught fish, with its unmistakable flavour and fine texture, can give. The bedrooms, both those in the hotel and those above the restaurant, are comfortably furnished and most command fine views over the harbour. Several of the bathrooms are richly panelled with mahogany. A full English or continental breakfast is served in the restaurant. Closeby are lovely sandy beaches. Water sports, clifftop walks and golf are all leisure activities available in the vicinity. Closed from just before Christmas to end of January. **Directions:** Opposite the quay in Padstow. Free car parking opposite. Price guide: Single £25–£75.90; double/twin £52–£115.

    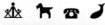

In association with MasterCard

TEMPLE SOWERBY HOUSE HOTEL

TEMPLE SOWERBY, PENRITH, CUMBRIA CA10 1RZ
TEL: 017683 61578 FAX: 017683 61958

Temple Sowerby House looks over at Cross Fell, the highest peak in the Pennines, noted for its spectacular ridge walk. This old Cumbrian farmhouse, formerly the principal residence of the village, is set in two acres of gardens and guests are assured of peace and quiet. The owners offer a warm, hospitable and friendly family service upon which the hotel prides itself. There are two dining rooms – the panelled room with its cosy atmosphere and the Rose Room which overlooks the garden. Delicious, home-cooked dishes might include a starter of avocado cheescake with piquant tomato sauce, followed by fillet of beef with a brandy and mixed peppercorn cream, rounded off with a pudding of warm fudge nut pie and butterscotch sauce. Individually furnished bedrooms all have private bathrooms. Four of the rooms are situated in the Coach House, just yards from the main house, overlooking the cobbled yard and garden. During the winter, apéritifs are taken by the fireside, while in the summer, guests can sip drinks on the terrace and enjoy views across the fells. Lakes Ullswater and Derwentwater, the Borders, Scottish Lowlands, Hadrian's Wall and Yorkshire Dales are within easy reach by car.
Directions: Temple Sowerby lies on the A66, five miles from exit 40 of the M6, between Penrith and Appleby. Price guide: Single £50–£55; double/twin £70–£80.

THE HAYCOCK

WANSFORD-IN-ENGLAND, PETERBOROUGH, CAMBRIDGESHIRE PE8 6JA
TEL: 01780 782223 FAX: 01780 783031

The Haycock, in a village happily skirted by the A1, is a handsome old hotel of great charm and character, where nothing is too much trouble for the staff. Overlooking the historic bridge that spans the River Nene, the hotel maintains much of its original personality while providing a full range of contemporary comforts. An award-winning restoration programme has created an additional 28 bedrooms. All are colourful, individually designed and furnished to a high standard. A purpose-built ballroom is a popular venue for a wide range of events, from May Balls, wedding receptions, Christmas parties and casino nights to the East Anglian Wine Festival. The Business Centre has also made its mark; it is well equipped with all facilities and offers the flexibility to cater for meetings, car launches, product seminars and national conferences. Amid this activity the Tapestry and Orchard Rooms, bar and terrace all provide traditional hospitality combined with great charm – as does the restaurant, with its wine list attracting particular attention. The Haycock offers such a diverse range of amenities – including a new country pursuits programme – that every need can be accommodated. **Directions:** Clearly signposted on A1 a few miles south of Stamford, on A1/A47 intersection west of Peterborough. Price guide: Single £72–£85; double/twin £95–£115.

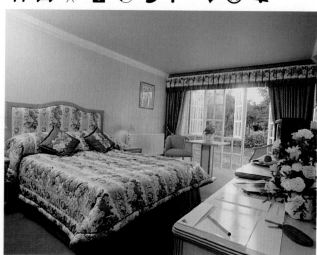

ALSTON HALL COUNTRY HOUSE HOTEL

ALSTON, HOLBETON, NR PLYMOUTH, DEVON PL8 1HN
TEL: 01752830 555 FAX: 01752830 494

Alston Hall is an impressive Edwardian manor house set in over four acres of lightly wooded parkland with expansive views across the soft rolling hills to the sea beyond. Located in one of the most beautiful, unspoiled regions of South Devon, midway between Plymouth and Kingsbridge near to the village of Holbeton in the South Hams, Alston Hall provides peace and comfort – the perfect place in which to relax and unwind. The oak-panelled Great Hall, with its balustraded minstrels gallery and stained-glass windows, acts as an elegant drawing room in which to dawdle with a drink or after-dinner coffee. The Peony Room Restaurant draws inspiration from traditional English and French culinary styles. The menu, which caters for all tastes, makes good use of fresh seafood and local farm produce. Alston Hall invites guests to enjoy the good life. In addition to the 20 delightful bedrooms, spacious public rooms and conference facilities, guests during their stay may use the Leisure Club where the amenities include both indoor and outdoor swimming pools, sauna, solarium, croquet and two all-weather tennis courts. AA Red Rosette. **Directions:** From A379, follow signs to Holbeton/Alston. Continue for about four miles to Battisborough Cross. Take first right signed Alston Hall. Price guide: Single £85; double/twin £100–£120.

MOORLAND LINKS HOTEL AND RESTAURANT

YELVERTON, NR PLYMOUTH, DEVON PL20 6DA
TEL: 01822 852245 FAX: 01822 855004

Surrounded by nine acres of well-kept grounds in a superlative setting, the Moorland Links Hotel is a dignified country retreat with spectacular views of remote and romantic moorland scenery. Over the past 10 years, since its takeover by Forestdale Hotels, the residence has been internally updated and extended with luxurious effect: stylishly decorated throughout with plush furniture, pastel walls and interesting prints, the Moorland guarantees a pleasurable and stress-free stay for business visitors and holidaymakers alike. All 45 en suite bedrooms have been individually designed and decorated with comfort in mind; little extras in each include trouser press, remote-control TV and hairdryers. After apéritifs in the lounge, guests may proceed to the restaurant overlooking the lawns, to sample first-class cooking prepared by chef Stephen Holmes, who can summon up everything from Japanese prawn dumplings to spicy vegetable tortillas, plus traditional dishes. Private and business functions are held in the various engagement rooms. The wildly beautiful Dartmoor National Park is a magnet for walkers; Plymouth, Buckland Abbey and golf are close by. **Directions:** A38 Exeter–Plymouth; A386 towards Tavistock for about five miles on to open moorland. Hotel signposted one mile on. Price guide: Single £61.95–£71.95; double/twin £79–£99; suite £115–£130.

THE MANSION HOUSE

THAMES STREET, POOLE, DORSET BH15 1JN
TEL: 01202 685666 FAX: 01202 665709

A sophisticated Georgian town residence, The Mansion House Hotel is set in a prime location just off Poole's busy quayside, in a quiet cul-de-sac adjacent to St James's Church – offering its visitors a calm retreat. Restored by its owners, The Mansion House provides every modern luxury. From the entrance hall a splendid staircase sweeps up to an elegant hallway featuring statuesque marble pillars. Pretty bedrooms demonstrate the personal touch; all are distinctively styled and named after a famous Georgian or Victorian character. A drink and a crudité in the Canadian Redwood Cocktail Bar – a popular haunt of local business people – is the ideal prelude to a fine meal. Good, English gourmet cooking is served in the panelled Dining Club restaurant. Lunches and lighter meals are also offered downstairs in the less formal Bistro, where stone walls and stripped oak furniture create a rustic atmosphere. Two conference rooms provide good private meeting facilities. For the sports enthusiast, all manner of water activities are available, while local places of interest include the harbour, sandy beaches, the Isle of Purbeck and Corfe Castle. **Directions:** Poole is reached from the M3 via the M27, A31, A349 and A350. Thames Street runs between The Quay and West Street by Poole Bridge. Price guide: Single £75–£80; double/twin £100–£120; suite £150.

THE LUGGER HOTEL

PORTLOE, NR TRURO, CORNWALL TR2 5RD
TEL: 01872 501322 FAX: 01872 501691

A 17th century inn by the sea – and reputed to have been the haunt of smugglers, it sits at the very water's edge in the picturesque fishing village of Portloe. Situated in a conservation area in the heart of the beautiful Roseland Peninsula, this internationally renowned hotel is like a solid rock in a changing world. The Lugger has been in the Powell family for three generations during which much thought and care have been taken to preserve it's welcoming intimate atmosphere. There are 19 tastefully furnished bedrooms, all with en suite facilities as well as personal safes and refrigerators. A skilled team of chefs offer varied and exciting menus of English and Continental dishes in the attractive restaurant overlooking the Cove. Local seafood is a speciality, with crab and lobster being particular favourites. The freshly made desserts on the sweet trolley, topped with clotted cream, are a delight to both the eye and the palate, whilst there is a wide choice of wines including Cornish wine from just a mile away. English Tourist Board 4 Crowns Highly Commended. Closed mid-November until early February. **Directions:** A390 from Plymouth, B3287 from St Austell to Tregony, then A3078 to Portloe. Price guide (including dinner): Single £60–£70; double/twin £110–£140.

THE BRIDGE HOTEL

PRESTBURY, CHESHIRE SK10 4DQ
TEL: 01625 829326 FAX: 01625 827557

The Bridge Hotel is situated in the centre of the village of Prestbury, one of the prettiest villages in the North West of England. Originally dating from 1626, The Bridge today combines the old world charm of an ancient and historic building with the comfort and facilities of a modern hotel, yet within easy reach of Manchester Airport and major motorways. The public rooms have retained much of the inn's original character, with oak panelling and beams in the bar and reception area. The bedrooms, many of which overlook the River Bollin, are decorated to the highest standard, with 5 rooms in the old building and a further 18 in a recently added wing. In the attractive galleried dining room, table d'hôte and à la carte menus offer traditional English cuisine. There is an extensive selection of wines to accompany your meal. Conference and banqueting facilities are available. Places to visit nearby include the Peak District National Park, Chatsworth, Tatton Park and Liverpool's Albert Dock. While enjoying a quiet location, the hotel is convenient for Manchester, just 30 minutes away, Liverpool, and the medieval city of Chester, which is under 40 minutes' drive. **Directions:** In the centre of the village next to the church. Prestbury is on the A538 from Wilmslow to Macclesfield. Price guide: Single £74; double/twin £84–£110.

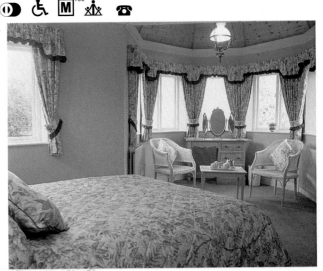

THE GIBBON BRIDGE HOTEL

NR CHIPPING, FOREST OF BOWLAND, LANCASHIRE PR3 2TQ
TEL: 01995 61456 FAX: 01995 61277

You will be 'Forever The Richer' having stayed at The Gibbon Bridge, set in award winning grounds abounding with trees, wildlife and a tarn. Now in their 13th year, Janet Simpson and her enthusiastic, attentive team provide a welcome retreat well placed for exploring Lancashire's heritage in the Forest of Bowland; yet only 20 minutes from the M6 and London/Glasgow railway at Preston. The 8 bedrooms and 22 suites include four-poster, half-tester, and Gothic brass beds, Jacuzzi baths and the Staple Oak Suite's private garden. The restaurant is renowned for its traditional and imaginative dishes using fresh herbs and vegetables from the kitchen garden and complemented by the extensive wine list. Elegant, unintrusive conference facilities incorporate up-to-date audio-visual and communication equipment. Leisure facilities include gymnasium, solarium, steam room, and an all-weather tennis court. Numerous sporting activities can be arranged. **Directions:** M6 exit 32, A6 to Broughton, B5269 to Longridge, follow signs to Chipping. Turn right at 'T' junction in village – hotel one mile outside the village on the right. Price guide: Single £70; double/twin £80; suite £95–£180.

NUTFIELD PRIORY

NUTFIELD, REDHILL, SURREY RH1 4EN
TEL: 01737 822066 FAX: 01737 823321

Built in 1872 by the millionaire MP, Joshua Fielden, Nutfield Priory is an extravagant folly embellished with towers, elaborate carvings, intricate stonework, cloisters and stained glass, all superbly restored to create an unusual country-house hotel. Set high on Nutfield Ridge, the priory has far-reaching views over the Surrey and Sussex countryside, while being within easy reach of London and also Gatwick Airport. The elegant lounges and library have ornately carved ceilings and antique furnishings. Unusually spacious bedrooms – some with beams – enjoy views over the surrounding countryside. Fresh fruit is a thoughtful extra. The cloistered restaurant provides a unique environment in which to enjoy the high standard of cuisine, complemented by an extensive wine list. Conferences and private functions can be accommodated in the splendid setting of one of the hotel's 10 conference rooms. The Priory sports and leisure club, adjacent to the hotel, provides all the facilities for exercise and relaxation that one could wish for, including a swimming pool, sauna, spa, solarium, gym, steam room and billiard room. **Directions:** Nutfield is on the A25 between Redhill and Godstone and can be reached easily from junctions 6 and 8 of the M25. From Godstone, the Priory is on the left just after the village. Price guide: Single £105; double/twin £125–£190; suite £225.

For hotel location, see maps on pages 473–479

251

THE RICHMOND GATE HOTEL AND RESTAURANT

RICHMOND HILL, RICHMOND-UPON-THAMES, SURREY TW10 6RP
TEL: 0181 940 0061 FAX: 0181 332 0354 – FROM USA TOLL FREE: 1-800 544 9993

This former Georgian country house stands on the crest of Richmond Hill close to the Royal Park and Richmond Terrace with its commanding views over the River Thames. The 66 stylishly furnished en suite bedrooms combine every comfort of the present with the elegance of the past and include several luxury four-poster rooms and suites. Exceptional and imaginative cuisine, complemented by prize-winning English country wines, is on offer in the sophisticated surroundings of 'Gates On The Park Restaurant'. Through the week a less formal alternative is available in the Bistro in the Victorian conservatory, overlooking the hotel's beautiful walled garden. Weddings, business meetings and private dining events can be arranged in a variety of rooms. A superb new leisure club includes a 20 metre swimming pool and extensive facilities for relaxation and recreation. Richmond is a unique town, close to central London and the West End yet in a country setting. The Borough offers a wealth of visitor attractions, including Hampton Court Palace, Syon House and Park and the Royal Botanic Gardens at Kew. Weekend breaks are inclusive of entry into one of the local attractions and are available from £98. **Directions:** Opposite the Star & Garter Home at the top of Richmond Hill. Price guide: Single £65–£95; double/twin £80–£155.

THE CHASE HOTEL

GLOUCESTER ROAD, ROSS-ON-WYE, HEREFORDSHIRE HR9 5LH
TEL: 01989 763161 FAX: 01989 768330

The Chase Hotel, just a few minutes' walk from the centre of Ross-on-Wye, is a handsome Regency country house standing in pleasant grounds. Careful restoration of the interiors has recaptured the elegance and craftsmanship of the past. After an apéritif in the Chase Bar, guests are ushered into the dining room where the tall windows and voluminous drapes make a striking impression. Chef Ken Tait favours a modern British approach to cooking, with a distinct Continental influence. He uses fine local produce, such as Herefordshire beef, game and fresh vegetables in combination, to create dishes that give an unexpected subtlety to traditional ingredients. When the bedrooms were renovated, great care was taken to preserve their original Georgian character: the effect was then softened with comfortable furniture and appealing fabrics. Unobtrusive, up-to-the-minute amenities have been provided in each room and en suite bathroom. The function suites can accommodate a host of events. The surrounding area offers an infinite variety of places to visit, including Hereford Cathedral, Symonds Yat, Monmouth and the Forest of Dean. **Directions:** From M50 exit 4 turn left at roundabout signposted Gloucester and right at first roundabout signposted 'Town Centre'. Hotel is ½ mile on left-hand side. Price guide: Single £65; double/twin £80; suite £110.

PENGETHLEY MANOR

NR ROSS-ON-WYE, HEREFORDSHIRE HR9 6LL
TEL: 01989 730211 FAX: 01989 730238

The first Baron Chandos, a favourite of Mary I Queen of England, reputed to have acquired Pengethley Estate in 1544, and here he built the original Tudor house. Although much of the building was ravaged by fire in the early 19th century, some parts survived – notably the oak panelling in the entrance hall – and it was rebuilt as a Georgian manor house in 1820. The en suite bedrooms reflect the traditional character of a former nobleman's country home. Drawing on the best produce that rural Herefordshire can offer, the menu includes Wye salmon, prime Hereford beef and tender Welsh lamb. Fresh herbs, grapes for future wine production and soft fruit are all grown within the manor boundaries. A complete vegetarian menu is also available. Throughout their stay at Pengethley, guests will find the service always attentive, but never intrusive. Chandos House is a purpose-built conference suite which can cater for business and social events. For leisure, there is a snooker room, a well-stocked trout lake, a 9-hole golf improvement course and an outdoor heated pool. Riding and hot-air ballooning can be arranged. The Wye Valley and Welsh border are not very far away and the Malvern Hills are nearby. **Directions:** Four miles from Ross-on-Wye, 10 miles from Hereford on the A49. Price guide: Single £70–£115; double/twin £100–£160.

BROOMHILL LODGE

RYE FOREIGN, RYE, EAST SUSSEX TN31 7UN
TEL: 01797 280421 FAX: 01797 280402

Imposing and ivy-bedecked, Broomhill is a dramatic mock-Jacobean construction towering above three green acres and dating back to the 1820s, when it was commissioned by a prominent local banker. Giving pleasing views over rolling East Sussex terrain, the hotel has been renovated with care by its new owners to offer a standard of accommodation as impressive as the architecture. Relaxed, informal, yet unerringly professional, the management and staff have quickly established an elegant, comfortable and warm place to stay. All 12 rooms are equipped with en suite bath or shower rooms and all modern conveniences. Four-poster bedrooms are available. A splendid new conservatory-style restaurant serves innovative cuisine expertly prepared. A fixed-price menu offers a wide choice (three-course lunch £14.50, dinner £18.50) and a typical menu might include calamares, then venison with cranberries followed by chocolate torte. Special tariffs apply for bookings of two or more nights. Sports available locally include windsurfing, sailing, angling, clay-pigeon shooting and golf on the famous links nearby. Hastings, Winchelsea, Romney Marsh and Battle Abbey are all nearby and worth visiting. **Directions:** $1\frac{1}{2}$ miles north of Rye on A268. Price guide: Single £52; double/twin £104.

BARNSDALE LODGE

THE AVENUE, RUTLAND WATER, NR OAKHAM, RUTLAND, LEICESTERSHIRE LE15 8AH
TEL: 01572 724678 FAX: 01572 724961

Situated in the heart of the ancient county of Rutland, amid unspoiled countryside, Barnsdale Lodge overlooks the rippling expanse of Rutland Water. Guests are invited to enjoy the hospitality offered by hosts The Hon. Thomas Noel and Robert Reid (who is also host at his sister hotel, Normanton Park). A restored 17th-century farmhouse, the atmosphere and style are distinctively Edwardian. This theme pervades throughout, from the courteous service to the furnishings – including chaises-longues and plump, upholstered chairs. The 29 en suite bedrooms, many of which are on the ground floor, including two superb rooms specifically designed for disabled guests, evoke a mood of relaxing comfort. Traditional English cooking and fine wines are served. A silver trolley of prime roast beef is always available. Elevenses, buttery lunches, afternoon teas and suppers may be enjoyed in the garden conservatory or courtyard. There are three conference rooms and facilities for wedding receptions and parties. A baby-listening service and safe play area are provided for children. Belvoir and Rockingham Castles and Burghley House are nearby. Rutland Water offers a wide range of water sports, as well as being of interest to nature lovers, including an Aquatic and Butterfly Centre. **Directions:** Barnsdale Lodge is situated on the A606 Oakham–Stamford road. Price guide: Single £49.50; double/twin £69.50; suite £79.

For hotel location, see maps on pages 473–479

NORMANTON PARK HOTEL

NORMANTON PARK, RUTLAND WATER SOUTH SHORE, RUTLAND, LEICESTERSHIRE LE15 8RP
TEL: 01780 720315 FAX: 01780 721086

Situated alongside the famous 'submerged' church overlooking England's largest man-made reservoir, Normanton Park Hotel has been meticulously restored from its origins as the coach house to Normanton Park Hall. The Grade II listed hotel is set in four acres of grounds, which were landscaped in the 18th century and have one of the country's oldest Cedar of Lebanon trees. Many of the bedrooms overlook the lake, which provides fly and coarse fishing, boat hire, wind-surfing, kite-flying, cycling, walking and birdwatching. The Sailing Bar offers a warm welcome, and a good variety of meals, snacks and drinks is served throughout the day. Designed on an orangery theme, the delightful restaurant offers a gourmet's choice of both à la carte and reasonably priced Sunday lunch table d'hôte menus. The cocktail bar, decorated with ancient bellows and a blazing log fire in cooler months, makes a relaxing lounge area for guests. Many stately homes and National Trust properties are nearby and the A1 is easily accessible. Helicopters may be landed at Barnsdale Lodge, sister hotel to Normanton Park, and guests transeferred from there. **Directions:** From the A1, take A606 at Stamford towards Oakham; turn along the south shore road towards Edith Weston. Price guide: Single £49.50; double/twin £69.50; suite/lake view £79.50.

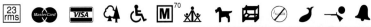

ROSE-IN-VALE COUNTRY HOUSE HOTEL

MITHIAN, ST AGNES, CORNWALL TR5 0QD
TEL: 01872 552202 FAX: 01872 552700

In recent years this 18th century Cornish manor house has been carefully upgraded, extended and refurbished and the sympathetic design of the extensions has successfully blended the old with the new. The decor throughout the bedrooms and the elegant public rooms reflects a restrained floral theme contrasting with dark mahogany and a new extension offers superior rooms with lovely views across the valley gardens. The new dining room is named after John Opie, the 18th century portrait painter born in the valley. Table d'hôte and à la carte menus are offered and Cornish seafood dishes are a speciality. The wine list represents a variety of countries and a Director's Bin of fine wines is also kept. The hotel hides away in a glorious secluded setting of 11 acres in a wooded valley of great natural beauty and there is a pervading atmosphere of peace and relaxation. The gardens feature ponds with a collection of waterfowl, woodland and pasture, with a stream running through. A heated swimming pool is located in the flower gardens. The magnificent Cornish coast, numerous gardens and National Trust properties, horseriding, watersports, walking, golf and flying are closeby. **Directions:** Via A30 through Cornwall. Two miles after village of Zelah turn right onto B3284. Cross A3075. Take third left turning to Rose in Vale. Price guide: Single £45–£55; double/twin £96–£110; suites £130.

ST MICHAEL'S MANOR HOTEL

FISHPOOL STREET, ST ALBANS, HERTFORDSHIRE AL3 4RY
TEL: 01727 864444 FAX: 01727 848909

The medieval foundations of this imposing privately owned manor house still form part of its cellars. Originally constructed in 1512, the fascinating history of St Michael's Manor is reflected in the diversity of architectural features – from its William and Mary structure to the recent Victorian-style conservatory – which blend together surprisingly well. Part of the early Tudor building, the Oak Lounge, makes a good reception area for private functions, with its fine Elizabethan plastered ceiling displaying *fleur de lys* and stylised floral bosses. Chintz fabrics and pastel colours together with an abundance of fresh flowers create a relaxing impression that complements the amiable welcome which has earned the hotel an RAC Merit Award for Hospitality. In the elegant, chandeliered restaurant an extensive menu offers international cooking with something to suit all tastes. The Bar Lounge leads to 5 acres of award-winning gardens, where the resident collection of wildfowl can be seen paddling about in the ornamental lake. The heart of Roman Verulamium is a 5-minute walk away, with its Roman theatre and hypocaust, museums, cathedral and antiques shops. Dogs accommodated by arrangement. **Directions:** Fishpool Street runs from the Abbey at the junction of the A5183 and A1081. The hotel is a few minutes walk from the town centre. Price guide from: Single £70; double/twin £80.

SOPWELL HOUSE HOTEL & COUNTRY CLUB

COTTONMILL LANE, SOPWELL, ST ALBANS, HERTFORDSHIRE AL1 2HQ
TEL: 01727 864477 FAX: 01727 844741/845636

The opening of a country club and health spa has firmly established Sopwell House among the area's leading hotels. An elegant Georgian manor, it offers a high degree of comfort and service while retaining a country house ambience. Peacefully set in 12 acres, surrounded by unspoiled countryside, Sopwell House is 30 minutes from London and 22 miles from Heathrow – ideal for executives or for a leisure break. The individually furnished bedrooms are all well equipped and many have four-poster beds. Overlooking the gardens, the distinctive Magnolia conservatory restaurant boasting 2 AA Rosettes provides modern cuisine from an imaginative seasonal menu. State-of-the-art health and leisure facilities include an ozone-purified swimming pool, fitness centre and a full range of specialist beauty treatments. Bejerano's Brasserie serves light, healthy dishes, including vegetarian options. A purpose-built conference centre, incorporating an impressive ballroom, offers excellent provision for banquets, dances and corporate events. Woburn Abbey, Hatfield House and St Albans' Roman sites are nearby. The hotel is convenient for the M1, M10, M25 and local railway station (Thameslink is 20 minutes to King's Cross). Dogs by arrangement. Special breaks available. **Directions:** Take A1081 from A414 Hatfield–St Albans road. Price guide: Single £68; double/twin £85; suite £129.

THE GARRACK HOTEL

BURTHALLAN LANE, ST IVES, CORNWALL TR26 3AA
TEL: 01736 796199 FAX: 01736 798955

This intimate, family-run hotel, secluded and full of character, is set in two acres of gardens with fabulous sea views over Porthmeor Beach, the St Ives Tate Gallery and the old town of St Ives. The bedrooms in the original house are in keeping with the style of the building. The additional rooms are modern in design. All rooms have private bathrooms and baby-listening facilities. Superior rooms have either four-poster beds or whirlpool baths. A ground-floor room has been fitted for guests with disabilities. Visitors return year after year to enjoy informal yet professional service, good food and hospitality. The restaurant specialises in seafood especially fresh lobsters. The wine list includes over 70 labels from ten regions. The lounges have books, magazines and board games for all, and open fires. The small attractive leisure centre contains a small swimming pool with integral spa, sauna, solarium and fitness area. The hotel has its own car park. Porthmeor Beach, just below the hotel, is renowned for surfing. Riding, golf, bowls, sea-fishing and other activites can be enjoyed locally. St Ives, with its harbour, is famous for artists and for the new St Ives Tate Gallery. Dogs by prior arrangement. **Directions:** A30–A3074–B3311–B3306. Go ½ mile, turn left at mini-roundabout, hotel signs are on the left as the road starts down hill. Price guide: Single £58–£61; double/twin £84–£122.

THE WELL HOUSE

ST KEYNE, LISKEARD, CORNWALL PL14 4RN
TEL: 01579 342001 FAX: 01579 343891

The West Country is one corner of England where hospitality and friendliness are at their most spontaneous, and nowhere more so than at The Well House, just beyond the River Tamar. New arrivals are entranced by their first view of this lovely Victorian country manor. Its façade wrapped in rambling wisteria and jasmine trailers is just one of a continuous series of delights including top-quality service, modern luxury and impeccable standards of comfort and cooking. The hotel is professionally managed by proprietor Nick Wainford, whose attention to every smallest detail has earned his hotel numerous awards, among them the AA 2 Red Stars. From the tastefully appointed bedrooms there are fine rural views, and each private bathroom offers luxurious bath linen, soaps and gels by Bronnley. Continental breakfast is served in bed – or a traditional English breakfast may be taken in the dining room. Chef Wayne Pearson selects fresh, seasonal produce to create his superbly balanced and presented cuisine. Tennis, swimming and croquet are on site, and the Cornish coastline offers matchless scenery and walking territory. St Keyne has a Mechanical Music Centre. **Directions:** Leave A38 at Liskeard, take A390 to town centre, then take B3254 south to St Keyne Well and hotel. Price guide: Single £60; double/twin £67.50–£105.

THE NARE HOTEL

CARNE BEACH, VERYAN-IN-ROSELAND, TRURO TR2 5PF
TEL: 01872 501279 FAX: 01872 501856

The Nare Hotel overlooks the fine sandy beach of Gerrans Bay, facing south, and is sheltered by The Nare and St Mawes headlands. In recent years extensive refurbishments have ensured comfort and elegance without detracting from the country house charm of this friendly hotel. All the bedrooms are within 100 yards of the sea, many with patios or balconies to take advantage of the outlook. While dining in the restaurant, with its colour scheme of soft yellow and green, guests can enjoy the sea views from three sides of the room. Local seafoods such as lobster, and delicious home-made puddings, served with Cornish cream, are specialities, complemented by an interesting range of wines. The Nare recently became the highest rated AA 4 Star hotel in the South West with a rosette for its food. Surrounded by sub-tropical gardens and National Trust land, the peaceful seclusion of The Nare is ideal for lazing or for exploring the coastline and villages of the glorious Roseland Peninsula. Facilities include concessionary golf and water sports. Guests arriving by train can be met by prior arrangement at Truro. Closed 4th January to 4th February (booking office open). Helipad within the grounds. **Directions:** Follow road to St Mawes; 3 miles after Tregony Bridge turn left for Veryan. The hotel is 1 mile from Veryan. Price guide: Single £50–£119; double/twin £100–£205.

BOLT HEAD HOTEL

SOUTH SANDS, SALCOMBE, SOUTH DEVON TQ8 8LL
TEL: 01548 843751 FAX: 01548 843060

Bolt Head Hotel occupies a spectacular position overlooking Salcombe Estuary, where the mild climate ensures a lengthy holiday season. New improvements have ensured that guests can enjoy a fine range of modern comforts during their stay. The bedrooms are furnished to a high standard, all with good en suite bathrooms, and there are family suites available complete with a baby-listening service. The light and sunny lounge is ideal for relaxation, or guests may sit on the adjoining sun terrace with sweeping views of the sea. In the air-conditioned restaurant special care is taken to cater for all tastes. Both English and French cuisine are prepared, with freshly caught fish, lobster and crab delivered daily, as well as wholesome farm produce and local cheeses. Palm trees surround the heated outdoor swimming pool on the sunny terrace. There is a good golf course within a few miles of the hotel. Riding, sailing and wind-surfing can be arranged. Sea fishing trips can be organised and private moorings are available. The hotel is directly adjacent to miles of magnificent National Trust cliff land at Bolt Head. Dogs by arrangement. Closed mid-November to mid-March. **Directions:** Please contact the hotel for directions. Price guide (including dinner): Single from £62; double/twin from £124; superior rooms available, as illustrated.

For hotel location, see maps on pages 473–479

SOAR MILL COVE HOTEL

SOAR MILL COVE, SALCOMBE, SOUTH DEVON TQ7 3DS
TEL: 01548 561566 FAX: 01548 561223

Soar Mill Cove Hotel is owned and loved by the Makepeace family who, with their dedicated staff, provide a special blend of friendly yet professional service. The hotel's spectacular setting is a flower-filled combe, facing its own sheltered sandy bay and entirely surrounded by hundreds of acres of dramatic National Trust coastland. While it is perhaps one of the last truly unspoiled corners of South Devon, Soar Mill Cove is only 15 miles from the motorway system (A38). All the bedrooms are at ground level, each with a private patio opening onto the gardens. Private guests will not find any conferences here. In winter, crackling log fires and efficient double glazing keep the cold weather at bay. Both the indoor and outdoor pools are spring-water fed, the former being maintained all year at a constant 88°F. This is the home of Keith Stephen Makepeace's award winning cuisine, imaginative and innovative reflecting the very best of the west of England; fresh crabs and lobster caught in the bay are a speciality. Soar Mill Cove is situated midway between Plymouth and Torquay and close to the old ports of Salcombe and Dartmouth. Dogs by prior arrangement. Closed 1 November to 9 February. **Directions:** A384 to Totnes, then A381 to Soar Mill Cove. Price guide: Single £58–£90; double/twin £98–£160.

NUNSMERE HALL

TARPORLEY ROAD, SANDIWAY, CHESHIRE CW8 2ES
TEL: 01606 889100 FAX: 01606 889055

Set in peaceful Cheshire countryside and surrounded on three sides by a lake, Nunsmere Hall epitomises the elegant country manor where superior standards of hospitality still exist. Wood panelling, antique furniture, exclusive fabrics, Chinese lamps and magnificent chandeliers evoke an air of luxury. The 32 bedrooms, with spectacular views of the lake and gardens, are beautifully appointed with king-size beds, comfortable breakfast seating and marbled bathrooms containing soft bathrobes and toiletries. The Brocklebank, Delamere and Oakmere business suites are air-conditioned, soundproofed and offer excellent facilities for boardroom meetings, private dining and seminars. The Garden Restaurant has a reputation for fine food and uses only fresh seasonal produce. County Restaurant of the Year in the 1993 Good Food Guide. A snooker room is provided, while there are several golf courses. Oulton Park Racing Circuit is nearby and the Cheshire Polo Club is next door. Archery and golf practice nets are available in the grounds. Although secluded, Nunsmere is convenient for major towns and routes. AA 3 Red Star and RAC 4 Star, ETB 5 Crowns Deluxe. **Directions:** Leave M6 at junction 18 northbound or 19 southbound, take A556 to Chester (approximately 12 miles). At second set of traffic lights turn left onto A49. Hotel is 1 mile on left. Price guide: Single £110; double/twin £140–£180; suite £200.

In association
with MasterCard

HACKNESS GRANGE

NORTH YORK MOORS NATIONAL PARK, SCARBOROUGH, NORTH YORKSHIRE YO13 0JW
TEL: 01723 882345 FAX: 01723 882391

The attractive Georgian Hackness Grange country house lies at the heart of the dramatic North York Moors National Park – miles of glorious countryside with rolling moorland and forests. Set in acres of private grounds, overlooking a tranquil lake, home to many species of wildlife, Hackness Grange is a haven of peace and quiet for guests. There are charming bedrooms in the elegant courtyard which have enjoyed a delightful refurbishment this year, together with de luxe rooms in the main house. For leisure activites, guests can enjoy 9-hole pitch 'n' putt golf, tennis, private fishing on the River Derwent and an indoor heated swimming pool. Hackness Grange is an ideal meeting location for companies wishing to have exclusive use of the hotel for VIP gatherings. The attractive Derwent Restaurant with its quality décor and paintings, is the setting for lunch and dinner and you will enjoy creatively prepared delicious cuisine, which is partnered by a wide choice of international wines. When you choose to stay at Hackness Grange you will find you have chosen well – a peaceful and relaxing location with so much to see and do: for example, visst Great Ayton, birthplace of Captain Cook. **Directions:** Take A64 York road until left turn to Seamer on to B1261, through to East Ayton. and Hackness. Price guide: Single £68–£83; double/twin £135–£165; suite £185.

WREA HEAD COUNTRY HOTEL

SCALBY, NR SCARBOROUGH, NORTH YORKSHIRE YO13 0PB
TEL: 01723 378211 FAX: 01723 371780

Wrea Head Country Hotel is an elegant, beautifully refurbished Victorian country house built in 1881 and situated in 14 acres of wooded and landscaped grounds on the edge of the North York Moors National Park just three miles from Scarborough. The house is furnished with antiques and paintings, and the oak-panelled front hall with its inglenook fireplace with blazing log fires in the winter, is very welcoming. All the bedrooms are individually decorated to the highest standards, with most having delightful views of the gardens. The elegant Four Seasons Restaurant is renowned for serving the best traditional English fare using fresh local produce and and the choicest ingredients,

supplemented by an interesting international wine list. There are attractive meeting rooms, each with natural daylight, ideal for private board meetings and training courses requiring privacy and seclusion. Scarborough is renowned for its cricket, music and theatre. Wrea Head is a perfect location from which to explore the glorious North Yorkshire coast and country, and you can take advantage of special English Rose breaks throughout the year. **Directions:** Follow the A171 north from Scarborough, past the Scalby Village, until hotel is signposted. Follow the road past the duck pond, and then turn left up the drive. Price guide: Single from £57.50–£75; double/twin from £115–£135; suite £165.

CHARNWOOD HOTEL

10 SHARROW LANE, SHEFFIELD, SOUTH YORKSHIRE S11 8AA
TEL: 0114 2589411 FAX: 0114 2555107

The Charnwood Hotel is a listed Georgian mansion dating from 1780. Originally owned by John Henfrey, a Sheffield Master Cutler, it was later acquired by William Wilson of the Sharrow Snuff Mill. Restored in 1985, this elegant 'country house in town' is tastefully furnished, with colourful flower arrangements set against attractive décor. The bedrooms are decorated in a country style, with the Woodford suite designed specifically to meet the requirements of a family. Two dining rooms are available for experiencing the gourmet skills of the chef and his brigade. Dignified and formal, Henfrey's Restaurant offers cuisine to match the surroundings, while traditional English/French fare is the order of the day at Brasserie Leo. The Library is ideal for private dining or small meetings and larger functions are catered for in the Georgian Room and Coach House. While approximately a mile from Sheffield city centre, with its concert hall, theatre and hectic night-life, Charnwood Hotel is also convenient for the Peak District National Park. Meadowhall shopping centre and Sheffield Arena are nearby. **Directions:** Sharrow Lane is near the junction of London Road and Abbeydale Road, 1$^{1}/_{2}$ miles from city centre. Junction 33 from the M1. Price guide: Single £45–£75; double/twin £60–£90.

WHITLEY HALL HOTEL

ELLIOTT LANE, GRENOSIDE, SHEFFIELD, SOUTH YORKSHIRE S30 3NR
TEL: 0114 245 4444 FAX: 0114 245 5414

Carved into the keystone above one of the doors is the date 1584, denoting the start of Whitley Hall's lengthy country house tradition. In the bar is a priest hole, which may explain the local belief that a tunnel links the house with the nearby 11th-century church. In the 18th century, the house was a prestigious boarding school, with Gothic pointed arches and ornamentation added later by the Victorians. Attractively refurbished, Whitley Hall is now a fine hotel with all the amenities required by today's visitors. Stone walls and oak panelling combine with richly carpeted floors and handsome decoration. A sweeping split staircase leads to the bedrooms, all of which have en suite bathrooms. Varied yet unpretentious cooking is served in generous portions and complemented by a wide choice from the wine cellar, including many clarets and ports. Peacocks strut around the 30-acre grounds, which encompass rolling lawns, mature woodland and two ornamental lakes. Banquets and private functions can be held in the conference suite. **Directions:** Leave M1 at junction 35, following signs for Chapeltown (A629), go down hill and turn left into Nether Lane. Go right at traffic lights, then left opposite Arundel pub, into Whitley Lane. At fork turn right into Elliott Lane; hotel is on left. Price guide: Single £58–£70; double/twin £80–£95.

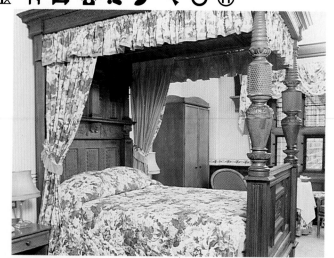

In association
with MasterCard

ROWTON CASTLE

SHREWSBURY, SHROPSHIRE SY5 9EP
TEL: 01743 884044 FAX: 01743 884949

Rowton Castle is mentioned in the Domesday Book and stands on the site of a Roman fort. Part of its large tower is reputed to date from the original castle, destroyed by Llewellyn, Prince of Wales in 1282. Residential parts date from 1696, with additions made in the early 19th century. In 1880 the property was made over to Baron Rowton, Disraeli's private secretary. Today it is a sympathetically restored and picturesque hotel set in 17 acres of formal gardens and grounds. From an armchair in the lounge guests are afforded wonderful views of the Welsh mountains through a spectacular avenue of lime trees. Each of the hotel's bedrooms has a unique charm and character and provides a full range of modern conveniences. The oak-panelled restaurant, centred on a 17th century carved oak fireplace, offers table d'hote and à la carte menus in a setting which is ideal for important business entertaining, celebrations and intimate dinners. The Cardeston Suite can accommodate 150 delegates and has a separate reception room and bar. Places of interest nearby include Shrewsbury Castle, Ironbridge and Llangollen. Golf, shooting. fishing and croquet are available. Shrewsbury, Shropshire's thriving historic market town, is within 10 minutes' drive. **Directions:** Five miles from Shrewsbury on the A458 Welshpool road. Price guide: Single £50; double/twin £65; suites £115.

HOTEL RIVIERA

THE ESPLANADE, SIDMOUTH, DEVON EX10 8AY
TEL: 01395 515201 FAX: 01395 577775

The Hotel Riviera is splendidly positioned at the centre of Sidmouth's esplanade, overlooking Lyme Bay. With its mild climate and the beach just on the doorstep, the setting mirrors the south of France and is the choice for the discerning visitor in search of relaxation and quieter pleasures. Behind the hotel's fine Regency façade lies an alluring blend of old-fashioned service and present-day comforts with a style and ambience that justly reflects its AA and RAC four-star rating. Glorious sea views can be enjoyed from the recently redesigned and refurbished en suite bedrooms, all of which are fully appointed and have many thoughtful extras like hairdryers, fresh flowers, bathrobes and complimentary toiletries. In the elegant bay-view dining room, guests are offered a fine choice of dishes from the extensive menus, prepared by French and Swiss trained chefs, with local seafood being a particular speciality. Arrangements can be made for guests to play golf, while bowls, croquet, tennis, putting, sailing and fishing are available nearby. Explore the many delightful villages of East Devon's rolling countryside and coastline, or just enjoy pottering around Sidmouth, with its enduring architectural charm. **Directions:** The hotel is situated at the centre of the esplanade. Price guide (including dinner): Single £67–£90; double/twin £118–£164; suite £162–£182.

THE FRENCH HORN

SONNING-ON-THAMES, BERKSHIRE RG4 OTN
TEL: 01734 692204 FAX: 01734 442210

For over 150 years The French Horn has provided a charming riverside retreat from the busy outside world. Today, it continues that fine tradition of comfortable accommodation and outstanding cuisine in a beautiful setting. The hotel nestles beside the Thames near the historic village of Sonning. The well appointed bedrooms and suites are fully equipped with modern amenities and many have river views. The old pannelled bar provides an intimate setting for pre-dinner drinks and the restaurant speciality, locally reared duck, is spit roasted here over an open fire. By day the sunny restaurant is a lovely setting for lunch, while by night diners can enjoy the floodlit view of the graceful weeping willows which fringe the river. Dinner is served by candlelight and the cuisine is a mixture of French and English cooking using the freshest ingredients. Jacket and tie is required for the restaurant in the eveing. The French Horn's wine list is reputed to be amongst the finest in Europe. Places of interest include Henley, Stratfield Saye, Oxford, Blenheim Palace and Mapledurham. There are numerous golf courses and equestrian centres in the area. **Directions:** Leave the M4 at junction 8/9 and follow the A4 to Sonning. The hotel is beside the bridge on the north side of the river. Price guide: Single £80–£110; double/twin £85–£130.

WHITECHAPEL MANOR

NR SOUTH MOLTON, NORTH DEVON EX36 3EG
TEL: 01769 573377 FAX: 01769 573797

Built in 1575 by Robert de Bassett, pretender to the English Throne, Whitechapel Manor a Grade I listed building is a vision of the past with terraced and walled gardens of lawns, roses and clipped yew hedges. The entrance hall has a perfect Jacobean carved oak screen. Elsewhere, William & Mary plasterwork and panelling, along with painted overmantles have been preserved. The large bedrooms at the front overlooking the gardens and the smaller, cosy rooms which overlook the woodlands are thoughtfully appointed for comfort. John Shapland, a north Devonian, can trace his family farming roots back further than the age of Whitechapel Manor and will provide anecdotes of both the Manor and North Devon. The restaurant combines the essence of modern French and English cuisine and is recognised as one of the best in the West Country. All around is tranquil, unspoilt countryside rising up to Exmoor National Park and the most dramatic coastline in England. Whitechapel is the ideal base from which to explore the moors, coast, ancient woodland valleys, Exmoor's villages and its wildlife. Also nearby are the RHS Gardens at Rosemoor. **Directions:** Leave M5 at junction 27. Follow signs to Barnstaple. After 30 minutes turn right at roundabout to Whitechapel. Price guide: Single £65; double/twin from £105. Special breaks and events all year round.

THE SWAN HOTEL

MARKET PLACE, SOUTHWOLD, SUFFOLK IP18 6EG
TEL: 01502 722186 FAX: 01502 724800

Rebuilt in 1659, following the disastrous fire which destroyed most of the town, The Swan was remodelled in the 1820s, with further additions in 1938. The hotel provides all modern services while retaining its classical dignity and elegance. Many of the antique-furnished bedrooms in the main hotel offer a glimpse of the sea, while the garden rooms – decorated in a more contemporary style – are clustered around the old bowling green. The drawing room has the traditional character of an English country house and the reading room upstairs is perfect for quiet relaxation or as the venue for a private party. The daily menu offers dishes ranging from simple, traditional fare through the English classics to the chef's personal specialities. An exciting selection of wines is offered. Almost an island, Southwold is bounded on three sides by creeks, marshes and the River Blyth – making it a paradise for birdwatchers and nature lovers. Hardly changed for a century, the town, built around a series of greens, has a fine church, lighthouse and golf course. Music lovers flock to nearby Snape Maltings for the Aldeburgh Festival. Winner of Country Living Gold Award for the Best Hotel 1993/94. **Directions:** Southwold is off the A12 Ipswich–Lowestoft road. The Swan Hotel is in the town centre. Price guide: Single £50–£68; double/twin £84–£118; suite £150.

For hotel location, see maps on pages 473–479

THE GEORGE OF STAMFORD

ST MARTINS, STAMFORD, LINCOLNSHIRE PE9 2LB
TEL: 01780 55171 FAX: 01780 57070

The George, a beautiful, 16th century coaching inn, retains the charm of its long history, as guests will sense on entering the reception hall with its oak travelling chests and famous oil portrait of Daniel Lambert. Over the years, The George has welcomed a diverse clientèle, ranging from highwaymen to kings – Charles I and William III were both visitors. At the heart of the hotel is the lounge, its natural stone walls, deep easy chairs and softly lit alcoves imparting a cosy, relaxed atmosphere, while the blazing log fire is sometimes used to toast muffins for tea! The flair of Julia Vannocci's interior design is evident in all the expertly styled, fully appointed bedrooms. Exotic plants, orchids, orange trees and coconut palms feature in the Garden Lounge, where a choice of hot dishes and an extensive cold buffet are offered. Guests may also dine alfresco in the courtyard garden. The more formal, oak-panelled restaurant serves imaginative but traditional English dishes and an award-winning list of wines. Superb facilities are incorporated in the Business Centre, converted from the former livery stables. Special weekend breaks available. **Directions:** Stamford is 1 mile from the A1 on the B1081. The George is in the town centre opposite the gallows sign. Car parking is behind the hotel. Price guide: Single from £72–£85; double/twin from £95–£115; suite £125–£160.

WHITEHALL

CHURCH END, BROXTED, ESSEX CM6 2BZ
TEL: 01279 850603 FAX: 01279 850385

Set on a hillside overlooking the delightful rolling countryside of north-west Essex is Whitehall, one of East Anglia's leading country hotels. While its origins can be traced back to 1151, the manor house is ostensibly Elizabethan in style, with recent additions tastefully incorporated. Traditional features such as beams, wide fireplaces and log fires blend well with the contemporary, fresh pastel shades and subtle-hued fabrics. A spectacular vaulted ceiling makes the dining room an impressive setting for dinner, with an à la carte or six-course set menu offering many delicious concoctions. For large private functions, the timbered Barn House is an ideal venue, where guests can enjoy the same high standards of cuisine found in the restaurant. Overlooked by the old village church is the attractive Elizabethan walled garden. Whitehall is only a short drive from London's newest international airport at Stansted and easily accessible from the M11 motorway, while Cambridge and Newmarket are only 30 minutes' drive away. **Directions:** Take junction 8 from the M11, follow Stansted Airport signs to new terminal building and then signs for Broxted. Price guide: Single £75–£95; double/twin £105–£155.

STAPLEFORD PARK

NR MELTON MOWBRAY, LEICESTERSHIRE LE14 2EF
TEL: 01572 787 522 FAX: 01572 787 651

Casual luxury is the byword in this pre-eminent 16th century house, which was opened as a hotel in 1988. It was once coveted by Edward, The Prince of Wales, but his mother Queen Victoria forbade him to buy it for fear that his morals would be corrupted by the Leicestershire hunting society! Today, Stapleford Park offers discerning guests supremely elegant surroundings and beautiful views over 500 acres of parkland. Described as "The Best Country House Hotel in the World" in Andrew Harper's Hideaway Report, it has received innumerable awards for its unique style and hospitality. The individually designed bedrooms have been created by famous names such as Tiffany, Wedgwood,

Crabtree & Evelyn and Range Rover. An exclusive cottage with four themed bedrooms is also available. Excellent cuisine,is carefully prepared to the highest standards. The wine list is presented by flavour and texture, an original approach which has met with universal approval. There are a host of sporting pursuits including falconry, clay and game shooting, golf, riding, tennis and fishing. There are facilities for private dinners, weddings, receptions and conferences. **Directions:** Stapleford Park is only $1^1/_2$ hours north of London, situated between the A1 and M1. Price guide: Double/twin £145-£215; suites from £230.

STONEHOUSE COURT

STONEHOUSE, GLOUCESTERSHIRE GL10 3RA
TEL: 01453 625155 FAX: 01453 824611

This outstanding Grade II listed manor is set in six acres of mature gardens in lovely countryside on the edge of the South Cotswolds. All the bedrooms are individually decorated and many feature original fireplaces and mullion windows. The John Henry Restaurant provides the perfect setting to enjoy a relaxed candlelit dinner or informal lunch and the traditional English cuisine is complemented by fine wines. A choice of outdoor pursuits includes fishing on the River Stour or golf at Stinchcombe Hill, while activity days within the grounds can include laser shooting, archery, quad biking and team building exercises. The conference facilities at Stonehouse Court are designed for all styles of meetings, from informal to boardroom. The self-contained Caroline Suite is well suited to holding product launches, training courses and conferences and the oak-panelled Crellin Room provides an appropriate atmosphere for small meetings or private dining. Among the numerous places of interest nearby are Cheltenham, Berkeley Castle and Slimbridge Wildfowl Trust and guests also have the chance to visit Cheltenham Races, polo at Cirencester or the Badminton horse trials. **Directions:** From junction 13 of the M5 Stonehouse Court is two miles on the A419 towards Stroud. Price guide: Single from £65; double/twin from £90; suites from £105.

LITTLE THAKEHAM

MERRYWOOD LANE, STORRINGTON, WEST SUSSEX RH20 3HE
TEL: 01903 744416 FAX: 01903 745022

One of the finest examples of a Lutyens Manor house, Little Thakeham is the home of Tim and Pauline Ractliff who have carefully preserved the feeling of a family home. Antiques, open log fires and a minstrel gallery all serve to enhance the authentic atmosphere of gracious living. There are two suites and seven bedrooms all furnished in character with the house. The restaurant, also open to non-residents serves traditional English food based on local produce such as Southdown lamb and shellfish from the South Coast. The set menu changes daily and there is an excellent cellar. Outside the gardens were created in the style of Gertude Jekyll and recently have been the subject of restoration. There is a heated swimming pool and croquet lawn in the grounds. The famous country houses of Goodwood, Petworth and Arundel Castle are nearby, racing enthusiasts are well served with Goodwood, Fontwell Park and Plumpton. Antique collectors will not be disappointed, there are shops in Arundel, Petworth and Chichester. **Directions:** From Storrington, take B2139 to Thakeham. After about one mile turn right into Merrywood Lane. Hotel is 400 yards on left. Price guide: Single £95; double/twin £150; suite £240.

THE GRAPEVINE HOTEL

SHEEP STREET, STOW-ON-THE-WOLD, GLOUCESTERSHIRE GL54 1AU
TEL: 01451 830344 FAX: 01451 832278

Set in the pretty town of Stow-on-the-Wold, regarded by many as the jewel of the Cotswolds, The Grapevine Hotel has an atmosphere which makes visitors feel welcome and at ease. The outstanding personal service provided by a loyal team of staff is perhaps the secret of the hotel's success – nothing is too much trouble for them. This, along with the exceptionally high standard of overall comfort and hospitality, earned The Grapevine the 1991 *Johansens Hotel Award for Excellence* – a well-deserved accolade. Beautifully furnished bedrooms, including six superb garden rooms across the courtyard, offer every facility. Visitors can linger over imaginative cuisine in the relaxed and informal atmosphere of the conservatory restaurant, with its unusual canopy of trailing vines. AA Rosette awarded for food. Whether travelling on business or for pleasure, The Grapevine is a hotel that guests will wish to return to again and again. The local landscape offers unlimited scope for exploration, whether to the numerous stone-cottaged villages tucked away in the Cotswolds or to the nearby towns of Cheltenham, Cirencester and Stratford-upon-Avon. Champagne breaks available from £47 per person d, b&b. Closed over Christmas/New Year. **Directions:** Sheep Street is part of the A436 in the centre of Stow-on-the-Wold. Price guide: Single from £74; double/twin from £108.

WYCK HILL HOUSE

WYCK HILL, STOW-ON-THE WOLD, GLOUCESTERSHIRE GL54 1HY
TEL: 01451 831936 FAX: 01451 832243

Wyck Hill House is a magnificent Cotswold mansion built in the early 1700s, reputedly on the site of an early Roman settlement. It is set in 100 acres of wooded and landscaped gardens, overlooking the beautiful Windrush Valley. The hotel has been elegantly restored and the bedrooms individually furnished to combine superb antiques with modern comforts. There is a suite with a large, antique four-poster bed, which is perfect for honeymoons and other special occasions. The cedar-panelled library is an ideal room in which to read, if you wish, and to relax with morning coffee or afternoon tea. The award-winning restaurant provides the highest standards of modern British cuisine from the freshest seasonally available local produce. The menus are complemented by a superb wine list. Wyck Hill House hosts several special events, including opera, travel talks, cultural weekends and a variety of theme activities. The hotel is an ideal base from which to tour the university city of Oxford and the Georgian city of Bath. Cheltenham, Blenheim Palace and Stratford-upon-Avon are just a short drive away. Special price 2-night breaks are available. **Directions:** One-and-a-half miles south of Stow-on-the-Wold on the A424 Stow–Burford road. Price guide: Single £78; double/twin £108–£130; suite £180.

BILLESLEY MANOR

BILLESLEY, ALCESTER, NR STRATFORD-UPON-AVON, WARWICKSHIRE B49 6NF
TEL: 01789 279955 FAX: 01789 764145

Three miles from Stratford-upon-Avon, Billesley Manor is set in 11 acres of delightful grounds with a typically English topiary garden and ornamental pond. Ten centuries of history and tradition welcome guests to this magnificent house in the heart of Shakespeare country. Billesley Manor has been extensively refurbished in recent years, blending old and new to create a hotel that is impressive, spacious and comfortable. Guests may stay in a suite, an oak-panelled four-poster room or one of the well-appointed modern rooms – all have a large bathroom and a good range of facilities. The panelled Tudor and Stuart Restaurants have won awards for their fine food and service,

including 3 AA Rosettes for the fifth year in a row. Billesley Manor is particularly suitable for residential conferences and meetings, offering self-contained amenities and seclusion. In addition to the many on-site leisure activities, like the attractive sun patio, pool, mini-golf and tennis courts, weekend breaks can include hot-air ballooning, shooting and riding. The hotel is ideal for visiting the Royal Shakespeare Theatre, Warwick Castle, Ragley Hall and the Cotswolds. **Directions:** From M40 (exit 15) follow A46 towards Evesham and Alcester. Three miles beyond Stratford-upon-Avon turn right to Billesley. Price guide: Single £99; double/twin £150; suite £190.

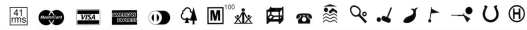

ETTINGTON PARK

ALDERMINSTER, STRATFORD-UPON-AVON, WARWICKSHIRE CV37 8BS
TEL: 01789 450123 FAX: 01789 450472

The foundations of Ettington Park date back at least 1000 years. Mentioned in the *Domesday Book*, Ettington Park rises majestically over 40 acres of Warwickshire parkland, surrounded by terraced gardens and carefully tended lawns, where guests can wander at will to admire the pastoral views. The interiors are breathtaking, their striking opulence enhanced by flowers, beautiful antiques and original paintings. Amid these elegant surroundings guests can relax totally, pampered with every luxury. On an appropriately grand scale, the 48 bedrooms and superb leisure complex, comprising an indoor heated swimming pool, spa bath, solarium and sauna, make this a perfect choice for the sybarite. The menu reflects the best of English and French cuisine, served with panache in the dining room, with its elegant 18th century rococo ceiling and 19th century carved family crests. The *bon viveur* will relish the fine wine list. Splendid conference facilities are available: the panelled Long Gallery and 14th century chapel are both unique venues. Riding is a speciality, while clay pigeon shooting, archery and fishing can also be arranged on the premises. **Directions:** From M40 junction 15 (Warwick) take A46 signposted Stratford, then left-hand turn onto A3400. Ettington is five miles south of Stratford-upon-Avon off the A3400. Price guide: Single £115; double/twin from £152; suites from £175.

SALFORD HALL HOTEL

ABBOT'S SALFORD, NR EVESHAM, WORCESTERSHIRE WR11 5UT
TEL: 01386 871300 FAX: 01386 871301

Between Shakespeare's Stratford-upon-Avon, the rolling Cotswolds and the Vale of Evesham is the Roman village of Abbot's Salford. Steeped in history, Salford Hall is a romantic Grade I listed manor house. It was built in the late 15th century as a retreat for the monks of Evesham Abbey and the imposing stone wing was added in the 17th century. Essentially unchanged, stained glass, a priest hole, exposed beams, oak panelling and original decorative murals are examples of the well-preserved features of the interior. The period charm is doubly appealing when combined with modern comforts, gracious furnishings, delicious food and an extensive selection of fine wines. Reflecting the past associations of the hall, the bedrooms are named after historical figures, and all are individually appointed with oak furniture and luxury fittings. Guests may relax in the Hawkesbury lounge, formerly a medieval kitchen, the conservatory lounge or on the sunny terrace within the walled flower garden. Facilities include snooker, a sauna and a solarium. Special weekends are arranged for hot-air ballooning, horse-racing, touring the Cotswolds, discovering Shakespeare and murder mysteries. Closed for Christmas. **Directions:** Abbot's Salford is 8 miles west of Stratford-upon-Avon on A439 towards Vale of Evesham. Price guide: Single £75; double/twin £95–£120.

WELCOMBE HOTEL AND GOLF COURSE

WARWICK ROAD, STRATFORD-UPON-AVON, WARWICKSHIRE CV37 0NR
TEL: 01789 295252 FAX: 01789 414666 TELEX: 31347

A splendid Jacobean-style mansion dating from 1869, the aptly named Welcombe Hotel stands in 157 acres of rolling parkland, much of which was owned by Shakespeare. One of the foremost hotels in the heart of England, it is also renowned for its fully equipped 18-hole golf course. The magnificent lounge, with its striking black marble fireplace, ornate floor-to-ceiling oak panelling, deep armchairs and bright flower arrangements, typifies the immaculate style of the hotel's interior. Exquisitely decorated, the restaurant is light, airy and spacious – an elegant setting overlooking the extensive formal gardens. The finest English and French cuisine is impeccably prepared, with particular emphasis on delicate sauces and presentation. A well-balanced wine list includes a wide selection of half bottles. Whether staying in one of the suites or bedrooms, guests will find the accommodation appointed to the highest standards. For small meetings or large-scale conferences, the Welcombe Hotel can offer every amenity to support the event. The centre of Stratford-upon-Avon is only 1 mile away. **Directions:** Five miles from exit 15 of M40, on A439. 1 mile from Stratford-upon-Avon. Price guide: Single £110; double/twin £150; suite £175–£375.

THE SWAN DIPLOMAT

STREATLEY-ON-THAMES, BERKSHIRE RG8 9HR
TEL: 01491 873737 FAX: 01491 872554

In a beautiful setting on the bank of the River Thames, this hotel offers visitors comfortable accommodation. All of the 46 bedrooms, many of which have balconies overlooking the river, are appointed to high standards with individual décor and furnishings. The elegant Riverside Restaurant, with its relaxing waterside views, serves fine food complemented by a good choice of wines. Moored alongside the restaurant is the Magdalen College Barge, which is a stylish venue for meetings and cocktail parties. Business guests are well catered for – the hotel has six attractive conference suites. Reflexions Leisure Club is superbly equipped for fitness programmes and beauty treatments, with facilities that include a heated 'fit' pool; rowing boats and bicycles may be hired. Squash, riding and clay pigeon shooting can all be arranged. Special theme weekends are offered, such as bridge weekends. Events in the locality include Henley Regatta, Ascot and Newbury races, while Windsor Castle, Blenheim Palace, Oxford and London's airports are easily accessible. **Directions:** The hotel lies just off the A329 in Streatley village. Price guide: Single £86–£99; double/twin £115–£126.

PLUMBER MANOR

STURMINSTER NEWTON, DORSET DT10 2AF
TEL: 01258 472507 FAX: 01258 473370

An imposing Jacobean building of local stone, occupying extensive gardens in the heart of Hardy's Dorset, Plumber Manor has been the home of the Prideaux-Brune family since the early 17th century. Leading off a charming gallery hung with family portraits are six very comfortable bedrooms. The conversion of a natural stone barn lying within the grounds, as well as the courtyard building, has added a further ten spacious bedrooms, some of which have window seats overlooking the garden and the Develish stream. Three interconnecting dining rooms comprise the restaurant, where a good choice of imaginative, well-prepared dishes is presented, supported by a wide-ranging wine list. Chef Brian Prideaux-Brune's culinary prowess has been recognised by all the major food guides. Open for dinner every evening and Sunday lunch. The Dorset landscape, with its picture-postcard villages such as Milton Abbas and Cerne Abbas, is close at hand, while Corfe Castle, Lulworth Cove, Kingston Lacy and Poole Harbour are not far away. Riding can be arranged locally: however, if guests wish to bring their own horse to hack or hunt with local packs, the hotel provides free stabling on a do-it-yourself basis. Closed during February. **Directions:** Plumber Manor is two miles south west of Sturminster Newton on the Hazelbury Bryan road, off the A357. Price guide: Single £65–£80; double/twin £84–£115.

BLUNSDON HOUSE HOTEL

BLUNSDON, SWINDON, WILTSHIRE SN2 4AD
TEL: 01793 721701 FAX: 01793 721056

Blunsdon House is thought to have been built as a hunting lodge at the beginning of the 19th century, although descriptions of the resident ghost predate this period! The house is set in 40 acres of gently undulating land on a ridge overlooking the Vale of Cricklade towards the distant Cotswolds. In 1958 the property was a farm guest house, becoming a licensed country club in 1960 and a fully licensed hotel in 1962. It was the first four star hotel in the county. The superbly appointed bedrooms are comfortable and well equipped, with "prestige" rooms offering a spa bath, reclining chair and a wall safe. Guests can choose a formal restaurant in which to enjoy delicious food and excellent service, or opt for the informality of the Carverie with its prime roast joints and sumptuous sweets. There are plenty of leisure activities to enjoy, ranging from a gentle stroll through the woods to a swim in the indoor pool. The 9-hole par 3 golf course is a gem. There is a ladies beautician as well as a steam room, sauna or hot spa. Nearby are the picturesque villages of the South Cotswolds and the ancient mysteries of the Wiltshire Downs and "White Horse Country." **Directions:** Leave M4 at junction 15, head north on A419 towards Cirencester. Blunsdon House Hotel is signposted on the right after seven miles. Price guide: Single £77.50; double/twin £92.50. Getaway breaks are also available.

TALLAND BAY HOTEL

TALLAND-BY-LOOE, CORNWALL PL13 2JB
TEL: 01503 72667 FAX: 01503 72940

This lovely old Cornish manor house, parts of which date back to the 16th century, enjoys a truly rural and unspoilt setting. The hotel is surrounded by over 2 acres of beautiful gardens with glorious views over the two dramatic headlands of Talland Bay itself. Bedrooms are individually furnished to a high standard, some having lovely sea views. Sitting rooms open to the south-facing terrace by a heated outdoor swimming pool. Dinner menus are imaginative and incorporate seafood from Looe, Cornish lamb, West Country cheeses. A choice of à la carte supplements changes with the seasons. Meals are complemented by a list of about 100 carefully selected wines. Leisure pursuits at the hotel include: swimming, putting, croquet, table tennis, sauna, painting courses and other special interest holidays. Talland Bay is a magically peaceful spot from which to explore this part of Cornwall – there are breathtaking cliff coastal walks at the hotel's doorstep, and many National Trust houses and gardens to visit locally – but most people come here just to relax and enjoy the view. This hotel provides old fashioned comfort in beautiful surroundings at exceptionally moderate prices. Resident owners: Barry and Annie Rosier. Closed January. **Directions:** The hotel is signposted from the A387 Looe–Polperro road. Price guide: Single £35–£70; double/twin £70–£140.

THE CASTLE AT TAUNTON

CASTLE GREEN, TAUNTON, SOMERSET TA1 1NF
TEL: 01823 272671 FAX: 01823 336066

The Castle at Taunton is steeped in the drama and romance of English history. Once a Norman fortress, it has been welcoming travellers to the town since the 12th century. In 1685, the Duke of Monmouth's officers were heard "roystering at the Castle Inn" before their defeat by the forces of King James II at Sedgemoor. Shortly after, Judge Jeffreys held his Bloody Assize in the Great Hall of the Castle. Today the Castle lives at peace with its turbulent past but preserves the atmosphere of its ancient tradition. The Chapman family have been running the hotel for over 40 years and in that time it has acquired a worldwide reputation for the warmth of its hospitality. Laurels in Michelin, Egon Ronay and the AA also testify to the excellence of the Castle's kitchen and cellar. Located in the heart of England's beautiful West Country, the Castle is the ideal base for exploring a region rich in history. This is the land of King Arthur, King Alfred, Lorna Doone's Exmoor and the monastic foundations of Glastonbury and Wells. Roman and Regency Bath, Longleat House and the majestic gardens of Stourhead. All this and much more can be discovered within easy driving distance of Taunton. **Directions:** Exit M5 junction 25 and follow signs for town centre. Alternatively from the south go by A303 and A358. Price guide: Single from £70; double/twin from £110.

RUMWELL MANOR HOTEL

RUMWELL, TAUNTON, SOMERSET TA4 1EL
TEL: 01823 461902 FAX: 01823 254861

Rumwell Manor Hotel, a magnificent Georgian Manor House, was built in 1805 by William Cadbury of Wellington. Standing in five acres of grounds, it looks south west across the peaceful Somerset countryside to the distant Blackdown Hills. The hotel's bedrooms are divided between the main house and the courtyard. All are individually decorated and furnished, although the main house bedrooms are superior in terms of their spaciousness and their spectacular views across the countryside. A full range of modern amenities is available in every bedroom. The beautifully proportioned public rooms provide an ideal environment in which to relax. The candlelit restaurant boasts an excellent range of imaginative dishes and there is a choice between table d'hôte and à la carte menus. An extensive wine list adds to the dining experience. The well stocked bar is the ideal place to sit. Guests of Rumwell Manor are given a warm and sincere welcome and an atmosphere of friendliness prevails throughout. Cheddar Gorge, the cathedrals of Exeter and Wells, the historic city of Bath, Exmoor, Glastonbury Abbey and Tor are just a few of the outings than can be enjoyed using Rumwell Manor as a base. **Directions:** Exit M5 junction 26. At next roundabout turn right onto A38 towards Taunton. The hotel drive is around three miles along on the right. Price guide: Single: £49–£55; double/twin £75–£105.

THE HORN OF PLENTY

GULWORTHY, TAVISTOCK, DEVON PL19 8JD
TEL: 01822 832528 FAX: 01822 832528

Nestling in the foothills of Dartmoor and overlooking the Tamar Valley is The Horn of Plenty. Built by the Duke of Bedford, Marquess of Tavistock, nearly 200 years ago, this charming house exudes warmth and welcome. Its four acres of gardens are ablaze with camellias, azaleas and rhododendrons from early spring. Inside, the furnishings are designed for comfort rather than fashion. Throughout the hotel, the smell of fresh flowers competes with the tang of wood smoke from the log fires that burn in the colder winter months. The Coach House has been converted into six lovely en suite bedrooms, all of which are well equipped and have balconies overlooking the walled garden. The heart of The Horn of Plenty is the kitchen, where great thought is put into the taste, texture, contrast and harmony of the food prepared there, whilst the eating experience is enhanced by the surroundings of the restaurant with its beautiful view of the Tamar Valley. Places of interest nearby include Cotehele House and the old market town of Tavistock. The hotel is an ideal base for those interested in active pursuits such as golf, riding on Dartmoor, fishing, walking, sailing and canoeing. **Directions:** At Tavistock take the A390 and after three miles turn right at Gulworthy Cross and follow the signs to the hotel. Price guide: Single £58–£78; double/twin £78–£98.

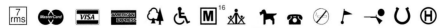

BUCKATREE HALL HOTEL

THE WREKIN, WELLINGTON, TELFORD, SHROPSHIRE TF6 5AL
TEL: 01952 641821 FAX: 01952 247540

Buckatree Hall Hotel, with its own lake and gardens, stands in woodland at the foot of Wrekin Hill in Telford, yet is only one mile from the M54. Many of the 62 bedrooms have balconies overlooking either the lake or the gardens, and some rooms have hi-tech waterbeds. All bedrooms are en suite with baths and aqua-lisa showers, garment presses, refreshment facilities, hairdryers, five-channel satellite TV and direct-dial telephone. Additional features in the Lady Executive Rooms include ironing facilities, double locks and door spy-holes. The two-storey Penthouse Suite has a whirlpool bath. The Terrace Restaurant, with its pink decorative theme, offers a wide choice of English and Continental dishes. The adjoining Fountain Room can be booked for private dinner parties. Enjoy a drink by the carved fireplace in the split-level Liszt Lounge or the Brahms Bar. The Champagne conference and banqueting suite is ideal for dinner dances or weddings. Foremost among the local attractions is the famous open-air museum at Ironbridge. As the birthplace of England's industrial revolution in the early 18th century, Ironbridge is a world heritage site. Weekend breaks from £96 p.p. for two nights dinner, bed and breakfast. **Directions:** Leave M54 at junction 7, turn left and first left again. Mid-week Price guide: Single £69–£75; double/twin £79–£85; suite £95–£125.

MADELEY COURT

TELFORD, SHROPSHIRE TF7 5DW
TEL: 01952 680068 FAX: 01952 684275

Madeley is a veritable gem of a residence. Its characteristic manor-house façade stands virtually unaltered since the 16th century when it was mainly built, while its interior has been recently expertly rejuvenated – with respect for its history – to provide accommodation suitable for all who stay there whether for pleasure or on business. Furnishings have been judiciously selected to enrich Madeley's period appeal: scatterings of fine fabrics, handsome antique pieces and elaborate fittings all accentuate the historic atmosphere, and ensure that every guest leaves with an indelible impression. Bedrooms, whether located in the old part of the Court or in the newer wing, are quiet and full of character; some offer whirlpool baths and views over the lake, all are en suite. At the heart of Madeley is the original 13th century hall, where the restaurant, awarded a coverted AA Rosette is now located, serving inventive food of the highest standard, with a wine list to match. The Brasserie offers a more informal setting. Business meetings and private functions are happily catered for in the three rooms available. Places of interest nearby include: Ironbridge Gorge, Shrewsbury, Powys Castle and Weston Park. Directions: Four miles from junction 4 of M54; follow A442 then B4373. Signposted Dawley then Madeley. Price guide: Single £79.50; double/twin £98; historic £110.

CALCOT MANOR

NR TETBURY, GLOUCESTERSHIRE GL8 8YJ
TEL: 01666 890391 FAX: 01666 890394

This delightful old manor house, built of Cotswold stone, offers guests tranquillity amidst acres of rolling countryside. Calcot Manor is situated in the southern Cotswolds close to the historic town of Tetbury. The building dates back to the 15th century and was a farmhouse until 1983. Its beautiful stone barns and stables include one of the oldest tithe barns in England, built in 1300 by the Cistercian monks from Kingswood Abbey. These buildings form a quadrangle and the stone glistening in the dawn or glowing in the dusk is quite a spectacle. Calcot achieves the rare combination of professional service and cheerful hospitality without any hint of over formality. The atmosphere is one of peaceful relaxation. All the cottage style rooms are beautifully appointed as are the public rooms. Recent additions are a discreet conference facility and a charming cottage providing four family suites with the sitting areas convertible into children's bedrooms equipped with toys, baby listening system and a safe outdoor play area. At the heart of Calcot Manor is its restaurant, dinner is very much the focus of a memorable stay. There is also a congenial lounge bar offering a range of traditional dishes. **Directions:** From Tetbury, take the A4135 signposted Dursley; Calcot is on the right after 3 1/2 miles. Price guide: Single £75–£100; double/twin £87–£125; family suites £125.

For hotel location, see maps on pages 473–479

THE CLOSE HOTEL

LONG STREET, TETBURY, GLOUCESTERSHIRE GL8 8AQ
TEL: 01666 502272 FAX: 01666 504401

This distinguished hotel, built over 400 years ago by a successful wool merchant, has been refurbished to the highest standard. The hotel is renowned for its luxury accommodation, and the individually styled bedrooms are truly elegant. All have superb hand-painted decorated bathrooms. The cuisine, served in the charming Adam dining room, is delicious and imaginative and there is an exceptional choice of wines from an extensive cellar. The restaurant overlooks a walled garden, and you can enjoy a quiet drink on the terrace. The hotel now has a purpose-built suite for top-level management meetings and corporate entertainment for up to 24 people. Many first-class sporting facilities are within easy reach, including racing at Cheltenham, motor racing at Castle Combe, golf, riding and hot-air ballooning. The Close can be booked for "Exclusive Use" and can hold small wedding services and receptions. It is also an ideal base for exploring the Cotswolds. **Directions:** The Close is on the main street of Tetbury, called Long Street. Tetbury is on the A433, 20 minutes from Bath. Private car park at rear of the hotel. Price guide: Single £90; double/twin £100.

THE SNOOTY FOX

MARKET PLACE, TETBURY, GLOUCESTERSHIRE GL8 8DD
TEL: 01666 502436 FAX: 01666 503479

This old coaching inn dating back to the 16th century is situated right in the heart of the quaint old market town of Tetbury. Built of mellow-hued stone, The Snooty Fox dominates the historic market place in the town centre. The hotel has been imaginatively refurbished by Hatton Hotels, who have carefully maintained its considerable period character. There are 12 individual and charming en suite bedrooms which are decorated to convey the warm and homely atmosphere of a bygone age. All are well appointed and comfortable. The public areas and restaurant are steeped in history and are full of antiques and fine oil paintings. The prints that decorate the walls depict the hotel's long association with the famous Beaufort Hunt. The Snooty Fox is still a favourite meeting place for the local community of this famous royal town. Guests can choose either to dine in the elegant restaurant or to enjoy the splendid food from the bar menu. Facilities for executive meetings can be arranged and the hotel is the perfect destination for business and short breaks throughout the year. **Directions:** The Snooty Fox is situated in the centre of Tetbury facing the market square. Price guide: Single £60; double/twin £80–£95.

CORSE LAWN HOUSE HOTEL

CORSE LAWN, NR TEWKESBURY, GLOUCESTERSHIRE GL19 4LZ
TEL: 01452 780479/771 FAX: 01452 780840

Though only 6 miles from the M5 and M50, Corse Lawn is a completely unspoiled, typically English hamlet in a peaceful Gloucestershire backwater. The hotel, an elegant Queen Anne listed building set back from the village green, stands in 12 acres of gardens and grounds, and still displays the charm of its historic pedigree. Visitors can be assured of the highest standards of service and cooking: Baba Hine is famous for the dishes she produces, while Denis Hine, of the Hine Cognac family, is in charge of the wine cellar. The service here, now in the hands of son Giles, is faultlessly efficient, friendly and personal. As well as the renowned restaurant, there are three comfortable drawing rooms, a large lounge bar, a private dining-cum-conference room for up to 45 persons, and a similar, smaller room for up to 20. A tennis court, heated swimming pool and croquet lawn adjoin the hotel, and most sports and leisure activities can be arranged. Corse Lawn is ideal for exploring the Cotswolds, Malverns and Forest of Dean. **Directions:** Corse Lawn House is situated on the B4211 between the A417 (Gloucester–Ledbury road) and the A438 (Tewkesbury–Ledbury road). Price guide: Single £70; double/twin £90; four-poster £100.

PUCKRUP HALL

PUCKRUP, TEWKESBURY, GLOUCESTERSHIRE GL20 6EL
TEL: 01684 296200 FAX: 01684 850788

Lying between the Cotswolds and the Malvern Hills, set in 140 acres of parkland, Puckrup Hall Hotel and Golf Club is the country house hotel of the future. The original Regency manor house, built in the 19th century has been tastefully extended to combine the most up-to-date hotel and leisure facilities with a taste of England's past. A superb 18 hole championship golf course complements the extensive hotel amenities and leisure complex, which includes aerobics studio, swimming pool, spa bath, solarium, steam room and gymnasium all supported by a beauty treatment centre and crèche. Each of the 84 luxury en suite bedrooms is furnished to the highest standard with all the facilities expected of a country house hotel. The 11 conference and private dining rooms can accommodate between 10 and 200 people for a meeting, presentation or dinner dance. An extensive range of cuisine is available from fine dining in the à la carte restaurant, a varied and exciting choice of menu in "Balharries Brasserie" or a light snack in the coffee shop. A refreshing drink in the "Limes" bar makes a welcome finish to a game of golf or as somewhere to relax. **Directions:** Puckrup Hall is 2 miles north of Tewkesbury on the A38, and only a few minutes from junction 8 of the M5, via junction 1 of the M50. Price guide: Single/double/twin from £75.50; suite from £110.

ORESTONE MANOR HOTEL & RESTAURANT

ROCKHOUSE LANE, MAIDENCOMBE, TORQUAY, DEVON TQ1 4SX
TEL: 01803 328098 FAX: 01803 328336

Orestone Manor is an elegant Georgian building set in two acres of secluded gardens in an area of outstanding natural beauty overlooking Lyme Bay. Run by resident proprietors, the atmosphere is welcoming and relaxed. The Manor has been substantially extended since it was built in the early-19th century. The main lounge has a unique pitch-pine ceiling and some bedrooms feature gables. Each en suite bedroom has a colour TV, direct-dial telephone and tea and coffee making facilities. All are individually furnished to a high standard, many with splendid sea views. Not only has Orestone Manor been ranked amongst the top few in Torbay by the AA (1994), it is only one of two hotels there to be awarded two AA Rosettes (1994) for cuisine. An imaginative menu changed daily always includes a vegetarian option. To enhance its growing reputation for fine food, the restaurant is non-smoking. There are five golf courses within seven miles, as well as sailing, horse-riding, tennis, squash and sailboarding. Dartmoor and many National Trust properties are nearby. Phone for details of special low-season breaks and Christmas and New Year packages. **Directions:** About three miles north of Torquay on B3199 (formerly A379) coast road towards Teignmouth. Price guide: Single £50–£75; double/twin £80–£130.

THE OSBORNE HOTEL & LANGTRY'S RESTAURANT

MEADFOOT BEACH, TORQUAY, DEVON TQ1 2LL
TEL: 01803 213311 FAX: 01803 296788

The combination of Mediterranean chic and the much-loved Devon landscape has a special appeal which is reflected at The Osborne. The hotel is the centrepiece of an elegant Regency crescent in Meadfoot, a quiet location within easy reach of the centre of Torquay. Known as a 'country house by the sea', the hotel offers the friendly ambience of a country home complemented by the superior standards of service and comfort expected of a hotel on the English Riviera. Most of the 23 bedrooms have magnificent views and are decorated in pastel shades. Overlooking the sea, Langtry's acclaimed award winning restaurant provides fine English cooking and tempting regional specialities, while Raffles Bar/Brasserie has a menu available throughout the day. Guests may relax in the attractive 5-acre gardens and make use of indoor and outdoor swimming pools, tennis court and putting green – all without leaving the grounds. Sailing, archery, clay pigeon shooting and golf can be arranged. Devon is a county of infinite variety, with its fine coastline, bustling harbours, tranquil lanes, sleepy villages and the wilds of Dartmoor. The Osborne is ideally placed to enjoy all these attractions. **Directions:** The hotel is in Meadfoot, to the east of Torquay. Price guide: Single £55–£89; double/twin £78–£128; suite £98–£138.

For hotel location, see maps on pages 473–479

THE PALACE HOTEL

BABBACOMBE ROAD, TORQUAY, DEVON TQ1 3TG
TEL: 01803 200200 FAX: 01803 299899

Once the residence of the Bishop of Exeter, the privately owned Palace Hotel is a gracious Victorian building set in 25 acres of beautifully landscaped gardens and woodlands. The comfortable bedrooms are equipped with every modern amenity and there are also elegant, spacious suites available. Most rooms overlook the hotel's magnificent grounds. The main restaurant provides a high standard of traditional English cooking, making full use of fresh, local produce, as well as offering a good variety of international dishes. The cuisine is complemented by a wide selection of popular and fine wines. Light meals are also available from the lounge and, during the summer months, a barbecue and buffet are served on the terrace. A host of sporting facilities has made this hotel famous. These include a 9-hole championship golf course, indoor and outdoor swimming pools, two indoor and four outdoor tennis courts, two squash courts, saunas and snooker room. A children's nanny is available to give guests extra freedom to enjoy themselves. Places of interest nearby include Dartmoor, South Hams and Exeter. Paignton Zoo, Bygone's Museum and Kent's Cavern are among the local attractions. **Directions:** From seafront follow signs for Babbacombe. Hotel entrance is on the right. Price guide: Single £50–£60; double/twin £90–£110; suites £160–£200. Special breaks available.

For hotel location, see maps on pages 473–479

In association
with MasterCard

PENDLEY MANOR HOTEL & CONFERENCE CENTRE

COW LANE, TRING, HERTFORDSHIRE HP23 5QY
TEL: 01442 891891 FAX: 01442 890687

The Pendley Manor was commissioned by Joseph Grout Williams in 1872. His instructions to architect John Lion were to build it in the Tudor style, reflecting the owner's interest in flora and fauna in the carved woodwork and stained glass panels. It stayed in the Williams family for three generations, but in 1987 the Manor was purchased by an independent hotel company, Craydawn Ltd. A refurbishment programme transformed it to its former glory and today's guests can once again enjoy the elegance and beauty of the Victorian era. The bedrooms are attractively furnished and well equipped, while the cuisine is appealing and well presented. Pendley Manor offers flexible conference facilities for up to 200 people. On its estate, which lies at the foot of the Chiltern Hills, sporting facilities include tennis courts, gymnasium; games rooms, buggy riding, laser shooting, archery and hot air balloon rides. Places of interest nearby include Woburn, Winslow Hall, Chenies Manor, Tring Zoological Museum and Dunstable Downs. **Directions:** Take Tring exit from new A41 and from roundabout take road marked Berkhamstead and London. Then take first turn on left. Price guide: Single £85; double/twin £95–£125; suites £130.

THE SPA HOTEL

MOUNT EPHRAIM, ROYAL TUNBRIDGE WELLS, KENT TN4 8XJ
TEL: 01892 520331 FAX: 01892 510575

The Spa was originally built in 1766 as a country mansion, with its own parkland, landscaped gardens and two handsome lakes. A hotel for over a century now, it retains standards of service reminiscent of life in Georgian and Regency England. All the bedrooms are individually furnished and many offer spectacular views. Above all else, The Spa Hotel prides itself on the excellence of its cuisine. The grand, Regency-style restaurant features the freshest produce from Kentish farms and London markets, complemented by a carefully selected wine list. Within the hotel is Sparkling Health, a magnificent health and leisure centre which is equipped to the highest standards. Leisure facilities include an indoor heated swimming pool, a fully equipped state-of-the-art gymnasium, cardiovascular gymnasium, aerobics dance studio, steam room, saunas, sunbeds, beauty clinic, hairdressing salon, flood-lit hard tennis court, childrens' adventure playground and ¹/₂ mile jogging track. The hotel is perfectly positioned for exploration of the castles, houses and gardens of Kent and Sussex. Special weekend bargain breaks are offered, with rates from £59.50 per person per night – full details available on request. **Directions:** Facing the common on the A264 in Tunbridge Wells. Price guide (excluding breakfast): Single from £69; double/twin from £84; suites from £130.

UCKFIELD (Little Horsted)

HORSTED PLACE SPORTING ESTATE AND HOTEL

LITTLE HORSTED, NR UCKFIELD, EAST SUSSEX TN22 5TS
TEL: 01825 750581 FAX: 01825 750240

Horsted Place enjoys a splendid location amid the peace and quiet of the Sussex Downs. This magnificent Victorian Gothic Mansion, which was built in 1851, overlooks the East Sussex National golf course and boasts an interior predominantly styled by the celebrated Victorian architect, Augustus Pugin. Guests are invited to enjoy the unobtrusive but excellent service offered by a committed staff trained to give fastidious attention to their requirements. The bedrooms in this lovely hotel are luxuriously decorated and furnished and offer every modern day comfort. Dining at Horsted is guaranteed to be a memorable experience. Chef Allan Garth offers a number of fixed priced and seasonally changing menus with his eclectic style of cooking. The Horsted Management Centre is a suite of air-conditioned rooms which have been specially designed to accommodate theatre-style presentations and training seminars or top level board meetings. Places of interest nearby include Royal Tunbridge Wells, Lewes and Glyndebourne. For golfing enthusiasts there is the added attraction of the East Sussex National Golf Club, one of the finest golf complexes in the world. **Directions:** The hotel entrance is on the A26 just short of the junction with the A22, two miles south of Uckfield and signposted towards Lewes. Price guide (including V.A.T.): Double/twin £130–£180; suites from £250.

LORDS OF THE MANOR HOTEL

UPPER SLAUGHTER, NR BOURTON-ON-THE-WATER, CHELTENHAM, GLOUCESTERSHIRE GL54 2JD
TEL: 01451 820243 FAX: 01451 820696

Situated in the heart of the Cotswolds, on the outskirts of one of England's most unspoiled and picturesque villages, stands the Lords of the Manor Hotel. Built in the 17th century of honeyed Cotswold stone, the house enjoys splendid views over the surrounding meadows, stream and parkland. For generations the house was the home of the Witts family, who historically had been rectors of the parish. It is from these origins that the hotel derives its distinctive name. Charming, walled gardens provide a secluded retreat at the rear of the house. Each bedroom bears the maiden name of one of the ladies who married into the Witts family: each room is individually and imaginatively decorated with traditional chintz and period furniture. The reception rooms are magnificently furnished with fine antiques, paintings, traditional fabrics and masses of fresh flowers. Log fires blaze in cold weather. The heart of this English country house is its dining room, where truly memorable dishes are created from the best local ingredients. Nearby are Blenheim Palace, Warwick Castle, the Roman antiquities at Bath and Shakespeare country. **Directions:** Upper Slaughter is 2 miles west of the A429 between Stow-on-the-Wold and Bourton-on-the-Water. Price guide: Single from £80; double/twin £115–£190.

THE LAKE ISLE

16 HIGH STREET EAST, UPPINGHAM, RUTLAND, LEICESTERSHIRE LE15 9PZ
TEL: 01572 822951 FAX: 01572 822951

This small personally run restaurant and town house hotel is situated in this pretty market town of Uppingham, dominated by the famous Uppingham School and close to Rutland Water. The entrance to the building, which dates back to the 18th century is via a quiet courtyard where a wonderful display of flowering tubs and hanging baskets greet you. In winter a log fire burns in the bar or relax in the upstairs lounge which overlooks the High Street. In the bedrooms, each named after a wine growing region in France, and all of which are en suite, guests will find fresh fruit, home-made biscuits and a decanter of sherry. Those in the courtyard are cottage-style suites. Under the personal direction of chef-patron David Whitfield the restaurant offers small weekly changing menus using fresh ingredients from far afield. There is an extensive wine list of more than 300 wines ranging from regional labels to old clarets. Special 'Wine Dinners' are held throughout the year, enabling guests to appreciate this unique cellar. Burghley House, Rockingham and Belvoir Castles are within a short drive. **Directions:** Uppingham is near the intersection of A47 and A6003. The hotel is on the High Street and is reached on foot via Reeves Yard and by car via Queen Street. Price guide: Single £45–£50; double/twin £60–£70; suite £70–£80.

THE SPRINGS HOTEL

NORTH STOKE, WALLINGFORD, OXFORDSHIRE OX10 6BE
TEL: 01491 836687 FAX: 01491 836877

The Springs is a grand old country house which dates from 1874 and is set deep in the heart of the beautiful Thames valley. One of the first houses in England to be built in the Mock Tudor style, it stands in six acres of grounds. The hotel's large south windows overlook a spring fed lake from which it takes its name. Many of the luxurious bedrooms and suites offer beautiful views over the lake and lawns, while others overlook the quiet woodland that surrounds the hotel. Private balconies provide patios for summer relaxation. The Fourways restaurant has an intimate, romantic atmosphere inspired by its gentle décor and the lovely view of the lake. The restaurant's menu is changed regularly to take advantage of fresh local produce and seasonal tastes. A well stocked cellar of carefully selected international wines provides the perfect accompaniment to a splendid meal. Leisure facilities include the swimming pool, a putting green, sauna bath and touring bicycles. Oxford and Windsor are nearby and the hotel is convenient for sporting events, racing at Newbury and Ascot and the Royal Henley Regatta. Directions: From the M40, take exit 6 onto the B4009, through Watlington to Benson; turn left onto A4074 towards Reading. After $^1/_2$ mile go right onto B4009. The hotel is $^1/_2$ mile further, on the right-hand side. Price guide: Single £85; double/twin £120–£150; suite £160.

BRIGGENS HOUSE HOTEL

BRIGGENS PARK, STANSTEAD ROAD, STANSTEAD ABBOTTS, NR WARE, HERTFORDSHIRE SG12 8LD
TEL: 01279 829955 FAX: 01279 793685

Briggens House Hotel, once a Georgian stately home, is set in 80 acres of lush countryside. Its lovely grounds include an Italian sunken garden, an arboretum containing trees from all over the world, and a charming walled kitchen garden. The hotel's artistically decorated bedrooms reflect the character and elegance of the 18th century building, while offering every modern amenity to ensure maximum comfort and convenience. Classical dishes and imaginative cuisine are features of the intimate Bridgeman Restaurant, where a wide variety of tastes and dietary requirements can be catered for. A nine hole professional golf course and two all weather tennis courts are available all year round, with a heated swimming pool open from April through to October. Clay pigeon and archery can be arranged upon request and an off site karting track is just minutes away. Briggens House is conveniently located between London and Cambridge. Attractions within the locality include Knebworth House, Hatfield House, The House on the Hill Toy Museum, Mountfitchet Castle and racing at Newmarket. **Directions:** Junction 7 from M11. Take A414 towards Hertford town, turn left at Eastwick Lodge roundabout still following A414. Exit at Briggens Park. Price guide: Single £85; double/twin £97–£130; suites £150.

HANBURY MANOR HOTEL

WARE, HERTFORDSHIRE SG12 0SD
TEL: 01920 487722 FAX: 01920 487692

A outstanding hotel, Hanbury Manor combines palatial grandeur with the most up-to-date amenities. Designed in 1890 in a Jacobean style, the many impressive features include elaborately moulded ceilings, carved wood panelling, leaded windows, chandeliers, portraits and huge tapestries. These create an elegant and comfortable environment. The three dining rooms vary in style from the formal Zodiac Restaurant to the informal Vardon Restaurant. All the cuisine is under the inspired guidance of Albert Roux of Le Gavroche. The health club includes an indoor swimming pool, Jacuzzi, squash courts, fully equipped gymnasium, crèche, sauna and steam baths. Professional treatments include herbal wraps, aromatherapy, mineral baths and massage, while specialists can advise on a personal fitness programme. There is an 18-hole golf course *par excellence* designed by Jack Nicklaus II. Outdoor pursuits include shooting, archery, horse-riding and hot-air ballooning. Ideal for conferences, ten rooms offer versatile business meetings facilities, including fax, photocopying, secretarial services and full professional support. Stansted Airport is 16 miles away. **Directions:** On the A10 25 miles north of London and 32 miles south of Cambridge. Price guide: Double/twin: £136–£197; suites £230–£405.

THE PRIORY HOTEL

CHURCH GREEN, WAREHAM, DORSET BH20 4ND
TEL: 01929 551666 FAX: 01929 554519

Dating from the early 16th century, the one-time Lady St Mary Priory has for hundreds of years offered sanctuary to travellers. In Hardy's Dorset, 'far from the madding crowd', it placidly stands on the bank of the River Frome in four acres of immaculate gardens. Steeped in history, The Priory has undergone a sympathetic conversion to a hotel which is charming yet unpretentious. Each bedroom is distictively styled, with family antiques lending character and many rooms have views of the Purbeck Hills. A 16th century clay barn has been transformed into the Boathouse, consisting of two spacious luxury suites at the river's edge. Tastefully furnished, the drawing room, residents' lounge and intimate bar together create a convivial atmosphere. The Greenwood Dining Room is open for breakfast and lunch, while splendid dinners are served in the vaulted stone cellars. There are moorings for guests arriving by boat. Dating back to the 9th century, the market town of Wareham has more than 200 listed buildings. Corfe Castle, Lulworth Cove, Poole and Swanage are all close by with superb walks and beaches. **Directions:** Wareham is on the A351 to the west of Bournemouth and Poole. The hotel is beside the River Frome to the east of Wareham. Price guide: Single £60–£105; double/twin £80–£185; suite £185.

BISHOPSTROW HOUSE

WARMINSTER, WILTSHIRE BA12 9HH
TEL: 01985 212312 FAX: 01985 216769

Built by John Pinch of Bath in 1817, Bishopstrow House offers its visitors the grace of a Georgian mansion together with all the benefits of modern facilities. Displayed in the finely proportioned public rooms is an impressive collection of antiques, 19th-century oil paintings and Persian carpets. Bedrooms feature canopied beds, festoon draperies and in some cases, private safes. Grandly furnished suites are available with luxurious bathrooms which have large, circular baths fitted with Jacuzzi whirlpools. The emphasis is on light, imaginative cooking in the modern style, with English and French dishes prepared by Chris Suter, winner of the 1990 Young Chef of the Year Award. A wide selection of carefully chosen wine is kept in the vaulted cellars. Guests may use the sauna, an indoor floodlit tennis court, perhaps followed by a leisurely swim in the heated pool, which is housed in an elegant, marble-pillared room. There is access to fishing within the hotel grounds, on the banks of the River Wylye. Longleat House, the beautiful gardens and arboretum of Stourhead, Bath, Shaftesbury and Stonehenge are close at hand. Less than one mile away is the West Wiltshire Golf Course. **Directions:** Bishopstrow House is just south-east of Warminster on the B3414 from London via the M3. Price guide: Single £98; double/twin £125–£250.

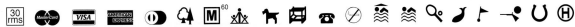

THE GLEBE AT BARFORD

CHURCH STREET, BARFORD, WARWICKSHIRE CV35 8BS
TEL: 01926 624218 FAX: 01926 624625

The Glebe at Barford was built in the 1820s as a rectory to the Church of St Peter, which stands next to the hotel gardens. Each of the 41 bedrooms has been tastefully decorated with soft, pastel fabrics and features either a coronet-style bed, a tented ceiling or a four-poster bed. The en suite bathrooms are all attractively finished with golden fittings and Italian marble floors. Pre-dinner drinks can be enjoyed in either the spacious lounge bar or the stylish cocktail bar with its flowing drapes and elegant seating. Overlooking the croquet lawn, the Cedars Conservatory Restaurant is the setting for dinner, where a wide selection of imaginatively prepared English and continental dishes is available. The showpiece of Glades Leisure Club is the heated swimming pool, fitted with the latest hydro swim jets and incorporating a massage spa pool. In addition, guests have free use of the sauna, steam room and trimnasium. The Bentley Suite can be tailored to suit conferences, weddings and dinners, while the Directors' Suite is a smaller executive-style meeting room. Stratford-upon-Avon, Leamington Spa, Warwick Castle, Birmingham and the Cotswolds are all accessible from The Glebe. **Directions:** From junction 15, M40 take A429 to Barford. At roundabout turn into Church Street. Price guide: Single £81–£105; double/twin £99–£150.

LINTON SPRINGS

SICKLINGHALL ROAD, WETHERBY, WEST YORKSHIRE LS22 4AF
TEL: 01937 585353 FAX: 01937 587579

Set in 14 acres of beautiful parkland, Linton Springs is an elegant country house hotel which successfully combines the grace of an English period house with modern day comforts. The house was built in the late 1700s as a shooting lodge for the nearby Harewood Estate. It has undergone extensive restoration work in recent times and boasts tasteful décor and furnishings throughout. The attractive and spacious bedrooms all feature oak panelling and are equipped with every modern amenity to ensure the highest level of comfort and convenience. Meals are served in the Gun Room Restaurant and excellent traditional English cuisine is complemented by a fine wine list. The menu features "special" dishes which are changed daily. The Linton Suite is an ideal setting for special occasions, while The Terrace Room and Boardroom provide privacy for business meetings and private dining. To help guests unwind, there is a 250 yard golf driving range and en-tout-cas tennis court within the grounds. There are also eight golf courses within a 20 minute drive. Nearby attractions include Leeds, York with its famous minster and the spa town of Harrogate. **Directions:** From A1 go through Wetherby towards Harrogate on the A661. After quarter of a mile turn left to Sicklinghall and the hotel is one mile on the left. Price guide: Single: £60; double/twin £80; suites £100.

WOOD HALL

LINTON, NR WETHERBY, WEST YORKSHIRE LS22 4JA
TEL: 01937 587271 FAX: 01937 584353

Off the A1 about 15 miles due west of York, built of stone from the estate, Wood Hall is an elegant Georgian house overlooking the River Wharfe. Its grounds, over 100 acres in all, are approached along a private drive that winds through a sweep of parkland. The sumptuously furnished drawing room and the oak-panelled bar, with its gentlemen's club atmosphere, lead off the grand entrance hall. Superb floral displays, gleaming chandeliers and immaculately designed interiors hint at the careful attention that has been lavished on Wood Hall. Gastronomes will relish the excellent à la carte menu, which combines contemporary Anglo-French style with attractive presentation. The mile-long private stretch of the Wharfe offers up trout and barbel to the keen angler, while miles of walks and jogging paths encompass the estate. There is a leisure club including a swimming pool, spa bath, steam room, gymnasium, solarium and treatment salon. Near to the National Hunt Race-course at Wetherby, York, Harrogate, Leeds, the Dales and Harewood House are only a short distance away. **Directions:** From Wetherby, take the A661 towards Harrogate. Take turning for Sicklinghall and Linton, then left for Linton and Wood Hall. Turn right opposite the Windmill public house; hotel is 1¹/₂ miles further on. Price guide: Single £90–£135; double/twin £98–£145; suite £280.

OATLANDS PARK HOTEL

146 OATLANDS DRIVE, WEYBRIDGE, SURREY KT13 9HB
TEL: 01932 847242 FAX: 01932 842252

Records of the Oatlands estate show that Elizabeth I and the Stuart kings spent time in residence in the original buildings. The present mansion dates from the late-18th century and became a hotel in 1856: famous guests included Émile Zola, Anthony Trollope and Edward Lear. The hotel stands in acres of parkland overlooking Broadwater Lake, with easy access to Heathrow, Gatwick and central London. Although it caters for the modern traveller, the hotel's historic character is evident throughout. The accommodation ranges from superior rooms to large de luxe rooms and suites. The elegant, high-ceilinged Broadwater Restaurant is the setting for creative à la carte menus with dishes to suit all tastes. A traditional roast is served every Sunday lunchtime. The professional conference team, six meeting rooms and up-to-date facilities make Oatlands Park a popular function venue. Theme evenings, such as Henry VIII banquets, are a speciality. Many sporting and leisure activities can be arranged, including golf, archery and shooting. There is a new fitness room. **Directions:** From M25 junction 11, follow signs to Weybridge. Follow A317 through High Street into Monument Hill to mini-roundabout. Turn left into Oatlands Drive; hotel is 50 yards on left. Price guide: Single £97–£108; double/twin £128–£143; suite £153. Special Break rate: Single £45; double/twin £70–£80.

KILHEY COURT

CHORLEY ROAD, STANDISH, WIGAN, LANCASHIRE WN1 2XN
TEL: 01257 472100 FAX: 01257 422401

Kilhey Court, with its wealth of Victorian features, offers a delightful environment for guests seeking high standards of comfort. The bedrooms provide a full range of facilities, while four luxurious suites complete with spa bath have been recently elegantly refurbished. The Laureate Restaurant, with its idyllic garden room setting and splendid Victorian conservatory, overlooks ten acres of carefully tended lawns and the picturesque Worthington lakes. It has been awarded two coveted Red Rosettes by the AA and its imaginative culinary dishes are carefully prepared using only the finest ingredients. An alternative dining experience is offered in the new Italian Pizza Oven Bistro. Guests seeking either a strenuous workout or some relaxation are invited to take advantage of the leisure centre, which offers guests a range of facilities including airconditioned aerobics studio, high tech gym, swimming pool, sauna, steam room and solarium. The impressive conference and seminar facilities at Kilhey Court are backed by a full range of support and technical services. The hotel owns the 18-hole Standish Court Golf Course which is just half a mile away. **Directions:** M6 exit 27 go into Standish, through traffic lights to T-junction, turn left and hotel is half a mile on right. Price guide: Single £70–£92; double/twin £85–£110; suites £135–£140.

WILLINGTON HALL HOTEL

WILLINGTON, NEAR TARPORLEY, CHESHIRE CW6 0NB
TEL: 01829 752321 FAX: 01829 752596

Built by Cheshire landowner Charles Tomkinson, Willington Hall was converted into a hotel by one of his descendants in 1977. Set in 17 acres of woods and parkland, the hotel affords wonderful views across the Cheshire countryside towards the Welsh mountains. There are both formally landscaped and 'wild' gardens, which create a beautiful backdrop for the handsome architectural proportions of the house. The hotel is a comfortable and friendly retreat for those seeking peace and seclusion. Under the personal supervision of Ross Pigot, Willington Hall has acquired a good reputation with local people for its extensive bar meals and à la carte restaurant, along with friendly and attentive service. The menus offer traditional English cooking, with dishes such as roast duckling with black cherry sauce. It is an ideal location for visiting the Roman city of Chester, Tatton Park, Beeston Castle and Oulton Park racetrack. North Wales is easily accessible from Willington Hall. The hotel is closed on Christmas Day. **Directions:** Take the A51 from Tarporley to Chester and turn right at the Bull's Head public house at Clotton. Willington Hall Hotel is one mile ahead on the left. Price guide: Single £44–£54; double/twin £80.

THE STANNEYLANDS HOTEL

STANNEYLANDS ROAD, WILMSLOW, CHESHIRE SK9 4EY
TEL: 01625 525225 FAX: 01625 537282

Privately owned and managed by Gordon Beech, Stanneylands is a handsome country house set in several acres of impressive gardens with an unusual collection of trees and shrubs. Some of the bedrooms offer lovely views over the gardens while others overlook the undulating Cheshire countryside. A sense of quiet luxury prevails in the reception rooms, where classical décor and comfortable furnishings create a relaxing ambience. In the restaurant, contemporary English cooking is prepared to a very high standard both in terms of composition and presentation, while live occasional music adds to the atmosphere. In addition, a private oak-panelled dining room can accommodate up to 50 people, while a larger suite is available for conferences and personal celebrations. The Stanneylands Hotel is conveniently located for tours of the rolling Cheshire plain or the more rugged Peak District, as well as the bustling market towns and notable industrial heritage of the area. Special corporate and weekend rates are available. **Directions:** Three miles from Manchester International Airport, Stanneylands is on a minor road which runs from the B5166 at Styal to the A34 between Wilmslow and Handforth. Bear right on this road to find the hotel just after crossing the River Dean. Price guide: Single £82.95; double/twin £91.35–£126; suite £126.

320
For hotel location, see maps on pages 473–479

HOTEL DU VIN & BISTRO

14 SOUTHGATE STREET, WINCHESTER, HAMPSHIRE SO23 9EF
TEL: 01962 841414 FAX: 01962 842458

Relaxed, charming and unpretentious are words which aptly describe the stylish and intimate Hotel du Vin & Bistro. This elegant hotel is housed in one of Winchester's most important Georgian buildings, dating back to 1715. It is jointly run by Gerard Basset, perhaps the UK's most famous sommelier, and Robin Hutson, whose career includes time with some of the country's finest hotels. The 13 individually decorated bedrooms feature superb beds made up with crisp, Egyptian cotton and offer every modern amenity, including telephone, trouser press, mini bar and tea and coffee making facilities. Each bedroom is sponsored by a wine house whose vineyard features in its decorations. Bathrooms boasting power showers, oversized baths and fluffy towels add to guests' sense of luxury and comfort. Quality food cooked simply with fresh local ingredients is the philosophy behind the Bistro, where an excellent and reasonably priced wine list is available. There is also a conference room available for special occasions. A welcoming and enthusiastic staff cater for every need. The hotel is a perfect base for exploring England's ancient capital, famous for its Cathedral and antique shops. The New Forest is a short drive away. **Directions:** M3 to Winchester. Southgate Street leads from the City centre to St. Cross. Price guide: Single: £60–£90; double/twin: £65–£95.

In association
with MasterCard

LAINSTON HOUSE HOTEL

SPARSHOLT, WINCHESTER, HAMPSHIRE SO21 2LT
TEL: 01962 863588 FAX: 01962 776672

The fascinating history of Lainston House is well documented, some of its land having been recorded in the *Domesday Book* of 1087. Set in 63 acres of superb downland countryside, this graceful William and Mary country house has been sympathetically restored to create a beautiful hotel. From the individually designed bedrooms to the main reception rooms, elegant and comfortable furnishings are the hallmark of Lainston House. Freshly prepared food, attentive service and views over the lawn make the restaurant one of the most popular in Hampshire. Facilities are available for small meetings in the Mountbatten Room or larger functions in the recently converted 17th century Dawley Barn. The charming grounds hold many surprises – an ancient chapel, reputedly haunted by the legendary Elizabeth Chudleigh, an 18th century herb garden and a dovecote. Historic Winchester is only $2^1/_2$ miles south, while Romsey Abbey, Salisbury and the New Forest are a short drive away. Other local activities include riding, country walking and good trout fishing on the River Test at nearby Stockbridge.
Directions: Lainston House is well signposted off the A272 Winchester–Stockbridge road, at Sparsholt $2^1/_2$ miles from Winchester. Price guide: Single from £95; double/twin £125–£225; suite from £245.

GILPIN LODGE

CROOK ROAD, NR WINDERMERE, CUMBRIA LA23 3NE
TEL: 015394 88818 FREEPHONE: 0800 269460 FAX: 015394 88058

Set in 20 acres of woodlands, moors and country gardens, surrounded by lakeland fells, Gilpin Lodge exudes tranquillity. Yet, only 12 miles from the M6 and two miles from Lake Winderemere, the area boasts a profusion of activities and sightseeing: walking and climbing, water sports, fishing, riding, golf (the golf course is almost opposite), historic houses, gardens and castles, and memorabilia of Beatrix Potter, Wordsworth and Ruskin. Guests have free use of a nearby private leisure club. This elegant yet relaxing hotel, a turn of the century Victorian house tastefully extended 90 years later, and modernised to incorporate every comfort, is replete with antiques, flowers, picture lined walls, real fires in winter, comfortable lounges, sumptuous en suite bedrooms (some with four-poster beds and all with sitting areas), and the warmest of welcomes from proprietors Christine and John Cunliffe. Service is attentive but unpretentious. The food, awarded two rosettes by the AA, is a pleasant obsession here. Dinner menus offer a wide choice of imaginative dishes. There is an extensive and varied wine list. Gilpin Lodge is graded 4 Crowns De Luxe and is highly acclaimed in most guides. Open throughout the year. **Directions:** M6 exit 36. A591 Kendal bypass then B5284 to Crook. Price guide: Single £50–£80; double/twin £80–£120; including dinner: single £65–£100; double/twin £110–£160

LAKESIDE HOTEL ON LAKE WINDERMERE

LAKESIDE, NEWBY BRIDGE, CUMBRIA LA12 8AT
TEL: 015395 31207 FAX: 015395 31699

Lakeside Hotel offers you a unique location on the water's edge of Lake Windermere. It is a classic, traditional lakeland hotel offering all the comforts and facilities you would expect. All the bedrooms are en suite and enjoy individually designed fabrics and colours, many of the rooms offer superlative views of the lake. Guests may dine in either the award-winning Lakeview Restaurant or Ruskin's Brasserie, where extensive menus offer a wide selection of dishes including Cumbrian specialities. The Lakeside Conservatory serves drinks and light meals throughout the day – once there you are sure to fall under the spell of this peaceful location. Berthed next to the lake you have cruisers which will allow you to discover the lake from the water. Guests are given free use of the Cascades Leisure Club at Newby Bridge. The hotel offers a fully equipped conference centre and many syndicate suites allowing plenty of scope and flexibility. Most of all you are assured of a stay in an unrivalled setting of genuine character. The original panelling and beams of the old coaching inn create an excellent ambience, whilst you are certain to enjoy the quality and friendly service.
Directions: From M6 junction 36 join A590 to Newby Bridge, turn right over bridge towards Hawkshead; hotel is one mile on right. Price guide: Single £75–£95; double/twin £110–£130; suites £150–£170.

LANGDALE CHASE

WINDERMERE, CUMBRIA LA23 1LW
TEL: 015394 32201 FAX: 015394 32604

Langdale Chase stands in five acres of landscaped gardens on the shores of Lake Windermere, with panoramic views over England's largest lake to the Langdale Pikes beyond. Visitors will receive good hospitality in this well-run country home, which is splendidly decorated with oak panelling, fine oil paintings and ornate, carved fireplaces. A magnificent staircase leads to the well-appointed bedrooms, many overlooking the lake. One unique bedroom is sited over the lakeside boathouse, where the traveller may be lulled to sleep by the gently lapping waters below. For the energetic, there is a choice of water-skiing, swimming or sailing from the hotel jetty. Guests can stroll through the gardens along the lake shore, in May the gardens are spectacular when the rhododendrons and azalias are in bloom. Guests have free access to the facilities of the adjacent leisure centre. Being pampered by attentive staff will be one of the many highlights of your stay at Langdale Chase. The variety of food and wine is sure to delight the most discerning diner. Combine this with a panoramic tableau across England's largest and loveliest of lakes and you have a truly unforgettable dining experience. **Directions:** Situated on the A591, three miles north of Windermere, two miles south of Ambleside. Price guide: Single from £40–£72; double/twin from £75–£110; suite £116–£150.

LINTHWAITE HOUSE HOTEL

CROOK ROAD, BOWNESS-ON-WINDERMERE, CUMBRIA LA23 3JA
TEL: 015394 88600 FAX: 015394 88601

Situated in 14 acres of gardens and woods in the heart of the Lake Distict, Linthwaite House overlooks Lake Windermere and Belle Island, with Claiffe Heights and Coniston Old Man beyond. Here, guests will find themselves amid spectacular scenery, yet only a short drive from the motorway network. The hotel combines stylish originality with the best of traditional English hospitality. The superbly decorated bedrooms, all en suite, offer glorious views. The comfortable lounge is the perfect place to unwind and there is a fire on winter evenings. In the restaurant, excellent cuisine features the best of fresh, local produce, accompanied by a fine selection of wines. Within the hotel grounds, there is a 9-hole putting green and a par 3 practice hole. Fly fishermen can fish for brown trout in the hotel tarn. Guests have complimentary use of a private swimming pool and lesiure club nearby, while fell walks begin at the hotel's front door. The area around Linthwaite abounds with places of interest: this is Beatrix Potter and Wordsworth country, and there is much to interest the visitor. **Directions:** From the M6 junction 36 follow Kendal by-pass (A590) for 8 miles. Take B5284 Crook Road for 6 miles. 1 mile beyond Windermere Golf Club, Linthwaite House is signposted on left. Price guide: Single £70–£95; double/twin £110–£150; suite £170.

OAKLEY COURT

WINDSOR ROAD, WATER OAKLEY, NR WINDSOR, BERKSHIRE SL4 5UR
TEL: 01753 609988 FAX: 01628 37011

The turreted towers of Oakley Court rise majestically over the banks of the Thames, where this handsome mansion has stood since 1859. The waterside location enables the hotel to offer a unique range of boating facilities, from a champagne picnic hamper for two on a chauffeured punt to a gastronomic feast for a hundred on a steamboat. The hotel's grandeur is quite awe-inspiring. Restored to their original splendour, the entrance hall, library and drawing room feature elaborate plasterwork, fresh flowers and elegant furnishings. An antique billiard table in the games room is kept in pristine condition. All of the bedrooms have views over the river or the 35-acre gardens. Gourmet cuisine is prepared by a skilled team, under chef Michael Croft, and is served with finesse in the candle-lit Oakleaf Restaurant, or in Boaters for lighter, less formal dining. Private dining can be arranged in the superbly equipped conference and banqueting suites. Activities organised for corporate parties include archery, laser clay pigeon shooting and falconry. There is a 9-hole par 3 golf course on site and the hotel has its own gym, sauna and solarium. Windsor Castle, Eton and Ascot are nearby, and Heathrow is 20 minutes' drive. **Directions:** Situated just off the A308, between Windsor and Maidenhead. Price guide: Single £104–£150; double/twin £104–£200; suites £260–£380.

LANGLEY HOUSE HOTEL

LANGLEY MARSH, WIVELISCOMBE, SOMERSET TA4 2UF
TEL: 01984 623318 FAX: 01984 624573

Conveniently located not far from the M5 junction 26, Langley House is a 16th century retreat set in four acres of beautifully kept gardens on the edge of the pretty Somerset town of Wiveliscombe. Modifications in Georgian times have invested this small, cosy hotel with a unique period charm, which explains its enduring popularity. Owners Peter and Anne Wilson have excelled in making Langley House a relaxed and comfortable place to stay. The eight bedrooms, all en suite, are individually decorated, with direct-dial telephone, TV and radio. Most have peaceful garden views and personal touches throughout including fresh flowers and mineral water, books and hot-water bottles.

Discreet good taste has been exercised in furnishing the public rooms with pastel sofas, traditional rugs, china and glass, antiques and paintings. (Langley House won the Wedgwood/British Tourist Authority Interior Design Award). In the beamed restaurant, Peter Wilson serves critically acclaimed cuisine and has been awarded a Michelin Red M. The wine list carries over 200 wines. Places of interest nearby include Exmoor, and famous gardens Knightshayes, Stourhead and Hestercombe. **Directions:** Wiveliscombe is 10 miles from Taunton on B3227. Langley House is half a mile north, signposted Langley Marsh. Price guide: Single £64.50–£70; double/twin £89–£115.

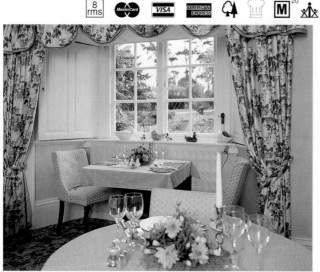

THE OLD VICARAGE HOTEL

WORFIELD, BRIDGNORTH, SHROPSHIRE WV15 5JZ
TEL: 01746 716497 FAX: 01746 716552

Standing in 2 acres of mature grounds, this Edwardian parsonage has been lovingly transformed into a delightful country house hotel. Awards abound – 3 AA Rosettes for food – English Tourist Board De Luxe Hotel and RAC 3 Merit Awards. The Old Vicarage offers guests an opportunity to enjoy a peaceful retreat in countryside of outstanding beauty. The spacious bedrooms are sensitively furnished in Victorian and Edwardian styles to complement the period features of the house. Four Coach House rooms offer complete luxury and comfort – and the Leighton suite has been specially designed with the disabled guest in mind. The

daily changing menu features the best of local produce and the award-winning cheeseboard and wine cellar will complete a wonderful evening. Local attractions include the world famous Ironbridge Gorge Museum complex, the Severn Valley preserved steam railway and the splendour of the border towns and villages. Half price golf is available at Worfield Golf Club. Two-day breaks available from £65 per person per day, which includes free Passport Tickets to Ironbridge Gorge. **Directions:** Eight miles west of Wolverhampton, one mile off A454, eight miles south of junction 4 of M54. Price guide: Single £65–£85; double/twin £98–£138.

SECKFORD HALL

WOODBRIDGE, SUFFOLK IP13 6NU
TEL: 01394 385678 FAX: 01394 380610

Seckford Hall dates from 1530 and it is said that Elizabeth I once held court here. The hall has lost none of its Tudor grandeur. Furnished as a private house with many fine period pieces, the panelled rooms, beamed ceilings, carved doors and great stone fireplaces are displayed against the splendour of English oak. Local delicacies such as the house speciality, lobster, feature on the à la carte menu. The original minstrels gallery can be viewed in the banqueting hall, which is now a conference and function suite designed in keeping with the general style. The Courtyard area was converted from a giant Tudor tithe barn, dairy and coach house. It now incorporates ten charming cottage-style suites and a modern leisure complex, which includes a heated swimming pool, exercise machines, solarium and spa bath. The hotel is set in 34 acres of tranquil parkland with sweeping lawns and a willow-fringed lake, and guests may stroll about the grounds or simply relax in the attractive terrace garden. There is a 18-hole golf course on a pay and play basis, where equipment can be hired. A walk along the riverside will take the visitor to picturesque Woodbridge, with its tide mill, antiques shops, yacht harbours and quaint old streets. Constable country and the Suffolk coast are nearby. **Directions:** Remain on the A12 Woodbridge bypass until you see the blue-and-white hotel sign. Price guide: Single £79–£99; double/twin £99–£135.

PETWOOD HOUSE HOTEL

STIXWOULD ROAD, WOODHALL SPA, LINCOLNSHIRE LN10 6QF
TEL: 01526 352411 FAX: 01526 353473

This fine hotel, set in 30 acres of secluded gardens and mature woodlands, was built at the turn of the century by Lady Weigall, the daughter of furniture stores magnate Sir Blundell Maple. It is said that the Maple craftsmen were responsible for the carving and building of the superb oak staircase and oak panelling. During World War II the Royal Air Force requisitioned the building and in 1943 several squadrons, including the famous 617 "Dambusters" Squadron, turned it into their Officers' Mess. "The Squadron Bar" has been recently reopened to the public. This is a wonderful memorial to the Dambusters. Full of memorabilia, it even contains the original piano. The traditional elegance of a period country house is evident in the spacious and well appointed en suite bedrooms. The restaurant serves the best of English, French and continental cuisine, augmented by a well-stocked cellar of wines, ports and liqueurs. Residents can take advantage of the facilities offered by a nearby leisure club. These include a swimming pool and 18-hole golf course. Petwood House is an ideal venue for conferences, banquets and receptions for up to 200. There is a choice of function suites, and a marquee can be set up on the lawn. **Directions:** From Lincoln take B1188, then B1189 and B1191 to Woodhall Spa. Price guide: Single £69.70–£81; double/twin £81–£120.

THE FEATHERS HOTEL

MARKET STREET, WOODSTOCK, OXFORDSHIRE OX20 1SX
TEL: 01993 812291 FAX: 01993 813158

The Feathers is a privately owned and run country house hotel, situated in the centre of Woodstock, a few miles from Oxford. Woodstock is one England's most attractive country towns, constructed mostly from Cotswold stone and with buildings dating from the 12th century. The hotel, built in the 17th century, was originally four separate houses. Antiques, log fires and traditional English furnishings lend character and charm. There are only 16 bedrooms, all of which have private bathrooms and showers. Public rooms, including the drawing room and study, are intimate and comfortable. The small garden is a delightful setting for a light lunch or afternoon tea and guests can enjoy a drink in the cosy courtyard bar, which has an open fire in winter. The antique-panelled restaurant is internationally renowned for its fine cuisine, complemented by a high standard of service. The menu changes daily and offers a wide variety of dishes, using the finest local ingredients. Blenheim Palace, seat of the Duke of Marlborough and birthplace of Sir Winston Churchill, is just around the corner. The Cotswolds and the dreaming spires of Oxford are a short distance away. **Directions:** From London leave M40 at junction 8; from Birmingham leave at junction 9. Take A44 and follow signs to Woodstock. The hotel is on the left. Price guide: Single £78; double/twin £99–£150; suite £185–£220.

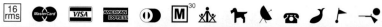

For hotel location, see maps on pages 473–479

WATERSMEET HOTEL

MORTEHOE, WOOLACOMBE, DEVON EX34 7EB
TEL: 01271 870333 FAX: 01271 870890

In a superb setting on the National Trust's North Atlantic coastline, Watersmeet Hotel commands dramatic views across Woolacombe Bay past Hartland Point to Lundy Island. Private steps lead directly from the hotel garden to the beach below. Resident owners Brian and Pat Wheeldon ensure that Watersmeet exudes the comfortable luxury of a country house. Attractive décor and floral fabrics in soft colours create a summery impression. The main bedrooms overlook the sea and visitors can fall asleep to the sound of lapping waves. Coffee, lunch and afternoon tea can be taken in the lounge, on the terrace or by the pool. Each evening the candles flicker in the Pavilion Restaurant and as the sun sets across the sea, guests can savour traditional English and continental dishes with a good choice of wines. That the hotel has been awarded two AA Rosettes for cuisine and all three RAC Merit awards for excellent hospitality, restaurant and comfort is indicative of its high standards. Locally, visitors can enjoy surfing, bathing, riding, bracing walks along coastal paths and exploring North Devon and Exmoor. Closed December to January. **Directions:** From Barnstaple follow A361 signed Ilfracombe for 8 miles. Turn left at roundabout and follow signs to Mortehoe. Price guide (including dinner): Single £55–£90; double/twin £90–£190.

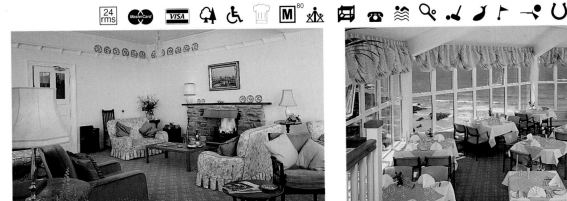

WOOLACOMBE BAY HOTEL

SOUTH STREET, WOOLACOMBE, DEVON EX34 7BN
TEL: 01271 870388 FAX: 01271 870613

Woolacombe Bay Hotel stands in 6 acres of grounds, leading to three miles of golden sand. Built by the Victorians, the hotel has an air of luxury, style and comfort. All rooms are en suite with satellite TV, baby listening, ironing centre, some with a spa bath or balcony. Traditional English and French dishes are offered in the dining room. Superb recreational amenities on site include unlimited free access to tennis, squash, indoor and outdoor pools, billiards, bowls, croquet, dancing and films, a health suite with steam room, sauna, spa bath with heated benches and high impulse shower. Power-boating, shooting and riding can be arranged, and preferential rates are offered for golf at the Saunton Golf Club. New "Hot House" aerobics studio, cardio vascular weights room, solariums, massage and beautician. However, being energetic is not a requirement for enjoying the qualities of Woolacombe Bay. Many of its regulars choose simply to relax in the grand public rooms and in the grounds, which extend to the rolling surf of the magnificent bay. A drive along the coastal route in either direction will guarantee splendid views. Exmoor's beautiful Doone Valley is an hour away by car. ETB 5 Crowns. Closed January. **Directions:** At centre of village, off main Barnstaple–Ilfracombe road. Price guide (including dinner): Single £53–£78; double/twin £106–£156.

BILBROUGH MANOR

BILBROUGH, YORK, NORTH YORKSHIRE YO2 3PH
TEL: 01937 834002 FAX: 01937 834724

This gracious manor house is situated on the edge of the conservation village of Bilbrough, just five miles from the centre of York. Since the time they acquired it in 1986, owners Colin and Susan Bell have transformed the manor from a private house into a comfortable hotel, with all the elements of the *Upstairs Downstairs* portrayal of service, comfort and fine food – including a butler! The 12 bedrooms are all individual in character with bathrooms en suite, colour television and direct dial telephone. Oak panelling, beautiful fireplaces with open fires in winter and comfortable furniture are features of the public rooms. In the formal dining room, New Classical French dishes are prepared by a team of young chefs, headed by Andrew Jones. The restaurant is managed by Antonio Esteve. Extensive gardens, where you can relax or play croquet on the lawn, and 100 acres of farmland and woodland surround the Manor. There are views to the Vale of York and Ilkley Moor beyond. Riding can be arranged locally and there are racecourses at York, Doncaster and Ripon. Also within reach are the Yorkshire Dales, Castle Howard, Whitby and Scarborough. Closed at Christmas. **Directions:** From A64 at Bilbrough (west of York), turn opposite the McDonalds Drive Thru, then take first left to the Manor. Price guide: Single £77; double/twin £85–£150.

THE GRANGE HOTEL

CLIFTON, YORK, NORTH YORKSHIRE YO3 6AA
TEL: 01904 644744 FAX: 01904 612453

Set near the ancient city walls, 4 minutes' walk from the famous Minster, this sophisticated Regency town house has been carefully restored and its spacious rooms richly decorated. Beautiful stone-flagged floors in the corridors of The Grange lead to the classically styled reception rooms. The flower-filled Morning Room is welcoming, with its blazing log fire and deep sofas, and double doors between the panelled library and drawing room can be opened up to create a dignified venue for parties, wedding receptions or business entertaining. Prints, flowers and English chintz in the bedrooms reflect the proprietor's careful attention to detail. The Ivy Restaurant has an established reputation for first-class gastronomy, incorporating the best in French and country house cooking. The Brasserie is open for lunch and dinner until after the theatre closes in the evening. For conferences, a computer, fax and telex are available as well as secretarial services. Brimming with history, York's list of attractions includes the National Railway Museum, the Jorvik Viking Centre and the medieval Shambles. **Directions:** The Grange Hotel is on the A19 York–Thirsk road, 1/2 mile from the centre on the left. Price guide: Single £89; double/twin £100–£155; suites £175.

MIDDLETHORPE HALL

BISHOPTHORPE ROAD, YORK YO2 1QB
TEL: 01904 641241 FAX: 01904 620176

Middlethorpe Hall is a delightful William III house, built in 1699 for Thomas Barlow, a wealthy merchant, and was for a time the home of Lady Mary Wortley Montagu, the 18th-century writer of letters. The house has been immaculately restored by Historic House Hotels who have decorated and furnished it in its original elegance and style. There are beautifully designed bedrooms and suites in the main house and in the adjacent classical courtyard. The restaurant offers the best in contemporary English cooking with an imaginative menu and a carefully chosen wine list. Middlethorpe stands in 26 acres of parkland where guests can wander and enjoy the walled garden, the white garden, the lake and the original ha ha's. The hotel overlooks York Racecourse – known as the 'Ascot of the North' – and the medieval city of York with its fascinating museums, restored streets and world-famous Minster is only 2 miles away. From Middlethorpe you can visit Yorkshire's famous country houses, like Castle Howard, Beningbrough and Harewood, the ruined Abbeys of Fountains and Rievaulx and explore the magnificent Yorkshire Moors. Helmsley, Whitby and Scarborough are nearby. **Directions:** Take A64 (T) off A1 (T) near Tadcaster, follow signs to York West, then smaller signs to Bishopthorpe. Price guide: Single £87–£108; double/twin £120–£179; suite from £190–£205.

For hotel location, see maps on pages 473–479

MOUNT ROYALE HOTEL

THE MOUNT, YORK, NORTH YORKSHIRE YO2 2DA
TEL: 01904 628856 FAX: 01904 611171

Two elegant William IV houses have been restored to their former glory to create the Mount Royale Hotel, which is personally run by resident proprietors Richard and Christine Oxtoby and their family. Comfortable bedrooms are furnished with imagination, all in an individual style. Each of the garden rooms opens onto the garden and has its own verandah. Downstairs, the public rooms are filled with interesting items of antique furniture, *objets d'art* and gilt-framed paintings. To the rear of the building, overlooking the gardens, is the restaurant, where guests can enjoy the best of traditional English cooking and French cuisine. Amenities include a snooker room with a full-sized table, steam room, sauna, solarium and trimnasium. With a delightful English garden and heated outdoor pool, the one acre grounds are a peaceful haven just minutes from York's centre. York is a historic and well-preserved city, famous for its Minster and medieval streets. Also within walking distance is York racecourse, where the flat-racing season runs from May to October. Lovers of the great outdoors will find the Yorkshire Dales and North York Moors a 45-minute drive away. Only small dogs by arrangement. **Directions:** From A64, turn onto the A1036 signposted York. Go past racecourse; hotel is on right before traffic lights. Price guide: Single £70–£90; double/twin £85–£115; suites £120.

Johansens Recommended Hotels in
Wales

Bodnant Gardens, Clwyd

Magnificent *scenery, a rich variety of natural, cultural and modern leisure attractions, and the very best accommodation awaits the Johansens visitor to Wales.*

Each year, millions of visitors head for Wales to discover or rediscover all that the country has to offer. An exceptionally high proportion come back year after year – a sure sign of satisfaction.

Wales has some of the most fabulous scenery imaginable, with much to see and do, and boasts three national parks covering nearly 1,600 square miles, as well as five areas designated as being of Outstanding Natural Beauty.

There are numerous large country parks, nature reserves, sites of special scientific interest and more than 700 miles of breathtakingly beautiful coastline to discover, plus delightful off shore islands, home to colonies of seals and rare birds.

But quite apart from the country's unspoilt natural beauty and endless scenic variety, the principality has a wealth of interesting and unusual attractions to enjoy.

There are a whole host of fascinating places to visit, many of them unique like the Centre for Alternative Technology, the green village of the future at Machynlleth in Mid Wales or Portmeirion, the dreamlike Italianate village in North Wales.

Visitors can take a ride on a narrow gauge steam railway, take a trip on a horse drawn canal boat, go to the summit of the Great Orme in the only cable hauled tramway in Britain, travel across Aberaeron harbour by the Aeron Express Aerial ferry or journey to the summit of Aberystwyth's Constitution Hill by cliff railway, one of the most spectacular in Britain.

In Wales there are working farms open to the public with rare breeds, and also fascinating factory workshops where visitors can watch glass being blown, carpets woven, candles being made and at several potteries visitors can enjoy a real hands-on experience by throwing a pot on a wheel.

The Industrial heritage of the past now provides fascinating visitor attractions like Big Pit in Blaenafon where ex-miners act as underground guides or the ever expanding Rhondda Heritage Park. In North Wales there are vast slate caverns and copper mines to explore, several narrow gauge steam railways to enjoy while in Mid Wales, visitors can tour a real goldmine, try their hand at panning and mining for gold – and keep anything they find!

Apart from these unique attractions, there are old working mills, art and craft centres, mountain and sea zoos, a hawking centre, sea aquariums, bird gardens, butterfly houses and wildlife parks.

There are exceptional museums like the 100 acre Welsh Folk Museum near Cardiff where buildings from all over Wales have been carefully reerected, and museums covering the maritime, motoring, industrial and aviation history of Wales, as well as those dedicated to the memory of famous personalities like Lloyd George and Dylan Thomas.

Wales also has her share of magnificent stately homes with priceless art treasures and antiques, world class gardens like Bodnant or Dyffryn, exciting new attractions like the haunted Llancaiach Fawr Manor in Rhymney Valley – a living history museum with guides dressed in costume, as well as vast medieval fortresses, castles and cromlechs.

There are also excellent leisure centres and sporting facilities throughout the country, in fact, Wales could have been tailormade for activity holidays and visitors can undertake virtually all types of outdoor activities and go abseiling or angling, ballooning or gliding, rafting or riding, climbing, canoeing or caving – to mention a few!

With family fun parks like Oakwood Park in West Wales, Starcoast World on the Llyn peninsula and Ocean Beach Amusement Park in Rhyl, famed for its whiteknuckle rides, Wales truly has something for everyone.

Centre for Alternative Technology
Machynlleth
Powys SY20 9AZ
Tel: 01654 702400

Great Little Trains of Wales
c/o The Station
Llanfair Caereinion
Powys SY21 OSF
Tel: 01938 810441

Big Pit
Blaenafon
Gwent NP4 9XP
Tel: 01495 790311

Rhondda Heritage Park
Lewis Merthyr
Coed Cae Road
Trehafod
Mid Glamorgan CF37 7NP
Tel: 01443 682036

Welsh Folk Museum
St Fagans
Cardiff CF5 6XB
Tel: 01222 569441

Bodnant Gardens
Tal y Cafn
Colwyn Bay
Clwyd LL28 5RE
Tel: 01492 650460

Dyffryn Gardens
St Nicholas
Nr Cardiff
South Glamorgan CF5 6SU
Tel: 01222 593328

Llancaiach Fawr Manor
Gelligaer Road
Nelson
Mid Glamorgan CF46 6ER
Tel: 01443 412248

For more information about Wales, please contact:-

Wales Tourist Board
Brunel House
2 Fitzalan Road
Cardiff CF2 1UY
Tel: 01222 499909

ALLT-YR-YNYS HOTEL

WALTERSTONE, HEREFORDSHIRE HR2 0DU
TEL: 01873 890307 FAX: 01873 890539

Allt-yr-Ynys straddles the border that runs between England and Wales – with rural Herefordshire on one side and the Black Mountains on the other. The original manor house on this site belonged to the estate of Robert Cecil, a Knight of the Court during the reign of King Henry II; however, the buildings that comprise today's hotel date from 1550. Many of the authentic features have been preserved, typically the moulded ceilings, oak panelling and massive oak beams. The bedrooms, some of which are situated in the converted outbuildings, have been beautifully appointed to complement their period character. Delicious British cooking features on the menu, and the chef can also prepare 'special dishes for special occasions' to cater for private functions of up to 60 people. In the bar, adjacent to the Jacuzzi and indoor heated pool, there is an ancient, horse-powered cider press. An undercover clay pigeon range is in the grounds, with all equipment – shotguns, cartridges and tuition. There are four golf courses within the vicinity. **Directions:** Midway between Abergavenny and Hereford, turn off A465 by Pandy Inn. Turn right at Green Park Barn crossroads as signposted to Walterstone. Price guide: Single £55–£65; double/twin £85–£100.

PORTH TOCYN COUNTRY HOUSE HOTEL

ABERSOCH, PWLLHELI, GWYNEDD LL53 7BU
TEL: 01758 713303 FAX: 01758 713538

Porth Tocyn is a friendly, family-owned hotel offering country charm and good food in a beautiful location. Situated in 25 acres of gardens and pasture, the house enjoys glorious views across Cardigan Bay to Snowdonia. In the 45 years that the Fletcher-Brewer family have owned the hotel, they have concentrated their efforts into creating a comfortable, attractive hotel without the stuffiness associated with some establishments. Children of all ages are welcomed: there are family bedrooms, a small children's sitting room, and high tea is provided for the younger ones every evening. However, this is very much a place where adults can relax. First-class home cooking has long been the cornerstone of Porth Tocyn's reputation. Focusing on the quality of each dish, dinner is a short-choice, five-course affair followed by coffee and home-made petits fours. The menu is changed completely each day. A dinner-party atmosphere brings a sense of occasion to the evening. Lunch is more informal and may be taken in the garden or by the pool. A variety of water sports and riding can be arranged locally, while the heritage coastline makes for ideal clifftop walks. Closed November to Easter. **Directions:** From Abersoch go 2¹/₂ miles, through Sarn Bach and Bwlchtocyn. 'Gwesty/Hotel' signs lead to Porth Tocyn. Price guide: Single £44.50; double/twin £58–£90.

CONRAH COUNTRY HOUSE HOTEL

RHYDGALED, CHANCERY, ABERYSTWYTH, DYFED SY23 4DF
TEL: 01970 617941 FAX: 01970 624546

One of Wales' much-loved country house hotels, the Conrah is tucked away at the end of a rhododendron-lined drive, only minutes from the spectacular rocky cliffs and sandy bays of the Cambrian coast. Set in 22 acres of rolling grounds, the Conrah's magnificent aspect affords views as far north as the Cader Idris mountain range. Afternoon tea and Welsh cakes or pre-dinner drinks can be taken at leisure in the drawing room or quiet writing room, furnished for comfort with plump chintz armchairs. Antiques, fresh flowers and books add to the relaxed country style. The cuisine is a marriage of classical and nouvelle forms, with fresh salmon and game among the specialities. An extensive

daily menu is provided for vegetarians. Resident proprietors John and Patricia Heading extend a warm invitation for a real 'taste of Wales', combined with old-fashioned, high standards of service. For recreation, guests may enjoy a game of table-tennis in the summer house or enjoy a walk around the gardens and the Conrah fields, where sheep and donkeys graze. Country pursuits such as pony-trekking, sea-fishing and birdwatching are available locally, while the university town of Aberystwyth is only 3 miles away. Closed Christmas. **Directions:** The Conrah lies 3 miles south of Aberystwyth on the A487. Price guide: Single £58–£60; double/twin £83–£110.

TREARDDUR BAY HOTEL

LON ISALLT, TREARDDUR BAY, NR HOLYHEAD, ANGLESEY LL65 2UN
TEL: 01407 860301 FAX: 01407 861181

This coastal hotel enjoys a magnificent location on the Anglesey coast, overlooking Trearddur Bay and close to a medieval chapel dedicated to the nun St Brigid. An extensive refurbishment programme in recent years has given the hotel a completely new look. Many of the spacious bedrooms, all of which are en suite, have panoramic views over the bay. All are furnished to a high standard. There are also nine studio suites, including one with four-poster bed. The comfortable lounge is the perfect place to relax and read the papers over morning coffee or afternoon tea. Before dinner, enjoy an apéritif in one of the hotel bars. Superb views apart, the hotel restaurant enjoys a reputation for excellent food – including locally caught fish and seafood – complemented by fine wines. Table d'hôte and à la carte menus offer a good choice of dishes. For those who find the Irish Sea too bracing, the hotel has an indoor pool. The beach is just a short walk away and there is an 18-hole golf course nearby. Anglesey is a haven for watersports enthusiasts and birdwatchers. Places of interest include Beaumaris Castle and the Celtic burial mound at Bryn Celi Ddu. Snowdonia is a little further afield. **Directions:** From Bangor, take A5 to Valley crossroads. Turn left onto B4545 for 3 miles, then turn left at garage. Hotel is 350 yards on right. Price guide: Single £70; double/twin £100–£110; studio suite £120–£140.

PALÉ HALL

PALÉ, LLANDDERFEL, BALA, GWYNEDD LL23 7PS
TEL: 01678 530285 FAX: 01678 530220

Palé Hall, a privately owned Victorian mansion, is nestled amongst 150 acres of parkland on the edge of the Snowdonia National Park. The house was built in 1870 for Mr Henry Robertson (a Scottish gentleman) who instructed his architects to spare no expense. Undoubtedly one of the most impressive buildings in Wales, notable guests included Queen Victoria, who described the house as enchanting and stayed. Other guests included Winston Churchill and members of the aristocracy. The house contains stunning interiors and exquisite features of a magnificent entrance hall with its galleried staircase, plus the boudoir with its hand-painted ceiling, marble fireplaces and bar.

The comfortable lounges (including a non-smoking lounge) enable quiet relaxation and contemplation. Each of the 17 suites are individually decorated and contain en suite bathrooms, TV, hospitality tray and luxury toiletries, plus a magnificent view of the surrounding scenery. The restaurant offers fine dishes and is complemented by an extensive cellar. Facilities for the pursuit of a number of outdoor activities are available; walking, riding, fishing, shooting, golf or white-water rafting. **Directions:** Palé Hall is situated off the B4401 Corwen to Bala road, four miles from Llandrillo. Price guide: Single £85–£95; double/twin £120–£135; Jacuzzi suite £160. (All prices include dinner).

BONTDDU HALL

BONTDDU, NR BARMOUTH, GWYNEDD LL40 2SU
TEL: 01341 430661 FAX: 01341 430284

Set in 14 acres of landscaped gardens with mixed woodland and a rhododendron forest, Gothic-styled Bontddu Hall commands a lofty position overlooking the Mawddach Estuary in Snowdonia National Park. Built in 1873 as a country mansion for the aunt of Neville Chamberlain, the hotel is reminiscent of the Victorian era and was frequented by several Prime Ministers during the days of the British Empire. The reception rooms are richly decorated in a fashion that complements the grandeur of the high, corniced ceilings and ornate, marble fireplaces. As well as the comfortable bedrooms in the main building, a number of suites are available in the Lodge, each with a private balcony facing the mountains.

Regional and classical cuisine are served in the Garden Restaurant. Lunch and afternoon teas can be taken on the sun terrace. Hill walking, climbing, pony-trekking, surfing, sail-boarding, skin-diving and bowling are available in the locality. The walks from Dolgellau are famous. Bontddu also has a gold mine. A tour of the area could include a trip on the famous narrow-gauge railways, or a visit to one of the many interesting castles, such as Harlech or Penrhyn. Closed November to Easter. **Directions:** Situated midway between Dolgellau and Barmouth on the A469. Price guide: Single £62.50; double/twin £90–£115; suite £150.

LLANGOED HALL

LLYSWEN, BRECON, POWYS, WALES LD3 0YP
TEL: 01874 754525 FAX: 01874 754545

The history of Llangoed Hall dates back to 560 AD when it is thought to have been the site of the first Welsh Parliament. Inspired by this legend, the architect Sir Clough Williams-Ellis, transformed the Jacobean mansion he found here in 1914 into an Edwardian country house. Situated deep in a valley of the River Wye, surrounded by a walled garden, the hotel commands breathtaking views of the Black Mountains and Brecon Beacons beyond. The rooms are warm and welcoming, furnished with antiques and oriental rugs and, on the walls, an outstanding collection of paintings acquired by the owner, Sir Bernard Ashley. Head Chef Ben Davies makes eating at Llangoed one of the principal reasons for visiting. Classic but light, his menus represent the very best of modern cuisine, complemented by a cellar of more than 300 wines. Tennis and croquet are available on site, and nearby there is golf, fishing, riding, shooting, and some of the best mountain walking and gliding in Britain. For expeditions, there are the Wye Valley, Hay-on-Wye and its bookshops, the border castles, Hereford and Leominster. Children over 8 are welcome. The hotel is a member of Welsh Rarebits and Small Luxury Hotels of the World. **Directions:** The hotel is 9 miles west of Hay, 11 miles north of Brecon on the A470. Price guide: Single £95; double/twin £155–£195; suite £195–£285.

PETERSTONE COURT

LLANHAMLACH, BRECON, POWYS LD3 7YB
TEL: 01874 665387 FAX: 01874 665376

Set in a tiny village on the eastern edge of the mysterious Brecon Beacons National Park, Peterstone is a carefully restored Georgian manor, swathed in history which can be traced back to the time of William the Conqueror. It was voted the best new hotel in Wales by the AA in 1992 and amongst a string of awards the hotel collected merits from the RAC and the Welsh Tourist Board. There are just 12 guest bedrooms at the court, eight beautifully proportioned period style rooms in the main house, and four split level rooms in the former stable that have all the things you expect and many you don't, such as tape players, video players and a welcoming decanter of sherry. Intimate parties and special occasions can be accommodated in one of the two small private rooms. The surrounding countryside has an abundance of walks, one of which starts at the end of the hotel drive and goes along the river and the canal back into Brecon. Alternatively, or perhaps even, after all the walking, there is in the hotel basement a fully equipped health club, with gymnasium, sauna, solarium and Jacuzzi. In the grounds are an outdoor heated pool, croquet and putting. **Directions:** Peterstone Court is located in the village of Llanhamlach, on the A40, three miles east of Brecon. Price guide: Single £79.50; double/twin £95–£130. Short breaks available all year round.

Coed-y-Mwstwr Hotel

COYCHURCH, NEAR BRIDGEND, MID GLAMORGAN CF35 6AF
TEL: 01656 860621 FAX: 01656 863122

Coed-y-Mwstwr is a country mansion of Victorian origin set in 17 acres of mature woodland, which is also home to an abundance of wildlife – kestrels, woodpeckers and buzzards all nest here, with foxes, rabbits and badgers never far away. Much thought has gone into ensuring that the décor and furnishings are in keeping with the style of the house. High ceilings, chandeliers and large fireplaces feature in the elegant public rooms. The 23 luxurious bedrooms all have en suite facilities and wonderful views. The elegant oak-panelled restaurant enjoys a good reputation locally and offers a blend of traditional and modern cuisine, with both table d'hôte and à la carte menus with 2 AA Rosettes. The wine list has more than 75 wines. Private functions for up to 130 people may be held in the Hendre Suite. In addition, there are two private dining rooms. A heated outdoor swimming pool, all-weather tennis court and snooker room are available for guests' use. For golfers, Royal Porthcawl and Southerndown courses are 10 minutes' drive from the hotel. The beautiful Gower and Pembrokeshire coastline and Brecon Beacons National Park are within easy reach. Open all year. **Directions:** Leave M4 at junction 35, take A473 towards Bridgend for 1 mile, turn right into Coychurch. At filling station turn right and follow signs uphill. Price guide: Single £80; double/twin £120; suite £140.

SEIONT MANOR HOTEL

LLANRUG, CAERNARVON, GWYNEDD LL55 2AQ
TEL: 01286 673366 FAX: 01286 672840

Set in 150 acres of parkland amid the majestic scenery of Snowdonia, Seiont Manor has been stylishly remodelled from original rustic buildings to create a unique luxury hotel offering guests every comfort. The oak-panelled bar and library, with its collection of leather-bound volumes, provide the perfect environment for relaxing with a drink before dinner. For lovers of good food, the excellent restaurant, overlooking the hotel's lake and grounds, serves classic French cuisine as well as superb local dishes, all prepared from the best ingredients. Each of the 28 bedrooms, with furnishings from around the world, is comfortable and spacious and has en suite facilities. The hotel is an ideal venue for conferences, functions and meetings of up to 120 people. A heated pool housed in the Victorian-style 'chapel' takes pride of place among the leisure facilities, which also include a sauna, solarium, multi-gym, aromatherapy and reflexology treatments. Mountain bikes and a jogging track are available for guests' use and there is fishing for salmon and trout in the river. Caernarvon golf course, with its stunning views over the Menai Straits, is nearby, as are the Snowdonia National Park, Ffestiniog Mountain Railway and Caernarvon Castle. **Directions:** 3 miles from Caernarvon on the A4086. Price guide: Single £75; double/twin £120–£150.

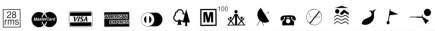

EGERTON GREY COUNTRY HOUSE HOTEL

PORTHKERRY, NR CARDIFF, SOUTH GLAMORGAN CF62 3BZ
TEL: 01446 711666 FAX: 01446 711690

A distinguished former rectory dating from the early-19th century, Egerton Grey is tucked away in seven acres of gardens in a secluded, wooded valley in the Vale of Glamorgan. Visitors can enjoy glorious views towards Porthkerry Park and the sea beyond. The interior design complements the architectural features of the house. The Edwardian drawing room has intricate plaster mouldings, chandeliers, an open fireplace and oil paintings. A quiet library overlooks the garden. All of the immaculately presented bedrooms are extremely comfortable, and several have Victorian baths and brasswork. Original Cuban mahogany panelling and candle-lit tables create an air of intimacy in the main restaurant. Egerton Grey has been described by one important guide as 'the definitive country house hotel for South Wales'. High-quality cuisine is presented with finesse on bone china, and wine is served in Welsh Royal Crystal glasses. Riding and sailing can be arranged and there is a pitch-and-putt course a short stroll away. The Welsh Folk Museum, Castle Coch and Cardiff Castle are nearby. **Directions:** From M4 junction 33, take A4050; follow airport signs for 10 miles. Take the A4226 towards Porthkerry; after 400 yards turn into the lane between two thatched cottages and hotel is at end of lane. Price guide: Single £55–£95; double/twin £85–£120.

MISKIN MANOR COUNTRY HOUSE HOTEL

MISKIN, MID-GLAMORGAN CF7 8ND
TEL: 01443 224204 FAX: 01443 237606

Although its history dates back to the 11th century, Miskin Manor first became a hotel only in 1986, following extensive restoration and refurbishment. Set amid 20 acres of undisturbed parkland, criss-crossed with streams, peace and seclusion are guaranteed. The uncommonly spacious reception rooms have fine fireplaces, panelled walls and elaborate plasterwork ceilings, all enhanced by rich drapery and comfortable furniture. All of the bedrooms have en suite bathrooms and full facilities. In the 1920s, one of the de luxe suites was occupied by the Prince of Wales (later King Edward VII), a room which is now aptly named the Prince of Wales suite. First-class Welsh cuisine is served in the AA Red Rosette awarded restaurant and complemented by a comprehensive wine list. Within the grounds is the popular sports and leisure club, Frederick's, which guests can use. It comprises three squash courts, badminton court, indoor heated swimming pool, gymnasium, snooker, spa, sauna, solarium, beautician, bistro and crèche. Celebrations, conferences and all manner of functions can be catered for at Miskin Manor, with reliable, professional support assured. Corporate activites held on site. **Directions:** From junction 34 of the M4, follow hotel signs, Drive is one mile from the motorway roundabout. Price guide: Single £80; double/twin £95; suite £175.

SOUGHTON HALL COUNTRY HOUSE HOTEL

NORTHOP, NR MOLD, CLWYD CH7 6AB
TEL: 01352 840811 FAX: 01352 840382

Built as a Bishops Palace in 1714, Grade I Soughton Hall set in beautiful landscaped gardens amidst 150 acres of parkland is approached via a spectacular half mile avenue of limes. Beautiful antique furniture adorns a house of unique history and architecture. With just 14 authentic bedrooms and the personal welcome of the Rodenhurst family, a memorable stay is assured. The hotel is also ideal for business use with a boardroom that is second to none. 1996 features the opening of a country inn within the old coach house and stables, a listed building of immense historical and architectural interest also. It will feature a beer parlour specialising in serving many real ales from local breweries and an informal wine and steak bar within the original haylofts. Special three day packages are available to include dinner in either the hotel restaurant (past awards include Welsh Restaurant of the Year) or the inn. Within the surrounding parkland is an 18-hole championship golf course. Golfing holidays are available. From the hotel, excursions can be made into North Wales and historic Chester. An exclusive, full-colour guide to selected holiday drives in the area is provided. **Directions:** From the M56 take the A55 towards North Wales, then the A5119 to Northop. Cross the traffic lights; the hall is one mile along the road on the left. Price guide: Single £70; double/twin £80–£119.

For hotel location, see maps on pages 473–479

TYDDYN LLAN COUNTRY HOUSE HOTEL

LLANDRILLO, NR CORWEN, CLWYD LL21 0ST
TEL: 01490 440264 FAX: 01490 440414

Tyddyn Llan is an elegant Georgian country house situated amid breathtaking scenery in the Vale of Edeyrnion. Owned and run by Peter and Bridget Kindred, the hotel is a quiet oasis in an area of outstanding natural beauty at the foot of the Berwyn Mountains. There are 10 bedrooms, all individual in style and elegantly furnished with antiques and period furniture. Each enjoys views of the gardens and the mountains beyond and has a bathroom en suite. The hotel is proud of the reputation it has established for the quality of the food served in the restaurant. Inventive and frequently changing menus feature dishes using fresh local ingredients and herbs from the kitchen garden. A carefully selected wine list complements the cuisine. In the gardens, guests may enjoy a game of croquet and tea is served on fine days. The hotel has rights to four miles of fly-fishing on the River Dee. Keen walkers can trace the ancient Roman road, Ffordd Gam Elin, which traverses the Berwyn Mountains. Here naturalists will find many different species of birds and wild flowers. Tyddyn Llan is well placed for exploring nearby Snowdonia, and the Roman city of Chester is only 35 miles away. **Directions:** Llandrillo is midway between Corwen and Bala on the B4401, four miles from the A5 at Corwen. Price guide (including dinner): Single £66–£86; double/twin £126–£147.

BRON EIFION COUNTRY HOUSE HOTEL

CRICCIETH, GWYNEDD LL52 0SA
TEL: 01766 522385 FAX: 01766 522003

This magnificent baronial mansion stands within five acres of glorious gardens and woodlands, yet only minutes from the sea. It was built by the millionaire slate owner John Greaves whose master craftsmen carved the spectacular pitch and Oregon pine panelled hallway, minstrels gallery and vaulted ceiling. The Conservatory Restaurant, which overlooks the floodlit gardens serves innovative cuisine, complemented by a superb selection of wines. All 19 bedrooms are en suite and are individually decorated, offering king-sized and four-poster beds, or you could choose a standard or de luxe room. The gardens provide interesting walks, from the stone walled terraces to the secluded herb garden or just laze on the verandah overlooking the lawns which abound in a variety of wildlife. Golf, shooting, riding and fishing are all nearby. A short drive will take you to the pretty villages of Criccieth, Porthmadog or the Italiante village of Portmeirion. The rugged beauty of the mountains of Snowdonia, together with castles, stately homes, Lloyd George's Museum and Ffestiniog Railway are all closeby. **Directions:** The hotel is on the A497 on the outskirts of Criccieth and stands at the top of a tree-lined drive, nestled in Woodland. Price guide: Single £51–£59; double/twin £78–£100. De luxe supplement £15 per room per night.

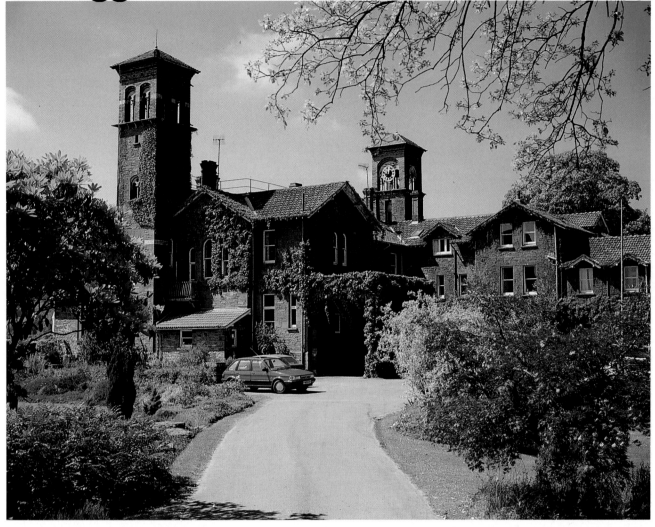

GLIFFAES COUNTRY HOUSE HOTEL

CRICKHOWELL, POWYS NP8 1RH
TEL: 01874 730371 FAX: 01874 730463

Visitors may be surprised to discover a hotel featuring distinctive Italianate architecture tucked midway between the Brecon Beacons and the Black Mountains. Gliffaes Country House Hotel is poised 150 feet above the River Usk and commands glorious views of the surroundings hills and valley. The elegantly furnished, Regency style drawing room is an ideal place to relax and leads to a large sun room and on to the terrace, from which guests may enjoy the magnificent scenery. In addition to a panelled lounge, there is a billiard room with a full-sized table. An informal atmosphere prevails in the dining room, where there is a choice of an excellent quality table d'hôte menu or an à la carte menu with a wide selection of dishes cooked to order and beautifully presented. The Gliffaes fishery includes every type of water, from slow-flowing flats to fast-running rapids, on $2\frac{1}{2}$ miles of the River Usk renowned for its wild brown trout and salmon fishing. The 33 acre hotel grounds have rare trees and shrubs as well as lawns for putting and croquet. Riding can be arranged nearby. Closed 5 January to 23rd February. **Directions:** Gliffaes is signposted from the A40, $2\frac{1}{2}$ miles west of Crickhowell. Price guide: Single £34.50–£44; double/twin £68–£102.

PENMAENUCHAF HALL

PENMAENPOOL, DOLGELLAU, GWYNEDD LL40 1YB
TEL: 01341 422129 FAX: 01341 422129

The splendour of Cader Idris and the Mawddach Estuary forms the backdrop for this handsome Victorian mansion which is in an exceptional retreat. Set within the Snowdonia National Park, the 21-acre grounds encompass lawns, a formal sunken rose garden, a water garden and woodland. The beautiful interiors feature oak and mahogany panelling, stained-glass windows, log fires in winter, polished Welsh slate floors and freshly cut flowers. There are 12 luxurious bedrooms, some with four-poster and half-tester beds, and all with interesting views. In the Gothic-style conservatory restaurant, guests can choose from an imaginative menu prepared with the best seasonal produce and complemented by an extensive list of wines. An elegant panelled dining room can be used for private dinners or meetings. Penmaenuchaf Hall is perfect for a totally relaxed holiday. For recreation, guests can fish for trout and salmon along ten miles of the Mawddach River, or take part in a range of water sports. They can also enjoy scenic walks, visit sandy beaches and historic castles and take trips on narrow-gauge railways. **Directions:** The hotel is off the A493 Dolgellau–Tywyn road, about two miles from Dolgellau. Price guide: Single £50–£95; double/twin £95–£140.

HOTEL MAES-Y-NEUADD

TALSARNAU, NR HARLECH, GWYNEDD LL47 6YA
TEL: 01766 780200 FAX: 01766 780211

This part-14th century house, built of granite and slate, is cradled by eight acres of landscaped mountainside. As a much-loved hotel it has been run by the Horsfall and Slatter families since 1981. Peace and tranquillity are all-pervasive, whether relaxing in the pretty, beamed lounge or reclining in a leather Chesterfield in the bar while enjoying an apéritif. Talented chefs create delicious English and Welsh dishes using fresh produce such as lamb, fish and a variety of Welsh farmhouse cheeses, along with vegetables and herbs from the kitchen garden. As an alternative dining venue for special occasions and parties, dinner can be provided on the world famous Ffestiniog railway. Also the hotel produces its own oils and vinegars which are stylishly presented for resale. Spring and autumn breaks are available. The bedrooms vary in style, from early beams and dormers to later Georgian elegance with full-length windows. For golfers, the Royal St David's Golf Course is located three miles away. Nearby attractions include the Italianate village of Portmeirion, slate caverns, beautiful beaches, Snowdonia, Edward I's castle at Harlech and the Ffestiniog railway. USA toll-free reservations: 1-800 635 3602. **Directions:** Hotel is 3¹/₂ miles north of Harlech, off the B4573, signposted at the end of the lane. Price guide: Single £72; double/twin £147–£198. (Including dinner)

KINSALE HALL HOTEL

LLANERCHYMOR, MR HOLYWELL, CLWYD CH8 9DX
TEL: 01745 560001 FAX: 01745 561298

Set in over 100 acres of lovely parkland, Kinsale Hall offers panoramic views of the Dee Estuary and the Wirral. Dating back to the 17th century it has been sympathetically restored and extended. Retention of original features including oak panelling, stained glass and decorative plaster ceilings together with traditional furnishings has created a welcoming and relaxed atmosphere. The spacious bedrooms have a full range of equipment to ensure maximum comfort and convenience for guests. Impeccable service and first class cuisine, French in inspiration, make the hotel's restaurant the perfect setting for lunch or dinner. Kinsale Hall is fully equipped to offer the latest in audiovisual technology for conferences and meetings for up to 300 people. The hotel's own golf course and golf driving range are complemented by a wide range or outdoor pursuits available locally. Clay shooting, archery and off-road driving can be arranged on site. Close by are the delights of the North Wales coastline and Snowdonia National Park. **Directions:** Follow A55 until Flint turn off. From the crossroad traffic lights in Flint turn left on to the A548 coast road for Prestatyn. After approximately seven miles turn left for Maes Pennant where the white ship is moored in the estuary. The hotel is 100 yards on left. Price guide: Single £65; double/twin £85–£105; suites £120.

LAKE VYRNWY HOTEL

LAKE VYRNWY, LLANWDDYN, MONTGOMERYSHIRE SY10 0LY
TEL: 01691 870 692 FAX: 01691 870 259

Situated high on the hillside within the 24,000 acre Vyrnwy Estate the hotel commands breathtaking views of mountains, lakes and moorland. It is also surrounded by lawns, an abundance of rhododendrons, woods and meadowlands. Built in 1860 its heritage has been maintained over 100 years on as a retreat for all lovers of nature and fine dining. There are 37 bedrooms all individually furnished and decorated, many with antiques and some with special features such as Jacuzzis, balconies, four-posters or suites. There are also dedicated meeting and private dining facilities. The award-winning candle-lit restaurant has a menu which changes 365 days of the year. Everything from the marmalade to the *petit fours* at dinner are created in the Vyrnwy kitchens. Its own market garden provides many of the seasonal herbs, fruits, vegetables and flowers. The hotel owns some of Wales' best fishing together with some 24,000 acres of sporting rights. Other pursuits include sailing, cycling, tennis and some beautiful walking trails. Also an RSPB sanctuary, the estate provides a wealth of wildlife and represents true peace and tranquillity. **Directions:** From Shrewsbury take the A458 to Welshpool, then turn right onto B4393 just after Ford (signposted to Lake Vyrnwy 28 miles). Price guide: Single £58; double/twin from £75; suite £122.50.

THE CAWDOR ARMS HOTEL

LLANDEILO, DYFED SA19 6EN
TEL: 01558 823500 FAX: 01558 822399

From the moment guests enter the flagstone entrance of The Cawdor Arms Hotel, they are reminded of the elegance of a time that is past. Leather chairs, comfortable furnishings, fresh flowers and original portraiture combine to create a restful atmosphere, echoed in the individually designed and named bedrooms. The hotel has offered hospitality, fine food and excellent wine to travellers and the neighbouring community since the early 1700s. An impressive reputation is enjoyed by the restaurant, which uses the freshest and finest local produce as the basis for a variety of memorable dishes. Llandeilo is a haven for the sporting enthusiast. Local shooting and fishing permits can be arranged by the hotel or guests may prefer to walk or ride a horse among the castles and peaks of the Beacons. Alternatively, why not take an unforgettable ballooning weekend over the Brecon Beacons National Park? The picturesque market town of Llandeilo stands on the banks of the River Tywi, one of Europe's finest salmon and sea trout rivers. It is the ideal touring base for those seeking the breathtaking scenery of the Gower Coast, Brecon Beacons and Pembrokeshire National Parks. Special places of interest nearby Carreg Cennen Castle and Talley Abbey. **Directions:** The Cawdor Arms Hotel is in the centre of Llandeilo on the A40. Price guide: Single £45; double/twin £65.

BODYSGALLEN HALL

LLANDUDNO, GWYNEDD LL30 1RS
TEL: 01492 584466 FAX: 01492 582519

Bodysgallen Hall, owned and restored by Historic House Hotels, lies at the end of a winding drive in 200 acres of wooded parkland and beautiful formal gardens. Magnificent views encompass the sweep of the Snowdonia range of mountains, and the hotel looks down on the imposing medieval castle at Conwy. This Grade I listed house was built mainly in the 17th century, but the earliest feature is a 13th century tower, reached by a narrow winding staircase, once used as a lookout for soldiers serving the English kings of Conwy and now a safe place from which to admire the fabulous views. The hotel has 19 spacious bedrooms in the house and 16 delightful cottage suites in the grounds. Two of the finest rooms in the house are the large oak-panelled entrance hall and the first floor drawing room, both with splendid fireplaces and mullioned windows. Head chef is Michael Penny, who produces superb dishes using fresh local ingredients. The Bodysgallen Spa comprises a spacious swimmng pool, steam room, sauna, solaria, gym, beauty salons, restaurant and bar. The hotel is ideally placed for visiting the many historic castles and stately homes in North Wales. **Directions:** On the A470 one mile from the intersection with the A55. Llandudno is a mile further on the A470. Price guide: Single £79–£95; double/twin £108–£165; suite £130–£145.

St Tudno Hotel

PROMENADE, LLANDUDNO, GWYNEDD LL30 2LP
TEL: 01492 874411 FAX: 01492 860407

Undoubtedly one of the most delightful small hotels to be found on the coast of Britain, St Tudno Hotel, a former winner of the *Johansens Hotel of the Year Award for Excellence*, certainly offers a very special experience. The hotel, which has been elegantly and lovingly furnished with meticulous attention to detail, offers a particularly warm welcome from owners, Martin and Janette Bland, and their caring and friendly staff. Each beautifully co-ordinated bedroom has been individually designed with many thoughtful extras provided to ensure guests' comfort. The bar lounge and sitting room, which overlook the sea, have an air of Victorian charm. Regarded as one of Wales' leading restaurants,

the air-conditioned Garden Room has won three AA Rosettes for its excellent cuisine. This AA Red Star hotel has won a host of other awards, including *Best Seaside Resort Hotel in Great Britain*, *Welsh Hotel of the Year*, national winner of the AA's *Warmest Welcome Award* and even an accolade for having the *Best Hotel Loos in Britain*! St Tudno is ideally situated for visits to Snowdonia, Conwy and Caernarfon Castles, Bodnant Gardens and Anglesey. Golf, riding, swimming and dry-slope skiing and tobogganing can be enjoyed locally. **Directions:** On the promenade opposite the pier entrance and gardens. Price guide: Single £69; double/twin £79–£145.

THE LAKE COUNTRY HOUSE

LLANGAMMARCH WELLS, POWYS LD4 4BS
TEL: 01591 620202 FAX: 01591 620457

The Lake Country House is hidden away in 50 acres of grounds, with sweeping lawns, thick woodlands, rhododendron-lined pathways and riverside walks. The spacious reception hall and drawing room are enhanced by log fires and antique furniture. Spectacular views of the surrounding countryside are offered by many of the comfortable, well-designed bedrooms. The hotel presents excellent food from a menu that is changed daily. Award winning hotel with 2 AA Rosettes for food. Meals are served in the elegant dining room and complemented by one of the finest wine lists in Wales. This is a fisherman's paradise – the hotel's own lake is well stocked with trout, or alternatively fish for salmon in the nearby Rivers Wye and Irfon. The Lake is renowned among birdwatchers, with 94 species of bird having been recorded here. For an exhilarating appreciation of the Welsh scenery, hacking and pony-trekking can be arranged. There are scenic drives in all directions, particularly towards the Brecon Beacons and Wye Valley. With a large billiard room in the hotel and a 6-hole practice golf course, there is no lack of recreational activity here. AA and RAC 3 Stars and Merit Award. **Directions:** From the A483, follow signs to Llangammarch Wells and then to the hotel. Price guide: Single £75; double/twin £115; suite £155.

BRYN HOWEL HOTEL AND RESTAURANT

NR LLANGOLLEN, CLWYD LL20 7UW
TEL: 01978 860331 FAX: 01978 860119

Bryn Howel, set in the magnificent Vale of Llangollen, was built in 1896. Although the hotel has been extended and regularly refurbished over the years, great care has been taken to preserve the original character and unique features of the building and its red brickwork, mullioned windows, oak panelling and intricate plaster mouldings still remain. The hotel is run by a brother and sister team, members of the Lloyd family who have owned the hotel for 30 years. They pride themselves on providing the highest standards of both comfort and service. Well appointed bedrooms, with a full range of modern amenities, offer splendid views of the surrounding countryside. Delicious food, featuring

Dee salmon, Welsh lamb and local game and poultry, is served in the Cedar Tree Restaurant, winner of many awards for its tempting cuisine. Alternatively, guests may dine in the intimacy of the Oak Room. The hotel's leisure facilities include a sauna and solarium. Reduced fees for the nearby golf club are available to residents, who may also enjoy free game fishing on a five mile stretch of the River Dee. Places of interest nearby include the historic city of Chester and town of Shrewsbury. Bryn Howel is closed at Christmas. **Directions:** On the A539 (three miles from Llangollen) between Llangollen and the A483. Price guide: Single £68.50; double/twin £90–£115.

YNYSHIR HALL

EGLWYSFACH, MACHYNLLETH, POWYS SY20 8TA
TEL: 01654 781209 FAX: 01654 781366

Once owned by Queen Victoria, Ynyshir Hall is a captivating Georgian manor house that perfectly blends modern comfort and old-world elegance. Its 12 acres of picturesque, landscaped gardens are set alongside the Dovey Estuary, one of Wales' most outstanding areas of natural beauty and the hotel is surrounded by the Ynyshir Bird Reserve. Hosts Rob and Joan Reen offer guests a warm welcome and ensure a personal service, the hallmark of a good family-run hotel. Period furniture and opulent fabrics enhance the eight charming bedrooms. The suites are particularly luxurious and, along with a four-poster room and ground floor room, are popular with many guests. The interiors are exquisitely furnished throughout with comfortable sofas, antiques, contemporary colour schemes, oriental rugs and many original paintings. These works of art are the creation of Rob, an established and acclaimed artist. Local seafood, game, and vegetables from the kitchen garden are used to create superb English, French and Welsh dishes. Dogs by prior arrangement. **Directions:** Off the main road between Aberystwyth and Machynlleth. Price guide: Single £65–£95; double/twin £90–£110; suite £120–£130.

THE CROWN AT WHITEBROOK

WHITEBROOK, MONMOUTH, GWENT NP5 4TX
TEL: 01600 860254 FAX: 01600 860607

A romantic auberge nestling deep in the Wye Valley, a designated area of outstanding natural beauty, The Crown is ideally situated for those seeking peace and tranquillity. Located in the wooded Whitebrook Valley on the fringe of Tintern Forest and only one mile from the River Wye, this is a place where guests can enjoy spectacular scenery. Roger and Sandra Bates offer their visitors a genuinely friendly welcome. Guests can relax in the cosy lounge and bar areas or in the Manor Room, with its ash furniture, hand-made locally. Sandra Bates' cooking has earned the Restaurant several awards, as well as recommendations from other guides. Dishes include local Welsh lamb and Wye salmon cooked with a classical French influence, followed by a choice of delicious home-made puddings and a selection of British farm cheeses. Most dietary requirements can be catered for as all food is freshly cooked to order. There is an extensive wine list. Tintern Abbey, Chepstow Castle and the Brecon Beacons National Park are nearby. **Directions:** Whitebrook is situated between the A466 and the B4293 approximately five miles south of Monmouth. Price guide: Single £39.50–£50; double/twin £53–£81.

THE CELTIC MANOR HOTEL & GOLF CLUB

COLDRA WOODS, NEWPORT, GWENT NP6 2YA
TEL: 01633 413000 FAX: 01633 412910

Consistently acknowledged as one of the finest hotels in Wales, this refurbished Victorian manor house is set in a 1000 acre estate of mature parkland. Spacious bedrooms are elegantly furnished with comfort in mind – a lounge for relaxation, two bars and a splendid terrace. Two fine restaurants – The Patio, located in the picturesque conservatory, and Hedleys, although differing in style, both benefit from the culinary skills of twice winner of the title, Welsh Chef of the Year, Trefor Jones and his award-winning team. A full range of banqueting and conference facilities caters for all requirements. Sports enthusiasts will enjoy the good recreational and leisure facilities available on site and in the locality. Two 18-hole championship golf courses designed by worlds leading golf-architect, Robert Trent Jones. Touring professional Ian Woosnam. An ancient woodland walk winds through Coldra Wood, with its rare flora and fauna. Activity weekends can be arranged for parties, including murder mysteries and hot-air ballooning. Of interest nearby are Tintern Abbey, the Wye Valley and the castles at Chepstow and Caerphilly. **Directions:** Leave M4 at junction 24; hotel is 400 yards along the A48 towards Newport on the right-hand side. Price guide: Single £85–£100; double/twin £99–£150; suite £150–£165.

For hotel location, see maps on pages 473–479

367

THE HOTEL PORTMEIRION

PORTMEIRION, GWYNEDD LL48 6ET
TEL: 01766 770228 FAX: 01766 771331

Portmeirion is a magical, private Italianate village, designed by the renowned architect Sir Clough Williams-Ellis, which was started in 1925 and completed in the 1970s. It enjoyed a celebrated clientèle from the start – writers such as George Bernard Shaw, H G Wells, Bertrand Russell and Noel Coward were habitués. It is set in 120 acres of beautiful gardens and woodland, including two miles of tranquil sandy beaches, and provides accommodation for visitors either in the village or in the main hotel. The Hotel Portmeirion, originally a mansion house, has been sensitively restored, retaining striking features from the past, such as the Victorian Mirror Room. The bedrooms are furnished to the highest standards, 14 rooms being in the hotel and 23 rooms and suites in the village while the restaurant offers the best French and British cooking, the seasonal menu relying on fresh, locally produced ingredients. AA Comfort & Care award. Swimming and tennis are available within the grounds as well as golf at Porthmadog (with complimentary green fees), and sailing is close at hand. The Ffestiniog and Snowdon mountain railways, slate caverns and Bodnant Gardens are nearby. Conference facilities can accommodate up to 100 people. Closed 7th January to 2nd February. **Directions:** Portmeirion lies off the A487 between Penrhyndeudrath and Porthmadog. Price guide: Single £57–£102; double/twin £67–£112; suite £96–£146.

WARPOOL COURT HOTEL

ST DAVID'S, PEMBROKESHIRE SA62 6BN
TEL: 01437 720300 FAX: 01437 720676

Originally built as St David's Cathedral Choir School in the 1860s, Warpool Court enjoys spectacular scenery at the heart of the Pembrokeshire National Park, with views over the coast and St Bride's Bay to the islands beyond. First converted to a hotel 30 years ago, the Court has undergone extensive refurbishments during the last 10 years. All 25 comfortably furnished bedrooms have en suite facilities and some have glorious sea views. The hotel restaurant enjoys a splendid reputation. Imaginative menus, including vegetarian, offer a wide selection of modern and traditional dishes. Local produce, including Welsh lamb and beef, is used whenever possible, with crab, lobster, sewin and sea bass caught just off the coast. Salmon and mackerel are smoked on the premises and a variety of herbs are grown. The hotel gardens are ideal for a peaceful stroll or an after-dinner drink on a summer's evening. There is a covered heated swimming pool (open April to end of October) and all-weather tennis court in the grounds. A path from the hotel leads straight on to the Pembrokeshire Coastal Path, with its rich variety of wildlife and spectacular scenery. Boating and watersports are available locally. St David's Peninsula offers a wealth of history and natural beauty and has inspired many famous artists. **Directions:** The hotel is signposted from St David's town centre. Price guide: Single £69–£79; double/twin £96–£144.

For hotel location, see maps on pages 473–479

NORTON HOUSE HOTEL AND RESTAURANT

NORTON ROAD, MUMBLES, SWANSEA SA3 5TQ
TEL: 01792 404891 FAX: 01792 403210

This elegant Georgian hotel, set in gardens near the shore of Swansea Bay, provides a comfortable and peaceful base from which to explore the countryside of South Wales. Resident proprietors Jan and John Power have earned a reputation for offering attentive, friendly service. The bedrooms all have private amenities, four of the more spacious rooms have four-poster beds, the majority are smaller rooms in a newer wing. The restaurant overlooks the terrace and gardens. The emphasis is on local produce and traditional flavours with starters such as 'bara lawr' – mushrooms filled with laverbread, cockles and bacon followed by main courses which include 'cig oen mewn pasteiod' – best end of

Welsh lamb coated in a duxelle of mushrooms, cooked in puff pastry and served with a minted gravy. Golf and riding can be arranged. The hotel has conference facilities for up to 20 people. The unspoiled Gower Peninsula is nearby, with its sandy bays and rugged cliffs. Mumbles village is a short walk away, while the city of Swansea is alive with galleries, theatres, a good shopping centre, its famous market and the maritime quarter. **Directions:** Leave the M4 at junction 42, take A483 to Swansea, then A4067 alongside Swansea Bay. A mile beyond the Mumbles sign, the hotel is signposted on the right-hand side. Price guide: Single £55–£65; double/twin £65–£80.

      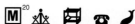

PENALLY ABBEY

PENALLY, TENBY, PEMBROKESHIRE SA70 7PY
TEL: 01834 843033 FAX: 01834 844714

Penally Abbey, a beautiful, listed Gothic-style mansion, offers comfort and hospitality in a secluded setting by the sea. Standing in five acres of gardens and woodland on the edge of Pembrokeshire National Park, the hotel overlooks Carmarthen Bay and Caldey Island. The bedrooms in the main building and in the adjoining coach house are well furnished, many with four-poster beds. The emphasis is on relaxation – enjoy a late breakfast and dine at leisure. Fresh seasonal delicacies are offered in the candle-lit restaurant, with its chandeliers and colonnades. Guests can enjoy a game in the snooker room or relax in the elegant sunlit lounge, overlooking the terrace and gardens. In the grounds there is a wishing well and a ruined chapel – the last surviving link with the hotel's monastic past. Water-skiing, surfing, sailing, riding and parascending are available nearby. Sandy bays and rugged cliffs are features of this coastline, making it ideal for exhilarating walks or simply building sandcastles on the beach. As its rates include the cost of dinner, this friendly hotel offers splendid value for money. **Directions:** Penally Abbey is situated adjacent to the church on Penally village green. Price guide (including dinner): Single £86; double/twin £140–£148.

TYNYCORNEL HOTEL

TAL-Y-LLYN, TYWYN, GWYNEDD LL36 9AJ
TEL: 01654 782282 FAX: 01654 782679

Situated in the magnificent Snowdonia National Park, Tynycornel Hotel overlooks its own 222-acre lake, whose waters reflect the grandeur of Cader Idris. Originally constructed as a farmhouse in the 16th century, the hotel has been extensively and sensitively refurbished so that none of the original ambience has been lost. The spacious lounge has views over the lake, with comfortable furniture, fine antiques, original prints and a blazing fire in winter. The 15 pretty bedrooms, all with bathrooms including a luxury suite, enjoy lakeside or garden views. The restaurant offers a high standard of cuisine and the set-price menu changes daily. Within the grounds there is a sauna and solarium. Tynycornel is an angler's paradise – wild brown trout, salmon and sea trout fishing are readily available – and the hotel is equipped with 10 petrol-powered boats and provides tackle hire, freezing facilities and a drying room. The stunning landscape offers many opportunities for those interested in birdwatching, walking and photography. Snowdonia and mid-Wales are steeped in history and a wide variety of leisure pursuits can be enjoyed. **Directions:** Tal-y-Llyn is signposted from the main A487 Machynlleth-Dolgellau road. The hotel is on the lake shore. Price guide: Single £46.50; double/twin £93; suite £125.

THE CWRT BLEDDYN HOTEL

LLANGYBI, NEAR USK, GWENT, SOUTH WALES NP5 1PG
TEL: 01633 450521 FAX: 01633 450220

Set in 17 acres of wooded grounds, this 14th century manor house, not far from the Roman town of Caerleon, is the perfect location from which to explore the Wye Valley and Forest of Dean. The hotel is a fine example of the traditional and the modern under one roof. Carved panelling and huge fireplaces in the lounge lend an air of classic country-house comfort. The 36 en suite bedrooms are spacious and offer guests every amenity, and most have wonderful views over the surrounding countryside. Cwrt Bleddyn's restaurant is renowned for its French-influenced cuisine, with both à la carte and table d'hôte menus. There is a good choice of vegetarian dishes. Light meals are also served in

the hotel's country club. Here, extensive leisure facilities include an indoor heated swimming pool, sauna, solarium, steam room and beauty salon. Alternatively, guests may just wish to stroll and relax in the grounds. Nearby is the local beauty spot of Llandegfedd, with its 434-acre reservoir. The hotel is open all year round. Private dining/function rooms are available. **Directions:** From Cardiff/Bristol, leave M4 at junction 25. Hotel is 3 miles north of Caerleon on the road to Usk. From the Midlands, take M5, then A40 to Monmouth. Turn off A449, through Usk, over stone bridge, then left towards Caerleon for 4 miles. Price guide: Single £85; double/twin £105.

PRODUCT OF SCOTLAND

Walkers
— ESTABLISHED 1898 —

The gift from the Highlands.

Like the Scottish Highlands themselves, once you have experienced Walkers shortbread, nothing else quite comes close to the original. This pure creamery butter shortbread is baked in the Highland village of Aberlour in Speyside to an original family recipe, first perfected by Joseph Walker in 1898. Guaranteed to be made from only the finest ingredients – with not an artificial flavouring, colouring or preservative in sight – just as it has always been. Can you imagine a better gift than that of the world's classic pure butter shortbread. Beautifully presented in its distinctive tartan packaging, Walkers irresistible range of varieties means it is always a welcome gift.

The world's classic pure butter shortbread

Walkers Shortbread Ltd Aberlour-on-Spey Scotland AB38 9PD Telephone +44 (0) 1340 871555 Fax +44 (0) 1340 871355

Johansens Recommended Hotels in Scotland

Drummond Castle, Perthshire

Scotland *offers the Johansens visitor a fine choice of recommendations amid breathtaking scenery. An abundance of outdoor pursuits will challenge the adventurous, blended with the warmth and charm of traditional hospitality.*

The Scottish Borders is one of the finest introductions to the nature and character of a country. The open space of green hills and rich farming plains with their network of well established fishing rivers indicate a land blessed with good agriculture and unpolluted water.

The picturesque ruins of several abbeys bear witness to the turbulence of centuries of Border wars and religious strife focusing attention on a tapestry of history, heritage, culture and recreation.

Small towns like Kelso and Peebles unspoiled in their rural setting unveil to the visitor the timeless appeal of Scotland - breathing space, charming locations, and people friendly, spirited and generous. All this is evident at the colourful festivals of the Border Ridings hosted in many towns.

Turn north to Scotland's capital, Edinburgh, a stunningly beautiful city. Here nature's gift of volcanic rock as a site for a castle and medieval town enhanced by enlightened municipal planning of magnificent gardens and Georgian architecture has created visual splendour which has escaped the ravages of time. There is no finer stage for the world's biggest festival of arts and music. Take time for a walk in the Royal Botanic Garden renowned for its plant collection, rock garden and with a Chinese garden in the making. There are gardens of all varieties throughout Scotland.

Edinburgh is beside the River Forth close to small towns and villages which hug the coastline to the North Sea. Seaside means golf courses, all challenging and most open to visitors at reasonable cost.

St Andrews, across the Forth, has several courses to test the enthusiast. The Home of Golf it is attractive and is home also to Scotland's oldest medieval university. The Fife coast has a ribbon of former fishing villages (the East Neuk) which are delightful and charming places to relax.

The pastoral landscape is marked in the neighbouring Perthshire which gives a first glimpse of the Highlands. Through Angus to the north east and Royal Deeside and the private home of the Queen and the Royal Family at Balmoral Castle with the gardens open to the public in summer. Nearby, at the eastern end of the Cairngorm Mountains, the village of Braemar, venue for the Braemar Gathering, the best known of the Highland Games.

Sixty miles along Deeside to Aberdeen, award winning Britain in Bloom city endowed with public gardens and parks, granite architecture and wedding its ancient culture of fishing and farming to the modern oil industry. From the overnight trip to the Shetland Isles is an ideal introduction to Scotland's network of passenger and vehicle ferries, most of which operate on the west coast. They reveal a unique world of mystical, timeless experience in the Western Isles. Lewis, Harris, Uist, Skye and Mull are but a few of these magical islands.

Aberdeen is also a base to embark on the adventure of the Malt Whisky Trail in the glens of the Livet and the Spey and their many famous distilleries where a dram awaits. Excellent fishing country, too.

Leave Speyside for Aviemore, premier winter sport resort, one of five in Scotland, and then to Inverness, the Highland capital. To the north the moors and hills of Ross-shire and Sutherland, to the west, Loch Ness with its famous inhabitant. Continue down the Caledonian Canal to Fort William and Britain's highest mountain, Ben Nevis.

The tour circle includes the Pass of Glencoe en route to Glasgow. Glencoe is a climbing and ski centre and notorious in clan history for the massacre of the Macdonalds.

Glasgow has impressive art galleries and museums and a vibrant music and theatre lifestyle. Fashion is a major keynote in its extensive shopping facilities.

Head for the Borders again through Ayrshire, home of the national poet Robert Burns who died in 1796. Many will respect his Immortal Memory on the bicentenary commemoration at his mausoleum in St Michael's Kirkyard, Dumfries.

Palace of Holyroodhouse
Canongate
Edinburgh EH8 8DX
Tel: 0131 556 7371

Inveraray Jail Visitor Centre
Church Square
Inveraray PA32 8TX
Tel: 01499 302 381

Balnain House Heritage Centre
40 Hunty Street
Inverness IV3 5HR
Tel: 01463 715 757

Drummond Castle Gardens
Muthill
Crieff PH7 4HZ
Tel: 01764 681 321

New Lanark Visitor Centre
New Lanark Mills
Lanark ML11 9DB
Tel: 01555 661 345

Discovery Point
Discovery Quay
Dundee DD1 4XA
Tel: 01382 201 245

Burns House
Burns Street
Dumfries DG1 2PS
Tel: 01387 255 297

Malt Whisky Trail
Grampian Highlands and Aberdeen
Migvie House
North Silver Street
Aberdeen AB1 1RJ
Tel: 01224 632727

For more information about Scotland, please contact:-

Scottish Tourist Board
23 Ravelston Terrace
Edinburgh EH4 3EU
Tel: 0131 332 2433

FARLEYER HOUSE HOTEL

ABERFELDY, PERTHSHIRE PH15 2JE
TEL: 01887 820332 FAX: 01887 829430

Farleyer House stands amid mature woodland overlooking the Tay Valley. The restaurant won the *Good Food Guide* Tayside Restaurant of the Year 1990 award for its wonderful cuisine, and is highly praised in the most prestigious food guides. A more relaxed and informal meal may be enjoyed in the new Scottish Bistro where the blackboard menu offers an outstanding choice. The house has a lengthy history, dating back to the 16th century. It has a warm luxurious feel with soft-pile carpets, full-bodied drapes, clusters of paintings and scattered *'objets d'art'*. Deer-stalking, fishing, riding, sailing and water sports can be arranged and there is a 6-hole practice golf course in the grounds. The central location makes this hotel a perfect base for touring the countryside and historic towns of Scotland. Dogs are accommodated separately from the main house and strictly by prior arrangement. **Directions:** Drive through Weem on the B846 past Castle Menzies and Farleyer is on the Kinloch–Rannoch road. Price guide: Single £75–£95; double/twin £140–£190.

SHIELDHILL HOUSE

QUOTHQUAN, BIGGAR, LANARKSHIRE ML12 6NA
TEL: 01899 220035 FAX: 01899 221092

Set amongst the rolling hills and farmlands of the Upper Clyde Valley lies Shieldhill House. This castle style country house hotel, parts of which date back to 1199, was the ancestral home of the Chancellor family for more than 700 years. It was transformed into a luxurious hotel in 1959. The 'old keep', the turreted roof and the secret staircase all conjure up bygone days, while open fires and deep soft furnishings ensure modern day comfort. The 11 individually designed, spacious bedrooms all have king, queen, twin or four poster beds and en suite facilities. The hotel's luxurious oak panelled lounge is the perfect place to relax, while in its spacious dining room exquisite cuisine can be enjoyed. An extensive and interesting wine list complements the delicious dishes on offer. For the energetic, the surrounding country provides plenty of opportunity to enjoy walking or a game of golf. Clay pigeon shooting or trout fishing can also be arranged. The three cities of Glasgow, Edinburgh and Carlisle are all easily reached by car. **Directions:** From Biggar take B7016 (signposted Carnwath), after two miles turn left into Sheildhill Road. The hotel is one and a half miles down on the right. Price guide: Single: £68–£89; double/twin: £104–£152.

SUMMER ISLES HOTEL

ACHILTIBUIE, ROSS-SHIRE IV26 2YG
TEL: 01854 622282 FAX: 01854 622251

An awe-inspiring wilderness of sea, mountains and islands is the setting for this unique hotel. It has been personally run for many years by proprietors Mark and Geraldine Irvine, and the atmosphere is relaxed and unstuffy – visitors unwind easily and soon find themselves among friends. So therapeutic is the combination of good food, comfortable accommodation and splendid surroundings that many guests return year after year. Nearly everything served in the restaurant is home-produced or caught locally. There are scallops, lobsters, langoustines, halibut, turbot, salmon and venison, along with home-made breads and pastries. Access to fresh ingredients allows award-winning chef Chris Firth-Bernard to produce superb menus – he strives for perfection with every course. Dinner is served at 8pm. After breakfast, Mark and Geraldine are happy to talk to guests about fishing, birdwatching, sailing around the islands to see the seal colonies or where to go exploring on foot. It is advisable to bring sensible outdoor clothing. Open from Easter to mid-October.
Directions: Ten miles north of Ullapool, turn along the twisting single-track road that skirts Lochs Lurgain, Badagyle and Oscaig under the eye of Stac Polly. Achiltibuie is 15 miles further; the hotel is just past the post office. Price guide: Single £44–£64; double/twin £67–£95.

In association with MasterCard

INVERCRERAN COUNTRY HOUSE HOTEL

GLEN CRERAN, APPIN, ARGYLL PA38 4BJ
TEL: 01631 730 414 FAX: 01631 730 532

The outstanding setting of Invercreran House is one of the many reasons for its popularity. Surrounded by mountains, it stands in 25 secluded acres of shrub gardens and woodland, overlooking the mature trees and meadows of Glen Creran. Guests can stroll through the grounds towards the River Creran which flows through the glen. Viewed from the outside, it is surprising to discover that the hotel has only nine guest bedrooms. The interiors, reception rooms and bedrooms alike are spacious. In the large lounge there is a free-standing fireplace where logs burn beneath a copper canopy. The Kersley family are involved in all aspects of the day-to-day running of the house. Their son Tony,

the master chef, prepares delicious dishes that emphasise the full flavour of fresh Scottish game, fish, vegetables and soft fruits. Meals are served in the semi-circular, marble-floored dining room. Invercreran House is well positioned for touring the Western Highlands, offering easy access to Oban, Fort William and Glencoe. Closed November to early March. **Directions:** Hotel is off the A828 Oban–Fort William road, 14 miles north of Connel Bridge, 18 miles south of Ballachulish Bridge. Travelling to Invercreran at the head of Loch Creran, stay on the minor road going north east into Glen Creran; hotel is 3/4 mile on left. Price guide: Single £64; double/twin £94–£130; suite £150.

LETHAM GRANGE HOTEL AND GOLF COURSES

COLLISTON, BY ARBROATH, ANGUS DD11 4RL
TEL: 01241 890373 FAX: 01241 890414

Letham Grange is a beautifully renovated Victorian mansion with its original sculptured ceilings, panelling, antique staircase, fireplaces and period paintings faithfully restored to their former splendour. With its splendid scenery, it is a perfect country retreat for either a sporting or leisure break. The sumptuous luxury of country house living that the hotel provides is enhanced by two excellent golf courses and a four-lane curling rink. The bedrooms are individually designed and spacious, with charming decor which reflects the original character of this lovely building. Dining in the restful Rosehaugh Restaurant is a gourmet experience. The finest fresh local foods are selected to create table d'hôte and à la carte menus of international standard. Even the most seasoned golfers will enjoy meeting the demands of the 18-hole championship standard Old Course, which surrounds the hotel. The New Course offers a more relaxing game. The curling rink is overlooked by the spacious Sweep 'n' Swing lounge where drinks are served. Some of Scotland's most majestic scenery within easy reach of the hotel. **Directions:** From Dundee take A92 and on the outskirts of Arbroath follow A933 to Colliston village. Turn right, signposted Letham Grange, and at Tjunction turn right and follow sign for half a mile. Price guide: Single £79; double/twin £125; suites £141.

BALCARY BAY HOTEL

AUCHENCAIRN, NR CASTLE DOUGLAS, DUMFRIES & GALLOWAY DG7 1QZ
TEL: 01556 640217 FAX: 01556 640272

The hotel takes its name from the bay on which it stands, in an area of Galloway that is romantic in its isolation and which was once full of intrigue. Heston Isle, the hide-out of 17th century smugglers, fronts the hotel's view across the Solway coast and the Cumbrian Hills beyond. Originally owned by a shipping firm, the hotel was known to harbour illegal loot in its secret underground passages. Nowadays, Scottish hospitality at Balcary Bay includes the provision of modern facilities with a traditional atmosphere. It offers local delicacies such as lobsters, prawns and salmon imaginitavely prepared, plus the reasurring intimacy of a family-run hotel. Despite its northerly aspect, Galloway benefits from the Gulf Stream and enjoys a mild and long holiday season. The area has great coastal and woodland walks. Closed from mid November to early March. Nearby are several 9 and 18 hole golf courses at Colvend, Kirkcudbright, Castle Douglas, Southerness and Dumfries. There are also salmon rivers and trout lochs, sailing, shooting, riding and bridwatching facilities. The area abounds with National Trust historic properties and gardens. **Directions:** Located off the A711 Dumfries–Kirkcudbright road, two miles out of Auchencairn on the Shore Road. Price guide: Single £50; double/twin £88–£100. Seasonal short breaks and reduced inclusive rates for 3 and 7 nights.

DARROCH LEARG HOTEL

BRAEMAR ROAD, BALLATER, ABERDEENSHIRE AB35 5UX
TEL: 013397 55443 FAX: 013397 55252

Four acres of leafy grounds and gardens surround Darroch Learg, sited on the side of the rocky hill which dominates Ballater. The hotel, which was built in 1888 as a fashionable country residence, offers panoramic views over the golf course, River Dee and Balmoral Estate to the fine peaks of the Grampian Mountains. The original house was converted into a hotel 50 years ago. Oakhall, an adjacent mansion built in Scottish baronial style and adorned with turrets, contains five of the 20 bedrooms available. All are individually furnished and decorated, providing every modern amenity. The reception rooms in Darroch Learg are similarly elegant and welcoming, a comfortable venue in which to enjoy a relaxing drink. Log fires create a particularly cosy atmosphere on chilly nights. Beautifully presented food is served in the dining room and the menu is changed daily. A wide choice of wines complements the cuisine, which is best described as modern and Scottish in style. To perfect the setting, there is a wonderful outlook south towards the hills of Glen Muick. The wealth of outdoor activities on offer include walking, riding, mountain-biking, loch and river fishing, gliding and ski-ing. Ballater itself is interesting with old ruined Kirk and Celtic stones. **Directions:** At the western edge of Ballater on the A93. Price guide: Single £45; double/twin £75–£100.

ARISAIG HOUSE

BEASDALE, BY ARISAIG, INVERNESS-SHIRE PH39 4NR
TEL: 01687 450622 FAX: 01687 450626

Princely redwoods rising above the sudden abundance of Arisaig's oak and rhododendron declare your journey done: now it is time to relax and enjoy the hospitality offered by your hosts, the Smither family. Natural light floods into the house, streaming through tall windows into the inner hall to warm the oak staircase and cast a gleam across polished furniture. The chef's epicurean offerings – supported by a lineage of fine château bottlings – give promise of the restoration of body and soul. Comprising game in season, crisp local vegetables, fruits de mer and pâtisserie baked daily, the cuisine is always a gastronomic delight. High above the ponticum and crinodendrons, the 14

spacious bedrooms afford a magnificent vista of mountains, sea and ever-changing sky. On some days, the clink of billiard balls or the clunk of croquet from the beautiful grounds are the only sounds to thread their way across the rustle of a turning page. On other days guests are hard to find, taking trips on ferries to Skye and the Inner Hebrides or discovering the landscape that has barely changed since Bonnie Prince Charlie's passage through these parts many years ago. Closed early November to mid-March. Arisaig House is a Relais et Châteaux member.
Directions: Three miles from Arisaig village on the A830 Mallaig road. Price guide : Single £65; double/twin £130–£215.

In association
with MasterCard

DALMUNZIE HOUSE

SPITTAL O'GLENSHEE, BLAIRGOWRIE, PERTHSHIRE PH10 7QG
TEL: 01250 885224 FAX: 01250 885225

Dalmunzie House is beautifully tucked away high in the Scottish Highlands, 18 miles north of Blairgowrie and 15 miles south of Braemar. Standing in its own mountainous 6,000-acre sporting estate, it is run by Simon and Alexandra Winton. Guests come to enjoy the relaxed family atmosphere which, together with unobtrusive service and attention, ensures a comfortable stay. The bedrooms are individual in character, some with antiques, others romantically set in the turrets of the house, all tastefully decorated. Delicately cooked traditional Scottish fare is created from local ingredients fresh from the hills and lochs. The menu changes daily and dishes are served in the dining room, accompanied by wines from the well-stocked cellar. Among the sporting activities available on site are golf (the 9-hole course is the highest in Britain) and shooting for grouse, ptarmigan and black game. Other country pursuits include river and loch fishing and stalking for red deer. Pony-trekking can be organised locally. Glenshee Ski Centre is 6 miles away: it offers cross-country and downhill skiing. Closer to home, the hotel games room provides more sedate pastimes for all the family. Closed early November to 28 December. **Directions:** Dalmunzie is on the A93 at the Spittal O'Glenshee, south of Braemar. Price guide: Single £48–£54; double/twin £72–£88.

BLAIRGOWRIE

KINLOCH HOUSE HOTEL

BY BLAIRGOWRIE, PERTHSHIRE PH10 6SG
TEL: 01250 884237 FAX: 01250 884333

Built in 1840, Kinloch House is an elegant example of a Scottish country home. Set in 25 acres of wooded parkland grazed by Highland cattle, it offers panoramic views to the south over Marlee Loch to the Sidlaw Hills beyond. It has a grand galleried hall with an ornate glass ceiling and fine paintings and antiques in the reception rooms. A carefully incorporated extension echoes the original style, with oak panelling and ornate friezes. Chef Bill McNicoll has built a reputation for good Scottish fare – lamb, fish, shellfish, wildfowl and game are all available in season. Choices from the menu such as sautéed breast of woodcock or roast partridge are complemented by an extensive wine list. The cocktail bar, which stocks over 140 malt whiskies, is adjacent to the conservatory and is a focal point of the hotel. David and Sarah Shentall offer a warm welcome to all the guests, whether they come simply to enjoy the beauty of the area, or to take advantage of the local pursuits of golf, hill walking, fishing and shooting. For the sightseer, Glamis Castle, Scone Palace and Blair Castle are among the area's attractions. 2 AA Rosettes and 3 AA Red Stars. Closed at Christmas. **Directions:** The hotel is 3 miles west of Blairgowrie, off the A923 Dunkeld road. Price guide (including dinner): Single £79; double/twin £159–£195.

ROMAN CAMP HOTEL

CALLANDER, PERTHSHIRE FK17 8BG
TEL: 01877 330003 FAX: 01877 331533

Roman Camp Hotel, originally built in 1625 as a hunting lodge for the Dukes of Perth, takes its name from a nearby Roman encampment. Reminiscent of a French château, the hotel's turrets house a myriad of period features, including a tiny chapel, linenfold wood panelling and ornate moulded ceilings. Set on the banks of the River Teith, the hotel is surrounded by 20 acres of superb grounds including a listed walled garden where herbs and flowers are grown for the hotel. The public rooms, drawing room, sun lounge and library are characterised by grand proportions, antique furnishings and fine views over the river and gardens. The bedrooms are individually and most becomingly furnished.

A richly painted ceiling, depicting traditional Scottish designs, is a unique feature of the restaurant, where the thoughtfully compiled menu is accompanied by a long and temting wine list. Guests are welcome to fish free of charge on the private stretch of the river, while all around there are plenty of interesting walks. Within easy reach are the Trossachs, Doune Motor Museum and Aberfoyle. Dogs are welcome by prior arrangement. **Directions:** Approaching Callander on the A84, the entrance to the hotel is between two cottages in Callander's main street. Price guide: Single £59–£85; double/twin from £85–£135; suite £115–£155.

For hotel location, see maps on pages 473–479

BARON'S CRAIG HOTEL

**ROCKCLIFFE BY DALBEATTIE, KIRKCUDBRIGHTSHIRE DG5 4QF
TEL: 01556 630225 FAX: 01556 630328**

Baron's Craig Hotel stands in wooded country overlooking Solway and Rough Firth, a tidal inlet biting deep into tree-covered and heathered hills. Thanks to the mild climate, the 12-acre grounds are ablaze with colour throughout much of the holiday season, especially in May, when masses of rhododendrons are in bloom. An imposing granite edifice, Baron's Craig was built in 1880 and harmoniously extended more recently. The 22 bedrooms have en suite facilities, both bath and shower; all have colour TV, radio, direct-dial telephone and baby-listening service. Tea and coffee making facilities are in all rooms for the convenience of guests but room service is available too. The original character of the building has been retained, with furnishings chosen to complement the period style. Excellent international cooking is augmented by a comprehensive wine list. Only three minutes from the hotel is a safe beach for swimming, while there is abundant scope for golf, fishing, boating, sailing and walking nearby. Among the local attractions are Castle Douglas, New Abbey, Glen Trool and Kirkcudbright. The new owner, Alberto Capaccioli, offers a warm welcome to all guests. Closed from November to Easter. **Directions:** Rockcliffe is a small village just off the A710 south of Dalbeattie. Price guide: (including breakfast) Single £57; double/twin £98. Reductions for stays of three days or more.

KINNAIRD

KINNAIRD ESTATE, BY DUNKELD, PERTHSHIRE PH8 0LB
TEL: 01796 482440 FAX: 01796 482289

Kinnaird is surrounded by a beautiful estate of 9,000 acres and offers breathtaking views of the moors and the Tay valley. Built in 1770, the house has been privately owned by the Ward family since 1927 and was completely renovated in 1990 by Mrs Constance Ward. Its friendly atmosphere has survived the centuries. The bedrooms are individually decorated with lovely fabrics and furnishings and each has a gas log fire and every modern convenience. The house is furnished almost entirely with fine and rare pieces of antique furniture, china and pictures, and decorated with fresh flowers. A ground floor bedroom with appropriate facilities is available for disabled guests. The dining rooms enjoy magnificent views and provide a stunning setting for a menu of carefully chosen and beautifully presented dishes. Kinnaird's cuisine has already won acclaim from local and international food critics. The original wine cellars are stocked with an extensive array of fine wines, liqueurs and malt whiskies. A wide variety of sporting facilities is available from salmon and trout fishing to shooting of pheasant, grouse, duck and partridge. The estate offers excellent walking, bird watching and a new all-weather tennis court. **Directions:** Two miles north of Dunkeld on A9, take B898 for four and a half miles. Price guide: Single £137–£210; double/twin £119–£220; suite £275.

For hotel location, see maps on pages 473–479

ENMORE HOTEL

MARINE PARADE, KIRN, DUNOON, ARGYLL PA23 8HH
TEL: 01369 702230 FAX: 01369 702148

Known as the jewel on the Clyde, the waterfront town of Dunoon on the Cowal peninsula is often regarded as the gateway to the Western Highlands. Enmore Hotel is an attractive house, built in 1785 as a summer retreat for a wealthy cotton merchant. It has since been fully restored by owners David and Angela Wilson. Pretty country wallpaper and bright fabrics characterise the bedrooms, with fluffy towelling robes and flowers among the extras. One of the bedrooms has a water bed and an invigorating whirlpool bath and another has a four-poster bed with a Jacuzzi. In the restaurant, the emphasis is on the use of fresh, local produce to create traditional Scottish dishes. Typical choices may include Arbroath smokies, haggis soup, kippers or steak served in a Drambuie and cream sauce. Chef-patron David Wilson offers a five-course table d'hôte menu each evening. Two international-standard squash courts are available. Dunoon is well equipped with recreational amenities, including bowling, tennis, sailing and a championship golf course. **Directions:** Kirn is on the A815, north-west of Dunoon (A885). In summer a car-ferry crosses to and from Gourock across the Firth. Price guide: Single £40–£50; double/twin £75–£130.

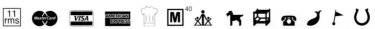

BORTHWICK CASTLE

BORTHWICK, NORTH MIDDLETON, MIDLOTHIAN EH23 4QY
TEL: 01875 820514 FAX: 01875 821702

To the south of Edinburgh, off the A7, stands historic Borthwick Castle Hotel, a twenty minute drive from Scotland's capital. Built in 1430 by the Borthwick family, this ancient stronghold has witnessed many of the great events of Scotland's history at first hand. Notably, the safe keeping of Mary Queen of Scots following her wedding to the Earl of Bothwell and a forceful visitation by Oliver Cromwell in 1650. At Borthwick Castle there are 10 bedchambers, each with en suite facilities and four with four-poster beds. In the evening, guests dine in the magnificent setting of the candle-lit Great Hall where a four-course set menu is prepared by gourmet chef Martin Russell, who describes his cuisine as "modern British with a strong bias for Scotland's natural larder". A comprehensive wine list is complemented by a fine selection of malt whiskies. While the castle caters for banquets of up to 50 guests, it especially welcomes those in search of that intimate dinner for two. In either case, the experience is unforgettable. Open from March to January 2nd. **Directions:** 12 miles south of Edinburgh on the A7. At North Middleton, follow signs for Borthwick. A private road then leads to the castle. Price guide: Single £80–£160; double/twin £95–£180.

CHANNINGS

SOUTH LEARMONTH GARDENS, EDINBURGH EH4 1EZ
TEL: 0131 315 2226 FAX: 0131 332 9631

Channings is located on a quiet cobbled street only 10 minutes' walk from the centre of Edinburgh, with easy access to the host of shops on Princes Street and the timeless grandeur of Edinburgh Castle. Formerly five Edwardian town houses, the original features have been restored with flair and consideration and the atmosphere is like an exclusive country club. Guests can relax in one of the lounges with a coffee or afternoon tea. For those who like to browse, the hotel has an interesting collection of antique prints, furniture, *objets d'art*, periodicals and books. The Brasserie (AA Rosette) offers varied menus from a light lunch to full evening meals. Five ground floor suites provide versatile accommodation for corporate requirements, small seminars and presentations, while both the Kingsleigh Suite and oak-panelled library make an ideal venue for cocktail parties and private dinners. At the rear of the hotel is a terraced, patio garden. Special weekend breaks are available throughout the year and offer good value. Closed for Christmas. **Directions:** Go north-west from Queensferry Street, over Dean Bridge on to Queensferry Road. Take third turning on right down South Learmonth Avenue, turn right at end into South Learmonth Gardens. Price guide: Single £85–£97; double/twin £115–£160.

DALHOUSIE CASTLE HOTEL AND RESTAURANT

EDINBURGH, BONNYRIGG EH19 3JB
TEL: 01875 820153 FAX: 01875 821936

The Dalhousie Castle nestles in hundreds of acres of forest, river pasture and parkland overlooking the banks of the South Esk. Over 800 years it has been host to numerous famous figures, including Edward I, Oliver Cromwell, Sir Walter Scott and Queen Victoria. Today, following sympathetic restoration, the family seat of the Ramsays of Dalhousie, it is a luxurious hotel which retains many fine features. Historically themed bedrooms include Robert the Bruce and others. Ornate plasterwork, fine panelling, stone walls and rich drapes adorn the public rooms, while the ancient barrel-vaulted dungeons offer a unique setting for candlelit dining. Both French and Scottish cuisine is served in the restaurant, complemented by attentive and personal service. Game and clay shooting, salmon and trout fishing, 'dry' skiing and golf at St Andrews, Muirfield and Gleneagles are all within easy reach. Archery and falconry can be arranged in the hotel's grounds. Carefully renovated banqueting and conference suites provide an excellent setting for conferences, meetings, banquets and weddings. The Castle is only 20 minutes drive from Edinburgh. 4 Crowns Highly Commended – Taste of Scotland Approved. **Directions:** From Edinburgh A7 south, through Lasswade and Newtongrange. Turn right at junction onto the B704 and the hotel is within $^1/_4$ mile. Price guide: Single £70–£105; double £125–£165.

THE HOWARD

32-36 GREAT KING STREET, EDINBURGH EH3 6QH
TEL: 0131-557 3500 FAX: 0131-557 6515

Since its conversion from private residence to hotel, The Howard has been sumptuously appointed throughout and offers a service to match the surroundings. The character of this Georgian town house prevails. The 16 bedrooms, including two suites, are beautifully furnished with antiques, while the drawing room centres on an elaborate crystal chandelier. The restaurant, Number 36, seats up to 50 people for business and private lunches, offering top Scottish cuisine, with a classical inspiration. The Oval and Cumberland suites offer quiet and elegant surroundings for either meetings or private dining, accommodating 12–30

guests. The Howard is an integral part of the largest classified historical monument in Britain: Edinburgh's New Town. Having a private car park to the rear, The Howard is an ideal city centre base from which to explore Edinburgh's cultural heritage, being in close proximity to such monuments as Edinburgh Castle, the Palace of Holyrood and the Royal Mile. **Directions:** Take the third road on the left off Princes Street into Frederick Street. Go right into George Street, left into Hanover Street. At third set of lights, right into Great King Street. Hotel is on left. Price guide: Single £65–110; double £130–180; suite £255.

JOHNSTOUNBURN HOUSE

HUMBIE, NR EDINBURGH, EAST LOTHIAN EH36 5PL
TEL: 01875 833696 FAX: 01875 833626

Dating from 1625, Johnstounburn House stands at the foot of the Lammermuir Hills, only 15 miles south of Edinburgh. Set amid lawns and parklands in a private estate, its grounds feature imposing yew hedges, an orchard, a patio rose garden and a herbaceons walled garden. Upon entering the house, guests will sense the depth of Scottish heritage preserved here. Refurbishments have enhanced the historical features while enabling guests to enjoy modern comforts. Of the 20 well-appointed bedrooms, 11 are in the house and nine in the tastefully converted coach house. There is a spacious cedar-panelled lounge where an open fire will warm you on chilly days. In the 18th-century, pine-panelled dining room, chef Bryan Thom prepares sumptuous fare from the finest Scottish produce. In the grounds guests can enjoy clay pigeon shooting, riding or fish in the trout-filled loch. Rough shooting and stalking can be arranged. There are also all-terrain vehicles which guests may drive over the Johnstoun 'burn' and through the fields. Muirfield and Gullane are among 15 golf courses nearby. Tantallon Castle, Abbotsford and Traquair House are a short drive away. **Directions:** From Edinburgh take A68 through Dalkeith and Pathhead to Fala. Turn left through Fala 1½ miles to T-junction; the hotel is on your right. Price guide: Single £95; double/twin £130; suite £155.

MALMAISON

ONE TOWER PLACE, LEITH, EDINBURGH EH6 7DB
TEL: 0131 555 6868 FAX: 0131 555 6999

Napoleon Bonaparte's first wife, Josephine, bought a house on the outskirts of Paris, not far from Versailles, in 1799. It became the couple's favourite home and very soon the model for the most fashionable way of life in its day. Almost two hundred years later Ken McCulloch's astutely converted old Seamen's Mission on the Leith waterfront is having a similar influence on contemporary fashion of rather a different kind, but under the very same name – Malmaison. Today's Malmaison Hotel Café Bar and Brasserie on the outskirts of Edinburgh is a trend-setter for townhouse hospitality of the 21st century. Downstairs a choice of informal first class catering, upstairs excellent practical accommodation in a self-contained luxury environment, into the bargain a room for meetings and somewhere to park your car outside. The bedrooms are a selection of suites and large doubles, some with panoramic views of the Firth of Forth, all perfectly designed, all at affordable prices. Edinburgh itself, the "Athens of the North", is rightly famed for its history, its buildings, its university, its galleries and nowadays also for its celebrated International Festival held each August. **Directions:** Malmaison is about 15 minutes drive from the centre of Edinburgh. Heading Northeast from the centre of the city follow Leith Street and then Leith Walk (A600) to Constitution Street and Tower Street near Albert Dock. Price guide: Single £75; double/twin £75; suites £105.

THE NORTON HOUSE HOTEL

INGLISTON, EDINBURGH EH28 8LX
TEL: 0131 333 1275 FAX: 0131 333 5305

This Victorian mansion, dating back to 1861, is a part of the Virgin Group. Situated in 55 acres of mature parkland, Norton House combines modern comforts with elegance. The 47 en suite bedrooms are bright and spacious, with many facilities, including a video channel and satellite TV. Influenced by the best Scottish and French traditions, the menu offers a balanced choice. Moments away, through leafy woodlands, a former stable block has been converted into a tavern, where drinks and snacks are available to families and friends. Set in a walled garden, it is an ideal venue for the barbecues which are a regular feature in the summer months. The Patio, Veranda and Usher Room lend a sense of occasion to small gatherings, while the Linlithgow Suite can cater for large-scale events such as banquets, weddings and conferences. Norton House is 1 mile from Edinburgh Airport and 6 miles from the city centre, making it a convenient base from which to explore the Trossachs, Borders and Lothians. Dogs accommodated by request. Special weekend rate, enquiries welcome. **Directions:** From Edinburgh take A8 past airport and hotel is 1/2 mile on left. From Glasgow, follow M8 to its close, take the first exit off the roundabout following signs for Ratho, then turn left at the top of the hill. Price guide: Single £99–£115; double/twin £120–£145; suite £165.

MasterCard In association with MasterCard

MANSION HOUSE HOTEL

THE HAUGH, ELGIN, MORAY IV30 1AW
TEL: 01343 548811 FAX: 01343 547916

Set within private woodland and overlooking the River Lossie stands the grand Mansion House Hotel. This former baronial mansion is only a minute's walk from the centre of the ancient city of Elgin. An elegant entrance hall boasts oak-panelled walls, fresh flowers and many antique curiosities. Its majestic staircase leads to the well appointed bedrooms, featuring four-poster beds and containing a welcoming glass of sherry. The Piano Lounge is an ideal place to relax before entering the elegant restaurant. Here the cuisine is creative, delicious and beautifully presented. The "Wee Bar" is in the centre of the house, well placed next to the Snooker Room, while a unique collection of whiskies gives the name to the Still Room. A purpose built function room, called the Haugh Room, has its own entrance, bar, toilets, and dance area. Guests at the hotel are invited to use the Country Club facilities which include a swimming pool, gymnasium, spa, steam room, sauna and sun bed. Complementing this is the Beauty Spot, which provides a multitude of unisex services. There is a choice of ten golf courses within ten miles, the opportunity to fish on the Spey and unlimited water sports in Findhorn Bay. **Directions:** In Elgin, turn off the main A96 road into Haugh Road. The hotel is at the end of this road by the river. Price guide: Single £70–£95; double/twin £100–£140.

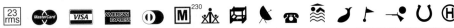

FORT WILLIAM (Onich)

In association
with MasterCard

ALLT-NAN-ROS HOTEL

ONICH, FORT WILLIAM, INVERNESS-SHIRE PH33 6RY
TEL: 01855 821210 FAX: 01855 821462

Situated on the north shore of Loch Linnhe, Allt-nan-Ros Hotel (Gaelic for 'Burn of the Roses') was originally built as a Victorian shooting lodge. It has been tastefully upgraded by its resident proprietors, the MacLeod family, and it offers both a high standard of comfort and exceptional views of the surrounding mountains and lochs. The design of the hotel takes advantage of its southerly aspect and all bedrooms and public rooms overlook the loch. Quality furnishings and a full range of amenities are provided in all the bedrooms, while the superior rooms available each incorporate a bay window. In the traditionally furnished lounges, dining room and bar a country house atmosphere prevails and guests are invited to relax and enjoy the lovely views. The cuisine served in the splendid restaurant is influenced by modern and French styles, but also adapts traditional Scottish recipes to today's tastes. A comprehensive and reasonably priced wine list incorporates wines from all around the world. Lying midway between Ben Nevis and Glencoe, the hotel is located in an area of unsurpassed scenery and history. Among the many local activities are climbing, walking, touring the towns and islands, sailing, fishing or taking a trip on the steam trains. **Directions:** Ten miles south of Fort William on the main A82. Price guide: Single £35–£55; double/twin £70–£110; suites £76–£130.

398

For hotel location, see maps on pages 473–479

CALLY PALACE HOTEL

GATEHOUSE OF FLEET, DUMFRIES & GALLOWAY DG7 2DL
TEL: 01557 814341 FAX: 01557 814522

Set in over 100 acres of forest and parkland, on the edge of Robert Burns country, this 18th-century country house has been restored to its former glory by the McMillan family, the proprietors since 1981. On entering the hotel, guests will initially be impressed by the grand scale of the interior. Two huge marble pillars support the original moulded ceiling of the entrance hall. All the public rooms have ornate ceilings, original marble fireplaces and fine reproduction furniture. Combine these with grand, traditional Scottish cooking and you have a hotel *par excellence*. The 56 en suite bedrooms have been individually decorated. Some are suites with a separate sitting room; others are large enough to accommodate a sitting area. An indoor leisure complex, completed in the style of the marble entrance hall, includes heated swimming pool, Jacuzzi, saunas and solarium. The hotel has an all-weather tennis court, a putting green, croquet, and a lake for private fishing or boating. Also, for exclusive use of hotel guests is an 18-hole golf course, par 70, length 5,500 yards set around the lake in the 150 acre grounds. Special weekend and over-60s breaks are available out of season. Closed January and February. **Directions:** Sixty miles west of Carlisle, 1-1$^{1}/_{2}$ miles from Gatehouse of Fleet junction on the main A75 road. Price guide: (including dinner): Single £70; double/twin £114–£140.

CASTLETON HOUSE HOTEL

GLAMIS, BY FORFAR, ANGUS DD8 1SJ
TEL: 01307 840340 FAX: 01307 840506

Castleton House stands on the site of an old fort and is set in extensive grounds. Its proprietors pride themselves on offering guests excellent accommodation and outstanding cuisine in an informal and refreshing country atmosphere. Each of the bedrooms has been furnished to the highest standards and includes a full range of modern amenities. Castleton House is at the heart of Scotland's larder with abundant, highly-prized local supplies of fresh fruit, vegetables, meat, poultry, game and fish. The hotel enjoys a reputation for fine cuisine, which is served both in the dining room and conservatory and its cellars are stocked with an outstanding selection of wines. There is no shortage of activities for sporting enthusiasts. Golf at St Andrews, Gleneagles, Carnoustie and Rosemount are all within a short distance, while game shooting and stalking can be arranged on a nearby estate. The Grampians offer hill walking and rock climbing and Britain's second largest ski area is only a 40 minute drive away. The surrounding area is rich in history and there are numerous standing stones, ancient houses, castles and forts to remind visitors of the past. Tayside offers many delights from the wild expanse of Rannoch Moor to the grandeur of the Grampians and the golden sands of Lunan Bay. **Directions:** Off A94, three miles from Glamis. Price guide: Single £60; double/twin £90.

GLEDDOCH HOUSE

LANGBANK, RENFREWSHIRE PA14 6YE
TEL: 01475 540711 FAX: 01475 540201

Once the home of a Glasgow shipping baron, Gleddoch House stands in 360 acres, with dramatic views across the River Clyde to Ben Lomond and the hills beyond. The individually appointed bedrooms all have en suite facilities and some have four-poster beds. Executive rooms and suites are also available. There are also refurbished self-catering lodges available for rent. There are a range of meeting rooms available to cater up to 50 delegates. The Garden restaurant is renowned for its award-winning modern Scottish cuisine, enhanced by a list of more than 300 wines. On the estate a series of activities are available such as golf, clay pigeon shooting, archery, off-road driving and falconry, making Gleddoch an ideal venue to host corporate events. Additionally the equestrian centre caters for all levels, from trekking to pony rides and individual tuition. Gleddoch's location offers an experience of a bygone era complemented with the sophistication today's traveller requires. A range of short breaks, golfing packages and gourmet events are available throughout the year. Glasgow Airport is only 10 minutes drive away and the City Centre 20 minutes. **Directions:** M8 towards Greenock; take B789 Langbank/ Houston exit. Follow signs to left and then right after ½ mile; hotel is on left. Price guide: Single £95–£100; double/twin £140–£150; suite £175.

MALMAISON

278 WEST GEORGE STREET, GLASGOW G2 4LL
TEL: 0141 221 6400 FAX: 0141 221 6411

In 1799, Josephine de Beauharnais, along with her husband, Emperor Napoleon I, bought a house near the Palace of Versailles just outside Paris. The house was called Malmaison and it soon became widely regarded as an example of the new chic contemporary style of its era. The Malmaison in Glasgow is today's equivalent of that independent style. A small contemporary hotel with spacious, stylish bedrooms, individually designed, complete with CD players and satellite televisions. With an art nouveau Brasserie and Café Bar serving traditional French cooking with an ever changing menu and an interesting list of wines by the glass, pot and bottle. Malmaison is situated in the heart of Glasgow, within easy walking distance of theatres, shopping, railway stations and only 20 minutes by road from the Airport. **Directions:** From south and east (Edinburgh) leave M8 at junction 17. Turn left at traffic lights into Sauchiehall Street and assume the right hand lane of the one way system. Take the third right, Pitt Street, and follow that road across three blocks until it turns round onto West George Street at the Strathclyde Police Headquarters. Malmaison is immediately on your left hand side. From the west (Glasgow Airport) leave M8 at junction 19. Price guide: Single £75; double/twin £75; suites £105.

21 rms MasterCard VISA AMERICAN EXPRESS ◑ ⚔ 📡 ☎

ONE DEVONSHIRE GARDENS

GLASGOW G12 0UX
TEL: 0141 339 2001 FAX: 0141 337 1663

Situated just ten minutes from the city centre, One Devonshire Gardens is set in the heart of a tree-lined Victorian terrace once the homes of the wealthy merchants and shipowners of Glasgow. This luxurious hotel prides itself of providing a caring, friendly service in relaxing surroundings. The bedrooms are superbly decorated and furnished and offer the ultimate in comfort and convenience. Fine cuisine, beautifully prepared and presented, is served in the elegant dining room. Try fillet of Angus beef with gratin dauphinoise, salsify, red wine jus and a shallot and basil butter, or roast stuffed quails with garlic and herbs on a crispy potato cake. These culinary delights are complemented by an extensive and interesting cellar. In the warmer months, afternoon teas may be enjoyed on the colourful terrace. There is plenty to do and see in Glasgow. Visit the cathedral the only complete medieval cathedral on the Scottish mainland or some of the fine museums such as Pollok House, which contains one of the best collections of Spanish paintings in Britain. **Directions:** From M8 junction 17 follow A82 (Great Western Road) for 1½ miles, turn left at traffic lights into Hyndland Road. Take first right into Hughenden Road, right at mini-roundabout then right again at end of road. Keep going – car park in front of hotel. Price guide: Single £135; double/twin £150; suites £180.

THE TOWN HOUSE

54 WEST GEORGE STREET, GLASGOW G2 1NG
TEL: 0141 332 3320 FAX: 0141 332 9756

The Town House, a Grade A listed building was originally built as The Glasgow Liberal Club and formerly used as part of The Royal Academy of Music and Drama. It has been tastefully and sympathetically restored to its former glory, with many original features still visible throughout. All 34 bedrooms are individually designed and furnished to the highest standards. Maximum priority has been given to security and each room has a card entry lock, security deadbolt and a spyhole. A comprehensive room service menu is available. In the Gordon Room bar on the first floor guests can sample the world famous Scottish hospitality. In the intimate Symphonies Restaurant, awarded an AA rosette for its standards of food and service, interesting and well presented dishes are served. The Music Room, where food is also offered, is an excellent example of a period ballroom and retains original features including two fireplaces and a minstrels gallery. Its menus are designed to suit all tastes and budgets. The hotel prides itself on its meetings and conferences facilities, with the availability of several private rooms enabling it to match size requirements of up to 180 delegates. **Directions:** The Town House Hotel is situated in the heart of Glasgow, opposite the Stock Exchange. Price guide: Single £85; double/twin £97–£110; suites £140–£160.

For hotel location, see maps on pages 473–479

GREYWALLS

MUIRFIELD, GULLANE, EAST LOTHIAN EH31 2EG
TEL: 01620 842144 FAX: 01620 842241

Greywalls, neighbouring Muirfield golf course, the home of the Honourable Company of Edinburgh Golfers, was designed for the cricketer, the Hon. Alfred Lyttleton, by Sir Edwin Lutyens. The hotel is a beautiful crescent shaped building made of warm, honey coloured stone from the local quarry. A delightful garden, believed to be the work of Gertrude Jekyll, provides secret enclaves where guests can escape to enjoy a good book and savour the delightful scents of roses and lavender. The hotel's bedrooms, all of varying size and design, are individually furnished and include many fine antiques. Downstairs is the peaceful panelled library, Edwardian tea room and small bar stocked with a selection of excellent brandies and whiskies. Hearty breakfasts of porridge, kippers from Achiltibuie, tasty sausages and freshly made croissants make an ideal start to the day while dinner is an outstanding feast provided by dedicated chefs. East Lothian has excellent golf courses, including Muirfield, where The Open is held regularly. Beautiful sandy beaches are within easy reach, along with nature reserves, ruined castles, villages, market towns and stately homes. The hotel is closed from November through to March. **Directions:** On A198 from city bypass which links to the M8, M9 and M90. Price guide: Single £95; double/twin £155–£170.

BUNCHREW HOUSE HOTEL

INVERNESS, SCOTLAND IV3 6TA
TEL: 01463 234917 FAX: 01463 710620

This splendid 17th century Scottish mansion, owned by Stuart and Lesley Dykes, is set amidst 20 acres of landscaped gardens and woodlands on the shores of Beauly Firth. Guests can enjoy breathtaking views of Ben Wyvis and the Black Isle, while just yards from the house the sea laps at the garden walls. Bunchrew has been carefully restored to preserve its heritage, while still giving its guests the highest standards of comfort and convenience. A further schedule of refurbishment began in 1995. The luxury suites are beautifully furnished and decorated to enhance their natural features. The elegant panelled drawing room is the ideal place to relax at any time, while during the winter log fires lend it an added appeal. In the candle-lit restaurant the traditional cuisine includes prime Scottish beef, fresh lobster and langoustines, locally caught game and venison and freshly grown vegetables. A carefully chosen wine list complements the menu. Local places of interest include Cawdor Castle, Loch Ness, Castle Urquhart and a number of beautiful glens. For those who enjoy sport there is skiing at nearby Aviemore, sailing, cruising and golf. **Directions:** From Inverness follow signs to Beauly, Dingwall on the A862. One mile from the outskirts of Inverness the entrance to Bunchrew House is on the right. Price guide: Single £55–£75; double/twin £75–£100; suites £105–£120.

CULLODEN HOUSE HOTEL

INVERNESS, INVERNESS-SHIRE IV1 2NZ
TEL: 01463 790461 FAX: 01463 792181 FROM USA TOLL FREE FAX 1 800 373 7987

Culloden House is a handsome Georgian mansion with a centuries-old tradition of hospitality. Among its famous visitors was Bonnie Prince Charlie, who fought his last battle by the park walls 250 years ago. The house stands in 40 acres of elegant lawns and parkland, where wild deer occasionally roam. Proprietors Ian and Marjory McKenzie have a high reputation with guests from all over the world. Thorough refurbishments of the décor and furnishings have enhanced the magnificent interiors. A good choice of accommodation is offered – from en suite single rooms to a four-poster double, or room with Jacuzzi – with the assurance that all rooms are appointed to the highest standards. New no-smoking suites are situated near the walled garden. In the Adam Dining Room, guests can savour superb cuisine prepared by acclaimed chef Michael Simpson, who trained at the Gleneagles Hotel and Hamburg Congress Centre. Business lunches, celebrations and functions can be held in the private dining room. Boat trips to Loch Ness can be arranged, while nearby are Cawdor Castle, the Clava Cairns burial ground and Culloden battlefield. Numerous routes lead to lovely glens. **Directions:** Take the A96 road and turn as signed to Culloden. Turn again at Culloden House Avenue. Price guide: Single £125–£175; double/twin £175–£220; suite £220.

KINGSMILLS HOTEL

CULCABOCK ROAD, INVERNESS, INVERNESS-SHIRE IV2 3LP
TEL: 01463 237166 FAX: 01463 225208

Built in 1785, this historic hotel has been extended and it offers guests both comfort and elegance. It is only a mile from the town centre, in three acres of gardens, adjacent to Inverness Golf Course. There is a choice of attractively appointed bedrooms, all with modern amenities. In addition to the standard rooms, as pictured below, there are seven beautifully furnished suite-style rooms, also family rooms with bunk beds and six self-catering villas. The Leisure Club incorporates a heated swimming pool, spa bath, steam cabin, sauna, sunbeds, mini-gym and pitch-and-putt. Hairdressing facilities are also provided. Throughout the year exceptionally good value is offered by special breaks which include local seasonal attractions. Golf, fishing, skiing, riding and pony-trekking can all be enjoyed nearby and, if required, arranged as part of an activity holiday. Christmas, Easter and New Year packages are also available. The Kingsmills Hotel is well placed for visiting the Highlands, Loch Ness, the Whisky Trail, Culloden battlefield and Cawdor Castle. USA representative – Thomas McFerran, telephone toll free: 1-800-215 443 7990. **Directions:** Turn left off A9 signposted Kingsmills and Culcabock. Turn right at the first roundabout, left at the second and the hotel is on the left just past the golf course. Price guide: Single £85–£97; double/twin £98–£145; suite £145.

MONTGREENAN MANSION HOUSE HOTEL

MONTGREENAN ESTATE, KILWINNING, AYRSHIRE KA13 7QZ
TEL: 01294 557733 FAX: 01294 850397

Set in 48 acres of wooded gardens, Montgreenan commands views towards Ailsa Craig and the Arran Hills, which make a spectacular sight at sunset. The history of the estate dates back to 1310, and the present mansion house was built in 1817 by Dr Robert Glasgow. The original features, including marble and brass fireplaces, decorative ceilings and plasterwork, have been retained. A family home until 1980, the hotel has a friendly atmosphere. The bedrooms are well appointed with antique and reproduction furniture and one of the bedrooms has a Jacuzzi bath. The elegant dining room, with burgundy-and-gold tapestried chairs, is the setting for dinner. Gourmet cooking features fresh Scottish salmon, lobster, game and Ayrshire beef. To accompany your meal, choose from 200 fine vintages. Glasgow and Prestwick Airport are only 30 minutes' drive away. Whatever the occasion, there are good facilities for conferences and entertaining. In addition to the 5-hole golf course on site, over 30 courses, including those at Royal Troon and Turnberry, are within 45 minutes' drive. Special rates available. **Directions:** 19 miles south of Glasgow, 4 miles north of Irvine. From Irvine take A736 towards Glasgow for 4 miles. Turn left at Torranyard Inn; hotel entrance is 2 minutes from there. Price guide: Single £66–£77; double/twin £92–£146.

ISLE OF ERISKA

LEDAIG, BY OBAN, ARGYLL PA37 1SD
TEL: 01631 720371 FAX: 01631 720531

Isle of Eriska was built in 1884, towards the end of the Scots Baronial period. Its imposing exterior of grey granite and red sandstone stands as a living monument to a bygone age. Inside, no two bedrooms are the same in size or outlook and each is named after one of the neighbouring Hebridean islands. With its bay window and chintz covered furniture, the Drawing Room is the perfect place to relax while there can be no better place than the library to enjoy a drink from the selection of malt whiskies. Internationally acclaimed standards of cuisine are meticulously maintained in the dining room, the garden supplying a wide range of herbs, vegetables and soft fruits. For energetic guests there are sports such as water-skiing and windsurfing, tennis on the all-weather courts and clay pigeon shooting. Surefooted ponies are available for trekking over the island, while croquet and the golf putting green are available for those who prefer leisurely pursuits. In addition, there is now a 9-hole, par 3 golf course, fitness suite and indoor swimming pool. Oban is 20 minutes away by car and from here steamers ply the islands. **Directions:** From Edinburgh and Glasgow, drive to Tyndrum, then A85 towards Oban. At Connel proceed on A828 for four miles, to north of Benderloch. Thereafter follow signs to Isle of Eriska. Price guide: Single £140; double/twin £175–£205; suites £305.

WESTERN ISLES HOTEL

TOBERMORY, ISLE OF MULL, ARGYLL PA75 6PR
TEL: 01688 302012 FAX: 01688 302297

Poised above Tobermory Harbour, the Western Isles Hotel combines friendly hospitality with breathtaking views over an ever-changing vista of mountain and sea. An appetite sharpened by the fresh sea air is certain to be sated in the elegant restaurant, with its spectacular outlook over the Sound of Mull. Special diets and vegetarians are well catered for with some notice. The lounge has an atmosphere of grace and comfort, while the now rebuilt conservatory, with a bar and magnificent views across the harbour, is delightful on scented summer evenings. The bedrooms are spacious. Off Mull's coast is the holy island of Iona, while Fingal's Cave can be seen on Staffa. Special rates for Easter,

Christmas and New Year. If bringing a dog, please say when booking and bring a basket/bed for it. **Directions:** Travelling to Mull is so pleasurable that it should be considered part of the holiday. On booking, contact ferry operators Caledonian MacBrayne, The Pier, Gourock; or ring 0631 62285 and book the Oban–Craignure ferry (40 minutes). There is an hourly Lochaline–Fishnish ferry. Oban is on the A82/A85 from Glasgow (two hours) or the A85 from Perth. At Craignure, turn right off ferry; Tobermory is 40 minutes' drive. A warm welcome awaits! Price guide: Single £36–£90; double/twin £72–£165.

UIG HOTEL

UIG, ISLE OF SKYE IV51 9YE
TEL: 01470 542205 FAX: 01470 542308

Grace Graham and her son David Taylor welcome guests to their hotel, set on the northern peninsula of the mystical Isle of Skye, where the golden eagle soars overhead and the once-familiar call of the corncrake can still be heard. The hotel is set in three acres of grounds on a hillside overlooking Uig Bay. Grace is responsible for the comfortable furnishings and decoration, which include a collection of watercolours and etchings by well-known artists. David ensures the smooth day-to-day running of the hotel and the good home cooking. Skye, nearly 70 miles long, is a wildlife haven of bays, moors and glens. Uig is the departure point for the ferry to the Outer Hebrides, North and South Uist, Harris and Lewis. The hotel has its own pony-trekking using sturdy, good natured Highland ponies. From time to time Bridge Congresses and Garden and Wild Life tours are organised, details on request. In the west, near Dunvegan Castle, the ancestral seat of the MacLeods, are beautiful white coral beaches. The nearby town of Portree has a heated swimming pool, squash and tennis courts. There is a 9-hole golf course at Sconser. Closed mid-October to 1st April. Dogs by arrangement. **Directions:** Skye can be reached by road-bridge via the A87 or by ferry via the A830. Approaching Uig from Portree, the hotel is on the right, beside a white church. Price guide: Single £35; double/twin £68–£84.

EDNAM HOUSE HOTEL

BRIDGE STREET, KELSO, ROXBURGHSHIRE TD5 7HT
TEL: 01573 224168 FAX: 01573 226319

Overlooking the River Tweed, in 3 acres of gardens, Ednam House is one of the region's finest examples of Georgian architecture. This undulating, pastoral countryside was immortalised by Sir Walter Scott. Ednam House has been owned and managed by the Brooks family for over 65 years, spanning four generations. Although the grandiose splendour may seem formal, the warm, easy-going atmosphere is all-pervasive. The lounges and bars are comfortably furnished and command scenic views of the river and grounds. All 32 bedrooms are en suite, individually decorated and well equipped. In the elegant dining room which overlooks the river, a blend of traditional and creative Scottish cuisine, using fresh local produce, is served. The wine list is very interesting and reasonably priced. Ednam House is extremely popular with fishermen, the Borders being renowned for its salmon and trout. Other field sports such as stalking, hunting and shooting can be arranged as can riding, golfing and cycling. Local landmarks include the abbeys of Kelso, Melrose, Jedburgh and Dryburgh. Closed Christmas and New Year. **Directions:** From the south, reach Kelso via A698; from the north, via A68. Hotel is just off market square by the river. Price guide: Single £47; double/twin £65–£120.

SUNLAWS HOUSE HOTEL

KELSO, ROXBURGHSHIRE TD5 8JZ
TEL: 01573 450331 FAX: 01573 450611

Converted by the owner, the Duke of Roxburghe, into a luxury hotel of charm and character, Sunlaws House is situated in 200 hundred acres of rolling grounds on the bank of the Teviot. There are 22 bedrooms which, like the spacious reception rooms, are furnished with care and elegance. The menu, which is changed daily, reflects the hotel's position at the source of some of Britain's finest fish, meat and game – salmon and trout from the waters of the Tweed, or grouse, pheasant and venison from the Roxburghe estate – complemented with wines from the Duke's own cellar. A fine selection of whiskies is served in the Library Bar, with its log fire and leather-bound tomes. The new Beauty Clinique *Elixir* brings to guests the régimes of Decleor of Paris. A full sporting programme can be arranged, including fly and coarse fishing, and falconry. The shooting school offers tuition in game and clay shooting. Cultural interest is also well served, with seven great country houses within easy reach. No stay would be complete without a visit to one of the many woollen mills to see tartans being made. The Christmas and New Year breaks are very popular. **Directions:** The hotel is at Heiton, just off the A698 Kelso–Jedburgh road. Price guide: Single £95; double/twin £140; suite £155–£175.

ARDSHEAL HOUSE

KENTALLEN OF APPIN, ARGYLL PA38 4BX
TEL: 01631 740227 FAX: 01631 740342

Ardsheal House is set high on a peninsula, commanding wonderful views of Loch Linnhe and the mountains of Morvern. The house is approached along a private drive that borders the loch and winds through ancient woodland. Set in 900 acres of hills, woods, gardens and shore front, this historic manor, built in 1760, has a charming, country house atmosphere. A friendly welcome is extended to all guests by resident managers Michelle and George Kelso. The interiors are cosy and decorative, with polished oak panelling and open fires on chilly evenings. Antique furniture and bright fabrics are to be found in all the en suite bedrooms. In the conservatory dining room, memorable dishes delight the eye and please the palate.

Fresh seafood, prime local meat and game, herbs and fruit from the hotel garden and home-made jellies, preserves and seasoned vinegars form the basis for innovative cooking. Dinner may be accompanied by a selection from the excellent wine list. Ardsheal House is open daily for lunch and dinner: non-residents are welcome. Using the hotel as a base, guests can visit islands, castles, lochs and glens or enjoy splendid walks in every direction. Closed 10 January to 10 February. **Directions:** Hotel is on the A828 four miles south of Ballachulish Bridge on the way to Oban. Price guide (including dinner): Single £85; double/twin £130–£180. Special reduced winter and spring rates. Special Christmas and New Year breaks.

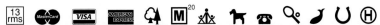

For hotel location, see maps on pages 473–479

ARDANAISEIG

KILCHRENAN BY TAYNUILT, ARGYLL PA35 1HE
TEL: 01866 833333 FAX: 01866 833222

Ardanaiseig stands on a wooded promontory beside Lock Awe at the point where the Loch turns west and spills into the River Awe. James Campbell, a younger son of the ancient family of Inverawe, commissioned the architect William Burn to build the mansion. It was completed in 1834 and over the next 40 years sheltering woods and parkland were laid out against a backdrop of the 3695 foot Ben Cruachan. The splendid woodland garden with its great rhododendron, azalea and rare shrubs came into existence in the 20th century. Although Ardanaiseig became a hotel in 1980, it remains essentially unchanged. The thoughtfully furnished bedrooms have retained their individuality and charm,

and the drawing room, dining room and library look south to wooded slopes and east to the Loch and its tree-clad islands. Good and plentiful food are offered as part of the fine tradition of a Scottish country house, with the young chef making inspired use of the fresh produce for which the west of Scotland is famed. Guests are invited to enjoy the lovely hill and lochside walks and woodland trails, boat trips and fishing which are available on the Ardanaiseig Estate, while nearby stunning islands, lochs and castles are also well worth discovering. **Directions:** On the A85 from Connel turn right onto the B845 towards Kilchrenan. Price guide: Single £78; double/twin £48–£80; suites £110.

KILDRUMMY CASTLE HOTEL

KILDRUMMY, BY ALFORD, ABERDEENSHIRE AB33 8RA
TEL: 019755 71288 FAX: 019755 71345

Set in the heart of Donside adjacent to the renowned Kildrummy Castle Gardens, and overlooking the ruins of the original 13th century castle from which it takes its name, Kildrummy Castle Hotel offers a rare opportunity to enjoy the style and elegance of a bygone era combined with all the modern comforts of a first-class hotel. Recent improvements have not detracted from the turn-of-the century interior, featuring the original wall tapestries and oak-panelled walls and high ceilings. The bedrooms, some with four-poster beds, all have en suite bathrooms. All have been refurbished recently to a high standard. In the restaurant, chef Kenneth White prepares menus using fresh, local produce – fish and shellfish from the Moray Firth, local game and, of course, Aberdeen Angus beef. Kildrummy Castle is ideally located for touring Royal Deeside and Balmoral, the Spey Valley, Aberdeen and Inverness, while the surrounding Grampian region has more castles than any other part of Scotland – 8 of the National Trust for Scotland's finest properties are within an hour's drive of the hotel. Also within an hour's drive are more than 20 golf courses. Visitors to the region can discover the 'Scotch Whisky Trail' and enjoy a tour of some of Scotland's most famous distilleries. **Directions:** Off the A97 Ballater/Huntly road, 35 miles west of Aberdeen. Price guide: Single £70; double/twin £120–£140.

CROMLIX HOUSE

KINBUCK, BY DUNBLANE, PERTHSHIRE FK15 9JT
TEL: 01786 822125 FAX: 01786 825450

The Cromlix estate of some 3,000 acres in the heart of Perthshire is a relaxing retreat. Built as a family home in 1874, much of the house remains unchanged including many fine antiques acquired over the generations. Proprietors David and Ailsa Assenti (previously nominated for excellence at Ballathie) are proud of their tradition of country house hospitality. The individually designed bedrooms and spacious suites have recently been redecorated with period fabrics to enhance the character and fine furniture whilst retaining the essential feeling of a much loved home. Unpretentious, relaxing and most welcoming. The large public rooms have open fires. In the restaurant, the finest local produce is used, including game from the estate, lamb and locally caught salmon. Cromlix is an ideal venue for small conferences and business meetings, and there is a small chapel – the perfect setting for weddings. Extensive sporting and leisure facilities include trout and salmon fishing and game shooting in season. Challenging golf courses within easy reach include Rosemount, Carnoustie and St Andrews. The location is ideal for touring the Southern Highlands, with Edinburgh and Glasgow only an hour away. **Directions:** Cromlix House lies four miles north of Dunblane, north of Kinbuck on B8033 and four miles south of Braco. Price guide: Single £95; double/twin £130; suite £180.

NIVINGSTON HOUSE

CLEISH, KINROSS-SHIRE KY13 7LS
TEL: 01577 850216 FAX: 01577 850238

Peacefully set in 12 acres of landscaped gardens at the foot of the Cleish Hills, this comfortable old country house and its celebrated restaurant offer the warmest of welcomes. Standing more or less half-way between Edinburgh and Perth the original 1725 building has benefited from several architectural additions and it is now further enlarged and refurbished with all the characteristics of an up-to-date hotel. Nivington House is particularly well known for its fine food, prepared from traditional Scottish produce such as Perthshire venison and locally caught salmon. The restaurant has regularly been commended in leading guides and deservedly it has "Taste of Scotland" status. The menus are changed daily. Scones and cream tea are however a permanent temptation. The attractive en suite bedrooms are decorated in soft, subtle colours, with Laura Ashley fabrics and wallpapers. In the grounds there are two croquet lawns and a putting green and practice net for keen golfers. Sporting facilities within easy reach include the famous golf courses at St Andrews, Gleneagles and countless others of lesser renown. Loch Leven is popular for trout fishing and there are boat trips to Loch Leven Castle. **Directions:** From M90 take exit 5 towards Crook of Devon. Cleish is 2 miles from motorway. Price guide: Single £75–£100; double/twin £95–£125.

CAMERON HOUSE

LOCH LOMOND, DUNBARTONSHIRE G83 8QZ
TEL: 01389 755565 FAX: 01389 759522

The splendour and location of this impressive baronial house has lured many famous visitors, from Dr Johnson and the Empress Eugénie to Sir Winston Churchill. Standing in over 100 acres of green lawns and wooded glades leading down to the shores of Loch Lomond, Cameron House offers luxurious accommodation and superlative recreational amenities. The indoor leisure club includes squash, badminton and aerobic facilities, three beauty treatment rooms, a games room with three full-size snooker tables and a state-of-the-art gymnasium. For children there is a games room, toddlers' pool, crèche and a children's club. Outside, another sporting world unfolds, with professional tennis coaching, 9-hole golf, clay pigeon shooting, archery, off-road driving, sailing, cruising and wind-surfing available. Each of the bedrooms and the five opulent suites is furnished in soft colours that complement the beautiful views from the windows. Guests can dine in the intimate Georgian Room or the Brasserie overlooking the loch. The conference, banqueting and function facilities are second to none and Glasgow, with its museums, art galleries and theatres, is less than 30 minutes' drive away. **Directions:** Cameron House is on the southern banks of Loch Lomond, via the A82 from Glasgow. Price guide: Single £125–£135; double/twin £150–£160; suite £225–£295.

In association with MasterCard

KIRROUGHTREE HOTEL

NEWTON STEWART, WIGTOWNSHIRE DG8 6AN
TEL: 01671 402141 FAX: 01671 402425

Situated in the foothills of the Cairnsmore of Fleet, on the edge of Galloway Forest Park, Kirroughtree Hotel stands in eight acres of landscaped gardens, where guests can relax and linger over the spectacular views. This striking mansion was built by the Heron family in 1719 and the rococo furnishings of the oak-panelled lounge reflect the style of that period. From the lounge rises the original staircase, from which Robert Burns often recited his poems. Each bedroom is well furnished – guests may choose to spend the night in one of the hotel's spacious deluxe bedrooms with spectacular views over the surrounding countryside. Many guests are attracted by Kirroughtree's culinary reputation – only the finest produce is used to create meals of originality and finesse. This is a good venue for small conferences. Pitch-and-putt, lawn tennis and croquet can be enjoyed in the grounds. Residents can play golf on the many local courses and also have use of our sister hotels new exclusive 18-hole course at Gatehouse of Fleet. Trout and salmon fishing can be arranged nearby, as can rough shooting and deer stalking during the season. Closed 3 January to 16th February. **Directions:** The hotel is signposted one mile outside Newton Stewart on the A75. Price guide: Single £70–£130; double/twin £116–£136; suite £170. (Including dinner)

KNIPOCH HOTEL

BY OBAN, ARGYLL PA34 4QT
TEL: 01852 316251 FAX: 01852 316249

Six miles south of Oban lies Knipoch, an elegant Georgian building set halfway along the shore of Loch Feochan, an arm of the sea stretching 4 miles inland. Wildlife is abundant in this area – rare birds of prey, deer and otters can often be seen. The hotel is owned and personally run by the Craig family, who go out of their way to ensure that their guests enjoy their stay. All the bedrooms are fully equipped and offer splendid views either of the loch or the surrounding hills. High standards of cooking are proudly maintained here. The daily menu features many Scottish specialities, prepared with imaginative flair. Not only is the choice of wines extensive – there are over 350 labels – but the list is informative, too: guests are given a copy to peruse at leisure rather than to scan hurriedly before ordering. In addition, the bar stocks a wide range of malt whiskies. Sporting activities available locally include fishing, sailing, yachting, golf, tennis, pony-trekking and skiing. A traditional Scottish event, the Oban Highland Games, is particularly renowned for its solo piping competition. The Knipoch Hotel makes a good base from which to visit the Western Isles and explore the spectacular scenery of the area. Closed mid-November to mid-February. **Directions:** On the A816, 6 miles south of Oban. Price guide: Single £60–£80; double/twin £130–£140.

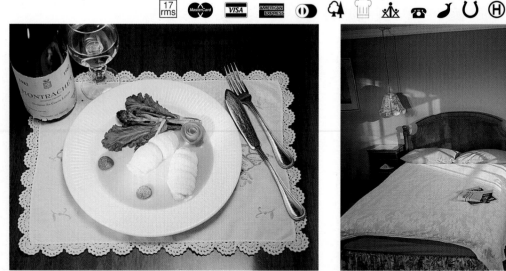

CRINGLETIE HOUSE HOTEL

PEEBLES EH45 8PL
TEL: 01721 730233 FAX: 01721 730244

This distinguished mansion, turreted in the Scottish baronial style, stands in 28 acres of beautifully maintained gardens and woodland. Designed by Scottish architect David Bryce, Cringletie was built in 1861 for the Wolfe Murray family, one of whom – Colonel Alexander Murray – accepted the surrender of Quebec after General Wolfe was killed. All of the bedrooms have fine views and many have been redesigned with attractively co-ordinated curtains and furnishings. The splendid panelled lounge has an impressive carved oak and marble fireplace, a painted ceiling and many oil portraits. The imaginative cooking, prepared with flair, attracts consistently good reports. The range and quality of fruit and vegetables grown in the 2-acre walled garden make this the only Scottish garden recommended in Geraldene Holt's *The Gourmet Garden*, which includes some of Britain's most distinguished hotels. On-site facilities include a new hard tennis court, croquet lawn and putting green. Golf can be played at Peebles and fishing is available by permit on the River Tweed. Aside from visits to Edinburgh, Cringletie is a good base from which to discover the rich historic and cultural heritage of the Borders. Closed 2 January to 10 March. **Directions:** The hotel is on the A703 Peebles–Edinburgh road, $2^{1}/_{2}$ miles from Peebles. Price guide: Single £52.50; double/twin £98–£104.

BALLATHIE HOUSE HOTEL

KINCLAVEN BY STANLEY, NR PERTH, PERTHSHIRE PH1 4QN
TEL: 01250 883268 FAX: 01250 883396

Set in an estate overlooking the River Tay, Ballathie House Hotel offers Scottish hospitality in a house of character and distinction. Dating from 1850, this mansion has a French baronial façade and handsome interiors. Overlooking lawns which slope down to the riverside, the drawing room is an ideal place to relax with coffee and the papers, or to enjoy a malt whisky after dinner. The premier bedrooms are large and elegant, while the standard rooms are designed in a cosy, cottage style. On the ground floor there are several bedrooms suitable for guests with disabilities. Local ingredients such as Tay salmon, Scottish beef, seafoods and piquant soft fruits are used by chef Kevin MacGillivray to create menus catering for all tastes. The hotel has a rosette for fine Scottish cuisine. Activities available on the estate include trout and salmon fishing and clay pigeon shooting. The Sporting Lodge adjacent to the main house is designed to accommodate sporting parties. The area has many good golf courses. Perth, Blairgowrie and Edinburgh are within an hour's drive. STB 4 Crowns De Luxe. Dogs in certain rooms only.
Directions: From A93 at Beech Hedges, signposted for Kinclaven and Ballathie, or off the A9, 2 miles north of Perth take the Stanley Road. The hotel is 8 miles north of Perth. Price guide: Single £62–£95; double/twin £115–£180; suite £200–£240.

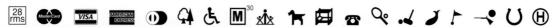

PARKLANDS HOTEL & RESTAURANT

ST LEONARD'S BANK, PERTH, PERTHSHIRE PH2 8EB
TEL: 01738 622451 FAX: 01738 622046

The Parklands Country Hotel and Restaurant, which overlooks Perth's South Inch Park, has benefited from an extensive programme of improvements. The hotel, with its classic lines, was formerly the home of John Pullar, who was Lord Provost of the City of Perth from 1867 to 1873. The 14 bedrooms all have en suite facilities and are immaculate. Each has been individually decorated to high standards under the personal supervision of proprietor Allan Deeson. In the main restaurant the accent is on light, traditional Scottish food. A full choice of à la carte and table d'hôte meals is available at both lunchtime and dinner. The boardroom opens off the hotel's entrance and overlooks the hotel gardens. It is a perfect venue for small private lunches or dinners or for business meetings and seminars, and has a large mahogany table and all the latest audio-visual equipment. Perth is a Royal Burgh of great age on the Tay Estuary, at the entrance to Strath Earn and Strath More, full of historical buildings, rich in story and legend. **Directions:** From the M90 head towards the station; Parklands is on the left at the end of the park. Price guide: Single £70–£100; double/twin £95–£135.

KNOCKINAAM LODGE

PORTPATRICK, WIGTOWNSHIRE DG9 9AD
TEL: 01776 810471 FAX: 01776 810435

On the beautiful West Coast of Scotland, surrounded on three sides by sheltering cliffs, lies Knockinaam. This delightful Lodge is perfectly situated to allow guests to enjoy magnificent views of the distant Irish coastline and to marvel at the stupendous sunsets and the changing moods of the sea and sky. In this atmosphere of timelessness and tranquillity, Sir Winston Churchill held a secret meeting here with General Eisenhower during the Second World War. Cheerful colour schemes and fabrics have been chosen for the comfortable bedrooms, while the public rooms are small and cosy. During cooler months residents can relax in front of their lovely open log fires. There is a daily changing menu offering sumptuous cuisine, which is beautifully prepared and presented. There is a particularly mild climate in the area round Knockinaam and there are many famous gardens within easy reach. Further inland, forests of spruce and larch lead into stunning countryside where amid the lochs, rivers and hills an abundance of wild game is to be found. There are several excellent golf courses close to the hotel. In the quiet season the hotel runs wine and cooking weekends. Off season there are also special prices available for both accommodation and dinner. **Directions:** On the A77 from Stranraer to Portpatrick look out for the roadside signpost to the hotel. Price guide: Single £80; double/twin £58–£80.

RUFFLETS COUNTRY HOUSE AND RESTAURANT

STRATHKINNESS LOW ROAD, ST ANDREWS, FIFE KY16 9TX
TEL: 01334 472594 FAX:01334 478703

One of the oldest country house hotels in Scotland, Rufflets has been privately owned and managed by the same family since 1952 and extends a friendly and personal service to its guests. Over the years the original turreted house, built in 1924, has been tastefully extended and upgraded to the optimum level of luxury and comfort. It faces south and overlooks ten acres of beautifully landscaped gardens. The hotel's 25 en suite bedrooms are individually designed, using a blend of contemporary and antique furnishings. Three of them are located in the charming Rose Cottage within the grounds of Rufflets. A well stocked kitchen garden supplies fresh herbs, vegetables and fruit for the award-winning restaurant. Featured on the menus are the finest quality Scottish beef, lamb, venison and East Neuk seafood. A carefully selected wine list is available to complement the cuisine. St Andrews is famous for its golf courses and among the many places of interest nearby is the British Golf Museum. Other places well worth a visit include Falkland Palace, Kellie Castle and Crail Harbour. **Directions:** Rufflets is situated $1\frac{1}{2}$ miles west of St Andrews. Price guide: Single £48–£79; double/twin £96–£158. Seasonal prices.

THE MURRAYSHALL COUNTRY HOUSE HOTEL

SCONE, PERTHSHIRE PH2 7PH
TEL: 01738 551171 FAX: 01738 552595

The Murrayshall Country House Hotel is set in 300 acres of undulating parkland and wooded hillside, with views sweeping across to the Grampians. Entering the hotel through the arched front door, visitors are welcomed by a friendly team of staff. The Old Masters' Restaurant, hung with Dutch 16th and 17th century oil paintings, is a visual delight, well suited to complement the artistry of the hotel's chef. Vegetables from the hotel's walled garden, and an abundance of local produce, form the basis of the menus, which have a Scottish flavour and a hint of modern French cuisine. The bedrooms have been designed to suit the varied demands of holiday-makers, honeymooners and fishermen, golfers and business travellers alike. With its own club house and bar, there is an 18-hole golf course adjacent to the hotel, where a golf professional is available to offer tuition. The Murrayshall offers special courses on golf. Guests may play croquet and bowls on the premises or follow one of the published walks that start from the hotel. Dogs by arrangement. Off season rates begin from £50 for dinner, bed and breakfast. **Directions:** Signposted a mile out of Perth on A94. Price guide: Single £50–£95; double/twin £100–£150; suites £130–£180.

For hotel location, see maps on pages 473–479

LOCH TORRIDON HOTEL

BY ACHNASHEEN, WESTER-ROSS IV22 2EY
TEL: 01445 791242 FAX: 01445 791296

Loch Torridon Hotel is gloriously situated at the foot of wooded mountains beside the loch which gives it its name. The hotel was built as a shooting lodge for the first Earl of Lovelace in 1887. The 58-acre estate contains formal gardens, mature trees and the shores of the loch. David and Geraldine Gregory, formerly of the Kinlochbervie Hotel, acquired the hotel in March 1992. They brought with them an excellent reputation for their brand of Highland hospitality and good cooking. A phased upgrading of the property has been completed to enhance the impact of the interiors and provide every comfort. Geraldine's cooking requires no such improvement – she is renowned for her inventive use of the finest local ingredients. She has been joined recently by Nicholas Green from the Chester Grosvenor, and together they make a formidable team. The hotel was chosen as the Best New Three Star Hotel in Scotland by the AA Inspector for 1993 and awarded two Rosettes for its food. Dinner is served between 7.15pm and 8.30pm. A starter of home-made Scotch broth or spinach roulade with prawns and cream could be followed by roast saddle of hare with caramelized onion tart or seafood kebab with tomato sauce and saffron rice. **Directions:** Ten miles from Kinlochewe on the A896. Do not turn off to Torridon village. Price guide: Single £50–£80; double/twin £80–£170; suites £180–£220.

PIERSLAND HOUSE HOTEL

CRAIGEND ROAD, TROON, AYRSHIRE KA10 6HD
TEL: 01292 314747 FAX: 01292 315613

This historic listed house, built for the grandson of Johnnie Walker, founder of the Scottish whisky firm, is as attractive inside as out. All the public rooms are spacious and inviting, with original features such as oak panelling and a frieze of Jacobean embroidery. Retaining their original charm, the bedrooms are formally decorated in a period style with soft colourings. Afternoon cream teas are served on the verandah, an airy sun-lounge opening on to beautiful gardens. The four acre grounds include immaculate lawns, a Japanese water garden and a croquet lawn. Guests can enjoy classically prepared gourmet dishes and Continental-style cooking in the warm, intimate atmosphere of the restaurant. The wine list is compiled from labels supplied by one of Scotland's oldest-established wine firms. For golfers, Royal Troon is across the road, and Turnberry and Old Prestwick are nearby. Ayr, the birthplace of Robert Burns, Kilmarnock and Irvine are a short drive and Culzean Castle, the seat of the Kennedy clan, is 19 miles away. Glasgow, Stirling and Edinburgh are easily accessible, as are Loch Lomond, the Trossachs and the isles of the Firth of Clyde. **Directions:** The hotel is on the B749, just beside Royal Troon Golf Club. Price guide: Single £59.50–£75; double/twin £97.50–£120.

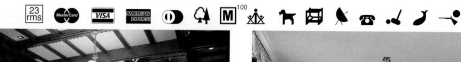

KNOCKIE LODGE HOTEL

WHITEBRIDGE, INVERNESS-SHIRE, IV1 2UP
TEL: 01456 486276 FAX: 01456 486389

Built originally as a shooting lodge in 1789, Knockie Lodge stands not far from Loch Ness, 25 miles south of Inverness, in an area of outstanding natural beauty and total peace and quiet. It is now very much the home of Ian and Brenda Milward. With its 10 spotlessly clean bedrooms, each comfortably and individually furnished, its drawing and dining rooms filled with antique furniture and family paintings, the billiard room and, of course, superb food prepared from a wide range of local produce, guests at Knockie Lodge can be assured of a real welcome and a very relaxed and hospitable atmosphere. For the brown trout fly-fisherman, there is excellent fishing on two lochs close to the house. It is also possible to cast for salmon on Loch Ness or, by arrangement, in the local salmon rivers. Other activities on offer locally include deerstalking in the autumn, bird-watching, sailing, ponytrekking and hill-walking. Knockie Lodge Hotel prides itself on its deserved awards: the AA 2 Red Stars, and the STB 3 Crowns deLuxe. The hotel is open from the end of April until the end of October and welcomes children aged ten and above. Those wishing to reserve from the USA can telephone 1-800-635 3603. **Directions:** Knockie Lodge Hotel is situated eight miles north of Fort Augustus on the B862. Price guide: Single: £55; double/twin: £100–£140.

EVERY DESTINATION SPEAKS MASTERCARD

Johansens Recommended
Hotels in
Ireland

St Patrick's Cathedral, Dublin

Celtic *treasures and legends, medieval architecture, racecourses and golf courses, great art collections and a richness of literature are found amongst the green landscapes of Ireland.*

Ireland today is not just the popular holiday location it has always been; it has now achieved the status of being Europe's fastest growing visitor destination and the graph continues to rise. The traditional, the cosmopolitan and the 'state-of-the-art' have been successfully combined, with nothing sacrificed to impersonal efficiency. The Irish welcome remains the same.

So much of Ireland's history is preserved in the architecture and ancient monuments of many of the towns and villages around the country that an umbrella body has been formed to assist the visitor in achieving the most comprehensive experience during a visit. Heritage Towns of Ireland has already designated 30 centres as of outstanding historic interest, and modern interpretative facilities have been provided in each to tell its story dramatically as well as entertainingly.

Dublin, the capital, is of modest size with a history spanning over a thousand years and is a centre of infinite variety and interest. The National Gallery houses Ireland's foremost collection of paintings, including works by Rembrandt, Reynolds, El Greco and Goya. The Royal Hospital Kilmainham and the Municipal Art Gallery in Dublin also have extensive collections of great quality. The Chester Beatty Library has some of the rarest oriental manuscripts in existence. The National Cathedral of St Patrick, where Jonathan Swift was once the Dean and now lies buried, maintains a choir school providing the great church's music continuously since 1492.

Arthur Guinness launched his now world-renowned black brew in Dublin in 1759. The tradition flourishes today and visitors are welcome to St James's Gate to explore the history and, of course, to sample the product. Not to be outdone, the Irish Whiskey Corner at Bow Street Distillery also welcomes visitors to learn the process and sample 'Uisge Beatha – the Water of Life'.

For the classical music lover, the National Concert Hall and the Royal Dublin Society offer a full range of recitals and concerts featuring the best of Irish and international talent.

Both Siamsa Tire – the National Folk Theatre of Ireland in Tralee, Co Kerry, and Bru Boru Heritage Centre in Cashel, Co Tipperary, are especially worth a visit for their interpretation in music, song and dance of the Irish folk tradition.

Heritage Towns of Ireland
92 Sandymount Road
Sandymount Village
Dublin 4
Tel: 00 353 1 668 9688

Irish Distillers Group Limited
Irish Whiskey Corner
Bow Street Distillery
Dublin 7
Tel: 00 353 1 872 5566

For more information about Ireland, please contact:

The Irish Tourist Board
Bord Failte
Baggot Street Bridge
Dublin 2
Tel: 00 353 1 676 5871

Northern Ireland is different. In an area which covers only one-sixth of the island of Ireland, the six counties of Ulster combine to present a wealth of unspoilt beauty, breathtaking coastlines, some of the best fishing in Ireland and a welcome that is second to none.

In addition, each county spreads its own rich tapestry of historical and scenic beauty. On uncongested roads the visitor can explore a varied landscape that changes from county to county. From the famous Giant's Causeway in Co. Antrim, to Benone Strand, the longest beach in Ireland in Co. Londonderry, and the lakeland landscape of Co. Fermanagh to 'Where the Mountains of Mourne Sweep Down to the Sea' in Co. Down.

The nature of the landscape provides the visitor with a feast of beauty and a superb environment for such activities as golf, fishing, walking, water sports, horse-riding and hire-cruising. For those whose interests lie in more leisurely pursuits, a varied cultural life is easily accessible by way of established theatres, museums, visitor and interpretative centres.

Belfast's most prestigious theatre is the Grand Opera House, a wonderful elaborate confection designed by Frank Matcham with a somewhat oriental theme celebrates its centenary in December 1995 with a year-long programme of special events planned, including two seasons of opera from Opera Northern Ireland in the spring and autumn.

Opera lovers are also well served by the annual season at Castleward. Taking place in mid-summer, this highly rated company presents its operas in the beautiful surroundings of a 700 acre National Trust country estate on the shores of Strangford Lough. Ariadne auf Naxos by Richard Strauss and Puccini's La Bohème are planned for the 1996 season.

Recent history may have obscured the essential character of Northern Ireland but nothing can eliminate the inherent friendliness of the people and the unique beauty of the surroundings.

Giant's Causeway Centre
44 Causeway Road
Bushmills BT57 8SU
Tel: 012657 31855

National Trust
Belfast Shop
86 Botanic Avenue
Belfast BT7 1JR
Tel: 01232 230018

For more information about Northern Ireland, please contact:-

Northern Ireland Tourist Board
St Anne's Court
59 North Street
Belfast BT1 1NB
Tel: 01232 246609

ADARE MANOR

ADARE, CO LIMERICK
TEL: 061 396566 FAX: 061 396124

Nestling in 840 acres of rolling countryside and gardens, Adare Manor is an architectural gem, originally built during the reign of George I and it is a proud reminder of the Earls of Dunraven who once resided here. In the 19th century the building was substantially enlarged and reconstructed in a Tudor style. Ornamental parterres were added. The magnificent public rooms range from the cosy library to the majestic Long Gallery – the venue for banquets and conferences. The purpose-built conference suite and boardroom are ideal for smaller gatherings. International and the best of Irish cuisine from Limerick is served in the beautiful dining room, with its views over the parterre and River Maigue. Afternoon tea is served in the elegant drawing room. To round off a relaxing day, guests will find a delightful retreat in one of the 64 sumptuously furnished bedrooms with en suite marble bathrooms. Country pursuits, including fishing, archery, clay pigeon shooting and riding, are offered on the estate. The leisure centre includes a heated indoor pool, sauna and gymnasium. An 18-hole golf course and a driving range are available for golfers. From UK phone 00 353 61 396566.
Directions: Adare Manor is 40 minutes from Shannon Airport, adjacent to Adare village. Price guide: Per room IR£110–IR£195.

GALGORM MANOR

BALLYMENA, CO ANTRIM BT42 1EA
TEL: 01266 881001 FAX: 01266 880080

This converted gentleman's residence is set amidst some of Northern Ireland's most beautiful lush scenery, with the River Maine running less than 100 yards from the main entrance. Most of the comfortable en suite bedrooms offer spectacular views of the surrounding countryside. The Dining Room offers a choice of table d'hôte or à la carte menus with local produce used wherever possible. For lighter eating there is a full bar menu in the Gillies Bar. There are six self-catering cottages available in the grounds which are perfect for weekend breaks or the longer stay. The Manor offers a varied choice of meeting rooms, all with the most modern facilities. Its estate includes 12 stables, a show jumping course and an eventing cross-country practice area, so there is plenty of scope for the equestrian enthusiast. Clay pigeon shooting is also available and there are opportunites to play golf on some of the best links courses in Ireland. Galgorm Manor is perfectly located for touring Northern Ireland. The lovely Antrim Coast, including the Giant's Causeway, is only a short drive away. **Directions:** Follow the A42 towards Ballymena. Shortly after passing Galgorm Castle on the right, turn left at Galgorm towards Cullybackey. Galgorm Manor is halfway between Galgorm and Cullybackey. Price guide: Single £89; double/twin £110; suites £125.

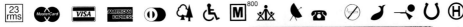

GLENLO ABBEY HOTEL

BUSHYPARK, GALWAY, IRELAND
TEL: 353 91 526666 FAX: 353 91 527800 E-mail: glenlo@iol.ie?

Situated some two and a half miles from the city of Galway on Ireland's west coast, Glenlo Abbey, built in 1740, was formerly the ancestral home of the Ffrench and Blake families, two of Galway's 14 great tribes who ruled over the city for centuries. The current owners, John and Peggy Bourke, have taken great care in their restoration of Glenlo Abbey, transforming it into a magnificent 5-Star hotel and conference centre. Spaciousness and tranquillity are the key notes in the accommodation at Glenlo Abbey, reflecting the very essence of Irish hospitality. The public rooms feature solid antique furniture and a beautiful collection of Irish art, in keeping with the character of the surroundings. All bedrooms have marbled en suite bathrooms and many have scenic views over Lough Corrib. Guests may relax over cocktails in the Kentfield or in the Oak Cellar Bar, before dining in the Ffrench Room restaurant. Here, fine Irish and international cuisine is served in an atmosphere reflecting the gracious living of the past. Glenlo Abbey offers a choice of conference rooms. The gentle slopes around the Glenlo Abbey reveal a challenging golf course. Tours through Connemara and fishing for trout and salmon on Lough Corrib can be arranged. **Directions:** The hotel is about two and a half miles north of Galway on the N59 to Clifden. Price guide: Single IR£100–IR£120; double/twin IR£120–IR£150; suite IR£175–IR£250.

NUREMORE HOTEL

CARRICKMACROSS, CO MONAGHAN, IRELAND
TEL: 042 61438 FAX: 042 61853

Set in 200 acres of glorious countryside on the fringe of Carrickmacross, the Nuremore Hotel has been extensively renovated. It offers guests all-round enjoyment, a vast array of activities and facilities and all that is best in a first-class country hotel. The bedrooms are well appointed and attractively designed to create a generous sense of personal space. Lunch and dinner menus, served in a spacious and elegant dining room, emphasise classic European cooking, with French and Irish dishes featured alongside. For sport, fitness and relaxation, guests are spoiled for choice by the range of amenities. A major feature is the championship-length, par 73, 18-hole golf course designed by Eddie Hackett to present an exciting challenge to beginners and experts alike. Maurice Cassidy has been appointed as resident professional and is on hand to give tuition. Riding nearby in Carrickmacross. The leisure club has a superb indoor pool, modern gymnasium, squash and tennis courts, sauna, steam room and whirlpool bath. Meetings, conferences and seminars held here are guaranteed a professional support service. Dublin is 90 minutes' drive away, while Drogheda and Dundalk are nearby for shopping. From the UK phone 00 353 42 61438. **Directions:** The hotel is on the main N2 road between Dublin and Monaghan. Price guide: Single IR£75–IR£90; double/twin IR£110–IR£130.

ASHFORD CASTLE

CONG, CO MAYO
TEL: 092 46003 FAX: 092 46260

Ashford Castle is set on the northern shores of Lough Corrib amidst acres of beautiful gardens and forests. Once the country estate of Lord Ardilaun and the Guinness family, it was transformed into a luxury hotel in 1939. The castle's Great Hall is lavishly decorated with rich panelling, fine period pieces, *objets d'art* and masterpiece paintings. Guest rooms are of the highest standards and many feature high ceilings, enormous bathrooms and delightful lake views. The main dining room offers superb continental and traditional menus, while the gourmet restaurant, The Connaught Room, specialises in excellent French cuisine. Before and after dinner in the Dungeon Bar guests are entertained by a harpist or pianist. Ashford Castle offers a full range of country sports, including fishing on Lough Corrib, clay pigeon shooting, riding and an exclusive 9-hole golf course. The hotel has just added a health centre comprising a whirlpool, sauna, steam room, fully equipped gymnasium and conservatory. Ashford is an ideal base for touring the historic West Ireland, places like Kylemore Abbey and Westport House, Sligo and Drumcliffe Churchyard, the burial place of W.B. Yeats.
Directions: 30 minutes from Galway on the shore of Lough Corrib, on the left when entering the village of Cong. Price guide from: IR£138–IR£235 (single, twin or double occupancy).

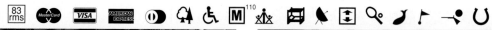

RENVYLE HOUSE HOTEL

CONNEMARA, CO GALWAY
TEL: 095 43511 FAX: 095 43515

Renvyle House Hotel has occupied its rugged, romantic position on Ireland's west coast for over four centuries. Set between mountains and sea on the unspoilt coast of Connemara, this hardy, beautiful building with its superlative views over the surrounding countryside is just an hour's drive from Galway or Sligo. Originally constructed in 1541, Renvyle has been an established hotel for over 100 years, witnessing in that time a procession of luminaries through its doors – among them Augustus John, Lady Gregory, Yeats and Churchill, drawn no doubt by an atmosphere as warm and convivial then as it is today. Renvyle now welcomes visitors with turf fires glowing in public areas, wood-beamed interiors and comfortable, relaxed furnishings in the easy rooms. The bedrooms are comfortably appointed and all have been refurbished in the past two years. In the dining room, meals from a constantly-changing menu are served with emphasis on local fish and Renvyle lamb. In the grounds activities include tennis, croquet, riding, bowls and golf. Beyond the hotel, there are walks in the heather-clad hills, or swimming and sunbathing on empty beaches. **Directions:** On the N59 from Galway turn right at Recess, take the Letterfrack turning to Tully Cross and Renvyle is signposted. Price guide: Single IR£21–IR£41; double/twin IR£42–IR£82.

THE HIBERNIAN HOTEL

EASTMORELAND PLACE, BALLSBRIDGE, DUBLIN 4
TEL: 01668 7666 FAX: 01660 2655

Tucked away in bustling downtown Dublin, the Hibernian Hotel is a magnificent architectural feat constructed just before the turn of the century in the commercial heart of the city. Refurbished and reopened in 1993 as a grand townhouse hotel, The Hibernian now prides itself on the elegance, style and warmth of service it can offer visitors to this vibrant metropolis: the hotel has a unique blend of modern ease and bygone atmosphere. David Butt, the general manager, is ably assisted by a professional team who ensure that the needs of both business and holiday guests are met quickly and efficiently. Luxury prevails at The Hibernian in soft furnishings, rich fabrics and deep upholstery; in each of the 30 individually designed bedrooms and suites. En suite bathrooms with a full range of toiletries are standard, as are fax/modem points, drinks facilities, individually controlled thermostats and and hairstyling appliances. In the restaurant, the luncheon and à la carte menus offer the full gamut of gastronomic dishes, from locally caught, artfully interpreted seafood to modern cuisine classics and fine wines to accompany them. The hotel makes an ideal base from which to explore the city. **Directions:** Turn right from Mespil road into Baggot Street Upper, then left into Eastmoreland Place; The Hibernian is on the left. Price guide: Single IR£95–IR£150; double/twin IR£120–IR£135; suite IR£160.

       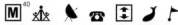

For hotel location, see maps on pages 473–479

THE KILDARE HOTEL & COUNTRY CLUB

AT STRAFFAN, CO KILDARE
TEL: 353 (1) 627 3333 FAX: 353 (1) 627 3312

Straffan House is one of Ireland's most elegant 19th century manor houses, set in 330 acres of beautiful countryside and overlooking the River Liffey. Just 17 miles from Dublin this is an international world class resort with its graceful reception rooms, totally luxurious bedrooms and palatial en suite bathrooms, also a superb leisure club with a sybaritic indoor pool. The public areas of the hotel are a treasure trove of contemporary paintings and works of art. There are excellent conference areas for business meetings, while corporate entertaining is dominated by facilities which include the Arnold Palmer course which is the venue for the Smurfit European Open, September 1995, 1996 and 1997,

indoor tennis and squash courts, a gymnasium, clay pigeon shooting, fishing and riding, croquet. Formal entertaining, meeting in the bar followed by a magnificent meal in the prestigious Byerley Turk Restaurant, with table d'hôte and à la carte menus complemented by an extensive wine list, is effortless, The Legend Bar and Restaurant in the Country Club offer less formality. The Arnold Palmer Room is available for gala functions and conferences at the Clubhouse. **Directions:** Leave Dublin on N7 driving south for 17 miles. Straffan is signposted on the left. Price guide: Single IR£190; double/twin IR£260; suite IR£325.

MARLFIELD HOUSE HOTEL

GOREY, CO WEXFORD
TEL: 055 21124 FAX: 055 21572

Staying at Marlfield House is a memorable experience. Set in 34 acres of woodland and gardens, this former residence of the Earl of Courtown, built in 1820 preserves the Regency lifestyle in all its graciousness. It is recognised as one of the finest country houses in Ireland, and is supervised by the welcoming hosts and proprietors, Raymond and Mary Bowe and their daughter Margaret. The suites all have period fireplaces where open fires cheerily burn in the cooler weather, and they have been built in a traditional, very grand style. All the bedroom furniture is of the Regency period and the roomy beds are draped with sumptuous fabrics. The bathrooms are made of highly polished marble and have large freestanding bathtubs. There is a luxurious drawing room, an impressive curved Richard Turner conservatory, and a regularly opulent dining room. The hotel's gastronomic delights have earned it numerous awards. Located two miles from fine beaches and Courtown golf club, the hotel is central to many touring high points: Glendalough, Mount Usher and Powerscourt Gardens and the medieval city of Kilkenny. When phoning from the British mainland dial 00 353 55 21124. Closed mid-December to mid-January. **Directions:** On the Gorey–Courtown road, just over a mile east of Gorey. Price guide: Single from IR£65; double/twin IR£120–IR£144; suites from IR£182–IR£400.

"Like your music?" Starr asked softly.

"Yes. Like my music." She drew in a breath. "I guess I'm saying I'm a complete and total mess."

"You're not. You're wonderful. You took me in."

"I'm lucky you put up with me. You're my sister, and I'm so grateful we're making a life together."

"Me, too." Starr bit her lower lip. "You're not going to stay married to Kipling, are you?"

"I don't think so. We don't want the same thing. I panicked when I found out I was pregnant. That wasn't really smart of me. I still want to stay in Fool's Gold. We're still going to be a family. Just you and me."

"And the baby." Starr leaned toward her. "I'll help. I can do things around the house."

"Good. One of us should know what she's doing." Starr laughed.

"We'll get a house," Destiny told her. "One we pick out together."

Not the one where she and Kipling made love, she thought. Those were memories she wanted to avoid.

"Are you going to get another job?" Starr asked tentatively. "Can you work with a baby?"

A really good question. Income would be required. She didn't doubt that Kipling would offer to pay child support, but that was money she would want to put away. In the meantime, she was perfectly capable and had a unique skill set.

"My mom's manager has always told me he wants to put me to work writing songs. I'm going to call him and find out if he's telling the truth." She touched

"You, too."

Destiny left the office and started home. As she walked toward home, she wondered how long she would be in love with Kipling. It had been two days since their last conversation. He'd tried to call her a couple of times, but she'd let him go to voice mail. When he'd texted, she'd asked for time. So far he was giving it to her.

She breathed in the warm air and wondered how she'd made such a mess of things. She'd fallen in love with a man who saw her as a project. Even more of a complication, she was pregnant with his child. It wasn't as if she and Kipling could simply break up. They were going to be connected for the rest of their lives.

The idea of that was both wonderful and terrifying. If she had to stay in touch with him, how could she ever stop loving him? Because she had to stop. She saw that now.

All her life she'd been running from exactly what she found herself in now. An emotional mess. She'd been so sure she'd made all the right choices, but she hadn't made any choices at all. She'd been hiding. From life. From herself. From her heart.

She arrived at the house just as Starr was walking up to the front door. They waved at each other.

"How was your day?" Destiny asked.

"Good."

"Any more kissing?"

Her sister rolled her eyes. "You're never letting that go, are you?"

"Probably not."

They stepped into the living room and flopped onto the sofa.

"You're not the type to kiss just any guy," Destiny added. "So you must really like Carter."

Starr blushed. "I do. He's so great. I know we're young, and I don't want things to get serious, but when I'm around him…"

"Magic?"

"Yeah. Just like they talk about in songs. You know, like your feelings for Kipling."

Destiny really hoped Starr wasn't experiencing any of *those* kinds of feelings.

"But we've talked," Starr continued. "There's not going to be any more kissing. We're going to hang out with friends and stuff. Be together, but not serious."

"That's a really smart decision."

"You think? I'm trying. I thought a lot about what you said. About my parents and how they reacted instead of thinking things through."

"You still have to have fun," Destiny told her. "Be a kid."

"I know, and I will. Just not so fast with boys. See. I'm learning from you."

"You are."

But Destiny wondered how much of the lesson was a good thing. Because it seemed to her, she might have gone too far in the sensible direction. It wasn't as if her personal life had turned out so great.

Their sensible marriage was no longer so sensible. In fact, in the cold light of day, it was a ridiculous

thing to have done. She was intelligent and capal She could raise a child on her own. Not that she v trying to shut Kipling out or keep him from his ba But marriage?

"I want to talk to you about something," she s

"What?"

"Kipling, mostly."

Starr leaned her head against the sofa. "I w dered. He hasn't been around."

"He's called but I haven't wanted to talk to hi

"Because he hurt your feelings?"

"Yes, and because I was confused. When I your age…"

Destiny wasn't sure how to explain something didn't quite make sense to her.

"I was determined not to be like my parent wanted a stable home. A sure thing. I got that fr my Grandma Nell, but when I went out on my o I was scared. What if I fell crazy in love and around the country, singing at honky-tonks and ing on a bus?"

Starr laughed. "That sounds fun."

"Not to me. It would have been a nightmare." paused, mentally feeling her way as she went. "I so afraid of what I could become, that I startec ignore who I actually was. It was safe, but now thinking it might not have been the right decisic

She smiled at her sister. "I never would have myself kiss a boy the way you did. I would h been too scared of what would happen. I ran fi so many things."

Starr's arm. "In fact, I was thinking of going through what I have after dinner. Want to help me with that?"

Starr's eyes widened. "Yeah. I'd love to."

"Good. Let's check out what's thawing in the refrigerator."

They rose, and Destiny led the way into the kitchen. But her mind was on the notebooks she'd stored in a box in her dresser. Notebooks filled with dozens of songs she'd written over the years. There were a few that would make beautiful duets. There might very well be some interest in a release sung by the daughters of Jimmy Don Mills.

She wasn't willing to go on tour or anything like that, but maybe a studio album wasn't out of the question.

"What's so funny?" Starr asked. "You're smiling."

"Am I? I was just thinking that life is nothing if not ironic. I've spent years running away from who I am only to find out that's the person I need to be."

FOR A WOMAN who owned a business smack in the middle of town, Jo Trellis was a difficult person to find. Kipling had been to her bar three times, left voice mail and texts, and he'd yet to connect with her. From what he could tell, she was avoiding him. Which seemed to be popular these days. Destiny was avoiding him, too.

This was not how he'd planned to spend the first couple of weeks of his marriage. Those nights had been so promising, he thought grimly, as he walked toward Destiny's house. They'd been all over each other. But more exciting than the physical chemistry had been how much they'd enjoyed each other's company. Or at least he'd enjoyed hers. By the way she was avoiding him, Destiny hadn't felt the same connection.

What he didn't get was how it had all gone to hell so quickly. One minute they were promising until death they did part, and the next he couldn't get her on the phone.

He knew the exact moment everything had changed with Destiny. It had happened after the incident with Starr and Carter. But the real trouble with everything else had begun long before that. That much he knew. But the exact when of it was more confusing.

He walked through the center of town. The Fourth of July festival was in full swing with booths and crafts and live music in the park. There was going to be a parade later, and fireworks. Normally, he found that kind of thing a lot of fun. But not today. Today he needed to see Destiny, and he had to figure out why he was so unsettled.

The Man Cave was part of the problem. If he couldn't fix things with Jo and his partners, then the bar wouldn't survive. Nick had shown him the books. Kipling had seen right away that while the bar could limp along for a few months, the end was inevitable. Without local support, they were doomed.

It wasn't the failure of the business that got to him, he thought. It was what that failure meant. Because

The Man Cave had been his way of fitting in. Of giving back. And he'd screwed it up royally.

He paused by Brew-haha and looked toward the
park. Even though it was still morning, there were
crowds everywhere. The sun was warm, the sky blue.

Little more than a year ago he'd been skiing down
a mountain in New Zealand, preparing to start serious training. He'd been fresh off his Olympic win
and totally unstoppable. Or so he'd thought.

After the crash, he'd been more worried about
whether he would walk again than thinking about
the end of his career. Then Mayor Marsha had shown
up, out of nowhere. She'd offered him a job and had
promised to take care of Shelby.

He still remembered how he hadn't believed her.
How he'd promised to follow her to hell if she would
protect his sister. He still remembered exactly what
she'd said.

*"You don't have to be alone in this, Kipling. Nor
do you have to go all the way to hell. Just come to
Fool's Gold when you're able. We'll be waiting for
you."*

She had kept her word. He knew now that Ford
Hendrix and Angel Whittaker had flown to Colorado
that very day. When Shelby's mother had died, they'd
brought Shelby to Fool's Gold. Kipling had followed
when he was able. In January, he'd accepted the job
as the head of HERO.

When he'd realized there wasn't a place for guys
to hang out, he'd thought of The Man Cave. He'd

gotten several business partners together, and they'd hired Nick.

He'd been so sure it was the right thing to do. It fixed a problem. He wanted to say it was the same with Destiny, only it wasn't. Because she was more important than all the rest of them put together.

He turned away from the park and walked the last couple of blocks to her house. When her door opened and he saw her, his whole body relaxed. Being with her was right.

"Hey," he said with a smile. "I wanted to see how you're doing."

"I'm glad you came by."

She had on cut-off jeans and a T-shirt. Her hair was back in a ponytail, and she was barefoot. Not overtly sexy, but she sure got to him.

He wanted to pull her close and kiss her. He wanted to do other things, too, but mostly he wanted to hold her. They sat on the sofa, facing each other. She looked good, he thought. Maybe a little tired, but all her.

His gaze dropped to the ring on her finger. The simple gold band looked lonely. He wanted to add a nice engagement ring. A sparkly diamond. Sure it was traditional, but he was mostly a traditional kind of guy.

"I've missed you," he told her. "Is everything okay with Starr?"

She nodded. "We're getting along well. We're sorting through songs I've written. My mom's manager is going to fly in next week to talk about the music."

"Good for you. You're too talented to ignore your abilities. How are you feeling?"

"Fine. I have a gynecologist appointment next week."

"With Dr. Galloway?" he asked, hoping the answer was no.

"How did you know?"

He shrugged. "I've met her." There was no need to go into the "flowering" conversation with Destiny. "Can I come with you?"

She nodded. "I want you to be as much a part of me being pregnant as you'd like."

It struck him that everything about this was wrong. They were married. They should be holding each other and heading to the bedroom to make love. Their conversation should be easy and natural—not stilted and informational. This was Destiny—they knew each other. Only right now it felt as if they were strangers.

"What's going on?" he asked. "You wanted time, so I gave it to you. Should I have pushed harder to talk to you?"

"No. You did the right thing. I've been thinking a lot about everything." She looked at him. "Kipling, I love you."

His first reaction was to jump up and yell the happy news as loud as he could. Destiny loved him. Destiny, who was kind and funny and sexy and determined. His second thought was that if she loved him, she would need so much more than he had to offer. He'd been unable to protect his own sister from his father's fists. How could he protect anyone else? Especially Destiny?

"I didn't expect it, either," she said wryly. "I had no idea. I've tried to be rational and calm in every situation. But that's not who I am. I don't have an answer to the nurture-nature question, but what I do know is that I can't pretend anymore. I can get a little crazy. Maybe I don't throw plates, but I'm not as rational as you think. I feel things. Deeply. And I'm not going to deny that anymore."

"I like that you feel things."

She smiled. "Good. Because we're having a baby together. We have a lot to work out."

He reached for her hands. "I want that. I want us to be a family, Destiny. I meant my vows. I'm in this for the long haul."

Her smile faded. "I believe you because me being pregnant is yet another problem for you to handle."

The unfair statement had him hanging on tighter. "It's more than that."

"I don't think it is. You don't love me back. It's okay. You don't have to. You like me, and we're friends, and I've seen how you take care of your sister. You'll be a good dad. Like I said before, I want you to be as much a part of my pregnancy as you want. I won't shut you out, but I won't be married to you. Not like this. I don't need fixing. I need to be loved, and you can't or won't." She squeezed his fingers before releasing them.

"Kipling, I want a divorce."

CHAPTER NINETEEN

"YOU OKAY?" CASSIDY ASKED.

No. I'm pregnant, getting a divorce, responsible for my teenage sister and I'm quitting my job in two weeks. Destiny told herself to breathe then smile. The phrase *fake it until you make it* had never sounded so right.

"I'm fine. Ready to get hiking."

She and Cassidy were heading out to map the last few areas on the grid. They'd already divided up the map. She figured each of the sections could be completed in less than a day. If everything went well, they would be done by the end of the week.

It was the Saturday of the July Fourth weekend, but neither she nor Cassidy had any reason not to work. Starr was with friends, and Destiny had no desire to sit home alone. Cassidy's husband was half a world away. Mapping the grid was a perfect solution.

"Radio in every couple of hours," Cassidy said as she collected her backpack. "I'll do the same." She grinned. "It would be humiliating for one of us to get lost."

"Tell me about it." Destiny picked up her own gear, and they headed for the door.

The timing of the work was perfect, she thought as she drove out of town. With everything going on, a few hours in nature were just what she needed to clear her head. She could enter data into the program and have a good cry at the same time. Because the tears were inevitable.

She could accept loving Kipling. She could accept that he didn't love her back. She was totally rational about the whole thing. The problem was, the news devastated her.

Until she'd told him she wanted a divorce, she hadn't realized how much she was hoping he was secretly in love with her, too. That he would turn to her, confess his feelings, and they would live happily ever after. But that hadn't happened. She'd said she wanted a divorce; Kipling had nodded once, said he would get his lawyer on that, and he'd left. There'd been no conversation, no whisper of emotion. Nothing. A big, fat nothing.

While she knew that staying married was a mistake, she couldn't help wishing that things had ended differently. After all those years of avoiding strong feelings, she'd finally gone and fallen in love, only to end up in an emotional face-plant. So much for acting rationally.

She pulled off the highway and into a rest area then consulted her map. When she'd confirmed she was where she was supposed to be, she got out and shrugged into her backpack then turned on the GPS tracker, along with her other equipment, and headed for the forest.

Time would heal, she reminded herself. She had a wonderful family and a baby on the way. Later, she would call her mother and tell Lacey that her wish for a grandbaby had been granted. This weekend she and Starr would continue to sort through Destiny's songs and pick the best twenty or so to play for her mom's manager. She would buy a house and get on with her life.

She had people who cared about her. She had good friends and lots of support. What she didn't have was the love of the man who had claimed her heart. That hurt, but she would survive.

For years Grandma Nell had been the benchmark by which she measured her actions. Would Grandma Nell do that? Would Grandma Nell be proud? While Destiny loved her grandmother, she knew she had to shift her thinking. Making Grandma Nell proud wasn't the point anymore. Now she had to learn to be proud of herself.

SKIING SEVENTY MILES an hour into a tree broke more bones than Destiny walking out on him, but being without her hurt a whole lot more. Kipling still couldn't figure out what to do with the information she'd clobbered him with before she'd left.

She loved him, and she was gone. Just like that. *I love you. I want a divorce.* It was the end of a bad movie. It was so extreme as to be ridiculous. But he wasn't laughing. Or sleeping or eating. In fact, it was all he could do to keep breathing.

It hurt. More than anything ever had. He who had

always believed that the words didn't matter—that only actions matter—had been ripped open by what he'd been told. Words killed, he thought grimly.

Just as bad, she was gone. Oh, sure, he would see her. They were having a kid together, and he knew that whatever happened between the two of them, she would never try to cut him out of his child's life. But he didn't want to be a part-time dad. He wanted to be a family. With her.

He started out of his rental to tell her just that, only to stop by the front door and turn around. What was he to say to convince her not to divorce him? He wanted them to stay married. He wanted to live with her and have his child with her. He thought he'd shown her how much he cared by his actions. He'd been there for her, had taken care of her.

He knew there was a solution to the problem. There had to be. But whatever it was, it eluded him. He ran different scenarios in his mind. He wrote letters. He'd considered renting a billboard, but had no idea what it would say.

Don't leave me was a start. *Marry me* was out of the question. They were already married. *Let's not get a divorce* was too twisted.

What he didn't understand was what had changed. If she loved him now, she'd probably loved him for a while. So wasn't their being married a good thing?

Someone knocked on his door. He pulled it open, eager to see Destiny. But instead his sister stood on the porch.

She put her hands on her hips. "Seriously, you could at least try not to be so disappointed it's me."

"Sorry."

"Hoping it was your new bride?"

He nodded and stepped back to let his sister in. She walked past him then turned to face him when he shut the front door.

"What's up?"

He asked the question in his best casual, "I'm fine. Ignore the signs of strain and tension" voice. Apparently, it worked because Shelby didn't ask any questions. Instead she said, "I've been thinking."

"About?"

"What you said before. About the business and me and us." She sighed. "You're a good big brother, and I love you."

It was obvious she had more to say, so he waited.

"And I'm sorry."

Not what he expected. "About?"

"I've sent you mixed messages. I ask your advice then get mad when you give it. I want you to rescue me but only sometimes. It's not clear to me, so it sure can't be clear to you, either."

He relaxed a little. "Okay. So where does that leave us?"

She smiled. "I would like to borrow the money from you, but only as a loan. I'll pay you back, with interest."

"What if I don't want to give you the money anymore?"

She laughed then hugged him. "You're a funny guy."

"Not everyone thinks so."

"Then they don't know you well enough."

He didn't think that was Destiny's problem.

Shelby studied him. "Want to talk about it?"

"There's nothing. I'm fine."

"Then why are you still living here instead of with Destiny?"

She had him on that one. "It's complicated. She's…" Not mad, he thought. Disappointed? Hurt? "Upset."

"Did you try to fix things too much? You do that, Kipling. You mean well, but sometimes people want to be more than a project."

"I don't see people as projects."

She raised her eyebrows as her hands returned to her hips.

He sighed. "Sometimes I do," he admitted.

"Enough that it's hard for the rest of us to be sure where we stand and if we matter. You're my brother, and I don't always know if you're excited about helping me or taking care of the problem."

Was that what had gone wrong with Destiny? He hadn't made it clear he cared about her and the baby?

"Doesn't what I do matter more than what I say?"

"Not always." Shelby hugged him. "You're a really good guy. If Destiny isn't seeing that right now, then give her a little time. You're not wrong to care."

"Thanks." Although he knew he had to be wrong

about something because Destiny didn't want to stay married to him. "You doing okay?"

"I am. I had a brief but horrible relationship with Miles, and I'm now officially over him."

"What? Miles the pilot? He's a player." And soon to be dead, Kipling thought grimly.

"Yes, I see that now." Shelby shook her head. "Don't go there. Don't take on my problem. I bought into his charm, and I learned a good lesson. I'll recover."

"You're my sister."

"Thanks for the clarification." She wrinkled her nose. "I mean it, Kipling. I have to figure this out on my own. Don't mess in my personal life, okay?"

He nodded slowly. "Sure. Come to me for money but not advice."

She flashed him a smile. "Exactly."

NOT SURE WHAT TO DO with himself, Kipling walked through town. Just his luck, no one was getting lost on a very busy holiday weekend.

Tourists mingled with locals. The smell of barbecue mingled with the scent of lemons and fresh churros. He nodded at people he knew, stepped out of the way of unsteady toddlers and rescued a balloon that nearly got away.

All of which should have made him feel better. Connected, maybe. But it didn't, and he wasn't.

He missed Destiny. Without her, he couldn't seem to think straight. Or sleep. Or know what was going on. He could have gone to see her. He knew that she and Cassidy were out mapping the last parts of the mountain. He could have joined them. But then what?

He crossed the street and headed for the park. Live music played. Music that made him think of Destiny performing at The Man Cave and how she'd lost herself in song.

She was amazing, he thought. Powerful and talented. Beautiful. She'd claimed to love him and then told him she wanted a divorce. What was he supposed to do with that?

The truth was, he wanted her back. He missed her and—

He turned at the sound of teenage boys laughing and saw Carter standing with his friends. The second Kipling spotted him, he knew what he had to do.

He walked toward the teen. Carter saw him approaching and straightened. While the festival spun on around them, Kipling felt the afternoon grow quiet—at least in his head.

"Hey," he said, when he was in front of Carter. "I wanted to tell you I'm sorry. I don't approve of you kissing Starr, but I get why it happened. Mills women are tough to resist." He raised one shoulder. "Yelling at you wasn't my finest hour."

Carter grinned. "It's okay. Felicia explained about the protective instincts of the alpha male in the clan." The teen chuckled. "Which might not make sense to you, but it's kind of how she talks. She's supersmart. Anyway, she's right. Starr's almost like your daughter. You have to be protective. I'm glad she has someone looking out for her, you know. Because it wasn't always like that."

Kipling stared at the kid. "You're not a jerk."

"Thanks, man. Neither are you."

Kipling shook his head. "No. I mean you're a good kid."

"Always have been. Does this mean I can—"

"No," Kipling told him firmly. "My protective instincts remain intact. But I now have more respect for Starr's selection process."

"I think that's a compliment, so thanks."

"You're welcome."

Carter turned back to his friends. Kipling looked around and tried to figure out what he should do next. Suddenly, a tall, brown-haired woman stepped in front of him.

"I hear you've been looking for me."

She was close to forty, fit, with just enough attitude to make a guy think she knew how to take care of herself.

Kipling had no idea who she was.

"Ma'am?"

The woman raised her eyebrows. "Not a very good way to start, Kipling. I've heard you're charming. Don't disappoint me."

Was it him, or had it gotten a little hot in here?

"I'm Jo Trellis," the woman said. "Of Jo's Bar."

"You," he said loudly. "Finally. I've been trying to talk to you for days. You won't take my calls or return them. You're never around when I stop by."

She looked more amused than chagrined. "What can I say? I'm elusive."

"You're putting me out of business."

"Back at you."

They stared at each other.

Kipling figured it had been her town first. "I'm sure we can find a solution to this problem."

"I've heard you like fixing things. So sure. Fix this one. We all take care of each other. If you wanted to open a bar that competed directly with me, you should have talked to me first. Or someone. But you didn't. You stomped in and did your thing without considering anyone else."

"Hey, wait. It wasn't like that. The guys around here don't have anywhere to go. Your place caters to women."

Her chin rose. "Tell me how that's bad."

Oops. "It's, ah, not. Women should have a bar where they can be comfortable. But so should guys. That's all I was doing." He thought about the town and how involved everyone was. "I didn't think about talking to you. I'm not from here."

"Not much of an excuse. You should learn how to have a conversation. Words matter."

He was starting to see that. They'd mattered with Carter, they mattered with Jo. Didn't it make sense they would matter with Destiny, too? She'd told him she loved him, and what had he said in return? Not a thing.

He thought about everything that was wrong right

now. "I'm sorry I didn't talk to you first. I should have. For what it's worth, you've won. My partners have pulled out, and Nick says we can't make it solely on tourist dollars."

Jo shifted from foot to foot. "Yeah, well, about that. I might have made a few phone calls. I wanted to make a little trouble, but I didn't anticipate how seriously my friends would take my concerns."

"You didn't mean to shut me down?"

"Hell, no. I was going to talk to you. Jo's does a good business, but I'm tired of working sixteen-hour days. I have a hot husband at home I'd like to spend more time with. I'm going to call off the ladies. Your partners will come slinking back. Jo's Bar is going to be open five days a week and close at seven in the evening. You can have the nights."

She held out her hand. He shook it. "Remind me never to go up against you again," he said.

"You got that right. Tell Nick to expect a crowd tonight. I'm going to make some calls."

DESTINY CROSSED THE shallow stream. On the other side, she confirmed the GPS signal was still strong. While she enjoyed a day hike as much as the next person, she didn't want to have to retrace her steps.

She paused for a drink of water. Tall trees offered shade overhead and kept the temperature comfortable, but she was in her third hour of hiking and getting a little tired.

She was out of shape, she thought. She hadn't been

exercising as regularly. That was going to have to change. She had to stay healthy for two. Something she couldn't mention to Kipling, she thought with a smile. Before she finished speaking, he would have designed a program and signed her up with a trainer.

No, he wouldn't, she thought, her smile fading. Because they weren't together anymore. She'd ended things pretty abruptly, and she hadn't heard from him since.

She missed him, she admitted. A lot. There was a hole in her life and maybe in her heart. A Kipling-size one. She missed how he visibly brightened when she walked in the room. How he listened and then offered advice whether she wanted it or not. She liked how easily he'd adjusted to being a mere mortal after years spent being a ski god.

He was a good man, she thought wistfully. Funny, charming, caring. Instead of getting mad when he'd found out she'd been a virgin, he'd wanted to help her learn to enjoy sex. He was dependable and caring. If only he loved her. Because without loving her, without her being able to—

Destiny stopped in midstride. She slowly lowered her raised foot to the ground and let the swirling thoughts settle. When they did, she nearly fell over from shock.

She was still doing it. She was still running from something—just like she always had. She'd run from her parents when she'd been younger. She'd run from her emotions, her passions, her talents.

She'd built up walls and hidden behind them, and she was still doing it. Right this second.

How did she know Kipling didn't love her? She hadn't asked. She hadn't given him a chance to talk or explain or even think. They'd never talked about their marriage or explored what either of them expected or needed to make the relationship work. She'd simply told him she wanted a divorce.

Running away from something wasn't the same as running to something. She'd spent so much of her life thinking about what she didn't want that she'd forgotten to figure out what was important to her. She was so worried about being unhappy that she never bothered to find what made her happy. Or who.

She loved Kipling. She knew that for sure. But did he love her? Maybe this was a good time to be asking that question. And not just of herself.

"What have I done?" she asked out loud.

There was no answer. Just the hum of insects and the call of a hawk.

She glanced down at her screen. Her exact location showed as a tiny dot. She could see the most direct route back to her car and immediately headed that way.

MEN HAD BEEN making fools of themselves over women for centuries, Kipling thought cheerfully. He was just one in a long line. If he was going to lose Destiny, he was going to do it in style. With everything on the table.

In the past hour he'd had a call from five of his

business partners asking to be a part of The Man Cave again, and a text from Nick saying he was expecting a big crowd. Felicia Boylan, Carter's mother, had found him and hugged him, all the while telling him how happy she was that he'd shown Carter the complete cycle of a male exchange, from misunderstanding to threatened violence, to apology and resolution. When he'd tried to explain that hadn't been his intent, she'd brushed off his comments.

He stood there, in the center of the festival, surrounded by people, and all he could think was that he wanted to tell Destiny all about it. Not just tell her, but have her share in it. He wanted to laugh with her and touch her and take care of her.

But the telling was important, too. Talking to her. Words. It came back to those damn words.

He got that actions were significant. Promising to be faithful was meaningless if you went out and cheated. His father hitting Shelby had a whole lot more meaning than the times he'd sworn he loved her. But maybe, just maybe, he'd taken the lesson he'd learned just a little too far. Maybe he'd dismissed the words too quickly. And if that were the case, he just might have a chance at winning Destiny back.

In the time it took him to jog home and grab the keys to his Jeep, he came to several more realizations. He realized that just because he'd never been in love before didn't mean he was necessarily flawed. He hadn't been holding back because he didn't believe saying he loved someone made a difference—he'd been waiting. For the right woman. The only woman.

Destiny had said she loved him, and now all he wanted was to say it back to her. Then convince her, because action was always going to be his thing. But he would say it, too.

Destiny loved him, he loved her, and there was no way he was going to let her go. Not without a fight. And if he made a fool of himself because of it, so be it.

He headed out of town. A quick call to Cassidy gave him the starting point. He had his tracking equipment and working knowledge of the STORMS program. He was supposed to be some kind of search and rescue expert. It was time he put that title to the test.

He pulled off into the rest area parking lot and pulled up next to Destiny's car. After getting out, he checked his equipment then started entering data. She was an experienced hiker, on a day trip. He knew the grid she would cover, just not which part she would be in right now.

"Looking for someone?"

He glanced up and saw Destiny heading toward him. He opened his driver's door, flung in his tablet then walked toward her.

There were so many things to say, he thought, but none of them mattered right this second. He cupped her face in his hands and kissed her on the mouth. She wrapped her arms around him and hung on as if she was never going to let go.

"I love you," he said when they came up for air.

"I had no right to say I wanted a divorce— What?" Her green eyes widened. "What did you say?"

"I love you. A lot. I have for a while. We're not getting a divorce without talking about it first. Once you agree to that, I'm going to convince you to stay with me for always."

"I do love a man with a plan." Her lips trembled. "Real love?"

"The forever kind." He kissed her again. "The kind that means I'm not leaving, so you should consider sticking around, too."

"I will. I am. I've been running away from what scared me for so long that I forgot what it was like to run to something. To you."

He held her close and breathed in the scent of her.

"Marry me," he whispered. "Not because you're pregnant or because it's the right thing to do. Marry me because you can't imagine spending another day without me. Marry me because we're a family. You, me, Starr, the baby. Marry me so we can be together always."

She looked into his eyes. "I already did, Kipling." She leaned against him. "I already did."

Kipling led her to his Jeep. She climbed inside. They would deal with her car later. They would deal with a lot of things. But the decisions would be easy, because they were together.

It wasn't flying down a mountain at seventy miles an hour, he thought as he started down the highway. It was better.

She took his hand in hers. "I'm going to write a song about this." She grinned. "After we have sex."

He was still laughing when they drove into town.

* * * * *

Okehampton (South Zeal)
The Oxenham Arms
South Zeal
Nr Okehampton
Devon EX20 2JT
01837 840244/577

Porthleven, Nr Helston
The Harbour Inn
Commercial Road
Porthleven
Nr Helston
Cornwall TR13 9JD
01326 573876

Sherborne (West Camel)
The Walnut Tree
West Camel
Nr Sherborne
Somerset BA22 7QW
01935 851292

Onneley
The Wheatsheaf Inn At Onneley
Barhill Road
Onneley
Staffordshire CW3 9QF
01782 751581

Preston (Goosnargh)
Ye Horns Inn
Goosnargh
Nr Preston
Lancashire PR3 27Y
01772 865230

Shipton-under-Wychwood
The Lamb Inn
Shipton-Under-Wychwood
Oxfordshire OX7 6DQ
01993 830465

Oxford (Banbury)
The Holcombe Hotel
High Street
Dedington
Oxfordshire OX5 4SL
01869 338274

Quorn
Quorn Grange
Wood Lane
Quorn
Leics LE12 8DB
01509 412167

Shipton-under-Wychwood
The Shaven Crown Hotel
High Street
Shipton-under-Wychwood
Oxfordshire OX7 6RA
01993 830330

Oxford (Middleton Stoney)
The Jersey Arms
Middleton Stoney
Oxfordshire OX6 8SE
01869 343234

Rosedale Abbey
The Milburn Arms Hotel
Rosedale Abbey
Pickering
North Yorkshire
YO18 8RA
01751 417312

Skipton (Elslack)
The Tempest Arms
Elslack
Nr Skipton
North Yorkshire BD23 3AY
01282 842450

Oxford (Minster Lovell)
The Mill and Old Swan
Minster Lovell
Burford
Oxfordshire OX8 5RN
01993 774441

Rugby (Easenhall)
The Golden Lion Inn of Easenhall
Easenhall
Nr Rugby
Warwickshire CV23 0JA
01797 223065

Southport (Formby)
Treetops Country House Restaurant
Southport Old Road
Formby
Nr Southport
Merseyside L37 0AB
01704 879651

Oxford (Stanton-St-John)
The Talkhouse
Wheatley Road
Stanton-St-John
Oxfordshire OX33 1EX
01865 351648

Rye
The Mermaid Inn
Mermaid Street
Rye
East Sussex TN31 7NU
01797 223065

Stonor (Henley-on-Thames)
The Stonor Arms
Stonor
Nr Henley-on-Thames
Oxfordshire RG9 6HE
01491 638354

Padstow
The Old Custom House Inn
South Quay
Padstow
Cornwall PL28 8ED
01841 532359

St Austell
The White Hart Hotel
Church Street
St Austell
Cornwall PL25 4AT
01726 72100

Stow-on-the-Wold
The Kingshead Inn And Restaurant
The Green
Bledington
Nr Kingham
Oxfordshire OX7 6HD
01608 658365

Pelynt (Nr Looe)
Jubilee Inn
Pelynt
Nr Looe
Cornwall PL13 2JZ
01503 220312

St Mawes
The Rising Sun
The Square
St Mawes
Cornwall TR2 5DJ
01326 270233

Stow-on-the-Wold
The Royalist
Digbeth Street
Stow-on-the-Wold
Gloucestershire GL54 1BN
01451 830670

Petworth (Sutton)
The White Horse Inn
Sutton
Nr Pulborough
West Sussex RH20 1PS
01798 869221

Saddleworth (Delph)
The Old Bell Inn Hotel
Huddersfield Road
Delph
Saddleworth
Lancashire OL3 5E6
01457 870130

Stratford-upon-Avon (Alveston)
Baraset Barn Restaurant
Pimlico Lane
Alveston
Stratford-upon-Avon
Warwickshire CV37 7RF
01789 295510

Pickering
The White Swan
The Market Place
Pickering
North Yorkshire YO18 7AA
01751 472288

Salisbury
The Milford Hall Hotel
206 Castle Street
Salisbury
Wiltshire SP1 3TE
01722 417411

Stratford-upon-Avon
The Blue Boar Inn
Temple Grafton
Alcester
Warwickshire B49 6NRE
01789 750010

Port Gaverne
Port Gaverne Hotel
Port Gaverne
Nr Port Isaac
North Cornwall PL29 3SQ
01208 880244

Scarborough (East Ayton)
East Ayton Lodge Country Hotel
Moor Lane
Forge Valley
East Ayton
Scarborough, North Yorkshire
01723 864227

Telford (Norton)
The Hundred House Hotel
Bridgnorth Road
Norton
Nr Shifnal, Telford
Shropshire TF11 9EE
01952 730353

Tewkesbury
The Bell Hotel
Church Street
Tewkesbury
Gloucestershire GL20 5SA
01684 293293

Thame, Nr Oxford
Thatchers Inn
29/30 Lower High Street
Thame
Nr Oxford
Oxfordshire OX9 2AA
01844 212146

Thelbridge
Thelbridge Cross Inn
Thelbridge
Nr Witheridge
Devon EX17 4SQ
01884 860316

Thorpe Market
Green Farm Restaurant And Hotel
North Walsham Road
Thorpe Market
Norfolk NR11 8TH
01263 833602

Torquay (Kingskerswell)
The Barn Owl Inn
Aller Mills
Kingskerswell
Devon TQ12 5AN
01830 872130

Totnes (Staverton)
The Sea Trout Inn
Staverton
Nr Totnes
Devon TQ9 6PA
01803 762274

Troutbeck, nr Windermere
The Mortal Man Hotel
Troutbeck
Nr Windermere
Cumbria LA23 1PL
015394 33193

Tunbridge Wells
Royal Wells Inn
Mount Ephraim
Tunbridge Wells
Kent TN4 8BE
01892 511188

Twyford (Knowl Hill)
The Bird in Hand
Bath Road
Knowl Hill
Twyford
Berkshire RG10 9UP
01628 826622/822781

Upton-upon-Severn, Nr Malvern
White Lion Hotel
High Street
Upton-upon-Severn
Worcestershire WR8 0HJ
01684 592551

Walberswick
The Anchor
Walberswick
Suffolk IP18 6UA
01502 722112

Weobley
Ye Olde Salutation Inn
Market Pitch
Weobley
Herefordshire HR4 8SJ
01544 318443

West Witton (Wensleydale)
The Wensleydale Heifer
West Witton
Wensleydale
North Yorkshire DL8 4LS
01969 622322

Whitewell
The Inn At Whitewell
Forest Of Bowland
Clitheroe
Lancashire BB7 3AT
01200 448222

Winchcombe
Wesley House
The High Street
Winchcombe
Gloucestershire GL54 5LJ
01242 602366

Winchester
The Wyckeham Arms
75 Kingsgate Street
Winchester
Hampshire SO23 9PE
01962 852824

Withypool
The Royal Oak Inn
Exmoor National Park
Withypool
Somerset TA24 7QP
01643 831236

Worthing (Bramber)
The Old Tollgate Restaurant & Hotel
The Street
Bramber
Steyning
West Sussex BN44 3WE
01903 879494

Wroxham
The Barton Angler Country Inn
Irstead Road
Neatishead
Nr Wroxham
Norfolk NR12 8YD
01692 630740

Yattendon
The Royal Oak Hotel
Yattendon
Newbury
Berkshire RG16 0UF
01635 201325

Chepstow
Castle View Hotel
16 Bridge Street
Chepstow
Gwent NP6 5E2
01291 620349

Dolgellau (Penmaenpool)
George III Hotel
Penmaenpool
Nr Dolgellau
Gwynedd LL40 1YD
01341 422525

Llanarmon DC
The West Arms Hotel
Llanarmon Dc
Nr Llangollen
Clwyd LL20 7LD
01691 600665

Llandeilo (Rhosmaen)
The Plough Inn
Rhosmaen
Llandeilo
Dyfed SA19 6NP
01558 823431

Montgomery
The Dragon Hotel
Montgomery
Powys SY15 6AA
01686 668359

Welshpool (Berriew)
The Lion Hotel And Restaurant
Berriew
Nr Welshpool
Powys SY21 8PQ
01686 640452

Banchory (Royal Deeside)
Potarch Hotel
By Banchory
Royal Deeside
Kincardineshire AB3 4BD
013398 84339

Comrie
Comrie Hotel
Comrie
Perthshire PH6 2DY
01764 670239/330

Drymen
The Winnock Hotel
The Square
Drymen
Stirlingshire G63 0BL
01360 60245

Glenisla
The Glenisla Hotel
Kirkton of Glenisla
By Alyth
Perthshire PH11 8PH
01575 582223

Isle Of Skye (Eilean Iarmain)
Isle Ornsay Hotel
Eilean Iarmain
Isle Of Skye IV43 8QR
01471 833332

Kylesku, Sutherland
Kylesku Hotel
Kylesku
By Lairg
Sutherland IV27 4HW
01971 502231/200

Loch Gilphead
Cairnbann Hotel
By Loch Gilphead
Argyll PA31 8SJ
01546 603668

MINI LISTINGS: JOHANSENS COUNTRY HOUSES AND SMALL HOTELS

Here in brief are the entries that appear in full in Johansens 1996 Guide to Country Houses and Small Hotels. On pages 456–461 is a similar list of Johansens Recommended Inns with Restaurants 1996 and on pages 469–472 a list of Johansens Recommended Hotels in Europe 1996. To order any of these guides see pages 487–496.

Ambleside
Laurel Villa
Lake Road
Ambleside
Cumbria LA22 0DB
015394 33240

Bakewell (Rowsley)
The Peacock Hotel at Rowsley
Rowsley
Nr Matlock
Derbyshire DE4 2EB
01629 733518

Bath
Paradise House
Holloway
Bath
Avon BA2 4PX
01225 317723

Ambleside (Clappersgate)
Nanny Brow Hotel
Clappersgate
Ambleside
Cumbria LA22 9NF
015394 32036

Bamburgh
Waren House Hotel
Waren Mill
Belford
Northumberland NE70 7EE
01668 214581

Bath (Bradford-on-Avon)
Widbrook Grange
Trowbridge Road
Bradford-on-Avon
Wiltshire BA15 1UH
01225 864750/863173

Appleton-le-Moors
Appleton Hall Hotel
Appleton-le-Moors
North Yorkshire YO6 6TF
01751 417227

Bath
Apsley House Hotel
141 Newbridge Hill Road
Bath
Avon BA1 3PT
01225 336966

Beaminster
The Lodge
Beaminster
Dorset DT8 3BL
01308 863468

Arundel (Burpham)
Burpham Country Hotel
Old Down
Burpham
Nr Arundel
West Sussex BN18 9RV
01903 882160

Bath (Norton St Philip)
Bath Lodge Hotel
Norton St Philip
Bath
Avon BA3 6NH
01225 723040

Beccles
St Peter's House
Old Market
Beccles
Suffolk NR34 9AP
01502 713203

Ashbourne
Beeches Farmhouse
Waldley
Doveridge
Ashbourne
Derbyshire DE6 1LS
01889 590288

Bath
Bloomfield House
146 Bloomfield Road
Bath
Avon BA2 2AS
01225 420105

Beer
Bovey House
Beer
Seaton
Devon EX12 3AD
01297 680241

Ashbourne (Biggin-by-Hulland)
Biggin Mill Farm
Biggin-by-Hulland
Nr Ashbourne
Derbyshire DE6 3FN
01335 370414

Bath (Box)
Box House
Box
Nr Bath
Wiltshire SN14 9NR
01225 744447

Belper (Shottle)
Dannah Farm Country Guest House
Bowmans Lane
Shottle
Nr Belper
Derbyshire DE5 2DR
01773 550273/630

Ashwater
Blagdon Manor Country Hotel
Ashwater
Devon EX21 5DF
01409 211224

Bath
Eagle House
Church Street
Bathford
Bath
Avon BA1 7RS
01225 859946

Bibury
Bibury Court
Bibury
Gloucestershire GL7 5NT
01285 740337

Atherstone
Chapel House
Friars Gate
Atherstone
Warwickshire CV9 1EY
01827 718949

Bath (Rode)
Irondale House
67 High Street
Rode
Bath
Avon BA3 6PB
01373 830730

Biggin-by-Hartington
Biggin Hall
Biggin-by-Hartington
Buxton
Derbyshire SK17 0DH
01298 84451

Badminton
Petty France
Dunkirk
Badminton
Avon GL9 1AF
01454 238361

Bath (Monkton Combe)
Monkshill
Shaft Road
Monkton Court
Avon BA2 7HL
01225 833028

Blockley (Chipping Campden)
Lower Brook House
Blockley
Moreton-in-Marsh
Gloucestershire GL56 9DS
01386 700286

Bakewell (Rowsley)
East Lodge Country House Hotel
Rowsley
Matlock
Derbyshire DE4 2EF
01629 734474

Bath
Newbridge House Hotel
35 Kelston Road
Bath
Avon BA1 3QH
01225 446676

Bolton-by-Bowland
Harrop Fold
Bolton By Bowland
Clitheroe
Lancashire BBY 4PY
01200 447600

Bournemouth
Langtry Manor
Derby Road
East Cliff
Bournemouth
Dorset BH1 3QB
01202 553887

Bourton-on-the-Water
Dial House Hotel
The Chesnuts
High Street
Bourton-on-the-Water
Gloucestershire GL54 2AN
01451 822244

Bridgnorth
Cross Lane House Hotel
Astley Abbots
Bridgnorth
Shropshire WV16 4SJ
01746 764887

Bristol (Chelwood)
Chelwood House
Achelwood
Nr Bristol
Avon BS18 4NH
01761 490730

Broadway
Collin House Hotel
Collin Lane
Broadway
Worcestershire WR12 7PB
01386 858354/852544

Broadway
Leasow House
Laverton Meadows
Broadway
Worcestershire WR12 7NA
01386 584526

Broadway (Willersey)
The Old Rectory
Church Street
Willersey
Nr Broadway
Worcestershire WR12 7PN
01386 853729

Brockenhurst
The Thatched Cottage
16 Brookley Road
Brockenhurst
New Forest
Hampshire SO42 7RR
01590 623090

Brockenhurst
Whitley Ridge and Country House
Hotel
Beaulieu Road
Brockenhurst
New Forest
Hampshire SO42 7QL
01590 622354

Bury St Edmunds
Bradfield House
Bradfield Combust
Bury St Edmunds
Suffolk IP30 OL3
01284 386301

Buttermere (Lorton)
New House Farm
Loreton
Cockermouth
Cumbria CA13 9UU
01900 85404

Cambridge (Duxford)
Duxford Lodge Hotel
Ickleton Road
Duxford
Cambridgeshire CB2 4RU
01223 836444

Cambridge (Melbourn)
Melbourn Bury
Melbourn
Nr Royston
Hertfordshire SG3 6DE
01763 261151

Carlisle (Crosby-on-Eden)
Crosby Lodge Country House Hotel
High Crosby
Crosby-on-Eden
Carisle
Cumbria CA6 4QZ
01228 573618

Cartmel
Aynsome Manor Hotel
Cartmel
Nr Grange-over-Sands
Cumbria LA11 6HH
015395 36653

Castleton (Hope)
Underleigh House
Off Edale Road
Hope
Derbyshire S30 2RF
01433 621372

Castleton (Hope)
Twitchill Farm Cottages
Edale Road
Hope
Derbyshire S30 2RF
01433 621426

Chagford
Easton Court Hotel
Easton Cross
Chagford
Devon TQ13 8JL
01647 433469

Cheltenham (Charlton Kings)
Charlton Kings Hotel
Charlton Kings
Cheltenham
Gloucestershire GL52 6UU
01242 231061

Cheltenham (Withington)
Halewell
Halewell Close
Withington
Nr Cheltenham
Gloucestershire GL54 4BN
01242 890238

Chester (Broxton)
Frogg Manor
Nantwich Road
Fullers Moor
Broxton
Chester
Cheshire CH3 9JH
01829 782629

Chester (Huxley)
Higher Huxley Hall
Huxley
Chester CH3 9BZ
01829 781484

Chipping Campden
(Broad Campden)
Malt House
Broad Campden
Chipping Campden
Gloucestershire GL55 6UU
01386 840295

Cirencester (Woodmancote)
Cotswold Park
Woodmancote
Cirencester
Gloucestershire GL7 7EL
01285 831414

Cirencester (Ablington)
Hinton House
Ablington
Cirencester
Gloucestershire GL7 5NY
01285 740233

Clovelly (Horn's Cross)
Foxdown Manor
Horn's Cross
Nr Clovelly
Devon EX39 5PJ
01237 451325

Colchester (Higham)
The Bauble
Higham
Colchester
Essex CO7 6LA
01206 337254

Colchester (Frating)
Hockley Place
Frating
Colchester
Essex CO7 7HF
01206 251703

Combe Martin (Berrynarbor)
Bessemer Thatch
Berrynarbor
Nr Combe Martin
North Devon EX34 9SE
01271 882296

Corbridge (Stocksbridge)
Glenview
6 Meadowfield Road
Stocksfield
Northumberland NE43 7QX
01661 843674

Cornhill-on-Tweed
Wark Farm House
Wark
Cornhill-on-Tweed
Northumberland TD12 4RE
01890 883570

Dartmoor (Leusdon)
Leusdon Lodge Hotel
Leusdon
Poundsgate
Nr Ashburton
Devon TQ13 7PE
01364 631304

Dartmoor (Lydford)
Moor View Hotel
Vale Down
Lydford
Devon EX20 4BB
01822 282220

Dedham
Maison Talbooth
Stratford Road
Dedham
Colchester
Essex CO7 6HN
01206 322367

Diss
Salisbury House
Victoria Road
Diss
Norfolk IP22 3JG
01379 644738

Dorchester (Lower Bockhampton)
Yalbury Cottage Hotel
Lower Bockhampton
Dorchester
Dorset DT2 8PZ
01305 262282

Dover (Temple Ewell)
The Woodville Hall
Temple Ewell
Dover
Kent CT16 1DJ
01304 825256

Dover (West Cliffe)
Wallett's Court
West Cliffe
St Margarets-at-Cliffe
Dover
Kent CT15 6EW
01304 852424

Evershot
Rectory House
Fore Street
Evershot
Dorset DT2 0JN
0193583 273

Evesham (Harvington)
The Mill at Harvington
Anchor Lane
Harvington
Evesham
Worcestershire WR11 5NR
01386 870688

Exeter (Dunchideock)
The Lord Haldon Hotel
Dunchideock
Nr Exeter
Devon EX6 7YF
01392 832483

Exford (Exmoor)
The Crown Hotel
Exford
Exmoor National Park
Somerset TA24 7PP
01643 831554/5

Fenny Drayton (Leicestershire)
White Wings
Quaker Close
Fenny Drayton
Nr Nuneaton
Leicestershire Cv13 6BS
01827 716100

Fordingbridge
Lions Court Restaurant and Hotel
Fordingbridge
New Forest
Hampshire SP6 1AS
01425 652006

Fressingfield (Diss)
Chippenhall Hall
Fressingfield
Eye
Suffolk IP21 5TD
01379 588180

Gatwick (Charlwood)
Stanhill Court Hotel
Stanhill Road
Charlwood
Nr Horley
Surrey RH6 0EP
01293 862166

Gissing (Diss)
The Old Rectory
Gissing
Diss
Norfolk IP22 3XB
01379 677575

Glossop
The Wind in the Willows
Level
Glossop
Derbyshire SK13 9PT
01457 868001

Grasmere (Rydal Water)
White Moss House
Rydal Water
Grasmere
Cunbria LA22 9SE
015394 35295

Great Snoring
The Old Rectory
Great Snoring
Fakenham
Norfolk NR21 0HP
01328 820597

Greenhill (Coalville)
Abbots Oak
Greenhill
Coalville
Leicester LE67 4UY
01530 832328

Guildford (Newlands Corner)
The Manor
Newlands Corner
Guidford
Surrey GU4 8SE
01483 222624

Hampton Court
Chase Lodge
10 Park Road
Hampton Wick
Kingston-upon-Thames
Surrey KT1 4AS
0181 943 1862

Harrogate
The White House
10 Park Parade
Harrogate
North Yorkshire HG1 5AH
01423 501388

Hawes
Rookhurst Georgian Country
  House Hotel
West End
Gayle
Hawes
North Yorkshire DL6 3RT
01969 667454

Helford
Tregildry Hotel
Gillan Manaccan
Helston
Cornwall TR12 6HG
01326 231378

Helston
Nanslow Manor
Meneage Road
Helston
Cornwall TR13 0SB
01326 574691

Hereford (Ullingswick)
The Steppes
Ullingswick
Nr Hereford
Herefordshire NR1 3JG
01432 820424

Keswick (Lake Thirlmere)
Dale Head Hall
Thirlmere
Keswick
Cumbria CA12 4TN
017687 72478

Keswick (Newlands)
Swinside Lodge Hotel
Grange Road
Newlands
Keswick
Cumbria CA12 8UE
017687 72948

Keswick-On-Derwent-Water
The Grange Country House Hotel
Manor Brow
Keswick-On-Derwent-Water
Cumbria CA12 4BA
017687 72500

Kirkby Lonsdale
Hipping Hall
Cowan Bridge
Kirkby Lonsdale
Cumbria LA6 2JJ
015242 71187

Lavenham
The Great House Restaurant
Market Place
Lavenham
Suffolk CO10 9QZ
01787 247431

Leominster
Lower Bache
Kimbolton
Nr Leominster
Herefordshire HR6 0ER
01568 750304

Lifton (Sprytown)
The Thatched Cottage
  Country Hotel
Sprytown
Lifton
Devon PL16 0AY
01566 784224

Lincoln (Washingborough)
Washingborough Hall
Church Hill
Washingborough
Lincolnshire LN4 1BE
01522 790340

Looe (Talland Bay)
Allhays Country House
Talland Bay
Looe
Cornwall PL13 2JB
01503 272434

Looe (Widegates)
Coombe Farm
Widegates
Nr Looe
Cornwall PL13 1QN
01503 240223

Ludlow (Downton)
The Brakes
Downton
Nr Ludlow
Shropshire SY8 2LF
01584 856485

Ludlow (Diddlebury)
Delbury Hall
Diddlebury
Craven Arms
Shropshire SY7 9DH
01584 841267

Luton (Little Offley)
Little Offley
Hitchin
Hertfordshire SG5 3BU
01462 768243

Lymington (Hordle)
The Gordleton Mill Hotel
Silver Street
Hordle
Nr Lymington
Hampshire SO41 6DJ
01590 682219

Maidstone (Boughton Monchelsea)
Tanyard
Wierton Hill
Boughton Monchelsea
Nr Maidstone
Kent ME17 4JT
01622 744705

Malton
Newstead Grange
Norton
Malton
North Yorkshire YO17 9PJ
01653 692502

Middlecombe (Minehead)
Periton Park Hotel
Middlecombe
Nr Minehead
Somerset TA24 8SW
01643 706885

Middleham (Wensleydale)
The Millers House Hotel
Market Place
Middleham
Wensleydale
North Yorkshire DL8 4NR
01969 622630

Minchinhampton
Burleigh Court
Burleigh
Minchinhampton
Gloucestershire GL5 2PF
01453 883804

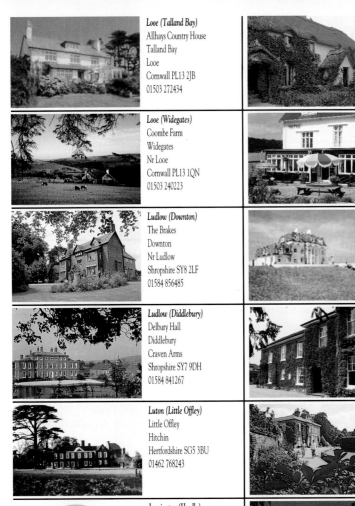

Morchard Bishop
Wigham
Morchard Bishop
Nr Crediton
Devon EX17 6RJ
01363 877350

Moretonhampstead (Lustleigh)
Eastbrey Barton Hotel
Lustleigh
Newton Abbott
Devon TQ13 9SN
01647 277338

New Romney (Littlestone)
Romney Bay House
Coast Road
Littlestone
New Romney
Kent TN28 8QY
01797 364747

North Walsham
Beechwood Hotel
Cromer Road
North Walsham
Norfolk NR28 0HD
01692 403231

Norwich
The Beeches Hotel & Victorian
   Gardens
4-6 Earlham Road
Norwich
Norfolk NR2 3DB
01603 621167

Norwich (Old Catton)
Catton Old Hall
Lodge Lane
Catton
Norwich
Norfolk NR6 7HG
01603 419379

Norwich (Drayton)
The Stower Grange
School Road
Drayton
Norwich
Norfolk NR8 6EF
01603 860210

Nutley
Down House
Down Street
Nutley
East Sussex TN22 3LE
01825 712328

Oswestry
Pen-Y-Dwffryn Hall
Rhydycroesau
Nr Oswestry
Shropshire SY10 7DT
01691 653700

Oxford (Kingston Bagpuize)
Fallowfields
Southmoor
Kingston Bagpuize
Oxford OX13 5BH
01865 820416

Porthleven, nr Helston
Tye Rock Hotel
Loe Bar Road
Porthleven
Cornwall TR13 9EW
01326 572695

Pulborough
Chequers Hotel
Church Place
Pulborough
West Sussex RH20 1AD
01798 872486

Redditch
The Old Rectory
Ipsley Lane
Redditch
Hereford & Worcester B98 0AP
01527 523000

Ross-on-Wye (Glewstone)
Glewstone Court
Nr Ross-on-Wye
Herefordshire HR9 6AW
01989 770367

Ross-on-Wye (Kilcot)
Orchard House
Astoningham Road
Kilcot
Gloucestershire GL18 1NP
01989 720417

Ross-on-Wye
Peterstow Country House
Peterstow
Ross-on-Wye
Herefordshire HR9 6LB
01989 562826

Ross-on-Wye (Yatton)
Rock's Place
Yatton
Ross-on-Wye
Hertfordshire HR9 7RD
01531 660218

Seavington St Mary (Nr
   Ilminster)
The Pheasant Hotel
Seavington St Mary
Nr Ilminster
Somerset TA19 0HQ
01460 240502

Sherborne
The Eastbury Hotel
Long Street
Sherborne
Dorset DT9 3BY
01935 813131

Simonsbath (Exmoor)
Simonsbath House Hotel
Simonsbath
Exmoor
Somerset TA24 7SH
01643 831259

South Molton
Marsh Hall Country House Hotel
South Molton
Devon EX36 3HQ
01769 572666

St Ives (Trink)
The Countryman At Trink
Old Coach Road
St Ives
Cornwall TR26 3JQ
01736 797571

Stamford (Ketton)
The Priory
Church Road
Ketton
Stamford
Lincolnshire PE9 3RD
01780 720215

Staverton, Nr Totnes
Kingston House
Staverton
Totnes
Devon TQ9 6AR
01803 762235

Stroud (Middle Lypiatt)
Middle Lypiatt House
Middle Lypiatt
Stroud
Gloucestershire GL6 7LW
01453 882151

Taunton (Hatch Beauchamp)
Farthings Hotel and Restaurant
Hatch Beauchamp
Taunton
Somerset TA3 6SG
01823 480664

Tewkesbury
Upper Court
Kemerton
Nr Tewkesbury
Gloucestershire GL20 7HY
01386 725351

Thetford
Broom Hall
Richmond Road
Sahamtoney
Thetford
Norfolk IP25 7EX
01953 882125

Tintagel (Trenale)
Trebrea Lodge
Trenale
Tintagel
Cornwall PL34 0HR
01840 770410

Uckfield
Hooke Hall
High Street
Uckfield
East Sussex TN22 1EN
01825 761578

Wareham (East Stoke)
Kemps Country House Hotel & Restaurant
East Stoke
Wareham
Dorset BH20 6AL
01929 462563

Wells
Beryl
Wells
Somerset
Avon BA5 3JP
01749 678738

Wells (Wookey Hole)
Glencot House
Glencot Lane
Wookey Hole
Wells
Somerset BA5 1BH
01749 677160

Whitby (Dunsley)
Dunsley Hall
Dunsley
Whitby
North Yorkshire YO21 3TL
01947 893437

Wimborne Minster
Beechleas
17 Poole Road
Wimborne Minster
Dorset BH21 1QA
01202 841684

Winchelsea
The Country House at Winchelsea
Hastings Road
Winchelsea
East Sussex TN36 4AD
01797 226669

Windermere (Bowness)
Fayrer Garden House Hotel
Upper Stores Road
Bowness-on-Windermere
Cumbria LA23 3JP
015394 88195

Witherslack
The Old Vicarage Country House Hotel
Church Road
Witherslack
Grange-over-Sands
Cumbria LA11 6RS
015395 52381

Woodbridge (Otley)
Otley House
Helmingham Road
Otley
Suffolk IP6 9NR
01473 890253

York
4 South Parade
York
North Yorkshire YO2 2BA
01904 628229

York (Escrick)
The Parsonage Country House Hotel
Escrick
York
North Yorkshire YO4 6LF
01904 728111

Abergavenny (Glancrwyney)
Glancrwyney Court
Glancrwyney
Nr Abergavenny
Powys
01873 811288

Abergavenny
Llanwenarth House
Govilon
Abergavenny
Gwent NP7 9SF
01873 830289

Abergavenny (Llanfihangel Crucorney)
Penyclawdd Court
Llanfihangel Crucorney
Nr Abergavenny
Gwent
01873 890719

Barmouth (Glandwr)
Plasbach
Glandwr
Nr Barmouth
Gwynedd LL42 1TG
01341 281234

Betws-Y-Coed
Tan-Y-Foel
Capel Garmon
Nr Betws-Y-Coed
Gwynedd LL26 0RE
01690 710507

Brecon (Three Cocks)
Old Gwernyfed Country Manor
Felindre
Three Cocks
Brecon
Powys LD3 0SU
01497 847376

Caernarfon
Ty'n Rhos
Llanddeiniolen
Caernarfon
Gwynedd
01248 670489

Conwy
Berthlwyd Hall Hotel
Llechwedd
Nr Conwy
Gwynedd LL32 8DQ
01492 592409

Conwy
The Old Rectory
Conwy
Llanrwst Road
Llansanffraid Glan Conwy
Gwynedd LL28 5LF
01492 580611

Corwen (Llandrillo)
Tyddyn Llan Country House Hotel
Llandrillo
Nr Corwen
Clwyd LL21 0ST
01490 440264

Criccieth
Myndd Ednyfed
Country House Hotel
Caernarfon Road
Criccieth
Gwynedd LL52 0PH
01766 523269

Dolgellau (Ganllwyd)
Dolmelynllyn Hall Hotel
Ganllwyd
Dolgellau
Gwynedd LL40 2HP
01341 440273

Fishguard
Plas Glyn-Y-Mel
Lower Town
Fishguard
Dyfed SA65 9LY
01348 872296

Fishguard (Welsh Hook)
Stone Hall
Welsh Hook
Haverford
WestPembrokeshire
Dyfed SA62 5NS
01348 840212

Llanfyllin
Bodfach Hall Country House
Hotel
Llanfyllin
Powys SY22 5HS
01691 648272

Forres
Knockomie Hotel
Grantown Road
Forres
Morray IV36 0SG
01309 673146

Pitlochry
Dunfallandy House
Logierait Road
Pitlochry
Perthshire PH16 5NA
01796 472648

Mold
Tower
Off Nercwys Road
Mold
Clwyd CH7 4ED
01352 700220

Grantown-on-Spey
Culdearn House
Woodlands Terrace
Grantown-on-Spey
Moray
Morayshire PH26 3JU
01479 872106

Port Of Menteith
The Lake Hotel
Port Of Menteith
Perthshire FK8 3RA
01877 385258

Tenby (Waterwynch Bay)
Waterwynch House Hotel
Waterwynch Bay
Tenby
Pembrokeshire
Dyfed SA70 8TJ
01834 842464

Inverness
Culduthel Lodge
14 Culduthel Road
Inverness
Inverness-shire IV2 4AG
01463 240089

Strath Brora
Sciberscross Lodge
Strath Brora
Rogart
Sutherland IV28 3YQ
01408 641246

Tintern
Parva Farmhouse
Tintern
Chepstow
Gwent NP6 6SQ
01291 689411

Isle Of Harris
Ardvourlie Castle
Aird A Mhulaidh
Isle Of Harris
Western Isles HS3 3AB
01859 502307

Birr, Co Offaly
Kinnitty Castle
Kinnitty
Birr
Co Offaly
353 509 37318

Ardelve (By Kyle of Lochalsh)
Conchra House
Ardelve
Kyle of Lochalsh
Inverness-shire IV40 8DZ
01599 555233

Isle Of Mull
Killiechronan
Killiechronan
Isle of Mull
Argyll PA72 6JU
01680 300403

Craigantlet, Newtownards
Beech Hill
23 Ballymoney Road
Craigantlet
Newtownards
Co Down
Northern Ireland BT23 4TG
01232 425892

Aviemore
Courrour House Hotel
Inverdruie
Inverness-shire PH22 1QH
01479 810220

Isle Of Skye (By Dunvegan)
Harlosh House
By Dunvegan
Isle of Skye
Inverness-shire IV55 8ZG
01470 521367

Letterkenny, Co Donegal
Castlegrove Country House
Ramelton Road
Letterkenny
Co Donegal
353 745 1118

Ballater (Royal Deeside)
Balgonie Country House
Braemar Place
Ballater
Royal Deeside
Grampian AB35 5RP
013397 55482

Killiecrankie, By Pitlochry
The Killiecrankie Hotel
Killiecrankie
By Pitlochry
Perthshire PH16 5LG
01796 473220

Malahide, Co Dublin
Belcamp Hutchinson
Balgriffin
Dublin
353 846 0843

Blairgowrie
Altamount House Hotel
Coupar Angus Road
Blairgowrie
Perthshire PH10 6JN
01250 873512

Moffat
Well View Hotel
Ballplay Road
Moffat
Dumfriesshire DG10 9JU
01683 220184

Nenagh, Co Tipperary
St David's Country House and
Restaurant
Ballycommon
Nenagh
Co Tipperary
353 672 4145

Drumnadrochit (Loch Ness)
Polmaily House Hotel
Drumnadrochit
Loch Ness
Inverness-shire IV3 6XT
01456 450343

Oban
The Manor House
Gallanach Road
Oban
Scotland PA34 4LS
01631 562087

Newtownards
(Co Down, Northern Ireland)
Edenvale House
130 Portaferry Road
Newtownards
Co Down BT22 2AH
01247 814881

Dunoon
Ardfillayne Hotel
West Bay
Dunoon
Argyll
Argyllshire PA23 7QJ
01369 702267

Perth
Dupplin Castle
Dupplin Estate
By Perth
Perthshire PH2 0PY
01738 623224

Portaferry
(Co Down, Northern Ireland)
Portaferry Hotel
The Strand
Portaferry
Co Down BT22 1PE
012477 28231

Fintry (Stirlingshire)
Culcreuch Castle Hotel
Fintry
Loch Lomond
Stirling & Trossachs
Stirlingshire
01360 860228

Pitlochry
Craigmhor Lodge
27 West Moulin Road
Pitlochry PH16 5EF
01796 472123

Riverstown, Co Sligo
Coopershill House
Riverstown
Co Sligo
353 716 5108

467

Skibbereen, Co Cork
Liss Ard Lake Lodge
Skibbereen
Co Cork
353 282 2365

Wicklow, Co Wicklow
The Old Rectory
Wicklow Town
Co Wicklow
343 404 67048

Guernsey (Fermain Bay)
La Favorita Hotel
Fermain Bay
Guernsey GY4 6SD
01481 35666

Sligo, Co Sligo
Markree Castle
Collooney
Co Sligo
353 716 7800

Guernsey (Castel)
Les Embruns Hotel
Route De La Margion
Vazon Bay
Castel
Guernsey
01481 64834

Jersey (St Helier)
Almorah Hotel
One Almorah Crescent
Lower Kings Cliff
La Pouque Lay
St Helier, Jersey JE2 3GU
01534 21648

Straffan, Co Kildare
Barberstown Castle
Straffan
Co Kildare
353 628 8157

MINI LISTINGS: JOHANSENS HOTELS IN EUROPE

Here in brief are the entries that appear in full in Johansens 1996 Guide to Hotels in Europe. On pages 456–461 is a similar list of Johansens Recommended Inns with Restaurants 1996 and on pages 462–468 a list of Johansens Recommended Country Houses and Small Hotels.

To order any of these guides see pages 487–496.

Austria (Bad Gastein)
Hoteldorf Grüner Baum
Kötschachtal 25
5640 Bad Gastein
Austria
43 64 34 25 160

Austria (Seefeld)
Hotel Viktoria
Geigenbühelweg 589
6100 Seefeld /Tirol
Austria
43 52 12 44 41

Belgium (Marche-En-Famenne)
Château d'Hassonville
6900 Marche-En-Famenne
Belgium
32 84 31 10 25

Austria (Bad Gastein)
Thermenhotel Haus Hirt
Kaiserhofstrasse
14 Bad Gastein
Austria
43 64 34 27 97

Belgium (Bruges)
Die Swaene
1 Steenhouwersdijk
8000 Bruges
Belgium
32 50 34 27 98

British Isles (London)
The Beaufort
33 Beaufort Gardens
Knightsbridge
London
England SW3 1PP
44 171 584 5252

Austria (Bregenz)
Hotel Deuring Schlössle
Ehre-Guta-Platz 4
6900 Bregenz
Austria
43 55 74 47 800

Belgium (Bruges)
Hotel De Tuilerieen
Dijver 7
B-8000 Bruges
Belgium
32 50 34 36 91

British Isles (London)
Blakes Hotel
33 Roland Gardens
London
England SW7 3PF
44 171 370 6701

Austria (Ellmar)
Hôtel Der Bär
Kirchbichl 9
6352 Ellmar
Austria
43 53 58 23 95

Belgium (Bruges)
Hotel Prinsenhof
Ontvangersstraat 9
8000 Bruges
Belgium
32 50 34 26 90

British Isles (London)
Cannizaro House
West Side
Wimbledon Common
London
England SW19 4UE
44 181 879 1464

Austria (Igls)
Schlosshotel Igls
Villersteig 2
6080 Igls
Austria
43 51 23 77 217

Belgium (Bruges)
Relais Oud Huis Amsterdam
Spiegelrei 3
8000 Bruges
Belgium
32 50 34 18 10

British Isles (London)
The Halcyon
81 Holland Park
London
England W11 3RZ
44 171 727 7288

Austria (Igls)
Sporthotel Igls
A-6080 Igls
Austria
43 51 23 77 241

Belgium (Bruges)
Romantik Pandhotel
Pandreitje 16
8000 Bruges
Belgium
32 50 34 06 66

British Isles (London)
22 Jermyn Street
22 Jermyn Street
London
England SW1Y 6HL
44 171 734 2353

Austria (Kitzbühel)
Romantik Hotel Tennerhof
6370 Kitzbühel
Griesenauweg 26
Austria
43 53 56 31 81

Belgium (De Panne)
Hostellerie Sparrenhof
Koninginnelaan 26
8660 De Panne
Belgium
32 58 41 13 28

British Isles (London)
The Leonard
15 Seymour Street
London
England W1H 5AA
44 171 935 2010

Austria (Salzburg)
Hotel Auersperg
Auerspergstrasse 61
A-5027 Salzburg
Austria
43 66 28 89 44

Belgium (Genval)
Chateau Du Lac
Avenue Du Lac 87
1332 Genval
Belgium
32 26 55 71 11

British Isles (London)
The Milestone
1-2 Kensington Court
London
England W8 5DL
44 171 917 1000

Austria (Salzburg)
Hotel Schloss Mönchstein
Mönchsberg Park, 26
5020 Salzburg City Center
Austria
43 66 28 48 55 50

Belgium (Habay-La-Neuve)
Les Ardilliéres Du Pont D'Oye
6 Rue Du Pont D'Oye
6720 Habay-La-Neuve
Belgium
32 63 42 22 43

British Isles (London)
Number Sixteen
16 Sumner Place
London
England SW7 3EG
44 171 589 5232

Austria (Schwarzenberg)
Romantik-Hotel Gasthof Hirschen
Hof 14
6867 Schwarzenberg im-
Bregenzerwald
Austria
43 55 12/29 44 0

Belgium (Malmedy)
Hostellerie Trôs Marets
Route Des Trôs Marets
4960 Malmedy
Belgium
32 80 33 79 17

British Isles (London)
The Savoy
The Strand
London
England WC2R 0EU
44 171 836 4343

Cyprus (Paphos)
The Annabelle
P.O. Box 401
Paphos
Cyprus
35 76 23 8 3 33

France (Chamonix)
Hotel Albert 1er
119 Impasse du Montenvers
74402 Chamonix-Mont Blanc
France
33 50 55 05 09

France (Gordes)
Hostellerie Le Phebus
Joucas
84220 Gordes
France
33 90 05 78 83

Czech Republic (Prague)
Hotel Palace Praha
Panska 12
11121 Prague
Czech Republic
42 22 40 93 111

France (Champigné)
Chateau Des Briottières
49330 Champigné
France
33 41 42 00 02

France (La Baule)
Le Castel Marie-Louise
1 Avenue Andrieu
44504 La Baule
France
33 40 11 48 38

Denmark (Faaborg)
Steensgaard Herregardspension
Steensgaard
5600 Millinge
Faaborg
Denmark
45 62 61 94 90

France (Chenehutte-Les-Tuffeaux)
Le Prieure
Chenehutte-Les-Tuffeaux
49350 Gennes
France
33 41 67 90 14

France (Lyon)
La Tour Rose
22 Rue du Boeuf
69005 Lyon
France
33 78 37 25 90

Denmark (GL. Skagen)
Strandhotellet
Jeckelsvej 2
9990 GL. Skagen
Denmark
45 98 44 34 99

France (Colmar)
Romantik Hostellerie Le Maréchal
4-6 Place Des Six Montagnes Noires
68000 Colmar
France
33 89 41 60 32

France (Monestier)
Château Des Vigiers
24240 Monestier
Dordogne
France
33 53 61 50 30

France (Arles)
Le Mas De Peint
Le Sambuc
13200 Arles
France
33 90 97 20 62

France (Connelles)
Le Moulin De Connelles
40 Route d'Amfreville-Sous-Les-Monts
27430 Connelles
France
33 32 59 53 33

France (Nancy)
Grand Hotel De La Reine
2 Place Stanislas
54000 Nancy
France
33 83 35 03 01

France (Avignon)
Auberge de Cassagne
450 Allée de Cassagne
84130 Le Pontet
Avignon
France
33 90 31 04 18

France (Courchevel)
Hotel Annapurna
73120 Courchevel (1850)
France
33 79 08 04 60

France (Nice)
Hotel La Pérouse
11 Quai Rauba-Capeu
06300 Nice
France
33 93 62 34 63

France (Avignon)
Auberge De Noves
13550 Noves
France
33 90 94 19 21

France (Courchevel)
Hotel Des Neiges
Rue de Bellecote
BP 96
73121 Courchevel (1850 Cedex)
France
33 79 08 03 77

France (Normandy)
Chateau Du Tertre
St Martin de Mieux
14700 Falaise
Normandy
France
33 31 90 01 04

France (Biarritz)
Hotel Du Palais
1 Avenue De L'Impératrice
64200 Biarritz
France
33 59 41 64 00

France (Courchevel)
Hôtel Des Trois Vallées
BP 22
73122 Courchevel (Cedex)
France
33 79 08 00 12

France (Paimpol)
Relais Brenner
Kergrist
Route de Saint-Julien
Pont de Lézardrieux
22500 Paimpol
France
33 96 20 11 05

France (Cannes)
Hotel L'Horset Savoy
5 Rue François Einesy
06400 Cannes
France
33 92 99 72 00

France (Deauville)
Hotel Royal
Boulevard Cornuché
14800 Deauville
Calvados
France
33 31 98 66 33

France (Paris)
Hotel Du Roy
8 Rue Francois 1er
75008 Paris
France
331 42 89 59 59

France (Cannes)
Hotel Majestic
14 La Croisette
06400 Cannes
France
33 92 98 77 00

France (Épernay)
Hostellerie La Briqueterie
4 Route de Sézanne
Vinay 51530
Épernay
France
33 26 59 99 99

France (Paris)
Hotel L'Horset Opera
18 Rue d'Antin
75002 Paris
France
331 44 71 87 00

France (Chambolle-Musigny)
Château Hôtel André Ziltener
Rue de la Fontaine
21220 Chambolle-Musigny
Côte d'Or
France
33 80 62 41 62

France (Eze Village)
Château Eza
Rue De La Pise
06360 Eze Village
France
33 93 41 12 24

France (Paris)
Hotel Lancaster
7 Rue de Berri
Champs Elysees
75008 Paris
France
331 40 76 40 76

France (Paris)
Hotel Royal Saint-Honoré
221 Rue Saint-Honoré
75001 Paris
France
331 42 60 32 79

France (Saint Paul)
Mas d'Artigny
Route de la Colle
06570 Saint-Paul
France
33 93 32 84 54

Germany (Dresden)
Bülow Residenz
Rähnitzgasse 19
01097 Dresden
Germany
49 35 14 40 33

France (Paris)
Montalembert
3 Rue de Montalembert
75007 Paris
France
331 45 48 68 11

France (Saint-Paul-De-Vence)
Le Saint-Paul
86 Rue Grande
06570 Saint-Paul-De-Vence
France
33 93 32 65 25

Germany (Garmisch-Partenkirchen)
Post-Hotel Garmisch Partenkirchen
Ludwigstrasse 49
8100 Garmisch-Partenkirchen
Germany
49 88 21 51 067

France (Paris)
Pavillon De La Reine
28 Place des Vosges
75003 Paris
France
331 42 77 96 40

France (St Rémy-de-Provence)
Château Des Alpilles
Route Départementale 31
Ancienne route du Grès
13210 St Rémy-de-Provence
France
33 90 92 03 33

Germany (Hamburg)
Kempinski Hotel Atlantic Hamburg
An Der Alster 72-79
20099 Hamburg
Germany
49 40 28 880

France (Paris)
Relais Christine
3 Rue Christine
75006 Paris
France
331 43 26 71 80

France (St Remy-de-Provence)
Hostellerie Du Vallon De Valrugues
Chemin Canto Cigalo
13210 St Remy-de-Provence
France
33 90 92 04 40

Germany (Kettwig)
Schlosshotel Hugenpoet
August-Thyssen Strasse-51
45219 Essen-Kettwig
Germany
49 20 54 12 040

France (Paris)
Relais St Germain
9 Carrefour de L'Odéon
75006 Paris
France
331 43 29 12 05

Germany (Alt Duvenstedt)
Hotel Töpferhaus
AM Bistensee
24791 Alt Duvenstedt
Germany
49 43 38 33 3

Germany (Oberwesel/Rhein)
Burghotel Auf Schönburg
55430 Oberwesel/Rhein
Germany
49 67 44 70 27

France (Paris)
Royal Hôtel
33 Avenue Friedland
75008 Paris
France
331 43 59 08 14

Germany (Bad Herrenbald)
Mönchs Posthotel
76328 Bad Herrenbald
Germany
49 70 83 74 40

Germany (Pegnitz)
Pflaums Posthotel Pegnitz
Nurmbergerstasse 12-16
91257 Pegnitz
Fränkische Schweiz
Germany
49 92 41 72 50

France (Paris)
Saint James-Paris
43 Avenue Bugeaud
75116 Paris
France
331 44 05 81 81

Germany (Bad Salzuflen)
Hotel Arminius
32105 Bad Salzuflen
Ritterstrasse 2-8
Germany
49 52 22 5 3 070

Germany (Plauen)
Hotel Alexandra
Bahnhofstrasse 17
08523 Plauen
Germany
49 37 41 22 67 47

France (Paris)
Les Suites Saint Honoré
13 Rue d'Aguesseau
75008 Paris
France
331 44 51 16 35

Germany (Baden Baden)
Der Kleine Prinz
Lichtentaler Strasse 36
76530 Baden Baden
Germany
49 72 21 34 64

Germany (Schlangenbad)
Parkhotel Schlangenbad
Rheingauer Strasse 47
65388 Schlangenbad
Germany
49 61 29 420

France (Port-en-Bessin)
La Cheneviére
Escures-Commes
14520 Port-en-Bessin
France
33 31 21 47 96

Germany (Baden Baden)
Schlosshotel Buhlerhöhe
Schwarzwaldhochstrasse 1
77815 Baden Baden/Bühl
Germany
49 72 26/55-0

Germany (Westerland/Sylt)
Hôtel Stadt Hamburg
Strandstrasse 2
D-25980 Westerland/Sylt
Germany
49 46 51 85 80

France (Roquebrune/Cap-Martin)
Vista Palace Hotel
Route De La Grande Corniche
06190 Roquebrune/Cap-Martin
France
33 92 10 40 00

Germany (Berlin)
Hotel Brandenburger Hof
Eislebener Strasse 14
10789 Berlin
Germany
49 30 21 40 50

Gibraltar
The Rock Hotel
3 Europa Road
Gibraltar
350 73 000

France (Saint-Emilion)
Hotel Château Grand Barrail
Route de Libourne
33330 Saint-Emilion
France
33 57 55 37 00

Germany (Berlin)
Kempinski Hotel Bristol
Kurfürstendamm 27
10719 Berlin
Germany
49 30 88 43 47 34

Hungary (Budapest)
Hotel Gellért
Gellért Tér 1
H-1111 Budapest
Hungary
36 11 85 22 00

Italy (Ferrara)
Ripagrande Hotel
Via Ripagrande 21
44100 Ferrara
Italy
39 53 27 65 250

Italy (Venice)
Hotel Cipriani & Palazzo Vendramin
Giudecca 10
30133 Venice
Italy
39 41 52 07 744

Spain (Mallorca)
Hotel La Residencia
Deia
Mallorca
Spain
34 71 63 90 11

Italy (Florence)
Hotel Albani
Via Fiume 12
50123 Florence
Italy
39 55 26 031

Italy (Venice)
Hotel Londra Palace
Riva degli Schiavoni
30122 Venice
Italy
39 41 52 00 533

Spain (Salamanca)
Residencia Rector
10 Rector Esparabé
Apartado 399
37008 Salamanca
Spain
34 23 21 84 82

Italy (Florence)
Hotel Regency
Piazza Massimo D'Azeglio 3
50121 Florence
Italy
39 55 24 52 47

Italy (Sicily)
Romantic Hotel Villa Ducale
Via Leonardo Da Vinci 60
98039 Taormina
Sicily
Italy
39 942/28 153

Spain (Seville)
Casa De Carmona
Plaza de Lasso
41410 Carmona
Seville
Spain
34 54 14 33 00

Italy (Marling/Meran)
Romantic Hotel Oberwirt
St Felixwegz 2
39020 Marling/Meran
Italy
39 47 32 22 020

Luxembourg (Berdorf)
Parc Hotel
16 Rue De Grundhof
L-6550 Berdorf
Luxembourg
35 27 91 95

Spain (Tenerife)
Gran Hotel Bahia Del Duque
Playa Del Duque
Tenerife
Canary Islands
34 22 71 30 00

Italy (Naples)
Albergo Miramare
Via Nazario Sauro 24
80132 Naples
Italy
39 81 76 47 589

Monaco (Monte Carlo)
Hotel Mirabeau
1 Avenue Princess Grace
98007 Monte Carlo
Monaco
33 92 16 65 65

Switzerland (Basel)
Hotel Basel
Am Spalenberg
Münzgasse12
4051 Basel
Switzerland
41 61 26 46 800

Italy (Porto Ercole)
Hotel Il Pellicano
Localita Lo Sbarcatello
58018 Porto Ercole (GR)
Italy
39 56 48 33 801

Netherlands (Amsterdam)
Hotel Ambassade
Herengracht 341
1016 AL
Amsterdam
Netherlands
31 20 62 62 333

Switzerland (Grindelwald)
Romantik Hotel Schweizerhof
3818 Grindelwald
Switzerland
41 36 53 22 02

Italy (Rome)
Hotel Farnese
Via Alessandro Farnese 30
(Anglo Viale Giulio Cesare)
00192 Rome
Italy
39 63 21 25 53

Portugal (Lisbon)
As Janelas Verdes
Rua das Janelas Verdes 47
1200 Lisbon
Portugal
35 11 39 68 143

Switzerland (Lucerne)
Hotel Wilden Mann
Bahnhofstrasse 30
6000 Lucerne 7
Switzerland
41 210 16 66

Italy (Rome)
Hotel Lord Byron
Via Guiseppe De Notaris 5
00197 Rome
Italy
39 63 22 04 04

Portugal (Madeira)
Reid's Hotel
P-9000 Funchal
Madeira
Portugal
44 1256 841155

Switzerland (Morges)
La Fleur Du Lac
70 Route de Lausanne
Quai I Stravinsky
1110 Morges
Switzerland
41 21 80 24 314

Italy (Rome)
Hotel Majestic Roma
Via Veneto 50
00187 Rome
Italy
39 64 86 841

Russian Federation (Moscow)
Hotel Baltschug Kempinski Moskau
UL Baltschug 1
113035 Moscow
Russian Federation
7 501 230 6500

Switzerland (Zous)
Posthotel Engiadina
Via Maistra
Zous
Switzerland
41 82 71 021

Italy (Rome)
Hotel Raphaël
Largo Febo 2
Piazza Navona
00186 Rome
Italy
39 66 82 831

Slovenia (Bled)
Hotel Vila Bled
Cesta Svobode 26
64260 Bled
Slovenia
38 66 47 915

Italy (Venice)
Albergo Quattro Fontane
Via Delle Quattro Fontane, N16
30126 (Lido di Venezia)
Italy
39 41 52 60 227

Spain (Ibiza)
Pikes
San Antonio De Portmany
Isla De Ibiza
Balearic Islands
Spain
34 71 34 22 22

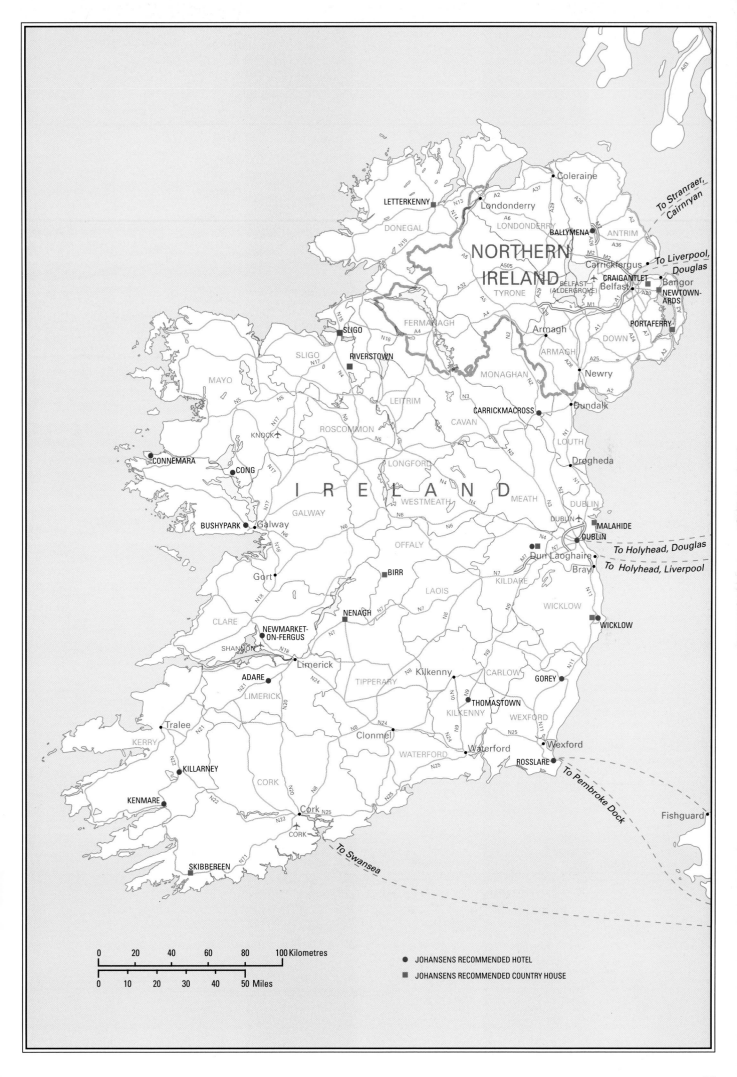

NORTHERN IRELAND

IRELAND

To Stranraer, Cairnryan

To Liverpool, Douglas

To Holyhead, Douglas

To Holyhead, Liverpool

To Pembroke Dock

To Swansea

- Coleraine
- LETTERKENNY
- Londonderry
- BALLYMENA
- Carrickfergus
- CRAIGANTLET
- Bangor
- Belfast
- BELFAST (ALDERGROVE)
- NEWTOWN-ARDS
- PORTAFERRY
- Armagh
- Newry
- Dundalk
- SLIGO
- RIVERSTOWN
- CARRICKMACROSS
- Drogheda
- CONNEMARA
- CONG
- Knock
- BUSHYPARK
- Galway
- DUBLIN
- DUBLIN
- MALAHIDE
- Dun Laoghaire
- Bray
- Gort
- BIRR
- NENAGH
- WICKLOW
- NEWMARKET-ON-FERGUS
- SHANNON
- Limerick
- ADARE
- Kilkenny
- GOREY
- Tralee
- THOMASTOWN
- Clonmel
- Waterford
- Wexford
- KILLARNEY
- ROSSLARE
- KENMARE
- Cork
- CORK
- SKIBBEREEN
- Fishguard

DONEGAL
ANTRIM
TYRONE
FERMANAGH
LONDONDERRY
DOWN
ARMAGH
MONAGHAN
SLIGO
MAYO
LEITRIM
CAVAN
ROSCOMMON
LONGFORD
LOUTH
MEATH
GALWAY
WESTMEATH
OFFALY
DUBLIN
LAOIS
KILDARE
CLARE
WICKLOW
TIPPERARY
LIMERICK
CARLOW
KILKENNY
WEXFORD
KERRY
WATERFORD
CORK

| 0 | 20 | 40 | 60 | 80 | 100 Kilometres |

| 0 | 10 | 20 | 30 | 40 | 50 Miles |

● JOHANSENS RECOMMENDED HOTEL

■ JOHANSENS RECOMMENDED COUNTRY HOUSE

ISLES OF SCILLY

JOHANSENS RECOMMENDED HOTEL
JOHANSENS RECOMMENDED INN OR RESTAURANT
JOHANSENS RECOMMENDED COUNTRY HOUSE

To Dublin/
Dun Laoghaire

To Rosslare

To Rosslare

To Cork

To Santander

To Roscoff

To Guernsey

0   20   40   60   80   100 Kilometres
0   10   20   30   40   50 Miles

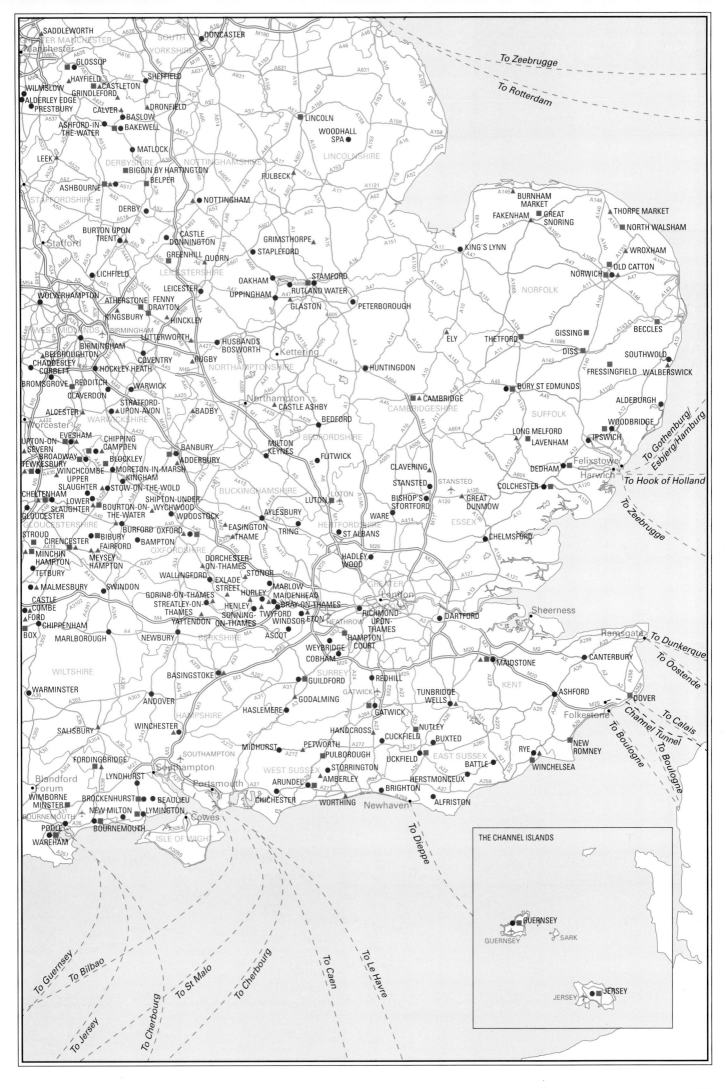

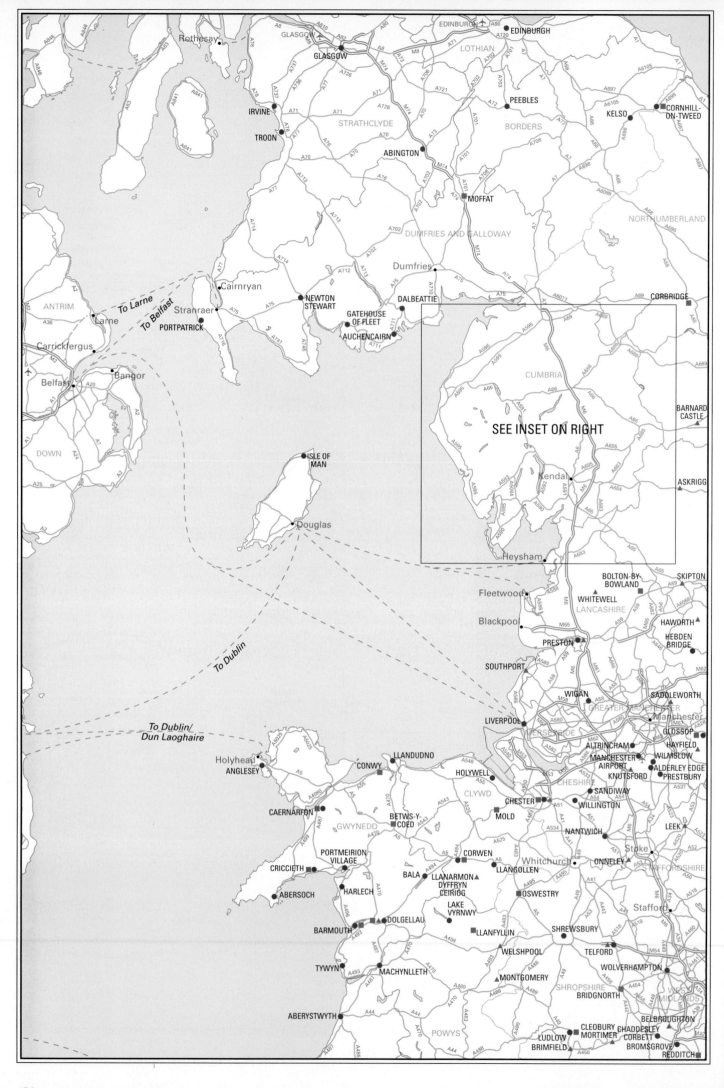

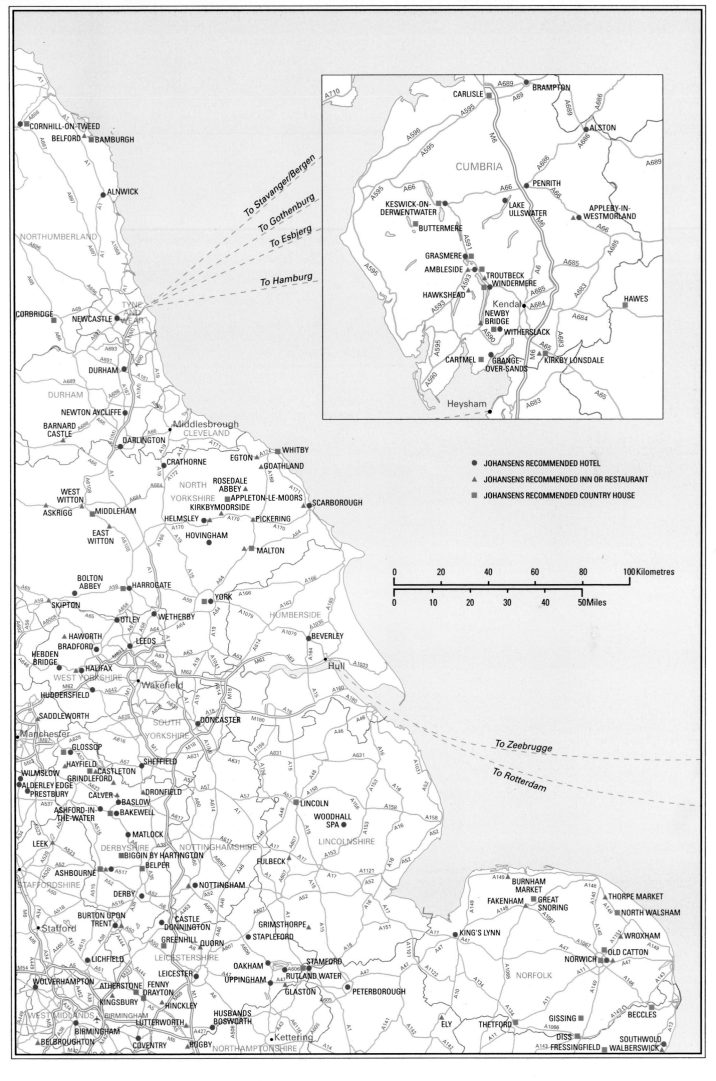

JOHANSENS RECOMMENDED HOTEL

JOHANSENS RECOMMENDED INN OR RESTAURANT

JOHANSENS RECOMMENDED COUNTRY HOUSE

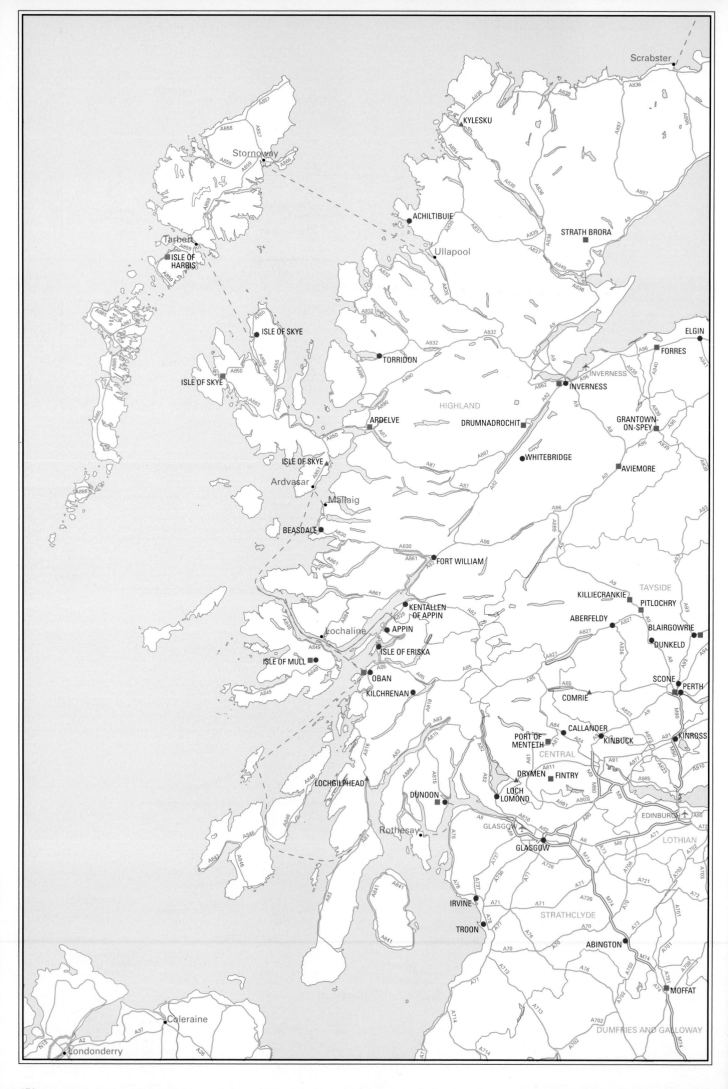

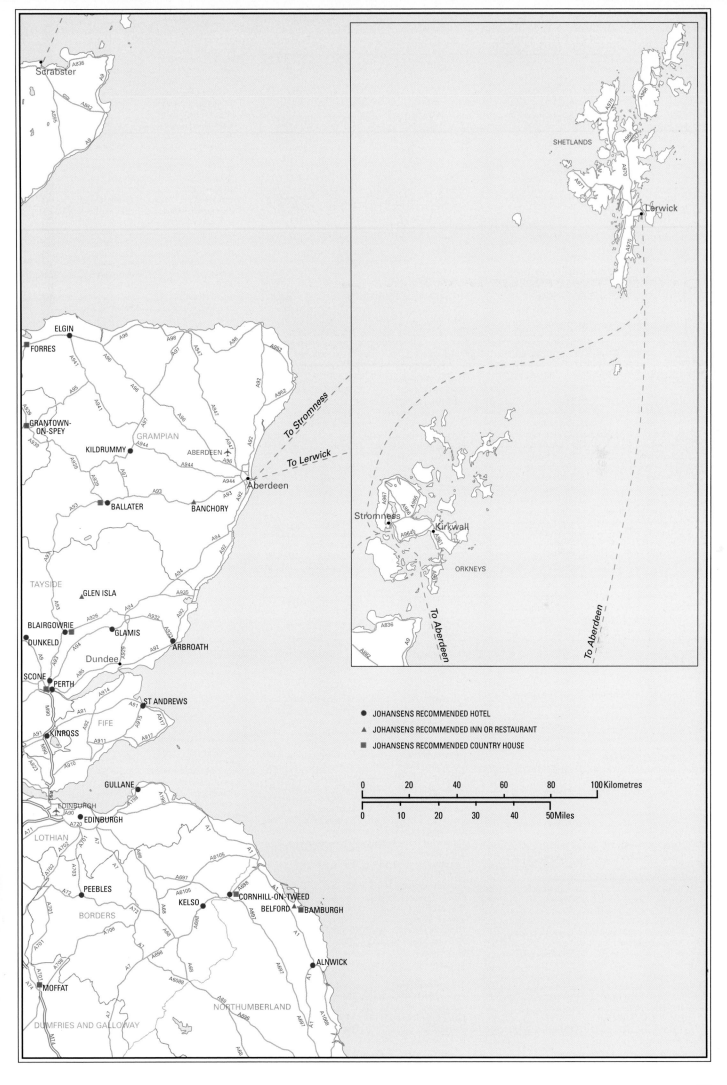

JOHANSENS RECOMMENDED HOTEL

JOHANSENS RECOMMENDED INN OR RESTAURANT

JOHANSENS RECOMMENDED COUNTRY HOUSE

| 0 | 20 | 40 | 60 | 80 | 100 Kilometres |

| 0 | 10 | 20 | 30 | 40 | 50 Miles |

To enable you to use your 1996 Johansens Recommended Hotels Guide more effectively the following pages of indexes contain a wealth of useful information about the hotels featured in the guide. As well as listing the hotels alphabetically by region and by county, the indexes also show at a glance which hotels offer certain specialised facilities.

The indexes are as follows:

- By region
- By county
- With a heated indoor swimming pool
- With a golf course on site
- With shooting arranged
- With salmon or trout fishing on site
- With health/fitness facilities
- With childcare facilities
- With conference facilities for 250 delegates or more

- Relais et Châteaux members
- Small Luxury Hotels of the World members
- Pride of Britain members
- Exclusive Hotels members
- Taste of Wales members
- Welsh Gold Collection members
- Index of advertisers

1996 Johansens Recommended Hotels listed by region

1996 Johansens Recommended Hotels by county

HOW TO ORDER YOUR JOHANSENS GUIDES

Our 24-hour FREEPHONE number may be used to place an order for copies of Johansens Recommended Guides.

FREEPHONE 0800 269397

Hotels with health/fitness facilities

At the following hotels there are health/fitness facilities available

LONDON

ENGLAND

WALES

SCOTLAND

IRELAND

CHANNEL ISLANDS

Hotels with childcare facilities

Comprehensive childcare facilities are available, namely crèche, babysitting and organised activities for children of all ages

LONDON

ENGLAND

SCOTLAND

IRELAND

Hotels with conference facilities

These hotels can accommodate theatre-style conferences for 250 delegates or over

LONDON

ENGLAND

WALES

SCOTLAND

IRELAND

Relais et Châteaux members

Small Luxury Hotels of the World members

Pride of Britain members

PLAY THE ROLE OF HOTEL INSPECTOR!

*A*t the back of this book you will notice a quantity of Guest Survey Forms. If you have had an enjoyable stay at one of our recommended hotels, or alternatively you have been in some way disappointed, please complete one of these forms and send it to us FREEPOST.

These reports essentially complement the assessments made by our team of professional inspectors, continually monitoring the standards of hospitality in every establishment in our guides.

Guest Survey reports also have an important influence on the selection of nominations for our annual awards for excellence.

'Diversity and excellence for the discerning traveller'.

GUEST SURVEY REPORT

Name and location of hotel: _____ Date of visit: _____

Name and address of guest: _____

_____ Postcode: _____

Please tick one box in each category below:	Excellent	Good	Disappointing	Poor
Bedrooms				
Public Rooms				
Restaurant/Cuisine				
Service				
Welcome/Friendliness				
Value For Money				

PLEASE return your Guest Survey Report form!

Occasionally we may allow other reputable organisations to write with offers which may be of interest.

If you prefer not to here from them, tick this box ☐

To: Johansens, FREEPOST (CB264), 175-179 St John Street, London EC1B 1JQ

Your own Johansens 'inspection' gives reliability to our guides and assists in the selection of Award Nominations

GUEST SURVEY REPORT

Name and location of hotel: _____ Date of visit: _____

Name and address of guest: _____

_____ Postcode: _____

Please tick one box in each category below:	Excellent	Good	Disappointing	Poor
Bedrooms				
Public Rooms				
Restaurant/Cuisine				
Service				
Welcome/Friendliness				
Value For Money				

PLEASE return your Guest Survey Report form!

Occasionally we may allow other reputable organisations to write with offers which may be of interest.

If you prefer not to here from them, tick this box ☐

To: Johansens, FREEPOST (CB264), 175-179 St John Street, London EC1B 1JQ

Your own Johansens 'inspection' gives reliability to our guides and assists in the selection of Award Nominations

GUEST SURVEY REPORT

Name and location of hotel: _____ Date of visit: _____

Name and address of guest: _____

_____ Postcode: _____

Please tick one box in each category below:	Excellent	Good	Disappointing	Poor
Bedrooms				
Public Rooms				
Restaurant/Cuisine				
Service				
Welcome/Friendliness				
Value For Money				

PLEASE return your Guest Survey Report form!

Occasionally we may allow other reputable organisations to write with offers which may be of interest.

If you prefer not to here from them, tick this box ☐

To: Johansens, FREEPOST (CB264), 175-179 St John Street, London EC1B 1JQ

Your own Johansens 'inspection' gives reliability to our guides and assists in the selection of Award Nominations

Order Coupon

To order Johansens guides, simply indicate which publications you require by putting the quantity(ies) in the boxes provided. Choose you preferred method of payment and return this coupon (NO STAMP REQUIRED). You may also place your order using FREEPHONE 0800 269397 or by fax on 0171 490 2538.

❏ I enclose a cheque for £_____ payable to Biblios PDS Ltd (Johansens book distributor).

❏ I enclose my order on company letterheading, please invoice me. (UK companies only)

❏ Please debit my credit/charge card account (please tick)

❏ MASTERCARD ❏ VISA ❏ DINERS ❏ AMEX

Card Number _____

Signature _____ Expiry Date _____
Name (Mr/Mrs/Miss) _____
Address _____
_____
_____ Postcode _____

(We aim to despatch your order with 10 days, but please allow 28 days for delivery)

Occasionally we may allow reputable organisations to write to you with offers which may interest you. If you prefer not to hear from them, tick this box ❏

CALL THE JOHANSENS CREDIT CARD ORDER SERVICE FREE ☎ 0800 269397

	WHEN YOU BUY A SET OF ALL THREE 1996 UK JOHANSENS GUIDES	PRICE	QTY	TOTAL
save £10		£35.80		
	Boxed presentation set of three 1996 UK Johansens guides with slip case	£39.00		
	Johansens Recommended Hotels in Great Britain & Ireland 1996	£21.90		
	Johansens Recommended Inns with Restaurants in Great Britain 1996	£11.95		
	Johansens Recommended Country Houses and Small Hotels in Great Britain & Ireland 1996	£11.95		
	Johansens Recommended Hotels in Europe 1996	£11.95		

ALL PRICES INCLUDE HANDLING AND UK POSTAGE ONLY 36J

Outside the UK add £3 for each single guide ordered, or £5 for a set or boxed set to cover additional postage. *PRICES VALID UNTIL 31/12/96*

Post free to:
JOHANSENS, FREEPOST (CB264), HORSHAM, WEST SUSSEX RH13 8ZA

Order Coupon

To order Johansens guides, simply indicate which publications you require by putting the quantity(ies) in the boxes provided. Choose you preferred method of payment and return this coupon (NO STAMP REQUIRED). You may also place your order using FREEPHONE 0800 269397 or by fax on 0171 490 2538.

❏ I enclose a cheque for £_____ payable to Biblios PDS Ltd (Johansens book distributor).

❏ I enclose my order on company letterheading, please invoice me. (UK companies only)

❏ Please debit my credit/charge card account (please tick)

❏ MASTERCARD ❏ VISA ❏ DINERS ❏ AMEX

Card Number _____

Signature _____ Expiry Date _____
Name (Mr/Mrs/Miss) _____
Address _____
_____
_____ Postcode _____

(We aim to despatch your order with 10 days, but please allow 28 days for delivery)

Occasionally we may allow reputable organisations to write to you with offers which may interest you. If you prefer not to hear from them, tick this box ❏

CALL THE JOHANSENS CREDIT CARD ORDER SERVICE FREE ☎ 0800 269397

	WHEN YOU BUY A SET OF ALL THREE 1996 UK JOHANSENS GUIDES	PRICE	QTY	TOTAL
save £10		£35.80		
	Boxed presentation set of three 1996 UK Johansens guides with slip case	£39.00		
	Johansens Recommended Hotels in Great Britain & Ireland 1996	£21.90		
	Johansens Recommended Inns with Restaurants in Great Britain 1996	£11.95		
	Johansens Recommended Country Houses and Small Hotels in Great Britain & Ireland 1996	£11.95		
	Johansens Recommended Hotels in Europe 1996	£11.95		

ALL PRICES INCLUDE HANDLING AND UK POSTAGE ONLY 36J

Outside the UK add £3 for each single guide ordered, or £5 for a set or boxed set to cover additional postage. *PRICES VALID UNTIL 31/12/96*

Post free to:
JOHANSENS, FREEPOST (CB264), HORSHAM, WEST SUSSEX RH13 8ZA

Order Coupon

To order Johansens guides, simply indicate which publications you require by putting the quantity(ies) in the boxes provided. Choose you preferred method of payment and return this coupon (NO STAMP REQUIRED). You may also place your order using FREEPHONE 0800 269397 or by fax on 0171 490 2538.

❏ I enclose a cheque for £_____ payable to Biblios PDS Ltd (Johansens book distributor).

❏ I enclose my order on company letterheading, please invoice me. (UK companies only)

❏ Please debit my credit/charge card account (please tick)

❏ MASTERCARD ❏ VISA ❏ DINERS ❏ AMEX

Card Number _____

Signature _____ Expiry Date _____
Name (Mr/Mrs/Miss) _____
Address _____
_____
_____ Postcode _____

(We aim to despatch your order with 10 days, but please allow 28 days for delivery)

Occasionally we may allow reputable organisations to write to you with offers which may interest you. If you prefer not to hear from them, tick this box ❏

CALL THE JOHANSENS CREDIT CARD ORDER SERVICE FREE ☎ 0800 269397

	WHEN YOU BUY A SET OF ALL THREE 1996 UK JOHANSENS GUIDES	PRICE	QTY	TOTAL
save £10		£35.80		
	Boxed presentation set of three 1996 UK Johansens guides with slip case	£39.00		
	Johansens Recommended Hotels in Great Britain & Ireland 1996	£21.90		
	Johansens Recommended Inns with Restaurants in Great Britain 1996	£11.95		
	Johansens Recommended Country Houses and Small Hotels in Great Britain & Ireland 1996	£11.95		
	Johansens Recommended Hotels in Europe 1996	£11.95		

ALL PRICES INCLUDE HANDLING AND UK POSTAGE ONLY 36J

Outside the UK add £3 for each single guide ordered, or £5 for a set or boxed set to cover additional postage. *PRICES VALID UNTIL 31/12/96*

Post free to:
JOHANSENS, FREEPOST (CB264), HORSHAM, WEST SUSSEX RH13 8ZA

GUEST SURVEY REPORT

Name and location of hotel: _____ Date of visit: _____

Name and address of guest: _____

_____ Postcode: _____

Please tick one box in each category below:	Excellent	Good	Disappointing	Poor
Bedrooms				
Public Rooms				
Restaurant/Cuisine				
Service				
Welcome/Friendliness				
Value For Money				

PLEASE return your Guest Survey Report form!

Occasionally we may allow other reputable organisations to write with offers which may be of interest.

If you prefer not to here from them, tick this box ☐

To: Johansens, FREEPOST (CB264), 175-179 St John Street, London EC1B 1JQ

Your own Johansens 'inspection' gives reliability to our guides and assists in the selection of Award Nominations

- -

GUEST SURVEY REPORT

Name and location of hotel: _____ Date of visit: _____

Name and address of guest: _____

_____ Postcode: _____

Please tick one box in each category below:	Excellent	Good	Disappointing	Poor
Bedrooms				
Public Rooms				
Restaurant/Cuisine				
Service				
Welcome/Friendliness				
Value For Money				

PLEASE return your Guest Survey Report form!

Occasionally we may allow other reputable organisations to write with offers which may be of interest.

If you prefer not to here from them, tick this box ☐

To: Johansens, FREEPOST (CB264), 175-179 St John Street, London EC1B 1JQ

Your own Johansens 'inspection' gives reliability to our guides and assists in the selection of Award Nominations

- -

GUEST SURVEY REPORT

Name and location of hotel: _____ Date of visit: _____

Name and address of guest: _____

_____ Postcode: _____

Please tick one box in each category below:	Excellent	Good	Disappointing	Poor
Bedrooms				
Public Rooms				
Restaurant/Cuisine				
Service				
Welcome/Friendliness				
Value For Money				

PLEASE return your Guest Survey Report form!

Occasionally we may allow other reputable organisations to write with offers which may be of interest.

If you prefer not to here from them, tick this box ☐

To: Johansens, FREEPOST (CB264), 175-179 St John Street, London EC1B 1JQ

Your own Johansens 'inspection' gives reliability to our guides and assists in the selection of Award Nominations

Order Coupon

To order Johansens guides, simply indicate which publications you require by putting the quantity(ies) in the boxes provided. Choose you preferred method of payment and return this coupon (NO STAMP REQUIRED). You may also place your order using FREEPHONE 0800 269397 or by fax on 0171 490 2538.

❑ I enclose a cheque for £_____ payable to Biblios PDS Ltd (Johansens book distributor).

❑ I enclose my order on company letterheading, please invoice me. (UK companies only)

❑ Please debit my credit/charge card account (please tick)

❑ MASTERCARD ❑ VISA ❑ DINERS ❑ AMEX

Card Number _____

Signature _____ Expiry Date _____

Name (Mr/Mrs/Miss) _____

Address _____

_____

_____ Postcode _____

(We aim to despatch your order with 10 days, but please allow 28 days for delivery)

Occasionally we may allow reputable organisations to write to you with offers which may interest you. If you prefer not to hear from them, tick this box ❑

CALL THE JOHANSENS CREDIT CARD ORDER SERVICE FREE ☎ **0800 269397**

save £10 WHEN YOU BUY A SET OF ALL THREE 1996 UK JOHANSENS GUIDES	PRICE	QTY	TOTAL
save £10 WHEN YOU BUY A SET OF ALL THREE 1996 UK JOHANSENS GUIDES	£35.80		
Boxed presentation set of three 1996 UK Johansens guides with slip case	£39.00		
Johansens Recommended Hotels in Great Britain & Ireland 1996	£21.90		
Johansens Recommended Inns with Restaurants in Great Britain 1996	£11.95		
Johansens Recommended Country Houses and Small Hotels in Great Britain & Ireland 1996	£11.95		
Johansens Recommended Hotels in Europe 1996	£11.95		

ALL PRICES INCLUDE HANDLING AND UK POSTAGE ONLY   36J

Outside the UK add £3 for each single guide ordered, or £5 for a set or boxed set to cover additional postage.   *PRICES VALID UNTIL 31/12/96*

Post free to:
JOHANSENS, FREEPOST (CB264), HORSHAM, WEST SUSSEX RH13 8ZA

Order Coupon

To order Johansens guides, simply indicate which publications you require by putting the quantity(ies) in the boxes provided. Choose you preferred method of payment and return this coupon (NO STAMP REQUIRED). You may also place your order using FREEPHONE 0800 269397 or by fax on 0171 490 2538.

❑ I enclose a cheque for £_____ payable to Biblios PDS Ltd (Johansens book distributor).

❑ I enclose my order on company letterheading, please invoice me. (UK companies only)

❑ Please debit my credit/charge card account (please tick)

❑ MASTERCARD ❑ VISA ❑ DINERS ❑ AMEX

Card Number _____

Signature _____ Expiry Date _____

Name (Mr/Mrs/Miss) _____

Address _____

_____

_____ Postcode _____

(We aim to despatch your order with 10 days, but please allow 28 days for delivery)

Occasionally we may allow reputable organisations to write to you with offers which may interest you. If you prefer not to hear from them, tick this box ❑

CALL THE JOHANSENS CREDIT CARD ORDER SERVICE FREE ☎ **0800 269397**

save £10 WHEN YOU BUY A SET OF ALL THREE 1996 UK JOHANSENS GUIDES	PRICE	QTY	TOTAL
save £10 WHEN YOU BUY A SET OF ALL THREE 1996 UK JOHANSENS GUIDES	£35.80		
Boxed presentation set of three 1996 UK Johansens guides with slip case	£39.00		
Johansens Recommended Hotels in Great Britain & Ireland 1996	£21.90		
Johansens Recommended Inns with Restaurants in Great Britain 1996	£11.95		
Johansens Recommended Country Houses and Small Hotels in Great Britain & Ireland 1996	£11.95		
Johansens Recommended Hotels in Europe 1996	£11.95		

ALL PRICES INCLUDE HANDLING AND UK POSTAGE ONLY   36J

Outside the UK add £3 for each single guide ordered, or £5 for a set or boxed set to cover additional postage.   *PRICES VALID UNTIL 31/12/96*

Post free to:
JOHANSENS, FREEPOST (CB264), HORSHAM, WEST SUSSEX RH13 8ZA

Order Coupon

To order Johansens guides, simply indicate which publications you require by putting the quantity(ies) in the boxes provided. Choose you preferred method of payment and return this coupon (NO STAMP REQUIRED). You may also place your order using FREEPHONE 0800 269397 or by fax on 0171 490 2538.

❑ I enclose a cheque for £_____ payable to Biblios PDS Ltd (Johansens book distributor).

❑ I enclose my order on company letterheading, please invoice me. (UK companies only)

❑ Please debit my credit/charge card account (please tick)

❑ MASTERCARD ❑ VISA ❑ DINERS ❑ AMEX

Card Number _____

Signature _____ Expiry Date _____

Name (Mr/Mrs/Miss) _____

Address _____

_____

_____ Postcode _____

(We aim to despatch your order with 10 days, but please allow 28 days for delivery)

Occasionally we may allow reputable organisations to write to you with offers which may interest you. If you prefer not to hear from them, tick this box ❑

CALL THE JOHANSENS CREDIT CARD ORDER SERVICE FREE ☎ **0800 269397**

save £10 WHEN YOU BUY A SET OF ALL THREE 1996 UK JOHANSENS GUIDES	PRICE	QTY	TOTAL
save £10 WHEN YOU BUY A SET OF ALL THREE 1996 UK JOHANSENS GUIDES	£35.80		
Boxed presentation set of three 1996 UK Johansens guides with slip case	£39.00		
Johansens Recommended Hotels in Great Britain & Ireland 1996	£21.90		
Johansens Recommended Inns with Restaurants in Great Britain 1996	£11.95		
Johansens Recommended Country Houses and Small Hotels in Great Britain & Ireland 1996	£11.95		
Johansens Recommended Hotels in Europe 1996	£11.95		

ALL PRICES INCLUDE HANDLING AND UK POSTAGE ONLY   36J

Outside the UK add £3 for each single guide ordered, or £5 for a set or boxed set to cover additional postage.   *PRICES VALID UNTIL 31/12/96*

Post free to:
JOHANSENS, FREEPOST (CB264), HORSHAM, WEST SUSSEX RH13 8ZA

GUEST SURVEY REPORT

Name and location of hotel: _____ Date of visit: _____

Name and address of guest: _____

_____ Postcode: _____

Please tick one box in each category below:	Excellent	Good	Disappointing	Poor
Bedrooms				
Public Rooms				
Restaurant/Cuisine				
Service				
Welcome/Friendliness				
Value For Money				

PLEASE return your Guest Survey Report form!

Occasionally we may allow other reputable organisations to write with offers which may be of interest.

If you prefer not to here from them, tick this box ☐

To: Johansens, FREEPOST (CB264), 175-179 St John Street, London EC1B 1JQ

Your own Johansens 'inspection' gives reliability to our guides and assists in the selection of Award Nominations

---

GUEST SURVEY REPORT

Name and location of hotel: _____ Date of visit: _____

Name and address of guest: _____

_____ Postcode: _____

Please tick one box in each category below:	Excellent	Good	Disappointing	Poor
Bedrooms				
Public Rooms				
Restaurant/Cuisine				
Service				
Welcome/Friendliness				
Value For Money				

PLEASE return your Guest Survey Report form!

Occasionally we may allow other reputable organisations to write with offers which may be of interest.

If you prefer not to here from them, tick this box ☐

To: Johansens, FREEPOST (CB264), 175-179 St John Street, London EC1B 1JQ

Your own Johansens 'inspection' gives reliability to our guides and assists in the selection of Award Nominations

---

GUEST SURVEY REPORT

Name and location of hotel: _____ Date of visit: _____

Name and address of guest: _____

_____ Postcode: _____

Please tick one box in each category below:	Excellent	Good	Disappointing	Poor
Bedrooms				
Public Rooms				
Restaurant/Cuisine				
Service				
Welcome/Friendliness				
Value For Money				

PLEASE return your Guest Survey Report form!

Occasionally we may allow other reputable organisations to write with offers which may be of interest.

If you prefer not to here from them, tick this box ☐

To: Johansens, FREEPOST (CB264), 175-179 St John Street, London EC1B 1JQ

Your own Johansens 'inspection' gives reliability to our guides and assists in the selection of Award Nominations

Order Coupon

To order Johansens guides, simply indicate which publications you require by putting the quantity(ies) in the boxes provided. Choose you preferred method of payment and return this coupon (NO STAMP REQUIRED). You may also place your order using FREEPHONE 0800 269397 or by fax on 0171 490 2538.

❏ I enclose a cheque for £_____ payable to Biblios PDS Ltd
(Johansens book distributor).
❏ I enclose my order on company letterheading, please invoice me.
(UK companies only)
❏ Please debit my credit/charge card account (please tick)
❏ MASTERCARD ❏ VISA ❏ DINERS ❏ AMEX

Card Number _____

Signature _____ Expiry Date _____
Name (Mr/Mrs/Miss) _____
Address _____
_____
_____ Postcode _____

(We aim to despatch your order with 10 days, but please allow 28 days for delivery)

Occasionally we may allow reputable organisations to write to you with offers which may interest you. If you prefer not to hear from them, tick this box ❏

CALL THE JOHANSENS CREDIT CARD ORDER SERVICE FREE ☎ 0800 269397

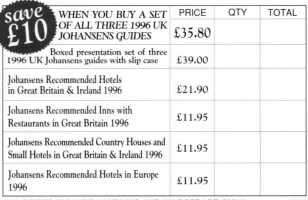

	PRICE	QTY	TOTAL
save £10 WHEN YOU BUY A SET OF ALL THREE 1996 UK JOHANSENS GUIDES	£35.80		
Boxed presentation set of three 1996 UK Johansens guides with slip case	£39.00		
Johansens Recommended Hotels in Great Britain & Ireland 1996	£21.90		
Johansens Recommended Inns with Restaurants in Great Britain 1996	£11.95		
Johansens Recommended Country Houses and Small Hotels in Great Britain & Ireland 1996	£11.95		
Johansens Recommended Hotels in Europe 1996	£11.95		

ALL PRICES INCLUDE HANDLING AND UK POSTAGE ONLY   36J
Outside the UK add £3 for each single guide ordered, or £5 for a set or boxed set to cover additional postage.   *PRICES VALID UNTIL 31/12/96*
Post free to:
JOHANSENS, FREEPOST (CB264), HORSHAM, WEST SUSSEX RH13 8ZA

Order Coupon

To order Johansens guides, simply indicate which publications you require by putting the quantity(ies) in the boxes provided. Choose you preferred method of payment and return this coupon (NO STAMP REQUIRED). You may also place your order using FREEPHONE 0800 269397 or by fax on 0171 490 2538.

❏ I enclose a cheque for £_____ payable to Biblios PDS Ltd
(Johansens book distributor).
❏ I enclose my order on company letterheading, please invoice me.
(UK companies only)
❏ Please debit my credit/charge card account (please tick)
❏ MASTERCARD ❏ VISA ❏ DINERS ❏ AMEX

Card Number _____

Signature _____ Expiry Date _____
Name (Mr/Mrs/Miss) _____
Address _____
_____
_____ Postcode _____

(We aim to despatch your order with 10 days, but please allow 28 days for delivery)

Occasionally we may allow reputable organisations to write to you with offers which may interest you. If you prefer not to hear from them, tick this box ❏

CALL THE JOHANSENS CREDIT CARD ORDER SERVICE FREE ☎ 0800 269397

	PRICE	QTY	TOTAL
save £10 WHEN YOU BUY A SET OF ALL THREE 1996 UK JOHANSENS GUIDES	£35.80		
Boxed presentation set of three 1996 UK Johansens guides with slip case	£39.00		
Johansens Recommended Hotels in Great Britain & Ireland 1996	£21.90		
Johansens Recommended Inns with Restaurants in Great Britain 1996	£11.95		
Johansens Recommended Country Houses and Small Hotels in Great Britain & Ireland 1996	£11.95		
Johansens Recommended Hotels in Europe 1996	£11.95		

ALL PRICES INCLUDE HANDLING AND UK POSTAGE ONLY   36J
Outside the UK add £3 for each single guide ordered, or £5 for a set or boxed set to cover additional postage.   *PRICES VALID UNTIL 31/12/96*
Post free to:
JOHANSENS, FREEPOST (CB264), HORSHAM, WEST SUSSEX RH13 8ZA

Order Coupon

To order Johansens guides, simply indicate which publications you require by putting the quantity(ies) in the boxes provided. Choose you preferred method of payment and return this coupon (NO STAMP REQUIRED). You may also place your order using FREEPHONE 0800 269397 or by fax on 0171 490 2538.

❏ I enclose a cheque for £_____ payable to Biblios PDS Ltd
(Johansens book distributor).
❏ I enclose my order on company letterheading, please invoice me.
(UK companies only)
❏ Please debit my credit/charge card account (please tick)
❏ MASTERCARD ❏ VISA ❏ DINERS ❏ AMEX

Card Number _____

Signature _____ Expiry Date _____
Name (Mr/Mrs/Miss) _____
Address _____
_____
_____ Postcode _____

(We aim to despatch your order with 10 days, but please allow 28 days for delivery)

Occasionally we may allow reputable organisations to write to you with offers which may interest you. If you prefer not to hear from them, tick this box ❏

CALL THE JOHANSENS CREDIT CARD ORDER SERVICE FREE ☎ 0800 269397

	PRICE	QTY	TOTAL
save £10 WHEN YOU BUY A SET OF ALL THREE 1996 UK JOHANSENS GUIDES	£35.80		
Boxed presentation set of three 1996 UK Johansens guides with slip case	£39.00		
Johansens Recommended Hotels in Great Britain & Ireland 1996	£21.90		
Johansens Recommended Inns with Restaurants in Great Britain 1996	£11.95		
Johansens Recommended Country Houses and Small Hotels in Great Britain & Ireland 1996	£11.95		
Johansens Recommended Hotels in Europe 1996	£11.95		

ALL PRICES INCLUDE HANDLING AND UK POSTAGE ONLY   36J
Outside the UK add £3 for each single guide ordered, or £5 for a set or boxed set to cover additional postage.   *PRICES VALID UNTIL 31/12/96*
Post free to:
JOHANSENS, FREEPOST (CB264), HORSHAM, WEST SUSSEX RH13 8ZA

GUEST SURVEY REPORT

Name and location of hotel: _____ Date of visit: _____

Name and address of guest: _____

_____ Postcode: _____

Please tick one box in each category below:	Excellent	Good	Disappointing	Poor
Bedrooms				
Public Rooms				
Restaurant/Cuisine				
Service				
Welcome/Friendliness				
Value For Money				

PLEASE return your Guest Survey Report form!

Occasionally we may allow other reputable organisations to write with offers which may be of interest.

If you prefer not to here from them, tick this box ☐

To: Johansens, FREEPOST (CB264), 175-179 St John Street, London EC1B 1JQ

Your own Johansens 'inspection' gives reliability to our guides and assists in the selection of Award Nominations

---

GUEST SURVEY REPORT

Name and location of hotel: _____ Date of visit: _____

Name and address of guest: _____

_____ Postcode: _____

Please tick one box in each category below:	Excellent	Good	Disappointing	Poor
Bedrooms				
Public Rooms				
Restaurant/Cuisine				
Service				
Welcome/Friendliness				
Value For Money				

PLEASE return your Guest Survey Report form!

Occasionally we may allow other reputable organisations to write with offers which may be of interest.

If you prefer not to here from them, tick this box ☐

To: Johansens, FREEPOST (CB264), 175-179 St John Street, London EC1B 1JQ

Your own Johansens 'inspection' gives reliability to our guides and assists in the selection of Award Nominations

---

GUEST SURVEY REPORT

Name and location of hotel: _____ Date of visit: _____

Name and address of guest: _____

_____ Postcode: _____

Please tick one box in each category below:	Excellent	Good	Disappointing	Poor
Bedrooms				
Public Rooms				
Restaurant/Cuisine				
Service				
Welcome/Friendliness				
Value For Money				

PLEASE return your Guest Survey Report form!

Occasionally we may allow other reputable organisations to write with offers which may be of interest.

If you prefer not to here from them, tick this box ☐

To: Johansens, FREEPOST (CB264), 175-179 St John Street, London EC1B 1JQ

Your own Johansens 'inspection' gives reliability to our guides and assists in the selection of Award Nominations

Order Coupon

To order Johansens guides, simply indicate which publications you require by putting the quantity(ies) in the boxes provided. Choose you preferred method of payment and return this coupon (NO STAMP REQUIRED). You may also place your order using FREEPHONE 0800 269397 or by fax on 0171 490 2538.

❏ I enclose a cheque for £_____ payable to Biblios PDS Ltd
   (Johansens book distributor).
❏ I enclose my order on company letterheading, please invoice me.
   (UK companies only)
❏ Please debit my credit/charge card account (please tick)
❏ MASTERCARD   ❏ VISA   ❏ DINERS   ❏ AMEX

Card Number _____

Signature _____ Expiry Date _____
Name (Mr/Mrs/Miss) _____
Address _____
_____
_____ Postcode _____

(We aim to despatch your order with 10 days, but please allow 28 days for delivery)

Occasionally we may allow reputable organisations to write to you with offers which may interest you. If you prefer not to hear from them, tick this box ❏

CALL THE JOHANSENS CREDIT CARD ORDER SERVICE FREE   ☎ 0800 269397

save £10	WHEN YOU BUY A SET OF ALL THREE 1996 UK JOHANSENS GUIDES	PRICE	QTY	TOTAL
		£35.80		
	Boxed presentation set of three 1996 UK Johansens guides with slip case	£39.00		
	Johansens Recommended Hotels in Great Britain & Ireland 1996	£21.90		
	Johansens Recommended Inns with Restaurants in Great Britain 1996	£11.95		
	Johansens Recommended Country Houses and Small Hotels in Great Britain & Ireland 1996	£11.95		
	Johansens Recommended Hotels in Europe 1996	£11.95		

ALL PRICES INCLUDE HANDLING AND UK POSTAGE ONLY   36J

Outside the UK add £3 for each single guide ordered, or £5 for a set or boxed set to cover additional postage.   *PRICES VALID UNTIL 31/12/96*

Post free to:
JOHANSENS, FREEPOST (CB264), HORSHAM, WEST SUSSEX RH13 8ZA

Order Coupon

To order Johansens guides, simply indicate which publications you require by putting the quantity(ies) in the boxes provided. Choose you preferred method of payment and return this coupon (NO STAMP REQUIRED). You may also place your order using FREEPHONE 0800 269397 or by fax on 0171 490 2538.

❏ I enclose a cheque for £_____ payable to Biblios PDS Ltd
   (Johansens book distributor).
❏ I enclose my order on company letterheading, please invoice me.
   (UK companies only)
❏ Please debit my credit/charge card account (please tick)
❏ MASTERCARD   ❏ VISA   ❏ DINERS   ❏ AMEX

Card Number _____

Signature _____ Expiry Date _____
Name (Mr/Mrs/Miss) _____
Address _____
_____
_____ Postcode _____

(We aim to despatch your order with 10 days, but please allow 28 days for delivery)

Occasionally we may allow reputable organisations to write to you with offers which may interest you. If you prefer not to hear from them, tick this box ❏

CALL THE JOHANSENS CREDIT CARD ORDER SERVICE FREE   ☎ 0800 269397

save £10 WHEN YOU BUY A SET OF ALL THREE 1996 UK JOHANSENS GUIDES £35.80
Boxed presentation set of three 1996 UK Johansens guides with slip case £39.00
Johansens Recommended Hotels in Great Britain & Ireland 1996 £21.90
Johansens Recommended Inns with Restaurants in Great Britain 1996 £11.95
Johansens Recommended Country Houses and Small Hotels in Great Britain & Ireland 1996 £11.95
Johansens Recommended Hotels in Europe 1996 £11.95

ALL PRICES INCLUDE HANDLING AND UK POSTAGE ONLY   36J
Outside the UK add £3 for each single guide ordered, or £5 for a set or boxed set to cover additional postage.   PRICES VALID UNTIL 31/12/96
Post free to:
JOHANSENS, FREEPOST (CB264), HORSHAM, WEST SUSSEX RH13 8ZA

Order Coupon

To order Johansens guides, simply indicate which publications you require by putting the quantity(ies) in the boxes provided. Choose you preferred method of payment and return this coupon (NO STAMP REQUIRED). You may also place your order using FREEPHONE 0800 269397 or by fax on 0171 490 2538.

❏ I enclose a cheque for £_____ payable to Biblios PDS Ltd
   (Johansens book distributor).
❏ I enclose my order on company letterheading, please invoice me.
   (UK companies only)
❏ Please debit my credit/charge card account (please tick)
❏ MASTERCARD   ❏ VISA   ❏ DINERS   ❏ AMEX

Card Number _____

Signature _____ Expiry Date _____
Name (Mr/Mrs/Miss) _____
Address _____
_____
_____ Postcode _____

(We aim to despatch your order with 10 days, but please allow 28 days for delivery)

Occasionally we may allow reputable organisations to write to you with offers which may interest you. If you prefer not to hear from them, tick this box ❏

CALL THE JOHANSENS CREDIT CARD ORDER SERVICE FREE   ☎ 0800 269397

save £10 WHEN YOU BUY A SET OF ALL THREE 1996 UK JOHANSENS GUIDES £35.80
Boxed presentation set of three 1996 UK Johansens guides with slip case £39.00
Johansens Recommended Hotels in Great Britain & Ireland 1996 £21.90
Johansens Recommended Inns with Restaurants in Great Britain 1996 £11.95
Johansens Recommended Country Houses and Small Hotels in Great Britain & Ireland 1996 £11.95
Johansens Recommended Hotels in Europe 1996 £11.95

ALL PRICES INCLUDE HANDLING AND UK POSTAGE ONLY   36J
Outside the UK add £3 for each single guide ordered, or £5 for a set or boxed set to cover additional postage.   PRICES VALID UNTIL 31/12/96
Post free to:
JOHANSENS, FREEPOST (CB264), HORSHAM, WEST SUSSEX RH13 8ZA

GUEST SURVEY REPORT

Name and location of hotel: _____ Date of visit: _____

Name and address of guest: _____

_____ Postcode: _____

Please tick one box in each category below:	Excellent	Good	Disappointing	Poor
Bedrooms				
Public Rooms				
Restaurant/Cuisine				
Service				
Welcome/Friendliness				
Value For Money				

PLEASE return your Guest Survey Report form!

Occasionally we may allow other reputable organisations to write with offers which may be of interest.

If you prefer not to here from them, tick this box ☐

To: Johansens, FREEPOST (CB264), 175-179 St John Street, London EC1B 1JQ

Your own Johansens 'inspection' gives reliability to our guides and assists in the selection of Award Nominations

---

GUEST SURVEY REPORT

Name and location of hotel: _____ Date of visit: _____

Name and address of guest: _____

_____ Postcode: _____

Please tick one box in each category below:	Excellent	Good	Disappointing	Poor
Bedrooms				
Public Rooms				
Restaurant/Cuisine				
Service				
Welcome/Friendliness				
Value For Money				

PLEASE return your Guest Survey Report form!

Occasionally we may allow other reputable organisations to write with offers which may be of interest.

If you prefer not to here from them, tick this box ☐

To: Johansens, FREEPOST (CB264), 175-179 St John Street, London EC1B 1JQ

Your own Johansens 'inspection' gives reliability to our guides and assists in the selection of Award Nominations

---

GUEST SURVEY REPORT

Name and location of hotel: _____ Date of visit: _____

Name and address of guest: _____

_____ Postcode: _____

Please tick one box in each category below:	Excellent	Good	Disappointing	Poor
Bedrooms				
Public Rooms				
Restaurant/Cuisine				
Service				
Welcome/Friendliness				
Value For Money				

PLEASE return your Guest Survey Report form!

Occasionally we may allow other reputable organisations to write with offers which may be of interest.

If you prefer not to here from them, tick this box ☐

To: Johansens, FREEPOST (CB264), 175-179 St John Street, London EC1B 1JQ

Your own Johansens 'inspection' gives reliability to our guides and assists in the selection of Award Nominations

Order Coupon

To order Johansens guides, simply indicate which publications you require by putting the quantity(ies) in the boxes provided. Choose you preferred method of payment and return this coupon (NO STAMP REQUIRED). You may also place your order using FREEPHONE 0800 269397 or by fax on 0171 490 2538.

❑ I enclose a cheque for £_____ payable to Biblios PDS Ltd
(Johansens book distributor).
❑ I enclose my order on company letterheading, please invoice me.
(UK companies only)
❑ Please debit my credit/charge card account (please tick)
❑ MASTERCARD ❑ VISA ❑ DINERS ❑ AMEX

Card Number _____

Signature _____ Expiry Date _____
Name (Mr/Mrs/Miss) _____
Address _____
_____
_____ Postcode _____

(We aim to despatch your order with 10 days, but please allow 28 days for delivery)

Occasionally we may allow reputable organisations to write to you with offers which may interest you. If you prefer not to hear from them, tick this box ❑

CALL THE JOHANSENS CREDIT CARD ORDER SERVICE FREE ☎ 0800 269397

save £10	WHEN YOU BUY A SET	PRICE	QTY	TOTAL
	OF ALL THREE 1996 UK JOHANSENS GUIDES	£35.80		
	Boxed presentation set of three 1996 UK Johansens guides with slip case	£39.00		
	Johansens Recommended Hotels in Great Britain & Ireland 1996	£21.90		
	Johansens Recommended Inns with Restaurants in Great Britain 1996	£11.95		
	Johansens Recommended Country Houses and Small Hotels in Great Britain & Ireland 1996	£11.95		
	Johansens Recommended Hotels in Europe 1996	£11.95		

ALL PRICES INCLUDE HANDLING AND UK POSTAGE ONLY   36J

Outside the UK add £3 for each single guide ordered, or £5 for a set or boxed set to cover additional postage.   *PRICES VALID UNTIL 31/12/96*

Post free to:
JOHANSENS, FREEPOST (CB264), HORSHAM, WEST SUSSEX RH13 8ZA

Order Coupon

To order Johansens guides, simply indicate which publications you require by putting the quantity(ies) in the boxes provided. Choose you preferred method of payment and return this coupon (NO STAMP REQUIRED). You may also place your order using FREEPHONE 0800 269397 or by fax on 0171 490 2538.

❑ I enclose a cheque for £_____ payable to Biblios PDS Ltd
(Johansens book distributor).
❑ I enclose my order on company letterheading, please invoice me.
(UK companies only)
❑ Please debit my credit/charge card account (please tick)
❑ MASTERCARD ❑ VISA ❑ DINERS ❑ AMEX

Card Number _____

Signature _____ Expiry Date _____
Name (Mr/Mrs/Miss) _____
Address _____
_____
_____ Postcode _____

(We aim to despatch your order with 10 days, but please allow 28 days for delivery)

Occasionally we may allow reputable organisations to write to you with offers which may interest you. If you prefer not to hear from them, tick this box ❑

CALL THE JOHANSENS CREDIT CARD ORDER SERVICE FREE ☎ 0800 269397

save £10	WHEN YOU BUY A SET	PRICE	QTY	TOTAL
	OF ALL THREE 1996 UK JOHANSENS GUIDES	£35.80		
	Boxed presentation set of three 1996 UK Johansens guides with slip case	£39.00		
	Johansens Recommended Hotels in Great Britain & Ireland 1996	£21.90		
	Johansens Recommended Inns with Restaurants in Great Britain 1996	£11.95		
	Johansens Recommended Country Houses and Small Hotels in Great Britain & Ireland 1996	£11.95		
	Johansens Recommended Hotels in Europe 1996	£11.95		

ALL PRICES INCLUDE HANDLING AND UK POSTAGE ONLY   36J

Outside the UK add £3 for each single guide ordered, or £5 for a set or boxed set to cover additional postage.   *PRICES VALID UNTIL 31/12/96*

Post free to:
JOHANSENS, FREEPOST (CB264), HORSHAM, WEST SUSSEX RH13 8ZA

Order Coupon

To order Johansens guides, simply indicate which publications you require by putting the quantity(ies) in the boxes provided. Choose you preferred method of payment and return this coupon (NO STAMP REQUIRED). You may also place your order using FREEPHONE 0800 269397 or by fax on 0171 490 2538.

❑ I enclose a cheque for £_____ payable to Biblios PDS Ltd
(Johansens book distributor).
❑ I enclose my order on company letterheading, please invoice me.
(UK companies only)
❑ Please debit my credit/charge card account (please tick)
❑ MASTERCARD ❑ VISA ❑ DINERS ❑ AMEX

Card Number _____

Signature _____ Expiry Date _____
Name (Mr/Mrs/Miss) _____
Address _____
_____
_____ Postcode _____

(We aim to despatch your order with 10 days, but please allow 28 days for delivery)

Occasionally we may allow reputable organisations to write to you with offers which may interest you. If you prefer not to hear from them, tick this box ❑

CALL THE JOHANSENS CREDIT CARD ORDER SERVICE FREE ☎ 0800 269397

save £10	WHEN YOU BUY A SET	PRICE	QTY	TOTAL
	OF ALL THREE 1996 UK JOHANSENS GUIDES	£35.80		
	Boxed presentation set of three 1996 UK Johansens guides with slip case	£39.00		
	Johansens Recommended Hotels in Great Britain & Ireland 1996	£21.90		
	Johansens Recommended Inns with Restaurants in Great Britain 1996	£11.95		
	Johansens Recommended Country Houses and Small Hotels in Great Britain & Ireland 1996	£11.95		
	Johansens Recommended Hotels in Europe 1996	£11.95		

ALL PRICES INCLUDE HANDLING AND UK POSTAGE ONLY   36J

Outside the UK add £3 for each single guide ordered, or £5 for a set or boxed set to cover additional postage.   *PRICES VALID UNTIL 31/12/96*

Post free to:
JOHANSENS, FREEPOST (CB264), HORSHAM, WEST SUSSEX RH13 8ZA

North American Order Coupon

To order Johansens guides in North America, simply indicate which guide(s) you wish by entering the quantity in the boxes provided. Select your preferred method of payment and forward whole Order Coupon by mail to Johansens at the address given at the bottom of this coupon.

SAVE $5

		Qty	US$ Total
When you buy all three 1996 UK Johansens guides	US$49.75 + $8.25 s&h		
Boxed presentation set of three 1996 UK Johansens guides	US$58.75 + $8.75 s&h		
Johansens Recommended Hotels in Great Britain & Ireland 1996	US$24.95 + $6.00 s&h		
Johansens Recommended Inns with Restaurants in Great Britain 1996	US$14.95 + $4.75 s&h		
Johansens Recommended Country Houses in Great Britain & Ireland 1996	US$14.95 + $4.75 s&h		
Johansens Recommended Hotels in Europe 1996	US$14.95 + $4.75 s&h		

PLEASE PRINT

Your Name

Street Address

Town/City

State/Province   Zip/Post Code

☐ I enclose a check for US $ _____ payable to JOHANSENS.

☐ Please debit my credit/charge card account the amount of US $ _____ in favor of JOHANSENS.

☐ MasterCard ☐ Diners ☐ Amex ☐ Visa ☐ Discover ☐ Carte Blanche

Card No

Expiry date

Signature   Date

All items shipped UPS Ground Service. Canadian customers or for experdited delivery details telephone 1-800 213 9628 (24 Hours). New Jersey customers, please add appropriate sales tax. Please allow 21 days for delivery.

BILLING ADDRESS OF CREDIT/CHARGE CARD, IF DIFFERENT FROM ABOVE

Street Address

Town/City

State/Province   Zip/Post Code

Mail to: JOHANSENS, 30 Edison Drive, Wayne, New Jersey 07470

✂ ···

North American Order Coupon

To order Johansens guides in North America, simply indicate which guide(s) you wish by entering the quantity in the boxes provided. Select your preferred method of payment and forward whole Order Coupon by mail to Johansens at the address given at the bottom of this coupon.

SAVE $5

		Qty	US$ Total
When you buy all three 1996 UK Johansens guides	US$49.75 + $8.25 s&h		
Boxed presentation set of three 1996 UK Johansens guides	US$58.75 + $8.75 s&h		
Johansens Recommended Hotels in Great Britain & Ireland 1996	US$24.95 + $6.00 s&h		
Johansens Recommended Inns with Restaurants in Great Britain 1996	US$14.95 + $4.75 s&h		
Johansens Recommended Country Houses in Great Britain & Ireland 1996	US$14.95 + $4.75 s&h		
Johansens Recommended Hotels in Europe 1996	US$14.95 + $4.75 s&h		

PLEASE PRINT

Your Name

Street Address

Town/City

State/Province   Zip/Post Code

☐ I enclose a check for US $ _____ payable to JOHANSENS.

☐ Please debit my credit/charge card account the amount of US $ _____ in favor of JOHANSENS.

☐ MasterCard ☐ Diners ☐ Amex ☐ Visa ☐ Discover ☐ Carte Blanche

Card No

Expiry date

Signature   Date

All items shipped UPS Ground Service. Canadian customers or for experdited delivery details telephone 1-800 213 9628 (24 Hours). New Jersey customers, please add appropriate sales tax. Please allow 21 days for delivery.

BILLING ADDRESS OF CREDIT/CHARGE CARD, IF DIFFERENT FROM ABOVE

Street Address

Town/City

State/Province   Zip/Post Code

Mail to: JOHANSENS, 30 Edison Drive, Wayne, New Jersey 07470

✂ ···

North American Order Coupon

To order Johansens guides in North America, simply indicate which guide(s) you wish by entering the quantity in the boxes provided. Select your preferred method of payment and forward whole Order Coupon by mail to Johansens at the address given at the bottom of this coupon.

SAVE $5

		Qty	US$ Total
When you buy all three 1996 UK Johansens guides	US$49.75 + $8.25 s&h		
Boxed presentation set of three 1996 UK Johansens guides	US$58.75 + $8.75 s&h		
Johansens Recommended Hotels in Great Britain & Ireland 1996	US$24.95 + $6.00 s&h		
Johansens Recommended Inns with Restaurants in Great Britain 1996	US$14.95 + $4.75 s&h		
Johansens Recommended Country Houses in Great Britain & Ireland 1996	US$14.95 + $4.75 s&h		
Johansens Recommended Hotels in Europe 1996	US$14.95 + $4.75 s&h		

PLEASE PRINT

Your Name

Street Address

Town/City

State/Province   Zip/Post Code

☐ I enclose a check for US $ _____ payable to JOHANSENS.

☐ Please debit my credit/charge card account the amount of US $ _____ in favor of JOHANSENS.

☐ MasterCard ☐ Diners ☐ Amex ☐ Visa ☐ Discover ☐ Carte Blanche

Card No

Expiry date

Signature   Date

All items shipped UPS Ground Service. Canadian customers or for experdited delivery details telephone 1-800 213 9628 (24 Hours). New Jersey customers, please add appropriate sales tax. Please allow 21 days for delivery.

BILLING ADDRESS OF CREDIT/CHARGE CARD, IF DIFFERENT FROM ABOVE

Street Address

Town/City

State/Province   Zip/Post Code

Mail to: JOHANSENS, 30 Edison Drive, Wayne, New Jersey 07470

MAIL TO:

JOHANSENS
30 EDISON DRIVE
WAYNE
NEW JERSEY 07470

MAIL TO:

JOHANSENS
30 EDISON DRIVE
WAYNE
NEW JERSEY 07470

MAIL TO:

JOHANSENS
30 EDISON DRIVE
WAYNE
NEW JERSEY 07470